Spaces of War, War of Spaces

Spaces of War, War of Spaces

Edited by
Sarah Maltby, Ben O'Loughlin,
Katy Parry and Laura Roselle

BLOOMSBURY ACADEMIC
NEW YORK · LONDON · OXFORD · NEW DELHI · SYDNEY

BLOOMSBURY ACADEMIC
Bloomsbury Publishing Inc
1385 Broadway, New York, NY 10018, USA
50 Bedford Square, London, WC1B 3DP, UK
29 Earlsfort Terrace, Dublin 2, Ireland

BLOOMSBURY, BLOOMSBURY ACADEMIC and the Diana logo
are trademarks of Bloomsbury Publishing Plc

First published in the United States of America 2020
This paperback edition published in 2022

Volume Editor's Part of the Work ©
Sarah Maltby, Ben O'Loughlin, Katy Parry and Laura Roselle
Each chapter © of Contributors

For legal purposes the Acknowledgements on p. xi constitute an
extension of this copyright page.

Cover image © Simon Norfolk

All rights reserved. No part of this publication may be reproduced or
transmitted in any form or by any means, electronic or mechanical,
including photocopying, recording, or any information storage or retrieval
system, without prior permission in writing from the publishers.

Bloomsbury Publishing Inc does not have any control over, or responsibility for,
any third-party websites referred to or in this book. All internet addresses given
in this book were correct at the time of going to press. The author and publisher
regret any inconvenience caused if addresses have changed or sites have ceased
to exist, but can accept no responsibility for any such changes.

Library of Congress Cataloging-in-Publication Data
Names: Spaces of war, war of spaces conference (2018 : Florence, Italy) |
Maltby, Sarah, editor. | O'Loughlin, Ben, editor. | Parry, Katy, 1973-editor. |
Roselle, Laura, editor.
Title: Spaces of war : war of spaces / edited by Sarah Maltby,
Ben O'Loughlin, Katy Parry and Laura Roselle.
Description: New York : Bloomsbury Academic, 2020. | Includes
bibliographical references and index.
Identifiers: LCCN 2019053917 | ISBN 9781501360312 (hardback) | ISBN
9781501360299 (pdf)
Subjects: LCSH: Mass media and war–Congresses. | Space and time in mass
media–Congresses.
Classification: LCC P96.W35 .S725 2020 | DDC 303.6/6–dc23
LC record available at https://lccn.loc.gov/2019053917

ISBN:	HB:	978-1-5013-6031-2
	PB:	978-1-5013-7224-7
	ePDF:	978-1-5013-6029-9
	eBook:	978-1-5013-6030-5

Typeset by Integra Software Services Pvt. Ltd.

To find out more about our authors and books visit www.bloomsbury.com
and sign up for our newsletters.

CONTENTS

List of Illustrations vii
Acknowledgements xi

Part I Spaces of War

Introduction Ben O'Loughlin and Laura Roselle 3

1 War art, digital media and the audience encounter *Jane Quinn* 13

2 The cadastral: Towards a visual forensics of in/visible spaces of war *Nicolette Barsdorf-Liebchen* 35

3 Digital spaces of war: Genre and affective investments in RT's representations of the Syrian conflict *Rhys Crilley and Precious Chatterje-Doody* 61

4 Conspiracy and the epistemological challenges of mediatized conflict *Eileen Culloty* 83

5 Command and control meet the decentralized network: Conventional militaries, social media and the information environment *Kevin Foster* 103

6 The myth of a thousand westerns: Media and just war theory *Sean Aday* 123

Part II War of Spaces

7 Liminality, gendering and Syrian alternative media spaces *Dina Matar and Kholoud Helmi* 143

8 #shaheed: A metaphotographic study of Kashmir's insurgency (2014–2016) *Nathaniel Brunt* 159

9   The Plain (a photographic work in progress)
    Melanie Friend 179

10 This is not a bomb: Matériel culture and the arms
    trade *Jill Gibbon* 187

11 Dialogic spaces in the situation of conflict: Stepping
    stones and sticking points *Liudmila Voronova* 205

12 Perfect war and its contestations *Jolle Demmers,
    Lauren Gould and David Snetselaar* 231

Conclusion: Where war inhabits *Sarah Maltby and Katy
    Parry* 247

Editor and contributor biographies in alphabetical order 261
Index 266

LIST OF ILLUSTRATIONS

Figures

1.1 *Distillation of Terror*, 2014. © John Keane. Courtesy of Flowers Gallery 17

1.2 Aluminium Waste Pond at Petkovici, from the *Bleed* series, 2005. © Simon Norfolk 19

1.3 Still taken from *Space Exodus*, 2008. Larissa Sansour. Reproduced with the kind permission of the artist 21

1.4 Computer visualization *Apparent Horizon*, 2012. David Cotterrell. Reproduced with the kind permission of the artist 23

1.5 *PhotoOp*, 2005. © kennardphillipps 24

1.6a Through 3D modelling, Forensic Architecture reconstructed the attack at the Iguala Palacio de Justicia in Mexico. The Ayotzinapa Platform enables users to explore the relationship between thousands of events and hundreds of actors from the night of 26–27 September 2014. *The Ayotzinapa Case: A Cartography of Violence*. Images: Forensic Architecture, 2017 28

1.6b After police left the scene at Periferico Norte, the remaining students attempted to protect evidence of the attacks. They held a press conference with journalists and teachers after state officials failed to help the students or process the crime scene. *The Ayotzinapa Case: A Cartography of Violence*. Images: Forensic Architecture, 2017 29

LIST OF ILLUSTRATIONS

2.1 *Negative Publicity*. 2011–2016 (series). © Edmund Clark. Reproduced with kind permission 44

2.2 *Negative Publicity*. 2011–2016 (series). © Edmund Clark. Reproduced with kind permission 45

2.3 *Negative Publicity*. 2011–2016 (series). © Edmund Clark. Reproduced with kind permission 46

2.4 *Negative Publicity*. 2011–2016 (series). © Edmund Clark. Reproduced with kind permission 50

2.5 *Negative Publicity*. 2011–2016 (series). © Edmund Clark. Reproduced with kind permission 51

2.6 *Negative Publicity*. 2011–2016 (series). © Edmund Clark. Reproduced with kind permission 54

8.1 Hundreds of people gather in Kakapora, Kashmir, for the funeral of 21-year-old Talib Ahmed Shah, a Kashmiri Lashkar-e-Taiba militant. © Nathaniel Brunt 160

8.2 Villagers document the funeral of 21-year-old Talib Ahmed Shah, a Kashmiri Lashkar-e-Taiba militant. Funerals of militants have become hyper-photographed events in the post-2013 period. © Nathaniel Brunt 160

8.3 A selection of photographs taken by the author in early 2013. © Nathaniel Brunt 164

8.4 Showkat Ahmed and his mother display a collage of family photographs in their home in Chittybandi. © Nathaniel Brunt 166

8.5 A memorial banner featuring militant photographs is displayed above a martyr's graveyard in Pulwama district south Kashmir. © Nathaniel Brunt 169

8.6 Kashmiri militants Davood Sheikh, Hilal Ahad Wani, Junaid Mattoo, Mushtaq Ahmed Mir and Farooq Ahmed pose for photographs with their weapons. All the young men, members of militant groups Hizbul Mujahideen and

Lashkar-e-Taiba, were later killed in 'encounters' with Indian security forces. The photographs were collected by Nathaniel Brunt in 2016. The collage was made by Nathaniel Brunt in 2017. Donated to the author by anonymous, Summer 2016   170

8.7   HM militants Davood Sheikh and Hilal Ahad Wani. Source: Donated to the author by anonymous, Summer 2016   171

8.8   Installation view of Nathaniel Brunt, #shaheed, 2017. Photo courtesy of Toni Hafkenscheid   173

9.1   From *The Plain*, © Melanie Friend. Original in colour   180

9.2   From *The Plain*, © Melanie Friend. Original in colour   181

9.3   From *The Plain*, © Melanie Friend. Original in colour   181

9.4   From *The Plain*, © Melanie Friend. Original in colour   182

10.1   Bomb stress ball. © Ricky Adam. Reproduced with kind permission   187

10.2   Grenade stress ball. © Ricky Adam. Reproduced with kind permission   188

10.3   'Welcome to Hell' sweet. © Ricky Adam. Reproduced with kind permission   189

10.4   Tank. © Ricky Adam. Reproduced with kind permission   189

10.5   Ammunition shell. © Ricky Adam. Reproduced with kind permission   190

10.6   Soldier stress ball. © Ricky Adam. Reproduced with kind permission   191

10.7   'The ultimate protection' condom. © Ricky Adam. Reproduced with kind permission   192

Tables

3.1 Summary of key features of each video 69

3.2 Audience engagement with each video 72

ACKNOWLEDGEMENTS

We are extremely grateful for the many people who made this book possible. We would like to thank the participants in the 2018 Spaces of War, War of Spaces conference which we held at the Accademia Europea Di Firenze (AEF), Florence, Italy, to mark the tenth anniversary of the *Media, War and Conflict* journal.

Our ambition for the conference was to provide a platform for relationship building among new generations of scholars and practitioners working in the field of media, war and conflict. To this end, our wonderful colleagues at AEF helped us design a unique and highly collegial conference that took into account both space and time. Working in one of the most beautiful cities in the world, we presented cutting-edge and contemporary ideas around the themes of space in rooms with historical frescoes on the ceiling, sharing meals in beautiful courtyard settings.

Significant amounts of time were provided for discussion, fostering an atmosphere of exceptional interdisciplinary and international collaboration. Throughout, there was space and time to breathe and think. We hope the book reflects this and indeed is a crystallization of all participants who presented, from twenty-five countries, many of whom were early and mid-career researchers. As editors this gives us great enthusiasm and confidence for the field in the years ahead.

We are especially grateful to Antonio Vanni and Elisabetta Santanni at AEF for their efforts in the Spaces of War, War of Spaces conference organization. Thank you also to Elon University, the New Political Communication Unit at Royal Holloway, University of London, the War and Media Network and to the journal publisher, Sage, for helping to fund the conference. Thanks also to the Universities of Leeds and Sussex for their continued support.

We would like to thank the publishing team at Bloomsbury; in particular, Katie Gallof and Erin Duffy for their assistance in the book development, and to the anonymous reviewers of the book proposal. We are also indebted to the photographers and artists who have kindly given us permission to include their images in the book. Finally, the book could not exist without our chapter contributors. We've very much enjoyed working with all sixteen authors presented here, whose approach to the themes of space and war was perceptive and varied. Our deepest thanks to them.

We look forward to continued collaborative work with all of the above people through the networks already formed through the conference and this book, and the ongoing work of the *Media, War and Conflict* journal.

PART ONE

Spaces of War

Introduction

Ben O'Loughlin and Laura Roselle

This volume is an intervention, not a handbook. It is motivated by a feeling that the ambition to provide broad perspectives on the transformation of war in new media environments, ecosystems and ecologies is distracting us from the richness of detailed work being conducted on specific cases. We feel an unease that macro-theorizations are flattening or ignoring the variety and intricacies of spaces. We worry that the insights from innovative thinking about space beyond the field of war and media have not found their way into this field. We also fear a dichotomy between 'grand' strategy of warfare on the one hand, and the everyday, the quotidian and the local on the other is obscuring a whole series of meso-level spaces and architectures of communication and conflict. This book is the first attempt to explicitly consider these concerns and the ways in which war is produced, enacted, negotiated, remembered and 'felt' in, through and with media spaces, and vice versa.

In fact, space has been under-theorized in the field of war and media while time and temporality have been absolutely central concerns. In the first decade of the twenty-first century, a body of research was published examining how the then 'new media' were affecting experience of acceleration and stasis, continuity and rupture, in the war on terror and through Western wars of intervention. Some work did examine how new forms of connectivity were shaping feelings of distance and proximity (Gillespie 2006; Silvestri 2015). Hoskins and O'Loughlin (2010) claimed war had 'diffused' across societies. But this work did not take the next step and seek to offer substantive theorizations that explain the mechanisms through which spaces of war were produced, sustained or challenged. This is a shame, because scales, mobilities and vectors were central to work on global political economy and how, for instance, sociotechnical systems that manage domains such as energy and transport are assembled and adapted (Eriksen 2016; Urry 2014).

And yet such studies of connectivity and war did provide a platform for enriching our understanding of space. Furthermore, since 2010 a decade of research on visibility and warfare has provided us with analytical tools to study how lines of sight and perspective and how layering and landscaping make space (Bousquet 2018; Galai 2017). Technologies such as drones and wearables transform experiences of proximity and the riskiness of spaces and our bodies in spaces. We have also seen focus on the air as a site of conflict and risk (Sloterdijk 2009). For instance, the Airspace Tribunal initiative in the UK seeks 'recognition of a new human right to protect the freedom to exist without physical or psychological threat from above' (Illingworth et al. 2018: 1). That initiative rests on a conception of the human being in the world, vulnerable and always perceiving possible risks, and a conception of military actors weaponizing that space that humans exist within. It connects to actors' use of media technologies as a means to target or hide, to de- or re-materialize in order to kill or stay alive (Bousquet 2018). At the same time, other trajectories of research renew the importance of space in other ways. The study of war and memory continues to place a focus on sites of memory rather than spaces (following important work by Maltby 2016; Nora 1989; Pshenychnykh, 2019; Winter 1995). Altogether, these theoretical resources can be used to bring much richer theorization of how the relations and practices of war and media are conditioned by space and create space.

Motivations: Why look at space?

Space matters to us for three reasons. First, it had become abundantly clear that, in matters of war and conflict, geographical space can help determine outcomes. Take radicalization, considered to be driven to a large extent by diffuse online dynamics. Following alarm that young British Muslims were travelling to Syria to fight for Islamic State in 2015, an anonymous intelligence officer told one of our editorial team that their agency believed nearly all those travelling came from three towns in Britain. If young people were being radicalized online then the geographical distribution would have been different. The social networks of particular situated communities mattered. For students of political communication this will come as no surprise: the reception of any individual to 'influence' by political narratives is explained to a large extent by the relationships they inhabit, and those relationships are still mostly local (Brown 2017). We must confront this. This is both an analytical and political task. 'Space has been replaced by time as the main ordering principle', Bruno Latour (2005: no page) writes; 'We can get rid of nothing and no one,' so the question becomes 'What should now be simultaneously present?' (ibid.). What practices and beliefs, what people and attachments? These are questions that drive antagonisms and create the conditions for war and conflict. How can spaces of war become spaces of cohabitation? How can shared vulnerabilities and dependencies be articulated in ways that can form stronger relations rather than drive insecurities (Cavavero 2009: 20–4)? What role can media technologies and media institutions play in that?

Second, and related, the humanities and social sciences have produced a lot of work on conceptual or metaphorical spaces: the gendered space, the stratified space, the securitized space, the racialized space and so on (Bodenheimer 2012). This presents an opportunity in the field of war and media because such conceptual spaces provide a normative benchmark for a type of space we either desire or reject. Do we want to encourage 'dialogic spaces' to encourage communication and possible diplomatic progress across enemy lines? Do we object to 'securitized spaces', in which certain people are classified primarily as security threats who must be stopped, because this leads to racial profiling, or do we genuinely think those being securitized are trying to kill us and securitization is justified?

Third, we wanted to push back on the primacy of time over space in studies of war and media. At the time satellite television became able to allow us to see live into distant spaces twenty-five years ago, the sociologist Barbara Adam argued: 'The traditional conceptual tools need to be supplemented and to some extent displaced by simultaneity, instantaneity, uncertainty and implication, all key features of global time, if social science is to become adequate to its contemporary subject matter' (Adam 1995: 9). All of that is true, and much of that work has been done (for an overview of the treatment of temporality in this field see Hoskins and O'Loughlin (2007)). However, we want to put back on the table the spatialities that have emerged alongside Adam's temporalities. We contend that it is of equal importance to ask questions about how experiences of presence, connectivity and relationships across spatial axes are developing and how these play a role in the perception of war and conflict. A decade ago research was exploring how individuals used traditional news media to construct senses of distance and proximity; how the 'closeness' or 'presence' of topographically distant 'things' (Weibel and Latour 2005) was felt topologically – that is, their closeness is understood not geometrically but affectively (Gillespie and O'Loughlin 2009). In the passing decade, in which we have witnessed widespread use of social media including encrypted apps like Whatsapp, do we understand how perceptions of distance and proximity function now to shape engagement with war and conflict? Given the increasing number of people displaced by war in recent years (BBC News 2019), and the continued moral concern that publics do not sufficiently care to help those suffering in war and conflict, these questions about how space operates are vital.

Lastly, a focus on space and spaces allows us to move away from a tendency in much scholarship in the field of media and war to focus on the West and its interactions with the non-West. The period of the war on terror extended this tendency, as the United States, UK and other Western nation states renewed their commitment to global surveillance, policing and punishment under a new narrative. Many scholars documented and critiqued the imaginaries and policies that enabled this global outreach; many critiques extended previous critical analysis of imperial and orientalist policy and press complicity but explained the new developments through new concepts too – for instance, securitization, mediatization, militarization among others – providing a new vocabulary to illuminate how power was exercised across space and through the management of spaces. Given that the war on terror reached into most if not all regions of the world, this was an opportunity to document the multiplicity of experiences and perspectives in that range of places. However, having surveyed the balance of scholarship throughout this period as editors of *Media, War & Conflict* there has been an absence of research exploring the perspectives of those 'on the receiving end' of the war on terror – those for whom the war on terror came looming over the horizon, whether silently and invisibly or through shock and awe tactics. Certainly this is partly because of an imbalance in resources and access to publication for scholars in those environments. And certainly there was a steady trickle of research on other, non-war on terror wars and conflicts that did expose readers to a wider set of spaces, experiences and perspectives. Ultimately, however, the multiple and varied textures of terrains and contexts in the world of war and media remained relatively cloaked.

While we embrace and seek out heterogeneity and multiplicity and all we can learn from that, this book is an opportunity to resist and refute the commonplace distinction that any local *place* is a site of authentic, desirable, 'real' life, while scaling up to global *spaces* brings a terrain that is abstract, cold and alienating or flat, borderless, seamlessly connective, and topological. We must resist this tendency, one that geographer Doreen Massey calls a 'retreat to place' (Massey 2005: 5). That axis is too simplistic. Latour (2018) has recently tried to reconceptualize the global as 'the terrestrial' in order to show how – in the context of addressing the climate emergency – this scale or space can be a place of normatively desirable action by actual people and communities still bound to the earth and its ecosystem. Equally, cold and alienating processes occur in local sites. This move negates any 'withdrawal' to the local (Massey 2005: 5).

A further challenge is how to analyse both material and non-material dimensions of spaces. The emergence of digital spaces has generated a proliferation of mapping, a mapping boom even (Oates and Gray 2019; Wilson et al. 2018). Again the figure of the forced refugee is central here. We know from studies of media and war that media play a world-making role for humans, creating visions of self and other on an international scale, positioning conflicts as 'distant' or 'close to home', and this is intensively the case for those moving countries (Georgiou 2006). Research has also established that for diasporic communities exiled by war or conflict, media are essential for surviving their forced journeys, for learning about their new destination and home and for staying in touch with news and personal ties in the place they were forced from (Gillespie et al. 2018). The materiality and availability of batteries, generators and phone chargers can play a critical role in the ability of refugees to keep moving in a safe and informed way and avoid illegal smugglers or border agents as they form their own trajectories and spaces.

Two concepts: Spaces of War, War of Spaces

We use 'Space' as a conceptual lens in order to consider, evaluate and reflect upon the convergence of war and media through two framing themes: **Spaces of War** and **War of Spaces**. The implications of this approach are threefold. First, it allows us to showcase cutting-edge scholarly and artistic work while also taking stock of how the field has developed and to identify the emerging challenges we face. Second, it allows us to foreground artistic work as part of this endeavour, particularly through the work of visual scholars and photographers. This is a unique quality of the book that brings a distinctly humanities approach to the subject matter, an issue that has gone previously unrecognized alongside more traditionally focused media, politics, and memory work. Third, it allows for a distinctly multidisciplinary approach to the subject. This volume is split into two parts, one on spaces of war and another on war of spaces. We encourage readers to think about how each conceptual approach can be developed, but also to think beyond this distinction and consider how else we can think about the relation between space and war.

Spaces of War

In our first part, **Spaces of War,** our contributors analyse how media spaces (traditional, digital, cultural, aesthetic, embodied, mnemonic) are used to position wars in space and time in a manner that transforms the conduct, outcomes and consequences of war for all involved. The volume thereby poses questions about the normative and empirical validity of a distinction between online spaces and physical ones.

Here, we present research exploring how actors use media to generate feelings and responses to conflict occurring in distance places. Media spaces are used to position a war for an audience. Quinn's (Chapter 1) examination of ways artists seek to engage audiences who are numbed by ubiquitous but distant conflicts separates a real, physical space of war from a detached public sphere geographically far away. The artists' use of digital technologies creates a different kind of public sphere, one marked by formats and techniques from journalism, art and cinema that inter-pollinate. But it remains in the West, far from war. Similarly, Barsdorf-Liebchen (Chapter 2) provides a radically alternative vision of the political-administrative space in which war is envisaged. She takes the term 'cadastral' space from town planning to explain how space is the product of technical, bureaucratic and practical procedures through which buildings and land are managed. She uses this concept to explore how post-photographic war imagery presents locations such as torture sites that are in many respects mundane, cadastral and even abstract. She asks what type of engagement is demanded of the audiences of such images. This becomes significant as these images become more widespread in twenty-first-century media culture.

In a slightly different framing of space, Crilley and Chatterje-Doody (Chapter 3) explore how an international news broadcaster, RT, presents the Syria conflict to distant audiences and how those audiences engage with RT's online space to register their comments and perspectives on that distant conflict. Like Quinn, the authors pay attention to the sometimes-creative representational practices made possible by these digitized environments.

We also present studies of communication in one space about another. Culloty (Chapter 4) provides an understanding of how rumours about actual physical events can mobilize and circulate transnationally through the internet. Foster's analysis (Chapter 5) indicates how efforts to undermine an enemy's military morale through online communication could bring advantages on the physical battlefield. Here, the distinct arenas become a condition that actors can leverage to gain advantage. Lastly, Aday (Chapter 6) maps out a moral and institutional space of war. Looking at the framing of US conflicts by US journalists as 'just wars', Aday reveals a network of organizations – news media, think tanks, offices of public administration – that sustain a space in which the idea of just war is used to legitimize military intervention. He goes further to argue that this space helps sustain a broader sense of the nation as just and benign and points out the irony that this moral space and national space help legitimize the conduct of war that is unjust. That harm and injustice is felt in another space, beyond the nation, beyond consideration.

War of Spaces

In our second part, we focus on **War of Spaces** where our contributors analyse how 'war' actors (political, military, survivors, victims) utilize, integrate and compete over (media) spaces, thereby recreating space and time in a manner that is *transformative* across political, social, cultural and personal spheres.

Matar and Helmi (Chapter 7) explore the spaces of alternative protest media in Syria since conflict began in 2011. Here the physical and media spaces of war overlap. They describe these as liminal spaces because new practices and subjectivities are created as the spaces themselves form. That liminality is constrained by the society's pre-existing institutions and norms, for instance assumptions about gender roles, as well as the conflict itself, but still actors in those spaces can push against social limits. Since what is at stake here is improved living conditions and a more emancipatory sociality, we might ask whether this politics of emerging spaces would have happened in Syria even if conflict had never begun.

We also find the transformation of space in Brunt's (Chapter 8) chapter on the space of insurgency in Kashmir. He finds a merging of physical and online spaces whereby combatants and civilians produce and publish their own media content and new opportunities emerge for documentary practitioners and researchers to access perspectives from 'the field'. Digital spaces such as encrypted social media group messaging services allow actors to perform a range of tasks, turning them into spaces for practices of memorialization, propagandizing, planning operations, signalling political resistance and making sense of unfolding history.

We appreciate that spaces of war can diffuse beyond the battlefield in less clear-cut ways and how war risks bleeding across spheres of life. Military violence can blur into domestic violence; harm on the battlefield can lead to harm in the streets and houses in home cities.

Through photography and interviews with local residents, Friend (Chapter 9) explores the landscape of a rural area of England used by military for exercises and testing. She finds a degree of complexity and ambivalence not immediately obvious to visitors to the area and argues that the landscape evidences a particular normalization of military presence and culture in the UK.

Gibbon (Chapter 10) deliberately moves objects out of war spaces and into other contexts. She takes gifts from arms fairs – stress balls in the shape of grenades, for instance – and displays them in a setting critical of war. These objects are signs that allow for a play of meaning, but they also signify actual destruction and suffering. This creates a dilemma. Audiences often react by laughing at these cartoonish objects, but this leads in turn to possible moments of unease and critical reflection. By turning elements of war into objects for speculation outside of their natural setting Gibbon asks whether they can still serve their original intention of promoting war.

In contrast, Voronova (Chapter 11) explores an effort to use space to de-normalize conflict. She examines how efforts to bring journalists from Ukraine and Russia into dialogue in neutral European cities might lead to less antagonistic framing of reporting of the conflict in Ukraine. Thus a distant space is created as a space for mediation. However, once those journalists return to their societies it is uncertain whether those dialogues can affect how the conflict is reported for and understood by ordinary citizens, let alone affect the possibilities for peace. Still, this is an instance of efforts to use space to engender transformation in the journalistic spaces of Ukraine and Russia which might in turn affect attitudes in their wider public spheres.

Lastly, Demmers, Gould and Snetselaar (Chapter 12) pose questions regarding how the hidden realities of warfare can be 'made visible' in and through war spaces, in this case by activists contesting the narratives of precision and care in 'remote warfare'. Drawing on Foucault's notion of 'regimes of truth', they investigate the ways in which 'war actors' negotiate, utilize and compete over media spaces, discussing the theoretical and political implications of the ways in which the spatial reconfiguration of contemporary warfare intersects with spaces of contestation and the ways in which 'perfecting warfare' further de-politicizes the violence executed.

Let us outline the typologies of spaces that the book investigates across all of these chapters. We find *institutional spaces*: governmental space where justifications for war are conceived, where legitimation practices are devised, alongside moral authority; journalistic institutional practices, traditionally seen as echoing official lines. Most contributors address *public spaces* – where opinion is formed and concerns arise about corruption of debate or where we find art gallery spaces that invite a particular way of looking. We find *resistant spaces* – through a focus on activism and ways to challenge narratives of war, through forensic practices but also making visible the arms fair trade that prefers to be invisible. And finally we find *ambivalent spaces* – a no-man's-land where art and media blur, for instance. These spaces are not distinct from each other, and the volume as a whole illustrates how they overlap and co-constitute each other.

What is noteworthy is the ways in which all these different kinds of spaces pose both opportunities and problems for a range of actors involved in the practice of media, war and conflict. They present challenges for those seeking to manage the perception of war and conflict, for instance. For military and policy practitioners they raise critical issues regarding the innovation and adaptation of techniques used to approach communities who might be spatially diffused globally, regionally, nationally or concentrated in towns and cities. For artists, digital technologies bring new formats and methods for representing an idea or situation and ways for engaging audiences. And for NGO staff these spaces present new opportunities to communicate, mobilize, fundraise and legitimize their work as well as to enact relief in the field or engage with local actors. Equally however, they present new risks regarding hacking and data loss as well as reputational damage from emergent images or other content that shows any illegal or norm-breaking actions by staff.

In short then, by bringing together artists and practitioners as well as scholars, this volume is not only multidisciplinary, cross-disciplinary and international in its approach, it is also relevant. Not only does it seek to further our understanding of the relevance of space in the theorization of war and media (practices, relations, processes), it also seeks to raise questions about how such a progressed understanding has relevance for those who operate in or engage with spaces of war.

References

Adam, B. (1995), *Timewatch: The Social Analysis of Time*, Cambridge: Polity Press.

BBC News (2019), 'Displaced People: Why Are More Fleeing Home Than Ever Before?', *BBC News*, 24 September. Available online: https://www.bbc.co.uk/news/world-49638793 (accessed 30 September 2019).

Bodenheimer, D. J. (2012), 'Beyond GIS: Geospatial Technologies and the Future of History', in A. Lünen and C. Travis (eds), *History and GIS: Epistemologies, Considerations and Reflections*, 1–15, Heidelberg, London and New York: Springer.

Bousquet, A. (2018), *The Eye of War: Military Perception from the Telescope to the Drone*, Minneapolis: University of Minnesota Press.

Brown, R. (2017), 'Public Diplomacy, Networks, and the Limits of Strategic Narratives', in A. Miskimmon, B. O'Loughlin and L. Roselle (eds), *Forging the World: Strategic Narratives and International Relations*, 164–89, Ann Arbor: University of Michigan Press.

Cavavero, A. (2009), *Horrorism: Naming Contemporary Violence*, New York: Columbia University Press.

Eriksen, T. H. (2016), *Overheating: An Anthropology of Accelerated Change*, London: Pluto Press.

Georgiou, M. (2006), *Diaspora, Identity and the Media: Diasporic Transnationalism and Mediated Spatialities*, Cresskill, NJ: Hampton Press.

Galai, Y. (2017), Narratives of redemption: The international meaning of afforestation in the Israeli Negev, *International Political Sociology*, 11(3): 273–91.

Gillespie, M. (2006), 'Transnational Television Audiences after September 11', *Journal of Ethnic and Migration Studies*, 32(6): 903–21.

Gillespie, M., and B. O'Loughlin (2009), 'News Media, Threats and Insecurities: An Ethnographic Approach', *Cambridge Review of International Affairs*, 22(4): 667–85.

Gillespie, M., S. Osseiran and M. Cheesman (2018). 'Syrian Refugees and the Digital Passage to Europe: Smartphone Infrastructures and Affordances', *Social Media+ Society*, 4(1): 1–12.

Hoskins, A., and B. O'Loughlin (2007), *Television and Terror*, Basingstoke: Palgrave.

Hoskins, A., and B. O'Loughlin (2010), *War and Media: The Emergence of Diffused War*, Cambridge: Polity.

Illingworth, S., N. Grief, A. Hoskins and C. Conway (2018), 'The Airspace Tribunal: Towards a New Human Right to Protect the Freedom to Exist without a Physical or Psychological Threat from Above', *European Human Rights Law Review*, 3: 201–7.

Latour, B. (2005), 'From Realpolitik to Dingpolitik – An Introduction to Making Things Public', Bruno Latour website. Available online: http://www.bruno-latour.fr/sites/default/files/downloads/96-MTP-DING.pdf (accessed 1 November 2019).

Latour, B. (2018), *Down to Earth: Politics in the New Climatic Regime*, Cambridge: Polity.

Maltby, S. (2016), *Remembering the Falklands War: Media, Memory and Identity*, Basingstoke: Palgrave.

Massey, D. (2005), *On Space*, London: Sage.

Nora, P. (1989), 'Between Memory and History: Les lieux de mémoire', *representations*, 26 (Spring): 7–24.

Oates, S., and J. Gray (2019), '# Kremlin: Using Hashtags to Analyze Russian Disinformation Strategy and Dissemination on Twitter', SSRN. Available online: https://ssrn.com/abstract=3445180 (accessed 1 November 2019).

Pshenychnykh, A. (2019), 'Leninfall: The Spectacle of Forgetting', *European Journal of Cultural Studies*, 1–22. DOI: 1367549419871345.

Silvestri, L. E. (2015), *Friended at the Front: Social Media in the American War Zone*, Oklahoma: University Press of Kansas.

Sloterdijk, P. (2009), *Terror from the Air*, Los Angeles: Semiotext(e).

Urry, J. (2014), *Offshoring*, Cambridge: Polity.

Weibel, P., and B. Latour (2005), *Making Things Public: Atmospheres of Democracy*, Cambridge, MA: The MIT Press.

Wilson, T., K. Zhou and K. Starbird (2018), 'Assembling Strategic Narratives: Information Operations as Collaborative Work within an Online Community', *Proceedings of the ACM on Human-computer Interaction*, 2(183): 1–25.

Winter, J. (1995), *Sites of Memory, Sites of Mourning: The Great War in European Cultural History*, Cambridge: Cambridge University Press.

1

War art, digital media and the audience encounter

Jane Quinn

Since Gulf War 1 (1990–1991), war artists have created their work in an environment dominated by news images of conflict. All pervasive, online, on the television news and the pages of newspapers, the media create the Western perception of 'otherness' or 'over there' conflicts through a narrow repertoire of visual representations. Suffering relatives of the dead, the lifeless bodies of children, the destruction of buildings and artefacts, the soldiers with their guns at the ready, the car exploding in a crowded street, blood-spattered clothing, frightened families holding each other in the face of death and injury, overcrowded sinking refugee boats have

The term 'war art' is used in this chapter to describe the output of artists from different disciplines who create images of conflict. The author is aware of the controversy surrounding this usage, that the term 'war art' suggests a colonialized Western perspective, that the world is now characterized by different conflicts rather than the large-scale wars of the twentieth century, and that it can be seen as an old-fashioned description referring in the past to military might and only to paintings. However, alternative terminology also has weaknesses: 'the imagery of conflict' does not sufficiently differentiate art from media images, and 'conflict artists' lacks impact and specificity. On reflection therefore the decision has been made to reclaim the term 'war art' and apply it within a post-digital environment. This enables a sharp distinction to be made between the different types of images and is used here to include art which encompasses human rights and autonomous warfare and its effects as well as direct combat.

all come to define these wars, and their effects, for the West. Often the audience is overwhelmed and doesn't know what their response should be, provoking a wide critical debate (Assman and Detmers 2016; Bloom 2016; Chouliaraki 2006; O'Doherty 1986; Sontag 2003). Sometimes viewers are driven to take action, a response which was evident in the humanitarian aid initiatives in the 1980s and 1990s and, in the UK, the 2015 movement of aid over to the refugee camps in Calais.

Faced with this image glut, enabled by digital technologies and delivered onto multiple media platforms, how have artists of conflict reacted? The relationship, between conflict, the media and art, is the subject of this piece. It reaches from Gulf War 1 in 1991, when images from the battlefield were, for the first time, instantaneously broadcast on television screens, and continues through the immediate past to the ongoing present.

The transition period from analogue to digital is my lived experience, working in the media as it adapted to the move from analogue to digital production and distribution methods. While the artist John Keane was demonstrating the increasing importance of the presence of the media in conflict zones with *PhotoCall (Brothers in Arms)* 1991 and *Zapatista Jungle* 1995, I was involved in testing out the establishment of a common European metatagging system for digital content. While artists were still being embedded with the armed forces, before it became too dangerous to be in the 'theatre of war', I was starting to commission websites in place of, or alongside books to supplement television programmes, demonstrating the changing 'balance of power' at that time between the different media elements, television, online, books and live events.

The impact of digital media on the operation of war has been well covered (Hoskins and O'Loughlin 2010; Mirzoeff 2005; Mitchell 2011) with the use of drones, long-distance rockets and hidden surveillance meaning that conflicts around the world have become more dangerous to report on. Yet in terms of representations of war, through the introduction of digital media, more people can access more images of conflict more easily and in more places than ever before.

Within this environment of systemic change, practising war artists have been adapting to and usurping the opportunities and artefacts which the digital revolution has opened up, through the tools they use, their output, their assumptions and expectations of the audience, but fundamentally through their relationship with media images. And this has a deeper resonance. The media do not show the 'hidden' in war – that which is too dangerous to reach, that which is disguised or not explicit, that which is mundane and not 'newsworthy'. Art which enables us to see the nature of war and which releases its meaning slowly can shed a new light on our understanding of conflict. It has found ways of showing subterfuge, surveillance, secrecy and distortion: the present-day mechanics of war which the media ignore. As the political axis of the West shifts, and amidst the speeding, frenetic production of images, news flashes and headlines, art which enables us to think and reflect has an increasingly important role to play.

In order to bear witness, 'for it to be known. For it to be seen. For it to be felt. Maybe to compel people to act. But it all begins with witnessing, the least that one can do' (Meiselas cited in Lubben 2008: 118), war artists, whether painters, photographers, video or installation artists, have found themselves grappling with this changing technological environment over the last quarter century. The artists of this period have moved on a trajectory which acknowledges the media and the impact of media images on the perceptions of war, to experimenting with ways in which they can represent war meaningfully in an environment which has become defined by the fast-moving, online imagery of conflict, to one where they engage directly through the use of complex digital tools. This has not been a linear development, but there are some discernible phases in the nature of the aesthetic response to war art which has been produced since 1991. The media and the relationship of journalists and artists with the media are central to these developments.

The media

After the precedent set in Gulf War 1, the media increasingly became part of the waging of war in the West, their images defining conflict for readers, users and viewers. Journalists and photojournalists were frequently embedded with the military, and 'official war artists', commissioned by the Imperial War Museum (IWM), were embedded alongside them. Although this relationship was appreciated by some artists like John Keane (Gulf War 1, 1991), it caused others, such as Steve McQueen (Iraq, 2003), real problems as they felt restricted and removed from observing any real action. Whereas the role of journalists in the 'theatre of war' was well understood by the military, the role of artists was less well-defined, and many of them felt they had to repeatedly explain and justify their presence. In conflict zones there has always been a balance between embedded photojournalists and 'unilaterals', and the same is true of artists. Keane, McQueen and Mark Neville worked within a closely defined situation, hosted and managed by the military, while others such as Simon Norfolk and (after his Wellcome Trust commission) David Cotterrell took a much more independent route to observe conflict and its aftermath. This was in direct contrast to the 'packages' constructed for the media by the military, with time limits on visits, group briefings and restricted access to the country outside army camps. News reports all tended to cover the same ground, which was carefully managed by the military.

This was the situation official war artists encountered up until Rosalind Nashashibi's video *Electrical Gaza* 2010–2015. Faced with multiple problems around Nashashibi's Gaza Strip project, including security issues, difficulties with insurance, return visits, and budget, the IWM stopped sending artists out to war zones, and together with the changing nature of war, the subject matter and the approach to war art changed.

What had happened in the years since 1991 to precipitate this change, and how did the artists respond? Although the internet seemed to offer the opportunity to reach new audiences, to established artists (non-net-art practitioners) it threatened their ability to make a living from selling their images. Very few, and kennardphillipps with images like *PhotoOp* (2005) are an exception, are happy for their images to be taken and shared and changed. There is a sharp distinction between photoshopping and superimposition by the artists themselves to create a desired aesthetic effect, and file sharing online involving many different users, often distorting the artist's original intention. With the cessation of the official war artist scheme, the closure of newspapers and low prices paid for online images, sources of commissions became increasingly hard to find. And the production of the art changed too as digital tools became available. But the starting point was the glut of media images of conflict and the way which artists of conflict subverted and appropriated these images in their work. There are several discernible aspects to this subversion strategy which were adopted by artists in a bid to create an alternative space where emerging aspects of contemporary warfare could be explored.

The complex image

One established method pursued by artists to make connections between different conflicts is to reference past aesthetic interpretations of war. This is a technique used, for instance, by Paul Seawright in his *hidden* sequence from Afghanistan in 2002, where he re-images Roger Fenton's 1855 *Valley of the Shadow of Death* from the Crimean War. John Keane referenced Paul Nash's bleak and destroyed landscape in *Making a New World* from the First World War in 1918 in his own *We Are Making a New World Order*, 1991. Here, the burning oilfields of Kuwait are in the background, and a grinning US soldier occupies another, different wasted war landscape.

But after 1991, media images became the main reference point. As a way of responding to the multiplicity yet somehow sameness of these images, artists brought a new dimension to their work and their relationship with the audience by creating single images and imbuing each one with different allusions, relying on the viewer to bring their own visual experience to their interpretation. Importantly this became an interdependent relationship with the media, with the artist as interpolator, making assumptions about what images their audience would be familiar with.

This loading of meanings onto individual images became a distinctive approach among war artists working in the UK in the 1990–2000s, referencing the growing complexity of the visual context in which they were creating. They worked in an outward-looking, experimental way within a rapidly changing technological environment, using tools which could enhance and deliver their understanding through a carefully thought-through aesthetic. Instead of images from journalists which were driven by the editorial stance of their proprietors, artists were free to explore the possibilities of digital media in relation to the representation of the changing images of conflict. In this way the interpretative image gained its power from the shortcomings of the exhausted stereotype, the one existing alongside the other in a symbiotic relationship.

John Keane demonstrated the loading of multiple meanings in *Distillation of Terror*, created in 2014. The image shows abstract orange and black upended rectangles set within a white square against a beige-and-grey

FIGURE 1.1 *Distillation of Terror*, 2014. © John Keane. Courtesy of Flowers Gallery.

desert background. The oil on linen painting represented a struggle for the artist – at a time when Daesh's power was rising he wanted to focus on the beheadings in the desert without showing the graphic reality of media images. Eventually, through moving away from the figurative, and combining the abstract with the political, he found a way of creating a facsimile, which depended upon the viewer having seen the propagandizing videos released by the terrorist group (shown in an edited version on the television news and in its entirety online) yet necessitating the use of their imagination. As spectators, there is an implicit responsibility to complete an image of the kneeling figure in orange with the black-clad jihadist towering over them in the moment before their death. *Distillation of Terror* may provoke, in a global audience, a sense of fear, despair and injustice: or maybe achievement in redressing a perceived grievance or oppression. Its effects may include research leading to a deeper understanding of the desert beheadings or a feeling of sympathy, compassion or empathy for the victim. No universal response can be predicted; there is a limited commonality or consensus across the world. Yet for Westernized audiences, familiar with news and internet images of the brutality and violence emanating from Daesh, it gave the awful familiarity of the images a permanent, framed, aesthetic presence, counterbalancing the transience of the internet age.

Using beauty

Originally a photojournalist, Simon Norfolk rejected the repetitive coverage of violence and death which newspaper editors requested and started to use beauty as a way of drawing the viewer into the horror of war, taking inspiration from the seventeenth-century baroque landscape artists Claude Lorrain and Nicolas Poussin among others. Norfolk's *Bleed* sequence from the Bosnian War (1992–1995) illustrates this.

His photograph of the aluminium waste pond at Petkovici, an exquisitely beautiful, dramatic and ominous photograph, shows the lake where in 1995 hundreds of Bosnian men and boys were executed on the edge of the dam that holds back the waste water. Some of their bodies were thrown into the lake – others buried. This photograph draws its power from the violent contrast between the snow and the red, blood colour of the lake. The quiet, almost-deserted country scene is disjointed by the suspicion that all is not what it seems. The realization of what happened there replaces the extreme beauty with the horrors of mass murder, in the same way as the pretty but ominous water photographs (*Untitled 1, 4 and 6*) and subsequent prints from Crni Vrh in the same *Bleed* sequence do.

In this instance, Norfolk helps the audience to find out more of the violent background to these images through the description on his website – outlining

FIGURE 1.2 Aluminium Waste Pond at Petkovici, from the *Bleed* series, 2005. © Simon Norfolk.

the political origins of the conflict and providing hyperlinks for more information – as an alternative narrative to the news media. He sees beauty as a way of getting under the 'carapace' which the viewer carries with them, developed by over-exposure to the sameness of media images, so that he can begin a conversation with them. He assumes that they are familiar with the conflicts he covers, and that that knowledge is drawn from media coverage. Once this baseline of familiarity is established, he is able to play upon their knowledge like a jazz theme, introducing new twists and challenges to their perceptions as he creates.

This approach is a long way from military artists who, in the past, worked mainly under 'contract' to particular regiments or went out to war zones on spec as unilaterals, selling their images to the military on their return home. Now, due to the changing nature of warfare and the growing danger which artists experience in conflict zones, military artists such as David Rowlands are increasingly working in an historical context. They seek commissions from the armed forces to visually recreate particular battles from past wars through a process of research, consultation, interviews with survivors and military experts. Digital media minimally affect this process: the resulting pictures are often hung in the officers' mess and have a military audience rather than reaching the general public, emphasizing regimental continuity, honour and valour.

Fictional narratives

The re-creation process adopted by military artists is a long way from the critical arguments about the ability of documentary photography to realistically represent conflict. Critics such as Judith Butler (2010), Ariella Azoulay (2008) and Dora Apel (2012) challenged the belief that a photograph could show the reality of war and envisaged other roles for it, allied to issues of citizenship, and new visual contracts between the photographer and the photographed. As the sharing, photoshopping, manipulating possibilities of digital media became mainstream, this argument shifted to a different sphere as artists exploited this potential and also recoiled from it. Jeff Wall's *Dead Troops Talk* (1992) can on one level be seen as an elaborate photographic re-creation of an incident at Moqor, Afghanistan, in 1986. Yet it was a carefully constructed photograph drawing on war images, horror movies and art historiography to create its effect. Wall used techniques drawn from different media to create the visual narrative – multiple takes in a large studio, using special effects, costumes and make-up – moving beyond objectivity to a deliberately mediated, created experience, displayed as a digital montage, exploring people coming back to life.

Wall's approach, the creation of contrived, narrative spaces, anticipated artists like Larissa Sansour. Explicitly rejecting the victim/aggressor representation of Palestinians, Sansour draws on universal narratives and dreams, interweaving themes which have become familiar through media coverage, using digitally driven computer-generated imagery (CGI) to engage with issues of Palestinian dispossession and identity. Deliberately stepping away from documentary reality 'I want to make that myth and have the power to make that myth – I don't want to be the subject of documentary' (Sansour 2016), her aim is to recreate the Palestinian identity through digital fiction, created not in isolation, but through working with large, multi-skilled production teams.

In the short film *Space Exodus* (2009), Sansour takes the 1969 televised sequence of Neil Armstrong's first steps on the moon, embedded deeply in the audience's memory, and reinforced by cultural derivations such as Stanley Kubrick's *Space Odyssey* 2001 and David Bowie's *Space Oddity* 1969, she appropriates the iconography of the moon landing. Using the soundtrack to *Space Odyssey*, she replaces Neil Armstrong – a white, American male –

FIGURE 1.3 Still taken from *Space Exodus*, 2008. Larissa Sansour. Reproduced with the kind permission of the artist.

with herself, a Palestinian woman born in Jerusalem, claiming the moon as a space where Palestinians can build a new future.

Because of its multiple cultural references, *A Space Exodus* can immediately trigger recollections in the viewer of a personal memorialized experience of time and place, wonder or tension, shock or excitement, juxtaposed here with the issue of Palestinian identity. In *In the Future They Ate from the Finest Porcelain* (2015), Sansour takes this further through a rebel leader who is a 'narrative terrorist' aiming to subvert the established image of the Palestinians for the future. Using CGI the interweaving of references in the film to aspects of the Palestinian experience which are familiar to the audience through media coverage – terrorism, rebellion, death, family, loss – reinforces the complexity of the Palestinian conflict and the search for a new identity. Sansour uses digital tools in a science fiction genre to imagine a very different future and to create alternatives to the present.

New digital tools, new aesthetics

Because of the increasing unpredictability of conflict, its dispersion and hidden nature, as well as the omnipresence of the repetitive images of suffering and destruction shown in the media, artists moved to an approach which came to be known as 'aftermath art', where they showed the impact of war on countries, infrastructure and communities rather than portraying details of immediate combat. Within this space, they started to explore the potential of digital tools. Keane, for example, instead of working from sketches, made the transition to a small, digital camera as a way of capturing images in the field – a sketchbook of an instantaneous kind – using the photographs as records once he returned to his studio in London. Simon Norfolk initially used a large 4 × 5 field camera made of mahogany and brass, to film in the 'theatre of war', as he knew that smaller cameras could be mistaken for guns in the chaos of combat. But in 2010 due to the introduction of X-ray scanning equipment at Kabul airport which would have damaged the film in the older, heavier camera, he moved to using a more mobile digital camera.

The exploration by artists of the use of highly developed digital tools to develop their work is a recurrent theme in the early 2000s as they adapted to and exploited the new possibilities. Langlands and Bell, commissioned by the IWM, created the central piece to their triptych *The House of Osama bin Laden* (2003) using an interactive animation V/SpaceLAB virtual reality system designed by designer and academic Tom Barker. To explore *The House of Osama bin Laden* in the gallery the player or viewer stands at a podium with a flight simulator-style joystick, while the exhibit is projected on the wall several feet away. (The flight simulator joystick is particularly relevant, since several of the 9/11 hijackers trained with 'Microsoft Flight

Simulator.') And the animation was made available online and on mobiles, an experiment in the possibilities of art which is simultaneously available on different platforms.

David Cotterrell worked as artist in residence in SEOS, a UK-based flight simulation and advanced data projection company which was a major client of the Ministry of Defence, to fulfil his installation *Monsters of the Id* (2012). Cotterrell harnessed the use of digital technologies with a carefully thought-through aesthetic position and explicitly saw them as a way of increasing understanding in the audience. *Monsters of the Id* sustains Cotterrell's view that the role of the serious artist is to encourage the audience to participate in a work of art, with the artwork providing the structure for them to do so. Reserving the right, as an artist, to remain complex and incomprehensible, Cotterrell (2016) speaks of the need for empathetic engagement from the viewer and sees the artist's role as attempting to generate a 'pluralism of perspective', offsetting the failure of political dialogue and government policy statements and engaging with the 'sensationalised landscape of declared war'.

FIGURE 1.4 Computer visualization *Apparent Horizon*, 2012. David Cotterrell. Reproduced with the kind permission of the artist.

Cotterrell's pluralism of perspective includes the ability to feel empathy, and empathetic engagement is implicit in leading to an understanding of the distortion which propagandizing and inaccurate media images invoke. He encourages the audience to engage emotionally, increasing participation through the use of digital installations leading to a more developed critical cognitive awareness of conflict.

kennardphillipps' aesthetic political satire uses digital collages to highlight human rights abuses or demonstrate the hypocrisy of politicians. Determined opponents to war and capitalism, the artists explicitly aim to generate activism and change through their work by using media imagery. Their best-known Iraq image, *PhotoOp*, prompted this comment from Jonathan Jones (2013) in *The Guardian*: 'They wanted to change the world,

FIGURE 1.5 *PhotoOp*, 2005. © kennardphillipps.

not record it: "We were trying to portray Iraq as it happened, and not wait until afterwards and make a history painting".'

In order to galvanize their audience, their provocative image of Tony Blair gave him a maniacal, narcissistic quality, utilizing irony and satire with the aim of stimulating political change. This searing political attack is explicitly mocking in its tone, far removed from the critical debates about the evocation of sympathy or empathy in the audience discussed above. Lifting the copyright on the image for public usage means it has become ubiquitous, shown in diverse situations including Oxford Street in London, the *British Medical Journal* and on the covers of many books.

More recently, Richard Mosse has used a military surveillance, thermal imaging camera to create his video sequence *Incoming* (2016). He speaks about the process (Mosse 2017): 'Using a part of a weapon to figure the refugee crisis is a deeply ambivalent and political task...And building a new language around that weapon – one of compassion and disorientation, one that allows the viewer to see these events through an unfamiliar and alienating technology – is a deeply political gesture.'

Yet by doing so, Mosse reopened debates about objectivity and intrusion on the part of the photographer – now potentially even more possible because of the power, reach and surveillance capacity which drove the development of his digital camera. This kind of criticism has been levelled before: for instance, Sebastião Salgado was accused (Kimmelman 2001; Sontag 2015) of romanticizing and exploiting suffering, rendering the audience immobile by showing its universal nature. Now Mosse captures, from a distance, the day-to-day actions and experiences of refugees without asking their permission (although their identifying features cannot be seen) and then displays the video on soaring screens to maximize the details of the impact on their lives. Within a digital environment, and despite its enormous possibilities, the debates about the value systems involved in depicting conflict and its effects – the parameters of realism, how distortion can happen, the ethics of intrusion on grief, the role of the artist – remain the same.

The new infrastructure of conflict

The media may still aim to cover combat in contemporary conflicts, but it neglects the 'hidden', the lethal new infrastructure of wars enabled by digitization. As artists strive to create alternative visual perspectives on war and conflict, the 'hidden' is a major challenge to portray, requiring a different kind of aesthetic approach and sensibility. Trevor Paglen's *NSA – Tapped Undersea Cables, North Pacific Ocean, 2016* captures the hidden network of digital superhighways which stretch under the sea, carrying data around the world. Paglen carried out two years of painstaking background research following Edward Snowden's disclosures that the NSA tapped these cables, and after scuba-diving training, the artist completed thirty underwater dives to photograph them. Background information, maps and documents accompanied the resulting images, demonstrating the potential for government snooping via these cables. The context of the 'witnessing' might have changed, but the necessity for art to help the audience see the 'historical moment' of conflict remains the same.

In his series showing data centres and experimental facilities, Simon Norfolk demonstrates how a combination of extreme clinical destructive precision exists alongside day-to-day human fallibility. *While Modelling Physics inside an Exploding Nuclear Warhead (2000s)* reminds the viewer of the non-human nature of the weapons, *Designing Nuclear Weapons (2000s)* shows how digital technologies have produced the potential for weapons of destruction side-by-side with the capacity for human misjudgement which increases their power.

This 'technical sublime' underlines the increasing growth and power of the digital infrastructure which runs our lives and underpins the military industrial complex. Personal information is transported and stored, where we don't know, nor do we know by whom. The contrast between the personalized 'warm' nature of social media and the 'cold' sophistication of the alienating complexes where that data is held is demonstrated by these artists. Direct combat is far away from these digital storage factories, weapon development centres and hidden communication networks, underlining the insidious nature of control by the state and industry. But the hidden does not end here, and artists have turned their attention to how to capture the increasingly covert abuse of human rights as an adjunct to war and oppression.

Human rights and the digital

The aesthetic representation of human rights abuses has many different forms, filling the space left by media coverage, permeating this concealed effect of conflict. Within this variety, Abu Ghraib (2003) was a shocking exception, not only in the nature of the recorded physical abuses against the Iraqi prisoners, but also in the failed value systems among the US soldier-perpetrators and their own amusement at carrying out their degrading actions. Bemused and confused by the personal nature of social media, they adopted its characteristics while performing shocking humiliations and abuse – and saw nothing wrong in doing that. This lack of value systems is what made this event so monstrous, demonstrated by the very people who were meant to be bringing the now tarnished 'rightness' of the United States into enemy territory. Quite clearly, the widespread access to the Abu

Ghraib photographs would not have been possible without digital cameras and online digital distribution systems.

The deliberate recording of human abuse can be seen in John Keane's *Fear* sequence (2012–2013) where he painted Russian portraits of political prisoners, identified only by their prisoner number (*Fear 59744, Fear 9067*). These portraits show the desperation and resignation of the political prisoners, staring out at the viewer from the greyness of the canvas. Instead of the news reports on assassinations in or by Putin's Russia, or coverage of the clashes on the Russian-Ukraine border, a sense of desolation and despair infuses the images, as the prisoners contemplate their inevitable end at the hands of the Russian state. The vitality and energy of Pussy Riot in *Fear Not* (2013), a triumph of the human spirit over adversity, is in distinct contrast to the silent, incarcerated captives.

Now many abuses of human rights are behind closed doors, unreported on by the media, enshrined in the emergency legislation of the state. Edmund Clark's *Control Order House* (2016) shows the mundaneness of the life of an inhabitant suspected of terrorist activity whose every move is monitored and who lives his captive life in a characterless house according to a schedule defined by his captors (see the chapter by Barsdorf-Liebchen in this collection for further discussion of Clark's work). *Letters to Omar* (2010) used a deceptively simple collection of letters to Omar Deghayes during his years in Guantanamo Bay (he was released without charge in 2007) to illustrate how repression and distortion work when concealed beneath a surface of normality. Although these letters were originally sent to support him, principally by strangers, they were read, redacted and stamped by the authorities until Deghayes didn't know if they were the originals, copies or imagined. They became an instrument of control. Max Pinckers (2014) describes how Clark's work was 'made in an effort to document the spatial forms of control within the house with the intention to potentially re-create various spaces in collaboration with an architect, be it digitally or physically, in the form of an installation when exhibiting the work'. The aesthetic challenges of this aspect of war are not how to show bodies on the battlefield or engage in discussions over whether it is acceptable to show the actual moment of death; they are how you make the mundane threatening: how you capture day-to-day deadness. The deadness of captivity, of hopelessness and despair.

Is it art, human rights, judicial evidence – and does it matter?

There has been an extended debate (Stallabrass 2013; van Kesteren 2008) over the role and verisimilitude of citizen journalism in representing conflict. Some authors have used established media in an effort to unravel the arguments about the authenticity of images shot by participating audiences on mobile phones and cameras, for instance, van Kesteren in his book *Baghdad Calling* (2008). But it is the work of Forensic Architecture which has harnessed citizen journalism and made it into a vital force in the representation of conflict, bringing the power of digital media into issues of human rights in a new and effective way. Forensic Architecture's work reveals not only a precisely researched and created account of a situation, but, through multiple technological approaches, a sense of the unremitting futility and inequality of autonomous conflict and its effects on civilians. Through their work, which occupies a place somewhere between human rights and art, the use of high-technology apparatus and military processes offers no exemption to human rights abuses, and the careful construction of the results of conflict directly confronts the dominant media trope of war as face-to-face combat.

Whether it is the analysis of the US air strike on the Al-Jinah mosque in Syria in 2017 or the investigation into the forcible disappearance of the Ayotzinapa students in Mexico in 2014 or *Lethal Warning: The killing of Luai Kahil and Mair al-Nimrah*, which recomposes the evidence around the deaths of two Palestinian teenagers who were killed by a missile fired from an Israeli aircraft in the Gaza Strip in 2018, Forensic Architecture resists the status quo by addressing the increasing sophistication of the military conduct

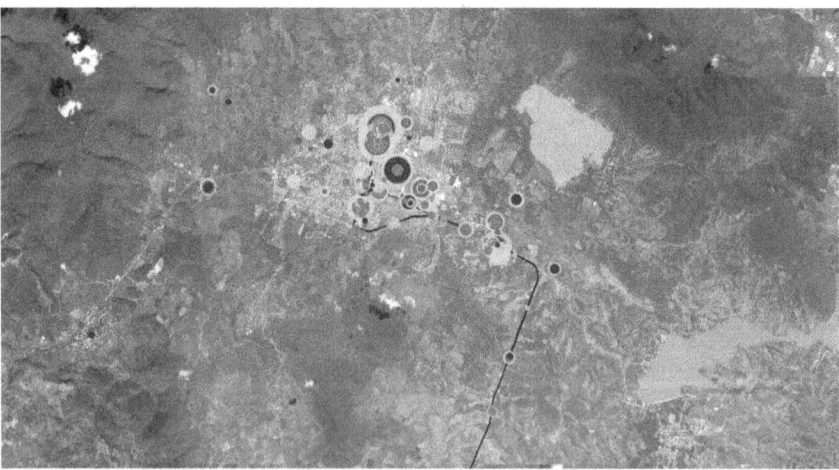

FIGURE 1.6a Through 3D modelling, Forensic Architecture reconstructed the attack at the Iguala Palacio de Justicia in Mexico. The Ayotzinapa Platform enables users to explore the relationship between thousands of events and hundreds of actors from the night of 26–27 September 2014. *The Ayotzinapa Case: A Cartography of Violence.* Images: Forensic Architecture, 2017.

FIGURE 1.6b After police left the scene at Periferico Norte, the remaining students attempted to protect evidence of the attacks. They held a press conference with journalists and teachers after state officials failed to help the students or process the crime scene. *The Ayotzinapa Case: A Cartography of Violence*. Images: Forensic Architecture, 2017.

and coverage of war on its own terms. Its work of remediation responds to the digital media habits of the audience: the productions reference the experience of looking at conflict on a computer, film or television; there is a celluloid intervention between viewer and artwork. With a contemporary audience, familiar with using screens on a daily basis, this increases the direct connectedness with the viewer in the same way as digitally distributed media images do. But these productions, imbued with inferences about human rights, suffering and the will to survive, are not defined by their ephemeral nature. They are about issues which have already had media coverage, and those which remain hidden, and their intention is clear – to show the impact and results of conflict on populations and individuals in a different way from the media, by using sophisticated digital instruments.

This suggests a new relationship between conflict and its representation which builds on the interaction with media imagery undertaken by the artists featured in this research. Forensic Architecture reconstructs acts of conflict, building forensically researched pictures of misrepresented or unrepresented incidents of violence or human rights abuses through using different media – sound, stills, videos, databases – to create a record of what happened. It takes the audience into the area of politics and human rights with explicit messages and meanings. Where the media may mention the lost refugee boat, this approach evinces pathos as the light tracking the boat's journey finally disappears from the database screen (*Left-to-Die Boat*, 2011), and with its loss demonstrates the institutional disregard for human rights. Forensic Architecture's integration of databases, film and citizen journalism to represent human rights violations is given longevity through its permanence on the Forensic Architecture website. However, it is displayed in galleries as well as used directly as evidence in truth commissions within a legal framework. Art galleries join online and judicial spaces as distribution routes for these projects: 'They are OPERATIVE MODELS, to paraphrase filmmaker Harun Farocki's concept of "operative images" – entities that not only represent, but "do" things in the world' (ICA 2018).

The range of responses to conflict using digital media is wide-ranging, creative and exploratory. The move from when conflict was about combat to where it is multifaceted – both obvious and hidden – has happened in the space of the last quarter century. The artists, photographers, filmmakers and installation artists who respond to this most difficult of subjects have created new genres, new approaches and new projects in a transformative digital environment.

Shaping the audience encounter

The audience for this imagery often hasn't always recognized the change. Some see the war art of the past, the representation of battles and wasted landscapes of the First World War (Nash, Singer Sargant, Wyndham Lewis) as real war art, and the diversity and range of current war art go unrecognized. Others see only the images of conflict online, or in citizen journalism, or form their views through the repetitive reports of the news media. And yet digitization has caused the relationship between creators and their audience to shift and change. No longer passive consumers of television programmes – viewers now have an extensive choice of programmes on multiple platforms beyond real-time broadcasts. There are choices to be made over which device to use and decisions to be made about which online content to access. Much of my time in the last five years of working at the BBC was spent analysing audiences, getting to know their likes, dislikes, viewing habits, interests and the possibilities for interaction with them.

It is different for the aesthetic representation of conflict. The audience response is difficult to predict and gauge, for digital media have for the first time levelled the visual playing field. A diverse, global audience may be looking at the same image on a mobile phone or computer in Kabul or Kenya or in an art gallery in London, but with very different reactions depending on their geographical location, age, religion and political beliefs. Within this global environment of accessible digital images (excluding those countries such as North Korea, China and Eritrea where government censorship is active) how is a Western audience reacting?

The artists' views

Artists do not have a view of a homogenous audience viewing their work. While Larissa Sansour (2016) comments, 'It is a different thing when you engage an audience and they are excited about what they are looking at rather than sympathetic. It's a different dynamic and in the long run it creates something completely different,' John Keane articulates a pragmatic view of the nature of the audience encounter with a strong sense of his own work and the importance of place. He acknowledges that his work might 'cause discomfort' if it is placed on the walls of a house or place of work. Yet he is explicitly 'making art objects which are to be seen within a room – in a relationship with that, hanging on a wall. So that is the ideal situation. I am making a one-off object which ideally people would engage with' (Keane 2016). This sense of place is evolving with digitization. His work is 'now much more widely available through technology as an image. Which is fine, I don't have a problem with that. I'd rather people saw the original but such is the quality of the technology now that things are much closer to what they should be than historically they were'. Keane is able to bring together his own practice with a developing sense of the nature of the audience encounter within the digital space.

Online and the art gallery

There are two main distribution channels for war art which shape the audience encounter – digital distribution and via the mediator (agent or artist, museum, gallery or publisher). And the encounter can take place in many different spaces – the gallery, on mobile phones, on a computer, in a museum, through a book.

Online spaces

Internet usage continues to grow at exponential rates in Africa and Asia particularly. Wearesocial.com (2019) reports there were 4.39 billion internet users in 2019, an increase of 366 million in comparison with January 2018, and 3.48 billion social media users globally. This growth cannot be ignored in economic terms, in increased access to new markets, or to different opinions. However, has it opened up new aesthetic spaces where audiences can have a meaningful encounter with an artists' image?

Although defined by concepts of personalization, it is arguable that the internet is not a medium which easily enables a unique encounter in a safe viewing space. Digital technologies act as both mediators and distribution channels. The internet is transient and static; it is place and delivery; it can offer interactivity, create intimacy and deliver personalized content. Yet there are limitations to the accessing of the image online. In certain online genres, such as news, the image disappears quickly and the viewer has to know where and how to reach it in the archive, assuming they knew it existed in the first place. It takes discriminating Google searches to find images and then be able to reflect upon them within the confines of the computer screen rather than on the walls of a gallery.

There are restrictions based on the framing of the image – the oblong shape and size of the computer, tablet or mobile phone screen; the speed of its delivery and recycling through file sharing on various platforms. Then there are the distractions of the 'constant other', other content, other points of view, and ease of switching between pages and sites.

The importance of a connection with the original (the aura) was spoken about by Walter Benjamin and John Berger, a unique interconnectedness which they saw photography and film destroying and which Suzanne Oberhardt (2001) refers to as 'the magical representation of immortality and human life that the painting can represent'. This special aesthetic space is threatened not only by the ephemeral nature of the internet, but by increased blurring between original art and reproduced art. Art libraries like Google's Cultural Institute's Art Project make available libraries of more than 45,000 artworks created through non-electronic means, which can be commented on and then shared by participants. 'Public' museums such as the Royal Academy are extending their retail activities and obliterating the distinctions between public and commercial as they sell prints on their online site, disconnected from their current exhibitions. This blurring is made possible by the particular constituents of the online experience – the ability to actively share and comment, and to purchase facsimiles, juxtaposing the internet's virtual communities of interest and its pretensions to fostering personal creativity with its increasing commerciality. This generates a very different kind of encounter than the user or viewer would have with the original.

Gallery spaces

In comparison with the extensive reach of the internet, art galleries and museums can be off-putting to the general population (O'Doherty 1986) and museum and gallery curators have a different perspective when creating a distinctive space which shapes the audience encounter. At both the Wellcome Trust and the IWM they speak about facilitating the audience's ability to make connections. For instance, Helen Sloan (2012) commented on David Cotterrell's *Monsters of the Id*, 'It asks the audience to consider the veracity of the image, their role in reading images and prevalent attitudes and the response that they might make to extreme experiences.'

The importance of surprising the spectator in the gallery is articulated by many curators including Hans Ulrich Obrist, Nicholas Serota and Glenn D. Lowry. Re-contextualized, this ambition can be interpreted as the creation of a special experience which might utilize digital media, but which speaks to the emotions and experience of the viewers. The appropriate use of multimedia has challenged the organizational cultures of war museums as immersive, digitally driven exhibitions have been mixed with more traditional displays. The unintended effect of this is not only to generate a backlash from the military establishment regarding the 'popularization' of war imagery through interactive displays, but less tangibly to create a hierarchy of importance between those conflicts and artists who are presented within a multimedia environment and those who aren't.

Although there may be a retreat from the optimism and expectations created by digital media and initially expressed by critics (Lovejoy 1989; Stallabrass 1997) in terms of a new relationship with the representation of war, exhibitions about conflict only gain from using a diversity of media to engage viewers' curiosity in a genre where it is easy to become overwhelmed as a spectator with the horror of war.

Conclusion

Despite the change in warfare, conflict is part of human life – something we fear, the other, the unknowable. Will the future see a retreat from the multiplicity of approaches to a search for single images which can tell a story of the horror of the effects of warfare, the suffering of the refugee, the destruction of a country? Or will the experimentation and complexity continue as digitization provides greater opportunities for engaging the viewer in challenging encounters with conflict through art? For the effects of digital media are ongoing and dynamic, evolving from day to day, non-linear, non-sequential, unpredictable – mirroring and helping to create the increasingly complex and dangerous world we live in.

References and further reading

Apel, D. (2012), *War, Culture and the Contest of Images*, Rutgers, NJ: Rutgers University Press.
Assman, A., and I. Detmers, eds (2016), *Empathy and Its Limits*, Basingstoke: Palgrave Macmillan.
Azoulay, A. (2008), *The Civil Contract of Photography*, New York: Zone Books.
Bloom, P. (2016), *Against Empathy*, London: Penguin.
Butler, J. (2010), *Frames of War: When Is Life Grievable?* New York: Verso.
Chouliaraki, L. (2006), *Spectatorship of Suffering*, London: Sage.
Cotterrell, D. (2012), *Monsters of the Id*, 11 February. Available online: https://cotterrell.com/exhibitions/4521/monsters-of-the-id/ (accessed 10 July 2018).
Cotterrell, D. (2016), 'Empathy and Risk: Inaugural Lecture at Brighton University', 17 November. Available online: https://cotterrell.com/talks/4665/empathy-risk/ (accessed 29 May 2018).

Hoskins, A., and B. O'Loughlin (2010), *War and Media*, Cambridge: Polity Press.
Institute of Contemporary Arts (2018), *Counter Investigations: Forensic Architecture*, 7 March–13 May.
Keane, J. (2016), Interview with Jane Quinn, London, 27 April.
Kesteren, G. van (2008), *Baghdad Calling, Reports from Turkey, Syria, Jordan and Iraq*, Rotterdam: Episode Publishers.
Kimmelman, M. (2001), 'Can Suffering Be Too Beautiful?', *New York Times* photography review, 13 July. A review of the exhibition *Migrations, Humanity in Transition: Photographs by Sebastião Salgado*. Available online: https://nytimes.com/2001/07/13/arts/photography-review-can-suffering-be-too-beautiful.html (accessed 29 May 2018).
Lovejoy, M. (1989), *Postmodern Currents: Art and Artists in the Age of Electronic Media*, Ann Arbor: UMI Research Press.
Lubben, K., ed. (2008), *In History: Susan Meiselas*, for the International Centre of Photography, New York: Steidl.
Mirzoeff, N. (2005), *Watching Babylon: The War in Iraq and Global Visual Culture*, New York: Routledge.
Mitchell, W. J. T. (2011), *Cloning Terror, The War of Images, 9/11 to the Present*, Chicago: University of Chicago Press.
Norfolk, Simon, website, https://simonnofolk.com.
Oberhardt, S. (2001), *Frames within Frames: The Art Museum as Cultural Artifact*, New York: Peter Lang.
O'Doherty, B. (1986), *Inside the White Cube: The Ideology of the Gallery Space*, Berkeley: University of California Press.
Pinckers, M. (2014), 'Control Order House by Edmund Clark, reviewed by Max Pinckers', *Photobookstore Magazine*, 4 March. Available online: https://photobookstore.co.uk/blog/photobook-reviews/control-order-house-by-edmund-clark-reviewed-by-max-pinckers/ (accessed 6 February 2018).
Sansour, L. (2016), Interview with Jane Quinn, London, 7 April.
Seymour, T. (2017), 'Richard Mosse – Incoming', *British Journal of Photography*, 15 February. Available online: https://bjp-online.com/2017/02/mosse/ (accessed 19 October 2019).
Sloan, Helen (2012), 'The Simulated and the Profane', David Cotterrell, *Monsters of the Id Exhibition Catalogue*, John Hansard Gallery/University of Southampton, 11 February–31 March.
Sontag, S. (2003), *Regarding the Pain of Others*, London: Penguin.
Sontag, S. (2015), *New York Photo Diary, Aesthetics and Ideology of Sebastião Salgado*, 13 June. Available online: https://ny-photography-diary.com (accessed 4 July 2017).
Stallabrass, J. (1997), 'Money, Disembodied Art and the Turing Test for Aesthetics', in J. Stallabrass, S. Buck-Morss and L. Donskis (eds), *Ground Control, Technology and Utopia*, London: Black Dog Publishing, pp. 62–111.
Stallabrass, Julian (2013), *Memory of Fire: Images of War and the War of Images*, Photoworks.
Wearesocial.com (2019), 'Global Digital Report 2019'. Available online: https://wearesocial.com (accessed 20 August 2019).

2

The cadastral: Towards a visual forensics of in/visible spaces of war

Nicolette Barsdorf-Liebchen

Introduction

In the twenty-first century, spaces of war are increasingly intangible, invisible, abstract. The spaces examined here are neither those of the physically direct, raw violence of war, nor the mediated scopo-centric violence of forms of media and entertainment. The focus here is rather upon the less visibly violent or invisible – in/visible – spaces of modern warfare in a globalized, neoliberal, transnationally corporatized, militarized and digitally hyper-connected dispensation.[1] Visually considered, these forms of violence are either concealed or in some way 'socially abstract' (Roberts 2014: 93). It is the civilian spaces that have become preoccupied by state-corporate-military power and their art-documentary photographic representation – or visualization – which is the focus of the reflections here. These are the contemporary spaces of war: the spaces where governance, corporatization and militarism converge to violate with impunity and hegemonic insouciance the emancipatory ethos of post–Second World War modernity, as judicially embodied in treaties such as the UN's 1948 Universal Declaration of Human Rights and the Geneva Conventions.

What is meant here is not the manifest violence of war and conflict, but the less obvious or concealed conditions subsuming or enabling overt violence:

its in/visibility. When power cynically arrogates to itself the right to flout its own rule of law, or contradicts its ostensible political ideology, it is power's abuse of power. It is not a phenomenon exclusive to twenty-first-century neoliberal capitalist democracy: historically conspicuous instances include the Reign of Terror during the French Revolution, German Nazism and the Shoah, and white-supremacist 'state of emergency' Apartheid South Africa in the mid-1980s. Of distinct theoretical relevance here is Carl Schmitt's 'state of exception' whereby a state acts ultra vires: beyond its legal powers or legitimacy – often violently so – and outside of an established normative constitutional framework, invoking a 'sovereign' power to do so (Schmitt [1932] 1996).

More specifically in a 'war on terror' context, such exceptionalism occurs where justification for state violence cannot be found constitutionally and within the rule of law. It is then 'pure violence without logos' (Agamben 2005: 40). In its post 9/11, digital, corporatist and militarist incarnation, this state of exception assumes more all-pervasive, diffuse, impenetrable shapes, lending a further level of abstraction to twenty-first-century power. Here I extend the meaning of the phrase to foreground corporate globalization. Reformulating it as a state-corporate exception, more emphasis is put on the *corporatization* of warfare. A twentieth-century US-led military-industrial complex has evolved in the twenty-first century into geopolitically decentred, globalized, normalizing, dehistoricizing and deeply systemic forms of state-corporate-military violence (Roberts 2014; Žižek 2009). A neoliberal power nexus with unrestrained corporatization and rampant militarization at its core 'pre-occupies' our spaces of civic and civilian being: a process designated here as 'cadastration'. The 'cadastral' is defined as '(of a map or survey) showing the extent, value and ownership of land, especially for taxation purposes'.[2] It is essentially an administrative, bureaucratic demarcation which apportions and secures space privately or publicly in the interest of those who own it, take charge of it or benefit from it.

Edmund Clark's image-making projects constitute a pioneering response to the challenges posed by state-corporate exceptionalism and its attendant, cadastrated spaces of war. They represent a deliberate turn away from the war-hero, humanitarian template of photojournalism in the interests of addressing these in/visible spaces of war. This focus is what distinguishes it from the tradition of iconic war photography archetypically represented by among others Robert Capa, Lee Miller, David Douglas Duncan, Don McCullin and James Nachtwey (Griffin 1999). Rather than the direct, raw violence of war, dissenting image-makers now are evolving their practices to focus on the publicly in/visible, socially abstract forms of violence which accrue within the nexus of neoliberal capitalist democracy, global corporatization, digital media and modern warfare.

Negative publicity: Decadastrating the clandestine spaces of war

Edmund Clark's *Negative Publicity* series is a project undertaken in collaboration with the counterterrorism investigator Crofton Black (Clark and Black 2016), which 'comprises photographs and documents that confront the nature of contemporary warfare and the invisible mechanisms of state control' (Clark 2016).[3] The work concerns itself with the Bush-Blair era between 2001 and 2008 and the 'war on terror'. The website summary (Clark 2011–2016) further describes the work as 'a paper trail' showing state-corporate-military:

> Activities via the weak points of business accountability: invoices, documents of incorporation, and billing reconciliations produced by the small-town American businesses enlisted in prisoner transportation. In conjunction with photographs of former detention sites, detainees' homes, companies and government locations this work recreates the network that links CIA 'black sites,' and evokes ideas of opacity, surface, and testimony in relation to this process: a system hidden in plain sight.[4]

The quotation provides direct insight into our commercial-quotidian enmeshment, as articulated above, with its references to 'small-town American businesses', 'companies (and government) locations' and 'documents of incorporation'. The excerpt tells us how the stuff and spaces of the CIA 'black sites' are right there under our noses: 'a system hidden in plain sight'. These are rather different sequestered black sites to the grandiose and majestic desert, sky- and seascapes in which they are visualized by Trevor Paglen[5] or the austere and cinematic sci-fi technologies captured to thrillingly sublime effect by Simon Norfolk.[6] Clark distinguishes his approach from theirs by way of emphatic contrast, explaining that they 'are linked by their shared use of the aesthetics of the sublime in their work – the artistic framing and presentation of the horrors they seek to represent', while his work is more about providing a glimpse for the viewer into their own 'everyday implication in this war on terror' (Clark 2016).

He is concerned above all to show how the control order houses or scenes of rendition may well be, or have been, in your very own neighbourhood; how the runway at the airport on which your plane en route to your holiday destination takes off or lands is the very same runway which an unmarked aircraft carrying a shackled detainee uses to refuel for further extraordinary rendition purposes. He says it is the sheer 'mundanity' and even 'domesticity' of these spaces, processes and activities, and our 'shared experience' of them that is the heart of what he seeks to visualize in his projects, to find new ways of visualizing the spaces and activities of modern warfare.

Clark thus seeks to present these hidden, clandestine activities and largely invisible structures and processes in a way that is 'relevant to us as individuals', he says. Clark says that the spaces hosting the activities, relations and networks of the state-corporate-military nexus do not require any aestheticization for them to be 'grasped', and he disagrees unequivocally that 'the horror' of state-corporate-military forms of violence is not representable. In fact, he argues quite the opposite. He insists that 'it' must at all costs be represented, whatever the medium and the means. This view can be seen as a staunch defence of representation to the question of the 'unrepresentability' (of, for example, violence and war, of the 'social totality', of trauma and private pain). For Rancière, the question as to whether some things are simply unrepresentable can only be answered by attending to the relation between art (aesthetics) and political violence (Rancière 2009: 109). Clark's commitment to representation is an avowedly pragmatic one and unconcerned with philosophical perspectives which may or may not be compatible with his ostensive definition – non-verbal and abstract pointing towards – of the visualization of 'war' in its cadastral configuration. Clark's maps of war spaces are neither artful nor philosophical: they are conceptual and forensic hooks for the furtherance of dissident practices of purposeful representation.

The cadastral

This more conceptual and investigatory mode of (art-documentary) image-making challenges traditional, iconizing modes of war representation. In their relative abstraction and absence of human figuration, they gesture towards these in/visible spaces we may well be walking or travelling through, living and working in, but not 'seeing' as spaces of 'war'. 'War' in quotation marks denotes here the peculiar kind of violence which attends these in/visible, intangible spaces in and through which the state-corporate-military-media-security-surveillance-techno-scientific nexus functions.[7]

What I attempt to build here via my readings is a 'cadastral' construct, or methodology, which reveals, and insistently reinstates, the human being at the centre of the non-human 'war' landscape. This also flushes out from their deep corporate embedding the (perfectly legal) commercial contracts for supply of military goods and services, ostending a morally arraigning finger towards the neoliberal state-corporate exception at the heart of the imperialist cadastration of others, then, now and – it is to be surmised – for a long while to come.

The rationale for the use of cadastral as a conceptual and methodological tool is best understood in the context of its relation to the more conventional notions of mapping, cartography and topography, and I propose the term as an adjunct to or augmentation thereof. In this respect, a foundational place to begin would be the map and its burgeoning significance for arts and humanities scholarship and creativity. Lize Mogel (2011: 187) observes:

> Maps have become part of a pop-culture kit-of-parts within the cultural sphere, used as a form, an aesthetic, or as a methodology. The rising number of college-level art, architecture, and design courses that teach "mapping" is a testament to this, as is the number of art exhibitions about maps concentrated in the last few years.

The rise of the map as methodological tool in the arts and humanities, she goes on to write, is due to a shift in the way we think about representation and space, itself largely as a result of the radical evolution of the way we obtain, communicate and understand information: that is, digitally. She writes that 'for artists and designers, maps are a highly aesthetic form, able to articulate and spatialize complexity' (Mogel 2011:187). So how is the term 'cadastral' to be understood as a tool for the spatialization of the complexity of 'war' or within the context of the visualization of spaces of war?

This term functions here as both a quasi-empirically fitting and more nuanced and evocative term to describe the spatial politics and sinister bureaucracy of the imperialist, colonial, neoliberal corporatist power that is the chief instigator of state-military violence. This conceptual modification to spatial analytics within the context of the visualization of 'perpetual war' (Kennedy 2016) addresses those aspects of twenty-first-century war not properly distinguished by the more generic cartography or topography paradigm: the in/visible spaces of war. In the contemporary context to which Mogel refers, image-makers have turned increasingly since the emergent postmodern mapping ambitions of the 1980s to the spatial visualization of socially abstract power and its forms of violence in response, not least, to the sheer complexity of the hyper-connected realm of power and its myriad spaces of 'war' in which we now live.

Indispensable to the 'perpetual war' aims of state-corporate-military power is the involvement ('complicity') of so many actants: principals and agents, executive and ancillary, to encompass all those in the socio-economic theatre of 'war'. The list is open-ended and extensive: aerospace, military and media-tech CEOs, arms manufacturers, engineers, technicians, software specialists, pilots, drivers, caterers, internet service providers and social media, broadcasters, bloggers, cleaners, logistics personnel, and so on, encompassing myriad sectors of civil-commercial society. There is something further contained in the concept of a 'cadastre' that is neither evoked nor specified by the others. 'War' and its forms of violence are certainly conceivable. However, while war and conflict in their brute 'eventality' might be mappable, 'war' as a diffuse, systemic 'Event' constitutive of an immersive of state-corporate-military existential order is not definitively measurable, and its 'audit trail' is often invisible. It poses an immense challenge for visual apprehension.

The Event

Vocabulary is significant here. I capitalize the Event here to distinguish it from the way in which it has been conceived in the theoretical adoption of the word by philosophers such as Alain Badiou and Slavoj Žižek, and I refer to tangible, material events of war as its 'eventality'. The latter philosophers conceptualize 'the event' in neo-Marxist fashion as a kind of radical historical rupture with the hegemonic order – in the most obvious case, a revolution (Badiou and Žižek [2005] 2010). I conceive of the Event not as a happening, a rupture or revolution, but rather as an ongoing agglomeration of both material and abstract, interconnected events. The Event is the systemic, structural, molecular condition of possibility whereby neoliberal corporatist-militarist hegemony is maintained amidst the violent order of 'events' it plays a major role in producing. Apart from war and conflict, 'Cold' or 'Great', hybrid, proxy, or attritional, 'war' encompasses too the making of mass refugee movements, socio-economic exploitation and injustice, dispossession and inequality, grave environmental and habitat depredation, deep social and political discontent, and so forth. The Event is the index of a global state-corporate-media-military nexus which shows no signs of contracting in the twenty-first century – quite the opposite. This is the ongoing, pervasive and diffuse, real and concrete, systemic and structural, socially abstract but essentially violent hegemony of 'perpetual war' (Kennedy 2016).

War is comprised of events. It has an ontic measurability, even where not all events are known about: its eventality. However, 'war' – as 'perpetual' – is of the order of the Event. It is simultaneously a very real but highly abstract Event which in our hegemonic and virtually (digitally speaking) existential immersion we have difficulty in seeing, visualizing and measuring.

In the ensuing I argue how, paradoxically, Clark's cadastral way of seeing points towards the Event by way of imagery which focuses microscopically on singular events, eventality. His imagery, while ostensive of the Event, pinpoints precise events, with spatio-temporal, (extra)judicial, cultural, political, social and economic coordinates, both visible and invisible, concealed but forensically discoverable, and critically 'knowable' through strategic visualization. The cadastral is a marker of the inaugural violence of the 'owned' spaces of war. It brings with it a strategic mathematical triangulation towards the thorough convergence of state-corporate interests: the CIA could do nothing without its business or corporate partners – the private military and security contractors (PMSCs) – in the rendition flights, the detention, torture or targeted killings of designated enemies of the state with which Clark's *Negative Publicity* is concerned.

Corporate lobbying of government has long been a feature of politics and power but the emergence of the media-tech giants such as Google and Amazon has entailed an increasing 'corporate capture' of governments, with states mimicking corporate models of governance. As Powers and Jablonski argue, the 'internet freedoms' we are sold and we espouse as our democratic right have less to do with Western principles of governance and foreign policy and their ostensibly humanitarian ethos and rather more to do with rank economic and geopolitical calculation. In this light, the state rhetoric of cyberwar – notably that emanating from the United States – can be regarded as a kind of decoy narrative to deflect attention from the 'real cyberwar', which is the West's use of digital networks to further its own neoliberal corporate-militarist agenda (Powers and Jablonski 2015). A cadastral visualization implicitly adopts this insight as methodological cornerstone. Cadastral visualization places thus more of a pointed emphasis on the state-corporate-managerial-military contiguity of space, place and being at even the most quotidian levels of society to include 'internet freedom' and hyper-networked digital practices.

It is, of course, also a state-corporate-bureaucratic-military tool of information and control. Both the state and its enabling corporate service providers require the apolitical and amoral function of bureaucracy for their ends, whatever they may be. No black site of rendition could coordinate its territorial or neighbourhood designation and concealment without a detailed, quantity-surveyor-produced cadastral map. The Registers of Scotland: Cadastral Mapping Overview explains as follows:

> [It is a map] showing all registered geospatial data relating to registered plots. The cadastral map consists of cadastral units, each of which represents a single registered plot of land. The cadastral map is not limited to defining ownership boundaries, but includes geospatial references for other rights or burdens that affect the registered plots of land.
> (ROS 2017)

The 'ownership boundaries' and the 'geospatial references' here indicate the kind of quantity surveying empirical precision which the more vague concepts of cartography or topography do not automatically suggest. The legal rights and burdens all have to do with how the space is used and who is entitled to use it. Beyond that, it is either a commercial, a public or a private space, subject – or not – to varying levels of policing or surveillance. Cartography/topography lacks the legal, bureaucratic, quotidian quality of the cadastral, which is considered here to be a more forensically, heuristically and hermeneutically productive tool for the visualization of some very particular, geo-locally sited spaces of 'war'. In addition, the adoption of such a quotidian, bureaucratic and technical triangulation or town planning tool invites a purposively engaged interaction of the viewer with the image and through this portal visualization of twenty-first-century spaces of war outside of and beyond still dominant photojournalistic representational frames.

War visioning: From forensic architecture to proxy measure

As observed above, the spaces of twenty-first-century warfare and modern power are myriad: physical and abstract, political, administrative/ bureaucratic, psycho-social, commercial, judicial, mundane, 'extraordinary', clandestine, private, public and so forth. Fleshed out further, as is discussed below, a room in a building in a city in which a 'detainee' is tortured can be (re)configured not only as an 'eventual' space, but as a 'cadastral' space: one that has geographical, technical, town planning, property development, politico-economic, foreign policy and state-military coordinates.

Clark's dissident image-making practices mark a significant departure from socially 'realistic' representations of war to their more abstract and conceptual, but paradoxically, more grounded visualization. Clark presents an aniconic eschewal of an aesthetics of the sublime (frequently deployed by Simon Norfolk and Trevor Paglen) in favour of the less spectacular, more mundane face/s of perpetual war. This sleight of frame inversion re-centres the human being as actual subject of universal concern while critically emphasizing power as the actual object(ive) of twenty-first-century dissident war photography. The images in the *Negative Publicity* series, to include the ones selected for discussion below, showcase this in their decisively untraditional occlusion of violated or dead humans, which deliberate absence quietly, profoundly, abstractly re-presents the latter by way of haunting metonym. Such synecdochal resurrection of life is indexed by, for example, an extraordinary rendition aircraft, a declassified but redacted court transcript, a city ordnance survey-style map, or the empty indoor bathing pool of a 'control order house'. They are melancholic in their gesturing towards human trauma, inhuman violation and the loss of humanity: the succumbing of perpetrators to the hegemonic commercial orchestration of state violence. They are chilling in their ostension towards the bureaucratic banality and quotidian, workaday operation of state-corporate-military power right in the midst of the residential neighbourhood, the civilian city airport, the ordinary home. The absence of the human figure in this imagery lends it a variously sombre, haunting, sinister or austere quality, inviting a reflective, meditative viewing in the first instance and a desire to understand more at a forensic level as one's gaze lingers. The images ostend counterintuitively towards a far more extensive network of agents, actants, players and participants – to include ourselves – in the state-corporate-military violence against others than can be visualized in the weighty presence of human beings, either as individuals or collectively.

Clark's localized and piecemeal forensic approach to subjects of visualization invites the viewer to look very closely, sedulously, and to unravel the image cadastrally, so as to 'figure' out for herself what the event was, the ongoing Event is, what is being shown or ostended towards, withheld, or remains resolutely outside any frame. In this sense, his images can be seen as micro-political excavations of callow state-corporate-military cadastration. By selecting to represent the visually more abstract, less conspicuous and unspectacular facets of 'war', Clark performs an art-documentary decadastration of very real, specifically situated, concealed or public spaces of 'war' and the systemic – but effectively brute – forms of violence in which we are all immersed, wittingly or not.

The confluence of aesthetics, politics and 'data' in these cognitive mapping projects is significant, resonating with the data aesthetics of some of Paglen's image-making. Paglen maps the night sky and the earth's oceans for secret satellites and tapping choke points respectively, for which he makes use of astronomical and flight data, ordnance survey maps, navigational and maritime charts, in the same way that Clark makes use of building plans, city maps, house layouts and declassified documentation. One such mapping project of Trevor Paglen and John Emerson used data gleaned about the CIA extraordinary rendition flights for the former's 'torture taxis' project (Mogel 2011: 192–4). The work, entitled *CIA Rendition Flights* 2001–2006, was also produced in large billboard format and eventually installed on a major Los Angeles boulevard. It shows the continents, all shaded black in a grey ocean, criss-crossed by thin orange lines representing the flights between cities, reaching over a good two-thirds of the globe. It is this type of clandestine celestial cadastration by state-corporate-military power that resonates deeply with Clark's *Negative Publicity* project, as one of its chief concerns is with these extrajudicial, extraordinary rendition flights. However, while Paglen's map provides us with the overall, geopolitical, migratory bird's-eye view of these activities, Clark's images show us what is happening at nitty-gritty, ground level. Figure 2.1 shows a plane on a runway, at a commercial airport, for example.

But while these physical spaces can be precisely triangulated and cadastrally mapped, modern warfare can only be approximated. One can only speculate on the extents, depth and complexity of networks, systems and relations through the use of extant maps, surveys, registers, official (de)classified information or otherwise obtained data, and mathematical models. Such empirical quantitative research can provide any amount of information, but what it cannot do on its own is visualize how something looks or works experientially, or its plethora of unquantifiable cultural and

FIGURE 2.1 *Negative Publicity*. 2011–2016 (series). © Edmund Clark. Reproduced with kind permission.

political meanings, implications, functions and uses. Just as topography and de- or re-territorialization as conceptual tools to map, challenge or resist globalized neoliberal capitalist hegemony and post-colonial transnational corporate imperialism are insufficient terms, so too is the alternative proposed here, the cadastral. It is as blunt an instrument as topography in the attempt imaginatively to visually map 'war'. The cadastral, as insufficient as it is to measure the spaces of war, is nonetheless a bespoke tool with a limited but significant 'use value' for the visualization of modern warfare and its expressions of violence.

While the cadastral is the central star in the conceptual and forensic constellation deployed here, I have found for it a lesser but no less operative moon: in close partnership with the cadastral in the tactics of 'war' figuration is the somewhat technical or mathematical-sounding 'proxy measure', elucidated here in respect of Clark's macabre maps.

Figures 2.2 and 2.3 show 'topographies of terror'. Figure 2.2 is of a town or city where there is an ordinary-looking neighbourhood in which there is a 'black site'. This is a site very far from US soil, but one commandeered by

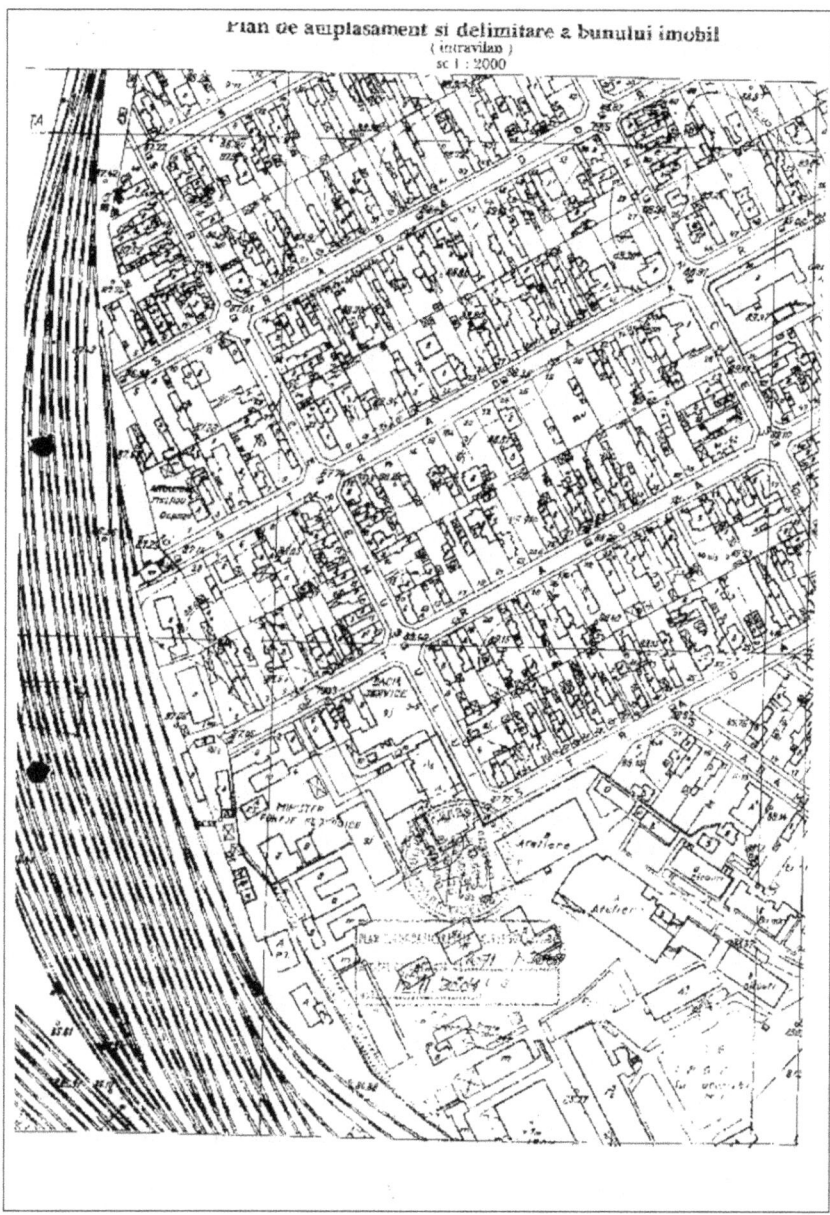

FIGURE 2.2 *Negative Publicity*. 2011–2016 (series). © Edmund Clark. Reproduced with kind permission.

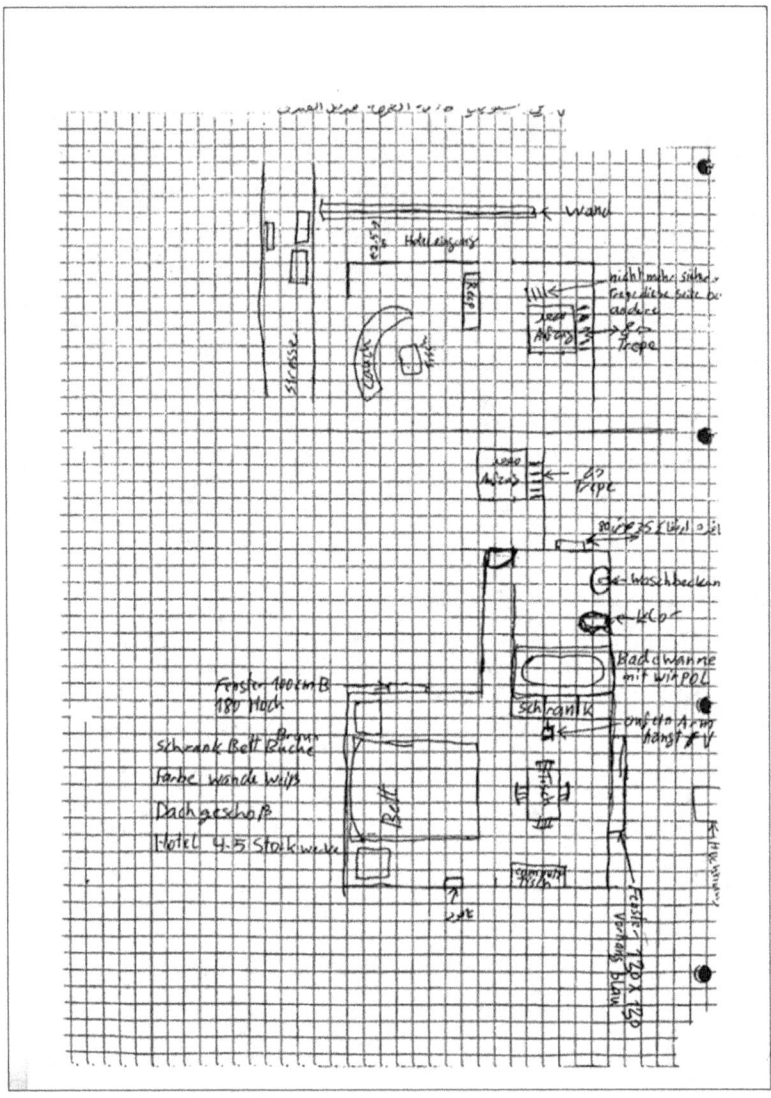

FIGURE 2.3 *Negative Publicity*. 2011–2016 (series). © Edmund Clark. Reproduced with kind permission.

the CIA. On the property is a house which is used for the interrogation and torture of those subject to extraordinary rendition: a 'control order house'.

Figure 2.3 is a hand-drawn sketch of the interior of such a residence among whose inhabitants were the prisoners and potentially the security contractors retained to detain, interrogate and torture. These images, apart from revealing something otherwise invisible to the neighbourhood, are also a cadastral and 'proxy measure' of the workings of 'war': the closest approximation of what is concealed beyond the images, outside the frame. A 'proxy measurement', a term more commonly used in statistics, information science or data analytics, is a method of predicting probable results when you cannot measure the exact value because it is unknown or unknowable, unpredictable, or because there is insufficient information. Proxy measure is used here more than metaphorically: it is a figural, forensic and cadastral approximation of the spatial and real coordinates of the violence of 'war'.

To explain further, Figure 2.2 is not a photograph: it is a reproduction, a copy of a document. Presumably drawn by a town planning draftsman, it shows an area of a fairly large city, judging by what appears to be an extensive railway network to the left of the image. The cadastral measurements are given as conforming to a scale of 1:2000 (although what exact unit of measurement – miles or kilometres – is not clear from this reproduction). To extract more from the image than is evident from the bare and uncommentaried presentation afforded by Clark, the viewer must supplement the viewing with her own further research. Upon feeding the title of the plan into an internet browser, one discovers that it originates from Romania and it is the easy to confirm that the language seen at the top of the image is Romanian. The city, if one peers more closely at the very faint names of buildings and streets, is the capital, Bucharest. The information the image provides is in the starkest (albeit faintest) way denotative, that is, indicative or indexical. We can infer from the fact that the map was part of a file of declassified information obtained by Clark and Black and that it probably represents the site of an act or acts of extraordinary rendition. In fact, further research reveals the 'meaning' of this map is confirmed by a press report of the Open Society Foundations advising of the fact that on 29 June 2016, the Strasbourg court held a public hearing in the case of Abd al-Rahim al-Nashiri, a Saudi national currently (at the time of writing) held at a US military prison at Guantánamo Bay. He has alleged that the Romanian government allowed his incommunicado detention and torture at a secret CIA base in Bucharest. It states:

> Despite a report from the Council of Europe identifying Romania as hosting one of the CIA's so-called 'black site' secret prisons, the Romanian government has persistently denied any knowledge of these operations. Romania was one of over 50 governments around the world that supported a program of secret rendition and torture launched by the CIA after the September 11, 2001, attacks on the United States.
>
> (Birchall 2016a)

The Open Society Foundations is joined by the investigatory efforts of the Associated Press and German media, which too discovered that extraordinary rendition had taken place in Bucharest. The building in which prisoners were held and tortured was owned by Romania's National Registry Office for Classified Information (ORNISS). The building also stores classified information from the EU and NATO.

If one regards at least one role of the image as a tutelary one, to instigate or inspire a desire in the viewer to know more and leading to further research, then by processes of both deduction and induction the viewer mops up the forensic 'excess' of the image. She pieces together a story about the involvement of one city in the 'war on terror', a city far from Washington, DC, in which Nicolae Ceausescu long ago established key ideological and political Spaces of War: numerous interrogation and torture facilities used by the communist regime, and now by the CIA, and which at least since the 'war on terror' is right in the very heart of twenty-first-century, globalized state-corporate-military power and its forms of violence.

The map is thus regarded a cadastral one, encompassing the proprietorial, technical, bureaucratic and legal facets denoted by (and delineated in) this administrative instrument. It is re-framed and re-(con)figured by Clark in the first instance and by the viewer as 'secondary witness' in her act of viewing and re-viewing the image as evidence. This image and its collaboration between image-maker and viewer are part of the post-photographic torture dispositif, as it were. It is one of a system of (re)distributed elements which go to make up rendition, itself a state-corporate torture assemblage. Critically and dissentingly reconfigured through this, it enacts a 'decadastration'. It locates the torture: sites it in a particular city and central rail transport hub of that city, not too far from government buildings.

In other words, the visual deconstruction of the 'war on terror' occurs through an interactive and dialectical nexus of image (re)production, image (re)viewing and visual data (re)configuration. It also shatters the proprietorial integrity and respectable legal codification of the civic allocation of property, exposing the brute impropriety of the uses to which transnational, state-corporate, cadastrated ('war') space is put. By extrapolation, we can take our own 'proxy measure' of what we do not know from what the image can 'tell' us. Viewed as part of the *Negative Publicity* series, and embedded in among the images of anonymous places, of rooms, boundary walls, redacted documents, house interior layout, a long low building in the woods, a swanky swimming pool, pixelated objects and subjects, a blurry aeroplane taking off from somewhere, and so forth, we 'realize' the global convergence of state and commercial activities, public and secret spaces, state-corporate and civilian activities.

Figure 2.3, the hand-drawn sketch imaged in Clark's series, is on an A4 page of block-lined notepaper and is the interior floorplan of parts of a house, labelled in the German language.

What we deduce is that the person who drew the floorplan was or spoke German, which is not enough, however, to tell us whether that person was an agent of the state or a security contractor retained, or the 'detainee', or someone else altogether. Clark does not disclose this, but he does reveal that he spent time with and interviewed ex-detainees. We are left to surmise what we will. Regardless of the source of the sketch, however, is the fact that an event took place, symptomal in its concreteness of the Event (the 'war on terror'). Again, the vague topography of the image nudges the viewer further into a kind of cadastral decoding of sorts – the location of the bed in relation to the interrogation area, for example. It compels consideration of the bathroom and where the prisoner may have been placed while undergoing torture. Slowly the denotative significance of the layout evokes in the mind's eye a compulsion to visualize what has happened and who was involved. Was the PMSC of German, Austrian, American, British or other nationality? Had the prisoner been resident in a German-speaking country before he was detained and subjected to rendition? Did the ex-detainee find his way to Germany, Austria or Switzerland and seek asylum? We do not learn any of this from either Clark or the image. The image of this reproduced and photocopied sketch thus acts as our proxy measure of what we do not know. What we do know is that constitutive events of the main Event – perpetual war – happen in very precise spaces and 'multinational' places, and yet they are nowhere to be seen or found (out), except in post-event reconstruction: via declassified documents, scribbles on paper or photographic audit trails showing the 'measure of things', such as these maps. The subjection of the map to a forensic and cadastral gaze both (con)figures and ostends towards the Event and its evental conditions of possibility, respectively. A simple line sketch, represented as an 'image', devoid of what one would formally or conventionally regard as aesthetic qualities, nonetheless becomes an ineffably poignant visualization of an index to twenty-first-century war spaces and, indeed, an art-documentary inquest into the state-sanctioned death of the extra-judicially executed Other. It is not least by virtue of a co-creative, critical 'collaboration' between imaging participants – the image-maker and the viewer – that strategies of visualization capable of exposing these in/visible war spaces can be optimally developed.

The next set of images we look at is textual in nature and so, literally, more revealing of the nature of the event that very probably took place within the walls of the control order house and its particular location, which can be identified in Bucharest town hall's cadastral map of an ordinary urban area of the city and, indeed, an invisible space of 'war'.

The images shown here of the *Negative Publicity* project bring into vernacular, everyday focus some war spaces in just this way. But they also show documents which are not usually accessible to the public, and while they constitute examples of the 'everyday' workings of 'war on terror' activities, the most heavily redacted of them (Figure 2.4) consisting of just consecutive black blocks (which puts one in mind of Malevich 1915) are actually at least

FIGURE 2.4 *Negative Publicity*. 2011–2016 (series). © Edmund Clark. Reproduced with kind permission.

obliquely suggestive of Norfolk's 'military sublime'.[8] Figure 2.5, an index to the torture guidelines applied in that very control order house in Bucharest, is only partially redacted. It is abominably fascinating in what it divulges: the use of a handgun and power drill in torture, waterboarding, mock execution, and so forth. If the state considers this information innocuous

FIGURE 2.5 *Negative Publicity*. 2011–2016 (series). © Edmund Clark. Reproduced with kind permission.

enough to disclose, to declassify, this begs the horrifying question as to what remains redacted, what is so heinous that it is rendered literally opaque.

The reproduction of this redacted document as an image which itself is already a photocopy removes it as evidence thrice or more (we see it on a computer screen or again as a further reproduction) from the space of its creation: its mis en scène. These levels of remoteness inhere in the image and in this sense it also ostends in abstract fashion towards its own creation and (re)productive function. Its reproduction or reproductive function is to provide us with our closest proxy measure of this particularly vicious aspect of 'war'. For the image-maker and viewer, the political and aesthetic 'use value' of the image lies precisely in what remains redacted in the original document. We see the Event horizon of where it is our eyes are permitted to roam, and we see what is subtracted from that 'space', of which we can never take the full measure.

However, the point is not just to stop at a proxy measure and then turn away, eyes averted, in a resigned slump. As with the Bucharest map, a little further effort is required to apprise oneself as amnesia-challenging, re-historicizing, concerned viewer of the sinister bureaucracy of torture these redacted documents literally point (as opposed to ostend) towards.

We already know from extant witness testimony, investigative journalism and the Abu Ghraib trophy photographs that other forms of torture aside from those involving mock execution, waterboarding and power drills were used. As alluded to earlier, what has been kept redacted was presumably considered not 'in the public interest' to reveal. We can speculate, but we can also deduce on the basis of the above that these forms of torture involved a social taboo of sorts, both in a liberal Western and other contexts, namely the use of sexual torture. This includes the sexual and moral degradation of prisoners such as the use of menstrual blood, urine and excrement, genital torture and electrocution, forcing prisoners to perform sex acts on each other, to include anal rape (Koenig 2017; Mowlabocus 2014). Extensive global state-corporate alliances were forged to undertake rendition, and in its investigations, the Council of Europe found that Romania had assisted the CIA to transfer al-Nashiri in and out of Bucharest and permitted his secret detention in the Bucharest CIA prison. It would seem at least very likely that there, perhaps in the hand-drawn room, the following occurred:

> In May 2004, during his detention in Bucharest, the Senate report confirms that al- Nashiri was subjected to 'rectal feeding' after an attempt at launching a hunger strike. He was forced to lie facing upwards with his head below his torso as CIA operatives infused a nutrition drink, Ensure, into him through his rectum. The Senate report refers to the practice of rectal rehydration as one that was imposed 'without evidence of medical necessity,' that CIA medical officers discussed as a 'means of behavior control.' Al-Nashiri was also subjected to abusive CIA conditions of confinement while held in Romania, including solitary incommunicado detention, blindfolding or hooding, continuous noise, continuous light, leg shackling and forced shaving. During the first month of detention

there, prisoners were subjected to sleep deprivation, water dousing, slapping and forcible standing in painful positions.

(Birchall 2016b)

This is where we depart definitively from the 'shared experience', the mundane and workaday aspect in our visualizations that Clark spoke of in his interview with me when articulating his aims in image-making. But while we are not there in the house, in those rooms, we are somewhere there – the airport, the train station, the road, the neighbourhood, the pharmacy (online perhaps) that stocks funnels and rubber tubes, and the grocery supplier that stocks Ensure.

In any event, none of these documents show any such image of torture. We are required to imagine the nature of the event. We are required to visualize also the burgeoning security business of the ex-combatant or the superannuated CIA agent reinvigorated by his top secret instruction from the highest echelons. We can visualize the domestic, civilian and professional spaces of 'war': comfortable homes and happy children of PMSC personnel or perhaps the Romanian Intelligence Service (SRI) operative who liaised with the CIA on the rendition. We can imagine the commercial aviator or proudly lapelled, honourably demobbed F-35 Lockheed Martin Lightning II stealth fighter pilot touching down on a landing strip designated for 'unusual' cargo at an airport somewhere in Eastern Europe. We can also imagine ourselves, back in 2004, having disembarked from a plane at said airport – as the above-mentioned pilot with her unusual cargo was landing – looking forward to our academic summer conference in a city visited for the first time. Resting thus one's gaze on such 'negative publicity', we can visualize richly the dastardly spaces of twenty-first-century 'war' and our purblind transits through and encounters with it.

Figure 2.6 is a page of a transcript of the cross-examination of a PMSC employee. The underlying trial was not a humanitarian matter, but a strictly commercial legal one. There had been a contractual dispute between the provider and the principal, the identity of which is not disclosed by Clark, but it could have been either an intelligence agency or another contractor or subcontractor. The 'image' literally invokes the queasily Hollywood-clichéd vocabulary of a lawyer conducting a cross-examination of a hapless PMSC employee concerning the rendition activities: 'A bad guy. A bank robber, or something else?' say the employee, to which the response is presumably 'terrorists'. In a darkly humorous typographical mistake on the part of the stenographer or transcriber, 'terrorists' has been erroneously recorded as 'theorists'. Further on, the lawyer continues to refer to the 'bad guys', neutering the impact of the word 'terrorist' to keep the matter contained within the amoral register of commercial legal discourse (in a different

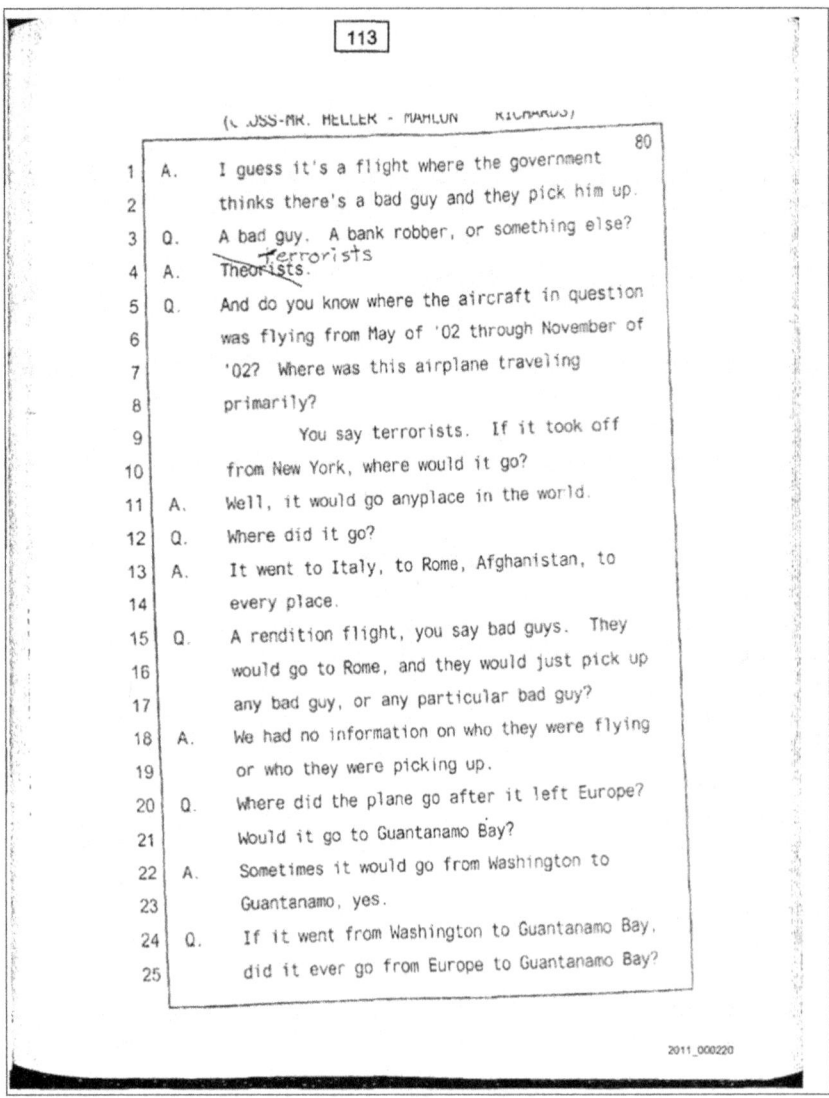

FIGURE 2.6 *Negative Publicity*. 2011–2016 (series). © Edmund Clark. Reproduced with kind permission.

way here, this is also a form of corporate veiling). As a visualization of the bizarre banality of the 'war on terror' for the everyday business of the judicial enforcement of contracts, it is a paradigmatically perfect instance: it is performative, allegorical, synecdochal and the de facto reality all at once. Once again, we see how the power of the image itself – as far from the aesthetic sublime or 'art' as one could conceive – resides in a combination of its post-photographic decontextualization and reframing, and its content both as process and product, the interwoven assemblage of which affords the work its critical impact.

Further, as above, a little more probing on the part of the concerned viewer facilitates a co-creative and collaborative intervention in the work's meaning and impact. Once one has realized that the respondent to the cross-examination in the trial is a private military and security contractor, it remains for the viewer to understand the place of the PMSC under the regulatory aegis of the law of armed conflict. In a percipient sketch of the military-contractual interface in twenty-first-century spaces of 'war', James Cockayne writes that PMSCs

> sit in a conceptual and physical position vis-à-vis the battlefield precisely where lines of accountability are weakened by jurisdictional barriers and contractual and informal – rather than command and control – relations. Figuring out how international law can be applied to these highly de-territorialized, networked commercial actors will remain a crucial task in the years ahead.
>
> (Cockayne 2012: 655)

We understand that the state-corporate-military nexus cannot do just what it wants; there are, as toothless as they may often prove to be, certain globally agreed checks and balances in the international laws of war to ensure that situations where a 'PMSC might itself become responsible for violations of international law by becoming a non-state party to a non-international armed conflict' are avoided as far as possible (Cockayne 2012: 654). The larger point here, however, is that 'war' is not only thoroughly mediatized, but it is ontologically corporatized. 'War' is no longer a Clausewitzian 'politics by other means', but business-as-usual. Like space exploration, the global security-surveillance axis upon which much systemic state-corporate-military and attendant foreign policy practices revolve constitutes the geopolitical and geo-local means of maintaining and surreptitiously extending and normalizing the spaces of war which envelope us and to a significant degree militarize our subjectivities, investment decisions and core values.

If strategies of visualization such as that adopted here by Clark are to pique the viewer into re-visioning her powers of strategic counter-visualization, they must be diligently attended to. It is not enough to appraise the work and to apply once again scholarly or art-world criteria of success/failure, or hermeneutic determinations in support of claims for a work's frame-busting powers. Clark adopts viewer-inclusive strategies of visualization which insist on what might be termed creative activism: his imagery may be read as an implicit invitation to the image viewer or user to continue to enquire into, to investigate, what it is (they think) they are viewing. This is a kind of sine qua non for the post-photographic visualization of 'war' as an essentially critical or dissenting activity which reaches beyond detached theorization, the cerebral stillness of the gallery or the cacophonic output of the press and social media. It is a way of seeing with which practitioners and scholars of the visual can actively collaborate. The viewer, compelled by an ethical 'ought', ought to be prepared to act collaboratively both within and beyond the 'moment' of the work's production, within and outside of its frame, curation and contexts. The piecemeal, guerrilla decadastration of spaces of war occurs in daily acts of strategic visualization, not only of art-documentary works, but of power-violence-person-image-text assemblages that we piece together through our vigilance as concerned citizen observers.

In summary, what Clark does with *Negative Publicity* is to take us into the dark heart of 'war on terror' extraordinary rendition and torture, both obliquely ostending towards or blatantly revealing the loci and (inter)locution of such heinous activities. Such an art of visualization still allows room for the viewer not only creatively to co-visualize, but also collaboratively to conduct her own forensic research with the help of his imagery. The challenges in viewing his work present an opportunity for some sleuthing. This strategy of spectator involvement invites a more active visualization of the 'war on terror' than simply viewing, say, an Abu Ghraib trophy picture. The visualization process as a collaborative effort also implicitly casts doubt on the perception that evidence of war and violence is ever 'self-evident'. Clark's strategies of visualization problematize the nature of visual 'evidence' or what counts as evidence, how we regard and treat evidence, and how we, for better or worse, co-create what then comes to be evidentially freighted.

His spaces of war are the clandestine, deliberately hidden ones. The imagery itself, in a strategy Clark shares with Trevor Paglen, both reveals and withholds its evidence, thereby alluding to the 'Janus face' of the neoliberal state: its simultaneous secrecy and transparency. This resonates with Michael Taussig's ethnological studies of 'public secrecy' in which he posits that secrecy in society and in communities functions dialectically as a process of deliberate, partial revelation of what is publicly known but cannot be openly articulated. Taboos are a case in point. Taussig describes how in 'primitive' societies masking and unmasking rites and rituals serve both to demystify and to re-enchant (Taussig 1999). It involves a pretence of not knowing what you know. As an 'ideological contrivance', the artifice of the public or open secret is a politically convenient fiction (Lee 2011).[9] The state deploys differential presentation to the public of 'evidence in support' of its policy decisions based on the nature of the legitimization required. Spaces of war are, and are represented as, both public and transparent, private and opaque at one and the same time.

This insight itself is an epistemologically crucial one for a more nuanced grasp of the role of ideology and strategic narratives in understanding the operation of the forms of violence of twenty-first-century 'terror-democracy' (Harrison 2008; Roselle et al. 2014). In war (as in commerce), attention is drawn towards either classification or publication: the official secret or public information. Spaces of war as objects of mediatization are frequently simultaneously secret and public, such as political espionage, or weapons of mass destruction. Pursuant to a state of exception understanding, war economics is couched in ideological terms as an existential necessity. Simultaneous conferral of state legitimacy and public absolvence of guilt for complicity in the measures that existential necessity demands is a fiat of statecraft. Spaces of war are not only physically, geopolitically mappable, but discursively, mediatically and imaginatively so.

To reiterate, state-military-corporate cadastration of lived-in spaces happens under our noses and where we live. Clark's *Negative Publicity* powerfully and poignantly ostends towards this brute fact. In engaging the non-human spaces of war rather than its spectacular eventality, Clark opens a window into the deceptively banal bureaucracy of surveillance, of state-military control, corporate-security exploitation and the general cadastration of our lived space into spaces primed for profitably perpetual war. We are immersed in the micro-mapping or cadastral visualization of war. The spectral absences of people lend a quotidian humanity to the non-human imagery. This is a performative paradox, whereby the act of creative visualization erases and distantiates only thereby to reintroduce more forcefully an expanded ambit of reference and renewed challenges for critical, concerned or dissident focus. It is an aesthetic which, while in no deliberate way proffering an 'anti-aesthetic', is in its focus quietly determined to bore into the deceptively workaday nature of the in/visible spaces of war we inhabit and, indeed, co-produce.

Notes

1 In/visible here is a simple form of shorthand for both less visible (unseen, unnoticed, covert or concealed from public view) and opaque or literally invisible (an intangible and abstract system, structure, or network of relationships).
2 The term derives from the French 'cadastre': a register of property. See Lexico.com. Available online: https://www.lexico.com/en/definition/cadastral (accessed 1 October 2019).
3 Unless otherwise cited, all the ensuing quotations are taken from this interview with Clark on 23 October 2016.
4 See Clark, Edmund. *Negative Publicity*. 2011–2016. Available online: https://www.edmundclark.com/works/negative-publicity/#1 [All images discussed here are available from this URL] (accessed 1 September 2019).
5 See Trevor Paglen NEWS. Available online: https://www.paglen.com/ (accessed 1 September 2019).

6 See Simon Norfolk. Available online: http://www.simonnorfolk.com/ (accessed 1 September 2019).
7 While Clark rejects any deterministic categorization of the type of photography he does, it could be regarded broadly as 'post-photography', in the sense that, firstly, the images are not necessarily made using a camera and rely upon archival, analogue or digital primary sources in their (re)production, and secondly, their subject matter is unconventionally conceptual, sometimes to the point of abstraction. Post-photography is not to be confused with the Aftermath photography of war-devastated urban- or landscapes, which may or may not feature a human presence. See Robert Shore (2014) for a useful introduction to the as yet unstable concept of the post-photographic.
8 A phrase coined by Simon Norfolk to describe the subject matter of his dissident image-making: the covert or in/visible machinery and systems of state-military neoliberal democracy.
9 See also Jodi Dean (2002, 2004) for an astute analysis of the public secrets of the state in a 'war on terror' context.

References

Agamben, G. (2005), *State of Exception*, trans. K. Attell, Chicago and London: University of Chicago Press.

Badiou, A., and S. Žižek ([2005] 2010), *Badiou and Žižek: Philosophy in the Present*, ed. P. Engelmann, trans. P. Thomas and A. Toscano, Cambridge, UK, and Malden, USA: Polity Press.

Birchall, J. (2016a), 'CIA Torture in Romania: Europe's Top Human Rights Court Hears Al-Nashiri Complaint', Press Release, *Open Society Foundations*, 29 June. Available online: https://www.opensocietyfoundations.org/newsroom/cia-torture-romania-europes-top-human-rights-court-hears-al-nashiri-complaint (accessed 1 October 2019).

Birchall, J. (2016b), 'Romania's Role in CIA Torture and Rendition Comes before European Court', Press Release of Open Society Justice Initiative, *Open Society Foundations*, 20 June. Available online: https://www.opensocietyfoundations.org/press-releases/romanias-role-cia-torture-and-rendition-comes-european-court (accessed 1 September 2019).

Clark, E. (2011–2016), 'Negative Publicity'. Available online: https://www.edmundclark.com/works/negative-publicity/ (accessed 1 September 2019).

Clark, E. (2016), 'Interview with Nicolette Barsdorf-Liebchen', Personal interview by phone, 23 October.

Clark, E., and C. Black (2016), *Negative Publicity: Artefacts of Extraordinary Rendition*. Co-published with Magnum Foundation.

Cockayne, J. (2012), 'Chapter 25: Private Military and Security Companies', in C. Finkelstein, J. D. Ohlin and A. Altman (eds), *Targeted Killings: Law and Morality in an Asymmetrical World*, 625–55, Oxford University Press.

Dean, J. (2002), *Publicity's Secret: How Technoculture Capitalizes on Democracy*, Ithaca, NY: Cornell University Press.

Dean, J. (2004), 'Secrecy since September 11', *Interventions: International Journal of Post-colonial Studies*, 6(3): 378.
Griffin, M. (1999), 'The Great War Photographs: Constructing Myths of History and Photojournalism', in B. Brennan and H. Hardt (eds), *Picturing the Past: Media, History, and Photography*, 122–57, Illinois: University of Illinois Press.
Harrison, K. (2008), 'Terror-democracy: An Iconology', PhD thesis, The Institute for Cultural Research, Lancaster University.
Kennedy, L. (2016), *Afterimages*, Chicago and London: University of Chicago Press.
Koenig, A. (2017), 'When Is a Cavity Search Not a Cavity Search? Rape at Guantánamo', *Lemming Cliff*, 11 January. Available online: https://medium.com/lemming-cliff/when-is-a-cavity-search-not-a-cavity-search-rape-at-guant%C3%A1namo-b2b320af05db (accessed 1 September 2019).
Lee, P. M. (2011), 'Open Secret: On the Work of Art between Disclosure and Redaction', *Artforum*, 49(9): 223.
Malevich, K. (1915), *Black Square* [Painting].
Mogel, L. (2011), 'Chapter 20. Disorientation Guides: Cartography as Artistic Medium', in M. Dear, J. Ketchum, S. Luria, and D. Richardson (eds), *Geohumanities: Art, History, Text at the Edge of Place*, 187–95, New York: Routledge.
Mowlabocus, S. (2014), 'Rectal Feeding Is Rape – but Don't Expect the CIA to Admit It', *The Conversation*, 12 December. Available online: http://theconversation.com/rectal-feeding-is-rape-but-dont-expect-the-cia-to-admit-it-35437 (accessed 1 September 2019).
Powers, S. M., and M. Jablonski (2015), *The Real Cyber War: The Political Economy of Internet Freedom*, Champaign, IL, USA: University of Illinois Press.
Rancière, J. (2009), *The Future of the Image*, London: Verso.
Roberts, J. (2014), *Photography and Its Violations*, New York: Columbia University Press.
ROS (2017), 'Cadastral Mapping: Overview', *Registers of Scotland*, 1 November. Available online: https://www.ros.gov.uk/services/registration/land-register/faqs/cadastral-mapping-overview (accessed 1 September 2019).
Roselle, L., A. Miskimmon and B. O'Loughlin (2014), 'Strategic Narrative: A New Means to Understand Soft Power', *Media, War & Conflict*, 7(1): 70–84.
Schmitt, C. ([1932] 1996), *The Concept of the Political*, trans. and intro G. D. Schwab, foreword T. B. Strong, notes L. Strauss, Chicago and London: University of Chicago Press.
Shore, R. (2014), *Post-photography: The Artist with a Camera*, London: Laurence King.
Taussig, M. (1999), *Defacement: Public Secrecy and the Labor of the Negative*, Stanford, CA: Stanford University Press.
Žižek, S. (2009), *Violence: Six Sideways Reflections*, London: Profile Books.

3

Digital spaces of war: Genre and affective investments in RT's representations of the Syrian conflict

Rhys Crilley and Precious Chatterje-Doody

Introduction

While research on media and war has provided sophisticated readings of narratives and images used to represent conflict, there is less attention given to how audiences interpret and feel about these representations. Yet recent scholarship (Solomon 2014) suggests that representations of war have political effects not only because of their content, but because of how audiences feel about them. In this chapter, we contribute to burgeoning discussions of affective investment, by analysing how different genres of video elicit different affective investments in representations of war. To do so we analyse a variety of genres of visual media produced by the Russian state-funded international broadcaster RT (formerly Russia Today) that cover the Syrian conflict. We begin by analysing how the visual representations apparent in breaking news reports, late-night parody shows, talk shows and short satirical social media videos frame Russia's involvement in the Syrian conflict and attempt to invoke emotional responses in the audiences that view them. In order to provide further insight into the extent to which different video genres elicit emotions, we then analyse online comments made on these four genres of video.

Russia in the Syrian conflict

In September 2015 the Russian military intervened in the Syrian conflict. Supporting the Assad regime, and labelling all opposition groups as 'terrorists', Russian airstrikes and military support seemingly turned the tide of the Syrian conflict in Assad's favour (Souleimanov and Dzutsati 2018: 42). While Russian intervention in Syria was partly motivated by economic and diplomatic interests, it arguably had a more fundamental strategic aim of helping 'to re-establish Russia's importance on the world stage' (Casula 2015; Wood 2018: 140). Indeed, through a combination of 'three years of nonstop bombing' (Frolovskiy 2019) and diplomatic summits, Russia has emerged as a key power broker in the Middle East, claiming that it has achieved what the 'West' could not – establishing the pathway to peace in Syria (Ellis-Petersen and Roth 2018). Such a pathway has been paved with civilian casualties, with some sources estimating that Russia has killed over 8100 Syrian civilians, including almost 2000 children (SOHR 2019).

Russian intervention in Syria, alongside the crisis in Ukraine, the Russian annexation of Crimea, and Russian interference in the 2016 US Presidential election (Jamieson 2018) have led to the claim that we have entered a 'New Cold War' (Osnos et al. 2017). In this supposedly new geopolitical era, one of the key means of confrontation between Russia and the 'West' takes place through media and communication – where an 'information war' (Hellman and Wagnsson 2017) sees Russia attempting to win the hearts and minds of global publics through various means. These include state-funded international broadcasting through media outlets such as RT and Sputnik (Chatterje-Doody and Crilley 2019b; Hutchings et al. 2015; Orttung and Nelson 2018; Yablokov 2015) as well as more nefarious methods such as spreading disinformation through shadowy online outlets (Hjorth and Adler-Nissen 2019; Jamieson 2018). We seek to build upon current studies, not by examining how 'truthful' Russia's reporting of the Syrian conflict is, but by exploring how audiences feel about that coverage. To do so, we draw upon recent scholarship on aesthetics and emotions to inform our study of Russia's representation of the Syrian conflict.

We argue that the use of different genres of video published by the Russian state-funded international broadcaster RT highlights how actors working under the broad umbrella of the state can, and do, produce multiple representations of the same conflict. By drawing upon theorizing of 'affective investments' (Solomon 2014) we ask three questions:

1 How does RT use different genres of video to frame Russia's involvement in the Syrian conflict?

2   How do these different genres of video serve to invoke emotions in their audiences?

3   How are audiences of these videos affectively invested in Russia's involvement in the Syrian conflict?

These questions provide important openings into considering the spaces of contemporary war and conflict. While the space of war has traditionally been conceptualized as limited to battlefields and their immediate surroundings, modern research has recognized the vital role that media play in bringing distant wars directly into our everyday lives, even when we may live half a world away from the battlefield (Gillespie 2006; Hoskins and O'Loughlin 2010; Sylvester 2010). In the digital age, political and media actors, social media platforms and, crucially, audiences interact and actively co-constitute the representation and meaning of the world and what happens in it (Chatterje-Doody and Crilley 2019b: 81; Merrin 2018; Miskimmon et al. 2017). Social media spaces, therefore, constitute sites at which society engages in representative practices – such as publishing, viewing and sharing comments, photographs, videos and memes – that give meaning to political, social and cultural phenomena such as war and conflict (Cottle 2006; Couldry 2008; Couldry and Hepp 2013).

Within the space of social media, political actors' representations of the wars they are engaged in flow together with audiences' own expressions of their thoughts and feelings about war. These multi-level engagements are visible to, and frame, the experience of subsequent viewers. Therefore, social media comments made by 'the people formerly known as the audience' (Rosen 2012: 13) produce interactions, commentary and framing that together shape understandings of war and conflict online. Our concern, then, is not purely with how physical spaces of war are represented by actors engaged in conflict. Rather, we engage directly with how audiences express feelings about those conflicts through the online comments they produce and share in the meaning-making space of social media.

In response to our research questions we analyse the visual representations apparent in examples of RT's breaking news reports, documentaries, satirical videos and talk shows that frame Russia's involvement in the Syrian conflict. In order to understand the audiences' affective investments in Russian involvement in the Syrian conflict we then analyse online comments made on these genres of video. We discuss the implications of these genres and different affective investments in Russian involvement in the Syrian conflict, and we argue that research must be attuned to the complex milieu of digital representations, genres and emotions that now form digital spaces of war, and which profoundly influence how audiences feel about the conflicts portrayed on-screen.

Media and war: From aesthetics to affective investments

It is important to understand how contemporary wars are represented through media because the words and images used to describe events, issues, actors and actions in global politics produce meanings that determine what can be thought, said and done in response to them (Bleiker 2001: 510). As the philosopher Jacques Rancière notes 'politics revolves around what is seen' (2006: 13) where visual media (such as photographs, news reports, movies and digital images) provide a 'distribution of the sensible' (2006: 12). In these terms, and in the context of war – as Judith Butler argues – visual media help to cultivate and sustain political violence by presenting war as 'an inevitability, something good, or even a source of moral satisfaction' (2010: ix).

Ultimately then, modern war and conflict cannot be made sense of 'unless one carefully accounts for the role of media in it' (Hoskins and O'Loughlin 2010: 4) especially given the emergence and spread of interactive digital communication technologies that permeate both the battlefield and the daily lives of people in places at a far remove from warzones (Cottle 2006; Merrin 2018). Central to understanding the significance of visual media and war has been an attention to how media representations invoke emotions (Åhäll and Gregory 2015; Maltby and Keeble 2007; Zollmann 2017). Some scholars have found that war reporting that features 'emotive and graphic coverage' has more influence over policymakers than non-graphic coverage (Robinson 2002: 25); others have paid attention to how 'suffering is portrayed on screen and how the suffering is narrated'(Chouliaraki 2006: 3), while Butler and others have analysed how visual media frame some lives as grievable and others as not (Butler 2010; Hutchison 2016).

We build upon studies of media representations of war and emotions by recognizing the importance of audiences (da Silva and Crilley 2017; Gillespie et al. 2010; O'Loughlin 2011; Pears 2016) and by using the concept of 'affective investments' (Solomon 2014) to help us analyse both the content of visual media and the responses of audiences that view them. While researchers often study the 'form' of the language or images used in media representations of identities and actions (Laclau 2004: 326), they often overlook the 'forces' by which such media appeal to those who view them (Laclau 2007: 111). As Ty Solomon suggests, media alone 'cannot carry the power that they often have – the force of affect is needed to explain how [they] resonate with audiences and have political effects' (2014: 729). Media representations of war do not only matter because of how they represent the world, but because of how audiences that view them feel about and respond to what they represent.

Following Solomon, we understand affective investments to be a linkage between the representation of identities in media and how these identities are given credence, significance and power due to how audiences feel that those representations express a 'deeper nerve or "essence"' to what is being represented (O'Loughlin 2011; Solomon 2014: 735).

We build upon the study of affective investments by exploring how the genre specificity of images of war and conflict may influence audiences' affective investments in their substantive content. Given that affective investments help to explain the linkage between media content and potential media effects, it is imperative to study not only *what* audiences say in response to online representations of war but also *how* different genres may shape those responses. With this in mind, we now introduce our case study and outline our methodology.

RT and the Syrian conflict: Recognizing the importance of genre

From the outbreak of the conflict in Syria, the government of President Bashar Al-Assad used a combination of physical threats and visa denial to constrain professional media reporting of events on the ground (Khamis et al. 2012). As a result, social media became the primary source of information about the conflict for many people (Lynch et al. 2014; Powers and O'Loughlin 2015). Various actors attempted to use social media to gain support and legitimacy for their causes, with the Syrian Opposition actively using citizen journalists to engage international audiences with their resistance to the Assad regime and revolutionary ambitions (Al-Ghazzi 2014; Andén-Papadopoulos and Pantti 2013; Crilley 2017; Saleh 2018).

What had initially started as a peaceful revolution against Assad and his regime escalated into a civil war between groups including government forces, the National Coalition of Syrian Revolutionary and Opposition Forces, and various Salafi Jihadi groups such as the Islamic State and al Nusra. The progression of the conflict took Syria from being 'a significant regional player into an arena in which a multitude of local and foreign players compete' (Hokayem 2013: 11). This competition was reflected by state-funded international broadcasters, which reported the conflict in ways that aligned with their host states' foreign policy interests (Matar 2014; Salama 2012). While 'Western' states supported the Syrian Opposition (Geis and Schlag 2017), Russia sought to maintain the Assad regime's control of Syria (Orttung and Nelson 2018).

Given Russia's substantial military engagement in Syria, RT's coverage of the conflict is a worthy object of study. The network's coverage reflects 'the Russian government's official position...one way or another' (Putin quoted in The Russian Presidential Executive Office 2013), and their representations of the Syrian conflict therefore serve to provide insight into how RT claims legitimacy for Russian foreign policy activities that have been widely condemned by members of the international community (Orttung and Nelson 2018: 3). We have chosen to study different genres of videos shared by RT's English-language channels on YouTube, because this provides chosen highlights of their broadcast reporting and thus gives an insight into their key messages and demonstrates how they attempt to set the news agenda and influence audiences (al Nashmi et al. 2017: 169–70). Furthermore, YouTube is at the heart of RT's social media strategy (al Nashmi et al. 2017; Chatterje-Doody and Crilley 2019a; Orttung and Nelson 2018) and also enables direct audience engagement via up- and down-voting functions and the ability to leave comments and replies on the video and in response to other audience members.

Studies to date have provided welcome insight into RT's use of YouTube and have accounted for differences between RT's different language services (Orttung and Nelson 2018). We build upon this research by focusing on RT's use of different genres of video across their English language YouTube channels. We do so because genres, as we understand them, are 'patterns/forms/styles/structures which transcend individual [media] products, and which supervise both their construction by [producer] and their reading by audiences' (Ryall 1975: 28). Genres provide a common 'repertoire of elements' (Lacey 2000: 133) that shape how media are produced and interpreted. Alongside news reports hosted by television anchors, RT produces media in a range of genres including, but not limited to, talk shows, documentaries and satirical short clips. However, studies of RT often remain focused on single genres of RT's output, such as their news broadcasts (Chatterje-Doody and Crilley 2019b; Hutchings et al. 2015; Hutchings and Tolz 2015; Miazhevich 2018; Rawnsley 2015), their coverage of conspiracy theories (Yablokov 2015) or their social media re-enactments (Crilley et al., 2019). Our study builds upon this work by placing genre at the heart of the analysis and exploring different forms of genre beyond those listed above. This helps us understand how media actors attempt to frame war and conflict in different ways in an attempt to invoke different emotions, and how in turn this may appeal to different audiences, thereby providing an insight into the complexity of how political actors claim legitimacy for their actions in multiple ways in the hybrid media ecology.

In order to understand how RT uses different genres of video to frame Russia's involvement in the Syrian conflict, we focus our analysis on one particular event: the chemical attack in Douma on 7 April 2018 which caused the deaths of approximately fifty people and injured one hundred more. The Organization for the Prohibition of Chemical Weapons (OPCW), USA, France and Britain, attributed the attack to the Assad regime. Despite this, the Syrian regime and their Russian allies argued that the attack was carried out, or staged, by opposition forces and their 'Western' allies. This event thus warrants attention because it marks a critical moment at which the Russian government sought to claim legitimacy for their own foreign policy in Syria while delegitimizing the policy of 'Western' states who conducted military airstrikes in response to the chemical attack. Our study explores examples of several different genres of video about the Douma chemical attack that RT published on YouTube. These are: (1) a breaking news video, (2) a late-night parody show, (3) a talk show and (4) a short satirical video (see Table 3.1 for an overview of each video).

Breaking news

On 13 April 2018 RT English uploaded a news broadcast to YouTube titled 'Solid Evidence Douma "Chemical Attack" Was Staged – Lavrov' (RT 2018c). The video follows the genre conventions of a news broadcast: introduction by news anchor; featured interview with official statement; interview with journalist; accompanying footage of the event. Throughout, a banner chryon at the bottom of the screen displays headlines such as 'Russian FM: Solid evidence Syria's Douma "chemical attack" staged'. At first glance, the video appears objective through the presentation of accounts from the Russian foreign secretary, other 'Western' media outlets (countering the Russian foreign secretary's claims) and the reactions of the US ambassador to the UN to the events. However, such a reading belies an inherent bias in favour of the Russian foreign minister's account noted through the anchor affirming that Lavrov has 'the solid proof...that pretty much one hundred percent goes against what you'll read and hear everywhere else'. The support of Russian claims is further emphasized by the dismissal of 'Western' news sources as deceptive, and the use of graphic imagery depicting the White Helmets as Islamist jihadists. Such characterizations serve as a portfolio of 'evidence' through which the news item can be seen to invoke mistrust and doubt in the United States, opening space for trust and credence in Lavrov and Russia.

Late-night parody show

The second video we examined is a late-night news parody show. This genre is perhaps most associated with shows such as *The Daily Show* and *Last Week with John Oliver*, which feature a news anchor-like presenter satirizing the news using a combination of humorous characterizations and images. Published on RT's documentary YouTube channel, the series *ClipaRT with Boris Malagurski* employs the conventions of this genre. In a video published on 12 September 2018 (RT 2018d), Malagurski uses sarcasm and expressive verbal and body language throughout. Excerpts from 'Western' media sources are used but Malagurski adopts a clear line of argument in favour of Assad and Russia, explicitly alleging that the Douma attack was staged. While the Syrian opposition and their backers are presented as untrustworthy proponents of 'propaganda' and terrorism, Assad is framed as a rational, trustworthy actor whose military are 'the real heroes in Syria'.

Talk show

On 16 April 2018, RT published a half-hour segment of their flagship talk show *CrossTalk* to YouTube. The episode, titled 'Syria Attacked' (RT 2018a), brings the regular presenter, Peter Lavelle, together with two guests to discuss US airstrikes in Syria in response to the Douma chemical attack. While typical genre characteristics of current affairs talk shows consist of debate between guests, *CrossTalk*'s guests often share a critical perspective on the 'West' and a supportive vision of Russia and its allies. This was precisely the case in this video. Guest Mark Sleboda is described as an 'international affairs and security analyst' and Dmitry Babich as 'a political analyst with Sputnik International'. While these introductions suggest trust in the guests' independence from RT, they can also be interpreted as obscuring their partisanship: Sputnik International is RT's sister outlet, and both Babich and Sleboda – previously described as 'a blatantly pro-Kremlin apologist' (Williams in Meade 2018) – are recurrent guests on RT.

Throughout the talk show, the participants depict the US-led airstrikes as illegitimate breaches of international law; 'dangerous' provocations against Russia; and a cynical 'distraction' from significant domestic crises faced by the leaders of the United States, UK and France. Russia, by contrast, it is claimed, 'hasn't reacted militarily'. The debate also focuses on how the Syrian opposition are 'jihadis' and 'terrorists' whose areas of Syria are 'just not safe'. Furthermore, the participants also speak to conspiracy theories, describing the chemical attack as 'a hoax' being used by the 'West' as 'a pretext... to attack everyone they want'. Lavelle says the West 'can dance on the global stage with impunity' and the participants agree, discussing how the strikes violate international law, how 'Western' justifications are 'gobbledygook', and further emphasizing how the 'West' should not be trusted.

Satirical social media short

The final video analysed for this study was uploaded by RT's most recent YouTube channel – ICYMI – a channel dedicated to publishing short satirical social media videos, designed for young audiences and featuring informal presenting, fast editing, bright colours, and the use of animation and memes. Published on 20 April 2018, 'ICYMI: Be reassured, people of Syria – the West has humanitarian missiles ready to intervene!' (RT 2018b) is hosted

TABLE 3.1 Summary of key features of each video

	Breaking news	Late-night parody show	Talk show	Satirical social media short
Conventions of genre	• Calm presenters • Impartial • Discussion of various views	• Expressive presenter • Humour/satire • Bias/subjective	• Impartial moderation • Discussion and debate of various views	• Expressive presenter • Humour/satire • Bias/subjective
Programme narrative	• Attack staged • Solid evidence • Earlier 'attacks' also appeared staged – conspiratorial insinuation • Biased mainstream media (MSM)	• Attack staged • Earlier 'attacks' were staged – explicit conspiracy theory • Complicit MSM	• The Syrian war is a proxy conflict • 'Western' intervention contravenes international law	• No humanitarian motive for 'Western' missile strikes • Financial motives (arms trade) • Political motives (distraction) • Prior Western use of WMDs
Framing of actors	• Lavrov: trustworthy • US government: untrustworthy • White Helmets: terrorist enablers • MSM: biased	• White Helmets: US-funded; US proxies; terrorist enablers • US government: untrustworthy; warmongering • Assad: rational actor • Syrian army: heroic	• Syrian opposition: terrorists • 'West': untrustworthy • Russia: effective; restrained; deserving of respect • Assad: legitimate; effective	• 'West': source of ridicule; hypocritical; untrustworthy; deceitful
Invocation of emotions	• Trust in Lavrov and Russia • Fear of Syrian opposition • Mistrust of the US • Suspicion of White Helmets	• Trust in Assad regime • Mistrust of White Helmets, Syrian opposition and the US • Fear of the Syrian opposition	• Fear of Syrian opposition • Mistrust of 'West' • Respect for Russia	• Mistrust of 'West'

by the RT UK news presenter Polly Boiko. The ICYMI channel adopts the conventions of satirical social media short videos, which are often limited to a few minutes in length, feature a presenter expressively talking to camera and using humour, alongside comedic images to report on and make light of a political issue. ICYMI's video on the Douma chemical attack begins with Polly Boiko's sarcastic assessment that 'after allegations of a chemical attack, Syrians were immediately reassured because, in case you missed it, heavily armed Western warplanes were on their way with a humanitarian intervention'.

The hypocrisy of 'Western' states is ridiculed by Boiko who reminds viewers of the global arms trade – with one section featuring the logos of 'Western' arms companies – while Boiko claims 'the message to despots and terrorists is stick to conventional weapons and if possible buy them from western arms dealers – because that way you can fire them safely from the moral high ground'. References are made to 'the Syrian clusterfuck', and by using humour the 'west' is framed as hypocritical, irresponsible and deceitful. The video ends by again emphasizing the hypocrisy and the untrustworthiness of 'Western' actors, as Boiko implies how the airstrikes on Syria are used as a distraction: 'Surgically striking a lesson into Syria makes for much better headlines at home than Stormy, Comey, Brexit, and Parisian protesters getting a police gassing of their own.'

Affective investments in different genres of RT's Syria coverage

Since analysis of RT's media content can only tell us about their emotive *representations* of the Douma attack, we now focus on comments made on each of these videos in order to establish how audiences of these video genres were affectively invested in Russia's involvement in the Syrian conflict. YouTube comments are socially significant, not just because of the site's mass user base (Thelwall et al. 2012: 617), but precisely because of their capacity to approximate a community-based negotiation of video content which, through the space of comments sections, brings particular identities and non-geographical connections between users to the fore (van Zoonen et al. 2010). In shaping the media space in which war is viewed and experienced, such discussions and negotiations are vital to understanding the affective investments of viewers in the video content: they form part of the media consumption of subsequent viewers, thus potentially shaping their perceptions of it.

In order to interrogate RT audiences' interpretations and expressions of emotion in response to RT's videos, we opened each YouTube video in an incognito web browser; gathered data on video views, upvotes, downvotes and comments; ordered according to YouTube's algorithm which determines how comments appear below videos. Factors such as the popularity of the comment maker, the date/time the comment was posted, the number of upvotes the comment receives, and the content of the comment determine the order in which comments appear (YouTube 2016). The top ten comments published therefore give an indication of how some of the audience has interpreted the video. While the expressions of emotions in these individual comments are not generalizable to all audience members, their prominence as top ten comments based on YouTube's algorithm suggests that the sentiments they express resonate with other audience members.

Given the fact that the majority of YouTube commentators choose to remain anonymous and register under pseudonyms (Thelwall et al. 2012: 617), it is difficult to discern who exactly is commentating on YouTube videos. YouTube purports to be effective at removing automated 'bot' accounts (YouTube 2018), and by viewing the profiles of those who published the top ten comments on each video we discern that the commentators – although mainly being anonymous and using pseudonyms – appear to be genuine YouTube users as they have published videos of their own and made playlists (not necessarily of political content, but of music videos, for example), and they also subscribe to other non-political channels. One commentator went by the name 'Pro Russian', and another user by the name of 'Supreme hatred' has 'Pro Russian!!' in their biography, but this is also followed by the statement that they 'support all forms of death metal worldwide'. Even so, given that the Russian state is often effective at making state-sponsored social media accounts appear to be from non-Russian users (Jamieson 2018), it is almost impossible for anyone other than social media platforms themselves to discern who may be making comments on behalf of the Russian state. Subsequently, this means first that the analysis below comes with the caveat that it could be shaped by actors associated with the Russian state itself, but second, and perhaps most importantly, it means that the analysis of social media comments should not be concerned with ascertaining their truthfulness or being caught up in unanswerable questions around the 'true' identity and intentions of the commenter. Rather, what we can study is how the comments published in response to videos of war are aspects of discourse that express feelings and represent identities in certain ways. In this way, social media comments such as those on YouTube are a space which provides a snapshot of audience sentiment to which subsequent audience members are subjected regardless of whether those sentiments are 'true' or not.

As can be seen in Table 3.2, audience engagement with RT's videos on the Douma attack and its aftermath displayed some interesting contrasts. First, while the breaking news video was the most-watched in absolute terms, it demonstrated the lowest net approval as a percentage of view count. Conversely, the satirical social media short, while least watched,

TABLE 3.2 *Audience engagement with each video*

	Breaking news	Late-night parody show	Talk show	Satirical social media short
Number of views	99,822	20,126	42,947	16,655
Number of upvotes	1900	555	1200	571
Number of downvotes	99	28	49	37
Net upvotes ('approval')	1801	527	1151	534
Net approval as % of views	1.8	2.6	2.7	3.2
Number of comments	894	82	551	184
Ratio views:comments	112:1	245:1	78:1	91:1

boasted the highest net approval as a percentage of views. As we discuss below this appears directly related to its perceived entertainment value. The talk show and late-night parody show enjoyed comparable net approval for views; yet, the talk show was three times more likely than the late-night parody to provoke viewers to comment, suggesting a greater intensity to their engagement. Our examination of the top ten comments on each of the videos gives an indication of the role of genre in stimulating audiences' affective investments in portrayals of conflict.

The high approval of the satirical short on 'humanitarian intervention' is reflected in top comments that engage not only with the video's content – 'Beating up the evil western media! Enlightening people!' – but express support for the genre, presenting and style of ICYMI's video, such as 'spot on and sweetly presented' and 'the one and only ICYMI'. This indicates that the audience enjoys the way in which ICYMI satirizes global politics, and the resonance of ICYMI's humour is demonstrated by comments including laughing emojis and 'hahahaaaaaaaa' designations. Others explicitly praised the effectiveness of the humour at conveying serious messages: 'Nothing like a good bit of British irony to get the message home. Nice video + subscribed.' Such comments reflect the fact that positive, humorous video content tends to be responded to in positive ways on YouTube (Thelwall et al. 2012: 619). Subsequently, the major affective investment in RT's satirical genre of videos appears to be one grounded in the comedic style and humour of these videos, rather than simply about the specific claims they make about the conflict in Syria. This affective investment creates a sense of community across the audience who share this sentiment and can be noted in the upvotes that comments such as the aforementioned one above receive, but also in replies such as:

> Yes RT is funded by the Russian government. Which makes one realise that they are also great at using a cute chick and Top Gear level irony as persuasion tactics. But to be frank, without the truth also, the irony and cute chick wouldn't actually work, so they have a triple whammy.

Comments like this reveal how audiences who may be critical of RT – recognizing it as being state funded and engaging in 'persuasion tactics' – are still affectively invested in their framing of the Syrian conflict because of their narrative claims and, importantly, the ironic style in which they present them.

The talk-show episode was the genre that enjoyed the highest ratio of comments to views, supporting Thelwall et al.'s (2012: 627) observation that audiences of controversial topics engage in more debates via comments due to the fact that such topics often provoke strong opinions. Here, too, the top comment engaged with the programme in form as well as content: 'It's programs like this that are making it increasingly difficult for the U.S. and its lackeys to justify their crimes.' Other top comments replicated the show's guests' mistrustful characterization of 'Western' actors and their motivations for involvement in Syria, suggesting that the 'West' is responsible for 'imperialist aggression' or motivated 'to kill Syrians and take away their resources'. Upvotes for these comments and replies that state their support such as 'you are absolutely right' highlight how, in this instance, social media comments – as a space in which the identities and actions of actors at war are debated and contested – resonate with RT's framing of the conflict through an overarching sense of conspiratorial mistrust.

In the discussion that emerged from this understanding of the conflict, shared anti-imperialist, 'Western'-sceptic and conspiratorially inclined identities came to the fore. So despite the video itself not having been anti-Semitic, its conspiratorial nature – and the 'conspiratorial' community that dominated the discussion space – facilitated the expression of overt anti-Semitism. Such sentiments are often associated with the kind of conspiracy theories that RT has been noted to have a tendency to explore (Yablokov 2015) and, in this case, were expressed by commenters declaring that the 'elephant in the room' is 'ISRAEL' or that 'Mossad' was responsible for the chemical attack and that the airstrikes against Syria were 'all to do with that pipeline going through Syria and the gas oil in Israel. Zionists'. Here, the significant affective investment in RT's talk-show depiction of the Syrian conflict concerns how the audience's sense of mistrust in the

'West' and belief in conspiracy theories aligns with, yet extends beyond, the conspiratorial, mistrustful views espoused by the talk-show guests.

Top comments on the breaking news and late-night parody show were devoid of anti-Semitism, which would be coherent with the likelihood that audiences of these genres were motivated less by a desire to engage in online discussion and more by immediate interest, and entertainment purposes respectively (see Thelwall et al. 2012). Nonetheless, their audiences displayed affective investment in RT's portrayals of key actors in the conflict, including by replicating those videos' disparagement of, and conspiracy theories about, the White Helmets and their origins. So comments on the breaking news video joked that the chemical attack was 'staged', that the 'White helmets live in [the] white house' and that 'the White Helmets could "stage" a lunar landing if you gave them enough money'. Late-night parody show viewers agreed that the White Helmets were 'THE REAL TERRORISTS', 'the propaganda arm of Al Qaeda' and 'as credible as CNN'. These kinds of assessments extended to expressions of affective investment in the identities of a trustworthy Russia and a deceitful 'West' in the top comments on both videos.

Those commenting on the breaking news video concluded that 'once again Russia proves to the world that the US government is doing what it does best which is lying' and 'the US leaders and their masters are definitely the terrible monster's [sic] to our world'. What is key here is the fearful emotion implied by this commenter which is echoed by another, who expresses concern over 'the Islambic [sic] invasion'. Again, such comments, alongside replies that state their agreement such as 'Agree 100%' and 'Yes. You are right,' as well as upvotes for these comments all highlight how RT's narratives resonate with audiences who feel mistrust towards 'Western' actors. Furthermore, they suggest that the audience also feels affectively invested in a sense of fear for 'outsiders' and others such as Muslims.

Meanwhile, top comments on Boris Malagurski's late-night parody show displayed similar affective investments in the notion of trustworthy Russian and deceitful Western identities, as in assessments that 'it is really tragic and sad how much evil USA is' and 'USA THE MORE THEY SPEAK THE MORE THEY LIE'. One commentator explicitly endorses Malagurski's characterization of Assad as the 'West's' scapegoat, opining that the Douma chemical attack 'was carried out by the UK and blamed on Assad'. Such comments highlight that these audience members are affectively invested in RT's framing of the 'West' as an actor that cannot be trusted and view it as a source of 'evil' that lies and commits atrocities while blaming them on others.

What emerges from this study is a typology of sorts concerning the affective investments audiences feel for RT's representations of the Syrian conflict. The first concerns how satirical videos – even when they concern war and conflict – solicit an affective investment in the humorous style of the video and the manner in which they make audiences laugh. Second, and as evidenced in response to the talk-show video featuring two guests who are mistrustful of the 'West', audiences appear to be affectively invested in a belief in conspiracy theories and the sense that the 'West' is evil and cannot be trusted, whereas they believe Russia is good and trustworthy. Third, the audience of the breaking news report and the late-night parody show appear to be mainly affectively invested in a sense of mistrust for the Syrian opposition and a sense of fear that the Syrian opposition forces are actually radical terrorists.

A complex milieu of representation, genre and emotion in war

All genres of RT's video outputs responding to the Douma attack and its aftermath reiterated both key pro-Russian narratives of those events and normatively loaded characterizations of the actors involved. Social media provided a space in which audiences could interact with both the video representations of war and with each other through upvotes and replies. The top comments on these videos indicated that RT's audiences had invested affectively in the identities of a trustworthy Russia contrasted with a deceitful 'West'. This indicates that RT's narration of the Syrian conflict, and the role of Russia within that, resonates with how their audiences feel about the conflict.

Our analysis suggests that the genre of video impacts how audiences engage with RT's representation of the Syrian conflict given the different rates of engagement, the intensity of engagement, and the audiences' propensity to replicate specific allegations about the actors and events portrayed on-screen. The genre of the videos also helped to shape the social media space in which they were discussed, echoing earlier findings of Thelwall et al (2012) and drawing attention to how different genres of videos invoke different affective investments in RT's representation of the Syrian conflict. It is not, however, possible to determine whether this is a result of having viewed a particular genre of content or whether it is because people likely to interact in particular ways are more likely to select certain genres of content to view.

Our first observation was that the breaking news video – a genre whose entire form is based around the stimulation of affect and immediacy – was the one with the highest total number of views. Yet compared to some of the genres that attract lower but more specific audiences, the breaking news video had relatively low levels of approval and of substantive engagement in the form of comments. This implies that a wider and more general audience may have viewed it but that it did not engage the majority of these viewers enough for them to comment on it.

Second, the specific content of the videos does have an impact on *how* audiences interact with it. In the case of the breaking news video and the late-night parody show, for instance, comments expressly replicated the conspiratorial allegations about the White Helmets, their motivation and their backing. On the videos not focused on such claims, they were similarly absent from the top comments. Furthermore, it appears that more in-depth programming such as talk shows are likely to stimulate more in-depth responses and that the emergence of community identities centred around a mistrust of the 'West' and a belief in conspiracy theories enables the extension of discussion beyond topics or framings included in the original video, but coherent with a perceived shared conspiratorial worldview. This was indicated by the increased propensity of viewers of the extended talk show to leave comments on the video and the emergence of anti-Semitic tropes in the comments, as well as replies to comments that stated their agreement and support. While there were examples of others replying to RT and other comments and challenging their claims, such as 'dont listen to these russian propaganda' and 'This video is sponsored by the Russian government. You've been goofed, ya big goof'; such comments and replies were a small minority across the comments on all four videos in our analysis. Thus, the discussion appears to lend itself to the promotion of further agreement and connectivity among RT's audience base, rather than a contestation and challenging of how they frame the Syrian conflict.

Third, audience approval for particular videos was not simply related to the extent to which they agreed with the arguments put forward within it, but also to their overall satisfaction with the entertainment experience. So, in this case, the satirical social media short was particularly successful at entertaining its target audience. While this is coherent with research indicating that some audience subsets are more motivated by entertainment objectives than political ones (Thelwall et al. 2012), it nonetheless suggests that the social media space enables international broadcasters to represent their narratives of war through genres such as satirical videos that blur the line between entertainment and politics – demonstrated here by the commenters noting not only their approval of the form in which the message was delivered, but also of the message itself. As humour plays an important role in creating and consolidating a shared sense of political community (Davies and Illot 2018; 1), RT's humorous framing of those involved in the Syrian conflict serves to be central to evoking an affective investment in the audience. However, while the late-night parody show also utilized a humorous genre, it proved less successful at generating audience approval. It is possible that this is due in part to the explicitly partisan nature of the parody show's pro-Assad message, the tone of which was one of advocacy rather than comedy. The ICYMI short, by contrast, did not so much support a pro-Russian reading of the Syrian conflict, as satirize the hypocrisy of the 'Western' actors involved.

Another possible reason for the disparity in the two comedy products' apparent success may be related to their closeness of fit with genre and audience expectations. The ICYMI satirical short video is a slick, punchy product fronted by a female millennial presenter with whom the average YouTube user can likely identify given that YouTube's audience is predominantly made up of millennial males (Thelwall et al. 2012: 626). As such, it is well calibrated for its intended dissemination on social media. ClipaRT, on the other hand, meshes an established parody-show format with a social media short form. In the late-night parody video, given his age, style of dress and mode of presenting – lecturing the viewer and talking down to them from behind a desk – Malagurski himself lacks the informal style common to parody videos and it is unclear how the video fits the preferences of any particular audience demographic.

Conclusion

When consuming images of war and conflict, audiences engage not only with the overall content of the narratives contained within, but also with the genre and form of the video content. So while breaking news videos have more of the urgency required to stimulate viral circulation to large number of potential audiences, other genres had greater ability to substantively engage their audiences. This might be in terms of stimulating greater levels of audience approval in the content or stimulating additional discussion within the parameters set out by the video. However, genres of output most suited to stimulating audience approval – such as the social media short video – are perhaps the least effective in projecting coherent strategic narratives. This is because successful political comedy writing involves questioning, criticism and disruption rather than the clear articulation of other political viewpoints and possibilities (Young 2017: 879).

As a digital space of war, YouTube enables actors who are engaged in war to represent themselves and their actions to audiences through the use of different genres of videos. Through the use of comments, audiences can interact with these representations, expressing their thoughts and feelings and, in doing so, shaping the viewing experience for others who also view the video and reply to comments. In our analysis we found that comments supported the claims of RT and that audiences generally shared the sentiments espoused in the videos as well as agreeing with the thoughts and feelings of others expressed through comments. This involved expressing support for the style used in the satirical video, invoking a sense that the 'West' is evil, deceitful and engaged in conspiracies in response to the talk-show video that expressed similar views and also sharing a mistrust and fear for the Syrian opposition like the breaking news video and the late-night parody video did. As such, the comments shared on social media sites become a space (of war) where meaning is given to the identities and actions of those at war. This matters because this enables a collapsing between the physical and affective spaces of war, where audiences come to feel strong feelings about wars and conflicts they experience in mediatized form, and then they express these feelings for others to view and engage with online. If spectatorship is one of the most significant ways in which many of us experience war (Sylvester 2010), then in the digital age it needs to be recognized that social media enables people to not only view war from afar but to comment, reply to, like, share and upvote media representations of war. Given that our study suggests that genre plays a key role in exerting an influence on audience emotions, it demands further comprehensive study of genres and audience engagement in these digital spaces of war. RT's willingness to innovate and utilize different genres of video as part of their remit to promote the interests, perspectives and actions of the Russian state is seeming to be effective in engaging the audiences who view their content. As viewers appear to be affectively invested in RT's different representations of the Syrian conflict across different genres of video, we require further research into not only the arguments and claims projected by actors at war, but the ways in which such claims are expressed through different genres in the digital age.

References

Åhäll, L., and T. Gregory (2015), 'Concluding Reflections', in L. Åhäll and T. Gregory (eds), *Emotions, Politics and War*, 222–33, London: Routledge.
Al Nashmi, E., M. North, T. Bloom and J. Cleary (2017), 'Promoting a Global Brand: A Study of International News Organisations' YouTube Channels', *The Journal of International Communication*, 23(2): 165–85.
Al-Ghazzi, O. (2014), '"Citizen Journalism" in the Syrian Uprising: Problematizing Western Narratives in a Local Context', *Communication Theory*, 24(4): 435–54.
Andén-Papadopoulos, K., and M. Pantti (2013), 'The Media Work of Syrian Diaspora Activists: Brokering between the Protest and Mainstream Media', *International Journal of Communication*, 7(0): 22.
Bleiker, R. (2001), 'The Aesthetic Turn in International Political Theory', *Millennium – Journal of International Studies*, 30(3): 509–33.
Butler, J. (2010), *Frames of War: When Is Life Grievable?* London: Verso.
Casula, P. (2015), 'The Syrian Conflict through Russian Eyes Revisited', *Russian Analytical Digest*, 175: 6–10.
Chatterje-Doody, P. N., and R. Crilley (2019a), 'Making Sense of Emotions and Affective Investments in War: RT and the Syrian Conflict on YouTube', *Media and Communication*, 7(3): 167–78.
Chatterje-Doody, P. N., and R. Crilley (2019b), 'Populism and Contemporary Global Media: Populist Communication Logics and the Co-construction of

Transnational Identities', in F. A. Stengel, D. Nabers, and D. B. Macdonald (eds), *Populism and World Politics: Exploring Inter- and Transnational Dimensions*, 73–99, London: Palgrave Macmillan.

Chouliaraki, L. (2006), *The Spectatorship of Suffering*, London and Thousand Oaks, CA: Sage.

Cottle, S. (2006), *Mediatized Conflict: Understanding Media and Conflicts in the Contemporary World*, Maidenhead: McGraw-Hill International.

Couldry, N. (2008), 'Mediatization or Mediation? Alternative Understandings of the Emergent Space of Digital Storytelling', *New Media & Society*, 10(3): 373–91.

Couldry, N., and A. Hepp (2013), 'Conceptualizing Mediatization: Contexts, Traditions, Arguments', *Communication Theory*, 23(3): 191–202.

Crilley, R. (2017), 'Seeing Syria: The Visual Politics of the National Coalition of Syrian Revolution and Opposition Forces on Facebook', *Middle East Journal of Culture and Communication*, 10(2): 133–58.

Crilley, R., M. Gillespie and A. Willis (2019), 'Tweeting the Russian Revolution: RT's# 1917LIVE and Social Media Re-Enactments as Public Diplomacy', *European Journal of Cultural Studies*, OnlineFirst: journals.sagepub.com/doi/abs/10.1177/1367549419871353.

da Silva, R., and R. Crilley (2017), '"Talk about Terror in Our Back Gardens": An Analysis of Online Comments about British Foreign Fighters in Syria', *Critical Studies on Terrorism*, 10(1): 162–86.

Davies, H., and S. Ilott (2018), 'Mocking the Weak? Contexts, Theories, Politics', in H. Davies and S. Ilott (eds), *Comedy and the Politics of Representation: Mocking the Weak*, 1–24, London: Springer.

Ellis-Petersen, H., and A. Roth (2018), 'Vladimir Putin Calls US-led Syria Strikes an "Act of Aggression"', *The Guardian*, 14 April. Available online: https://www.theguardian.com/world/2018/apr/14/insulting-russia-furious-over-syria-attacks-as-politician-likens-trump-to-hitler (accessed 10 September 2019).

Frolovskiy, D. (2019), 'What Putin Really Wants in Syria', *Foreign Policy*, 1 February. Available online: https://foreignpolicy-com.libezproxy.open.ac.uk/192019/02/01/what-putin-really-wants-in-syria-russia-assad-strategy-kremlin (accessed 12 August 2019).

Geis, A., and G. Schlag (2017), '"The Facts Cannot Be Denied": Legitimacy, War and the Use of Chemical Weapons in Syria', *Global Discourse*, 7(2–3): 285–303.

Gillespie, M. (2006), 'Security, Media, Legitimacy: Multi-ethnic Media Publics and the Iraq War 2003', *International Relations*, 20(4): 467–86.

Gillespie, M., J. Gow, A. Hoskins, B. O' Loughlin and I. Zveržhanovski (2010), 'Shifting Securities: News Cultures, Multicultural Society and Legitimacy', *Ethnopolitics*, 9(2): 239–53.

Hellman, M., and C. Wagnsson (2017), 'How Can European States Respond to Russian Information Warfare? An Analytical Framework', *European Security*, 26(2): 153–70.

Hjorth, F., and R. Adler-Nissen (2019), 'Ideological Asymmetry in the Reach of Pro-Russian Digital Disinformation to United States Audiences', *Journal of Communication*, 69(2): 168–92.

Hokayem, E. (2013), *Syria's Uprising and the Fracturing of the Levant* (1st edn), Abingdon: Routledge.

Hoskins, A., and B. O'Loughlin (2010), *War and Media*, Cambridge: Polity Press.
Hutchings, S., and V. Tolz (2015), *Nation, Ethnicity and Race on Russian Television: Mediating Post-Soviet Difference*, London: Routledge.
Hutchings, S., M. Gillespie, I. Yablokov, I. Lvov and A. Voss (2015), 'Staging the Sochi Winter Olympics 2014 on Russia Today and BBC World News: From Soft Power to Geopolitical Crisis', *Participations*, 12(1): 630–58.
Hutchison, E. (2016), *Affective Communities in World Politics*, Cambridge: Cambridge University Press.
Jamieson, K. H. (2018), *Cyberwar: How Russian Hackers and Trolls Helped Elect a President – What We Don't, Can't, and Do Know*, New York: OUP USA.
Khamis, S., P. B. Gold and K. Vaughn (2012), 'Beyond Egypt's "Facebook Revolution" and Syria's "YouTube Uprising:" Comparing Political Contexts, Actors and Communication Strategies', *Arab Media & Society*, 15: 1–30.
Lacey, N. (2000), *Narrative and Genre: Key Concepts in Media Studies*, New York: St. Martin's Press.
Laclau, E. (2004), 'Glimpsing the Future', in S. Critchley and O. Marchart (eds), *Laclau: A Critical Reader*, 279–328, London: Routledge.
Laclau, E. (2007), *On Populist Reason*. Reprint edition, London and New York: Verso.
Lynch, M., D. Freelon and S. Aday (2014), 'Syria's Socially Mediated Civil War', *United States Institute of Peace*, 13 January. Available online: http://www.usip.org/publications/syria-s-socially-mediated-civil-war (accessed 3 August 2015).
Maltby, S., and R. Keeble (2007), *Communicating War: Memory, Media and Military*. Bury St Edmunds: Arima Publishing.
Matar, D. (2014), 'A Critical Reflection on Aesthetics and Politics in the Digital Age', in A. Downey (ed), *Uncommon Grounds: New Media and Critical Practices in North Africa and the Middle East*, 163–8, London: I.B.Tauris.
Meade, A. (2018), 'Russia Analyst Interviewed by ABC a "Blatantly Pro-Kremlin Apologist"', *The Guardian*, 7 May. Available online: https://www.theguardian.com/media/2018/may/08/russia-analyst-interviewed-by-abc-a-blatantly-pro-kremlin-apologist (accessed 12 August 2019).
Merrin, W. (2018), *Digital War: A Critical Introduction*, London and New York: Routledge.
Miazhevich, G. (2018), 'Nation Branding in the Post-Broadcast Era: The Case of RT', *European Journal of Cultural Studies*, 21(5): 575–93.
Miskimmon, A., B. O'Loughlin and L. Roselle, eds (2017), *Forging the World: Strategic Narratives and International Relations*, Ann Arbor: University of Michigan Press.
O'Loughlin, B. (2011), 'Images as Weapons of War: Representation, Mediation and Interpretation', *Review of International Studies*, 37(1): 71–91.
Orttung, R. W., and E. Nelson (2018), 'Russia Today's Strategy and Effectiveness on YouTube', *Post-Soviet Affairs*, 35(2): 77–92.
Osnos, E., D. Remnick and J. Yaffa (2017), 'Trump, Putin, and the New Cold War', *The New Yorker*, 6 March. Available online: https://www.newyorker.com/magazine/2017/03/06/trump-putin-and-the-new-cold-war (accessed 30 January 2018).
Pears, L. (2016), 'Ask the Audience: Television, Security and Homeland', *Critical Studies on Terrorism*, 9(1): 76–96.

Powers, S., and B. O'Loughlin (2015), 'The Syrian Data Glut: Rethinking the Role of Information in Conflict', *Media, War & Conflict*, 8(2): 172–80.
Rancière, J. (2006), *The Politics of Aesthetics*, London and New York: Continuum.
Rawnsley, G. D. (2015), 'To Know Us Is to Love Us: Public Diplomacy and International Broadcasting in Contemporary Russia and China', *Politics*, 35(3–4): 273–86.
Robinson, P. (2002), *The CNN Effect: The Myth of News, Foreign Policy and Intervention*, London: Routledge.
Rosen, J. (2012), 'The People Formerly Known as the Audience', in M. Mandiberg (ed), *The Social Media Reader*, 13–16, New York: NYU Press.
RT (2018a), 'CrossTalk Bullhorns: Syria Attacked (Extended Version)', *YouTube*. Available online: https://www.youtube.com/watch?v=pfaQGCT5zAU&feature=youtu.be (accessed 12 August 2019).
RT (2018b), 'ICYMI: Be Reassured, People of Syria – the West Has Humanitarian Missiles Ready to Intervene!', *YouTube*. Available online: https://www.youtube.com/watch?v=_zUn2esjYK8&feature=youtu.be (accessed 12 August 2019).
RT (2018c), 'Solid Evidence Douma "Chemical Attack" Was Staged – Lavrov', *YouTube*. Available online: https://www.youtube.com/watch?v=LKE6YKw5Y40&feature=youtu.be (accessed 12 August 2019).
RT (2018d), 'The White Helmets: Clipart with Boris Malagurski', *YouTube*. Available online: https://www.youtube.com/watch?v=RkJ6N97cRLs&feature=youtu.be (accessed 12 August 2019).
The Russian Presidential Executive Office (2013), 'Visit to Russia Today Television Channel', Russian Presidential Executive Office, 11 June. Available online: http://en.kremlin.ru/events/president/news/18319 (accessed 12 August 2019).
Ryall, T. (1975), 'Teaching through Genre', *Screen Education*, 17(1): 27–33.
Salama, V. (2012), 'Covering Syria', *The International Journal of Press/Politics*, 17(4): 516–26.
Saleh, L. (2018), 'Civic Resilience during Conflict: Syria's Local Councils', *Journal of Arab & Muslim Media Research*, 11(2): 135–55.
SOHR (2019), '45 Months of the Russian Military Operations on the Syrian Territory Kill about 18550 People, Including 8114 Civilians and among Them There Are More Than 1970 Children', *The Syrian Observatory for Human Rights*, 30 June. Available online: http://www.syriahr.com/en/?p=132995 (accessed 12 August 2019).
Solomon, T. (2014), 'The Affective Underpinnings of Soft Power', *European Journal of International Relations*, 20(3): 720–41.
Souleimanov, E. A., and V. Dzutsati (2018), 'Russia's Syria War: A Strategic Trap?', *Middle East Policy*, 25(2): 42–50.
Sylvester, C. (2010), *Experiencing War*, London: Routledge.
Thelwall, M., P. Sud and F. Vis (2012), 'Commenting on YouTube Videos: From Guatemalan Rock to El Big Bang', *Journal of the American Society for Information Science and Technology*, 63(3), 616–29.
van Zoonen, L., F. Vis and S. Mihelj (2010), 'Performing Citizenship on YouTube: Activism, Satire and Online Debate around the Anti-Islam Video Fitna', *Critical Discourse Studies*, 7(4): 249–62.
Wood, T. (2018), *Russia without Putin: Money, Power and the Myths of the New Cold War*, London: Verso Books.

Yablokov, I. (2015), 'Conspiracy Theories as a Russian Public Diplomacy Tool: The Case of Russia Today (RT)', *Politics*, 35(3–4): 301–15.

Young, D. G. (2017), 'Theories and Effects of Political Humor', in K. Kenski and K. H. Jamieson (eds), *The Oxford Handbook of Political Communication*, 872–84, Oxford: Oxford University Press.

YouTube (2016), 'New Tools to Shape Conversations in Your Comments Section', *YouTube Creator Blog*, 3 November. Available online: https://youtube-creators.googleblog.com/2016/11/new-tools-to-shape-conversations-in.html (accessed 12 August 2019).

YouTube (2018), 'How Video Views Are Counted', *YouTube*, 30 January. Available online: https://support.google.com/youtube/answer/2991785?hl=en-GB (accessed 12 August 2019).

Zollmann, F. (2017), *Media, Propaganda and the Politics of Intervention*, New York: Peter Lang.

4

Conspiracy and the epistemological challenges of mediatized conflict

Eileen Culloty

Introduction

This chapter examines the epistemological challenges of defining and understanding conspiracy theories about mediatized conflict. Although there is a long, historical association between conspiracy and conflict, the production and circulation of conflict conspiracies has been undertheorized within research on conflict media. In part, this oversight reflects the long-established stereotype of conspiracy theorists as paranoid and isolated fanatics with little significance for public debate. This dismissive characterization is no longer tenable as conspiracy theories have become a ubiquitous feature of contemporary life. Fuelled by social media, conspiracy theories emerge in response to major breaking news stories and present interpretive narratives for understanding economic, political, scientific and social systems. A 2014 study found that half the US population endorsed at least one conspiracy claim (Oliver and Wood 2014). Since then, the salience of conspiracy theories has increased through the online activities of populist politicians, ideological extremists and propagandists. For their part, the major online platforms have recently imposed measures to reduce public exposure to conspiracy theories and their exponents (Dickson 2019; Hern 2018).

In tandem with these developments, scholarly interest in conspiracy theories has grown considerably. The rise of a mainstream conspiracy culture at the turn of the millennium has been attributed to many overlapping factors including the fallout of the War on Terror era; declining trust in experts and official institutions; and the affordances of digital media, which enable a range of actors to challenge official claims to truth and knowledge (Aupers 2012; Byford 2011). More recently, in the wake of revelations about online disinformation and strategic influence campaigns, conspiracy theories appear symptomatic of a post-truth era of political communication (Bennett and Livingston 2018; Lewandowsky et al. 2017).

Although a field of research is emerging around conspiracy theories, there is little consensus over the conceptualization of the subject. Moreover, conspiracy theories can be a challenging object of study because the boundaries between a conspiracy theory and a political opinion are often difficult to explicate (Huneman and Vorms 2018). This is clear in conspiracy theories about war and conflict as the claims produced by various actors – whether states, militaries, combatants, journalists, activists or civilians – intersect with conspiracy theories and the competing narratives of international relations. This is exemplified by the competing claims surrounding the Russian-Ukrainian conflict (e.g. the shooting down of Malaysia Airlines Flight 17 in 2014), the protracted Syrian conflict (e.g. the chemical weapons attacks on Ghouta in 2013 and on Khan Sheikhoun in 2017) and the claims of populist politicians (e.g. the Polish government's contention that the 2010 Smolensk air crash was orchestrated by Russia).

As contemporary conflict is heavily mediatized, it becomes more open to conspiracy claims because mediatization highlights doubts about the nature of evidence and the authority of experts (Leander 2014). These epistemological issues are not new. After all, there is a long history of academic research on, and public controversies about, perceptions of truth in conflict images (Morris 2004; Sontag 1977). What has changed is the influence of the digital environment. The shift from mass to digital media created a new ecology for war media (see Hoskins and O'Loughlin 2010) typified by the production of content from disparate sources and its unpredictable remediation across various platforms. In the process, digital media greatly weakened the capacity of governments, militaries and professional journalists to control the flow of information. Moreover, through mediatization, contemporary conflicts are globalized phenomena. Following Giddens's (1990: 19) concept of globalization as a 'dislocation of space from place', Volkmer (2008: 97) argues that online communication 'transforms place to space' by forging connections across different regional spheres. It is in this globalized media environment that contemporary conflicts are mediatized through 'terrains of symbolic power ... [which are] reshaping, defining and sometimes powerfully contesting the symbolic centre' of Western media culture. In the process, the capacity of powerful news media to influence how events are reported and understood has been undermined.

In this context, this chapter investigates the relationship between conspiracy and the reporting of mediatized conflict. Specifically, I argue that mediatized conflict presents epistemological challenges for news media. It generates uncertainty in news reporting, which creates a space for conspiracy *claims* or conspiracy-like suspicions of official narratives.

Although conspiracy-like suspicions may have merit – that is, they may be plausible considerations at a given time or genuine expressions of dissent – they also feed into the wider circulation of conspiracy *theories* (i.e. large-scale theories about the corrupt intentions of governments), which further reflect a deeper tendency towards conspiracy *thinking* (i.e. a worldview grounded in the rejection of official narratives). In the case of Syria, the uncertainty of news reporting was underpinned by a reliance on social media footage, the absence of journalists on the ground who could verify this information and the presence of a wide range of experts proffering competing interpretations of the online footage. These conditions were further complicated by the fact that the Syrian conflict became entangled with the conspiracy theories and influence campaigns that circulated on social media. In other words, the news media (inadvertently) facilitated the promotion of conspiracy claims, which were taken up by conspiracy theorists and propagandists.

Addressing the uncertainty of the available information and evaluating the merits of competing claims are thus a major challenge for conflict journalism. In this regard, the Syrian conflict saw the emergence of a new kind of journalism actor: the social media verification expert. However, verification takes time and, as illustrated below, investigations often only reach their conclusions long after the initial story has been reported. This suggests that the routine practices of conflict reporting may need to be adapted to accommodate uncertainty. This may involve affording greater attention to the evaluation of competing claims and competing experts – in particular, to distinctions between conspiracy-like claims on the one hand and conspiracy theories and conspiracy thinking on the other. In addition, as social-media verification becomes an institutionalized practice, journalists may need to communicate the nature of the verification process to their audiences while allowing that verification takes time and is itself open to debate and dispute.

This chapter first introduces how conspiracy theories have been conceived across several literatures and sets out a three-fold theorization of conspiracy claims, conspiracy theories and conspiracy thinking. I then examine how and why mediatized conflict creates conditions that enable the circulation of these dimensions of conspiracy. Using the Syrian War as a case, I illustrate this explanation in reference to the circulation of conspiracy claims in news media after the 2013 gas attack on Ghouta and the 2017 gas attack on Khan Sheikhoun. The conclusion identifies a set of challenges for conflict journalism and for researchers of war and media arising from the argument of this chapter.

Understanding conspiracy theories

Conspiracy theories have attracted interest from a range of academic disciplines including philosophy, psychology and sociology. Much research within philosophy is concerned with identifying the reasoning errors that underpin conspiracy thinking and, more recently, the difficulty of defining conspiracy theories (Cassam 2019; Cohnitz 2017; Denith 2014; Keeley 1999). While these contributions are valuable, they generally neglect to consider what makes conspiracy theories appealing for those who endorse them. Insights on this question come from psychology where researchers investigate the factors determining conspiracy beliefs (Goertzel 1994; Grzesiak-Feldman 2013; Swami et al. 2011; Wood et al. 2012). However, psychological researchers rarely question the plausibility of conspiracy claims because conspiracy theorists and their theories are generally dismissed as irrational actors (Cohnitz 2017; Leander 2014; Uscinski et al. 2016). On the other hand, researchers from the sociological and cultural tradition recognize conspiracy theories as a means of challenging authority (Aupers 2012; Fenster 2008; Harambam and Aupers 2017; Van Prooijen 2019; West and Saunders 2003). On this view, popular conspiracy theories are understood as a 'means of articulating an opposition to the forces of international capitalism, globalization, America's military and political supremacy, and the more general rise of a transnational political order' (Byford 2011: 3).

Each of these disciplinary perspectives is important for understanding conspiracy claims about conflict. Conspiracy theories, including accusations of conspiracy theorizing, highlight the inherent instability of truth claims about mediatized conflict. They amplify fundamental questions about the interpretation of conflict images and witness testimony and about the ideological underpinnings of conflict narratives. Conspiracy claims about conflict range from irrational beliefs in malign forces to plausible suspicions about the intentions of conflict actors. This distinction between irrational and plausible claims, and gradients of belief in between, supports a more nuanced understanding of conspiracy claims and their functions within specific sociopolitical contexts.

It is useful to clarify the differences between a set of related terms. A conspiracy may be defined as 'a secret arrangement between a small group of actors to usurp political or economic power, violate established rights, hide vital secrets, or illicitly cause widespread harm' (Uscinski et al. 2016: 58). It is an *act* that serves the interests of a select few while undermining the greater good and possibly also the law. In the 1970s, the Watergate scandal concerned a conspiratorial act to place the US Democratic Party under illegal surveillance for the political advantage of then US president Richard Nixon. For such secretive acts to be recognized as a conspiracy, they must be exposed as Watergate was by investigative journalists working for *The*

Washington Post. It is possible – even likely – that there are conspiracies which have not yet been revealed to the public.

While a conspiracy refers to an act, a *conspiracy theory* proposes the existence of a conspiratorial act. Typically, this conspiratorial act is proposed as a causal explanation for some troubling event. Conspiracy theorists, such as those involved in the 9/11 Truth movement, attempt to amass evidence that would prove the existence of the conspiracy.

Should evidence emerge that the 9/11 terror attack was in fact a false-flag operation orchestrated by the Bush administration, the conspiracy theorists would feel vindicated to a certain extent. However, this would not mean that the conspiracy theorists were correct in their reasoning or motivation if they based their judgements on conspiracy thinking over and above any available evidence. More generally, conspiracy theories reflect a deeper tendency towards *conspiracy thinking*, which designates a worldview in which events and circumstances are assumed to be the product of conspiracy (Brotherton et al. 2013). In other words, it is a predisposition to adopt 'the unnecessary assumption of conspiracy when other explanations are more probable' (Aaronovitch 2009: 5). The above distinctions open up the possibility that one may endorse a particular conspiracy claim or a particular conspiracy theory without also succumbing to a worldview in which events are generally assumed to be the product of conspiratorial acts.

However, these broad definitions are complicated by the sheer range of conspiracy theories and their wide variances in plausibility. For example, a claim about the existence of reptilian humanoids and a claim about 9/11 as a false-flag operation operate in very different spheres of plausibility. Claims about reptilian humanoids are bizarre and irrational because there has never been any scientific evidence to suggest the possible existence of shape-shifting reptilians. In contrast, the 9/11 conspiracy theory has a degree of plausibility insofar as proponents can point to the evidence of historical false-flag operations and to statements by leading Bush administration figures which appeared to welcome the opportunity of 'some catastrophic and catalysing event' (PNAC 2000: 51). Recognizing these differences does not excuse or endorse such claims. However, it is an important step to understanding what might motivate people to endorse different conspiracy claims and it highlights how different disciplinary perspectives may be useful when trying to understand the appeal of claims that have widely different levels of plausibility.

Endorsement of conspiracy theories appears to be a motivated process that serves various ideological, sociological and psychological needs (Miller et al. 2016; van Prooijen 2019). The appeal of conspiracy theories may be based on their capacity to explain random or complex events in terms of a simple narrative. In response to a shocking event – whether the death of a public figure, a natural disaster or a terror attack – conspiracy theories appear to fulfil the cognitive need for easily understood, causal explanations

(Swami 2012). In addition, research suggests that conspiracy beliefs may be influenced by feelings of fear and weakness (Grzesiak-Feldman 2013), by ideological orientations (Berinksy 2017; Miller et al. 2016) and by political affiliations (Berinsky 2017; Hofstadter 1964; Miller et al. 2016).

A growing body of psychological work investigates how individual differences in personality traits and cognitive thinking styles influence conspiracy theory endorsement (Brotherton et al. 2013; Bruder et al. 2013; Goertzel 1994; Gualda and Rúas 2019; Miller et al. 2016; Oliver and Wood 2014; Swami et al. 2011; Wood et al. 2012). However, it should be noted that this research has been hindered by the weak operationalization of measures (Brotherton et al. 2013) and the difficulty of comparing conspiracy beliefs across different temporal and geographical contexts (see Bruder et al. 2013). Nevertheless, existing studies suggest that endorsement of conspiracy claims is predicted by belief in other conspiracy theories. Significantly, these other theories may be unrelated theories (Goertzel 1994), fictitious theories invented by the researchers (Swami et al. 2011) or even mutually exclusive theories such as the contradictory claims that Princess Diana faked her own death and that she was murdered (Wood et al. 2012).

These findings indicate that conspiracy beliefs do not arise from a rational evaluation of particular conspiracy claims but from a general tendency towards conspiracy thinking or what Bruder et al. (2013) call a conspiracy mentality. Similarly, Hardin (2002) characterizes conspiracy thinking for its 'crippled epistemology' – a form of extreme doubt. More recent work has identified empirical links between conspiracy thinking and a tendency towards doubt and mistrust. For example, conspiracy thinking appears to be linked to the conviction that important information is hidden from the public (Gualda and Rúas 2019) and that the media is biased (Uscinski et al. 2016).

However, if conspiracy belief is a consequence of conspiracy thinking, this raises further questions about what influences the development of conspiracy thinking in the first place. As Van Prooijen (2019) argues, contributing factors to conspiracy theory belief may be epistemic (the desire to protect cherished beliefs), existential (the need to understand the world) or social (the desire to reinforce prior beliefs about in-groups and out-groups).

Moreover, social marginalization and discrimination may play a role in perceptions of plausibility. For example, Washington (2006) persuasively maintains that the covert history of medical testing on African Americans makes health care conspiracy theories seem plausible for members of that community. On this understanding, conspiracy theories are not necessarily irrational and may offer a means of contesting power relations (Aistrope and Bleiker 2018; Fenster 2008). On this basis, Fenster (2008: 1) contends that political conspiracy theories are 'a way of interpreting and narrating politics as part of an oppositional individual and collective project'. In such instances, the object 'conspiracy theory' is not clearly delineated because 'the boundary between social critique of science on the one hand, and conspiracy theorizing on the other hand, as easy to draw as it may seem, is rather fuzzy' (Huneman and Vorms 2018: 250). As argued below, this fuzziness is also a feature of claims about mediatized conflict.

Conspiracy theories and mediatized conflict

Historically, the secret activities of powerful elites have been the subject of much anxiety and there is a long history of conspiracy theorizing in relation to conflict and international affairs (Aaronvitch 2009; Aistrope and Bleiker 2018; Olmsted 2009). These tendencies are amplified by digital media and the mediatization of conflict. The mediatization of conflict is not simply about the increased volume of coverage but the multiple and overlapping media channels through which a conflict is relayed. It refers to an environment in which media are recognized as 'an instrument of war' (Payne 2005: 81) and one in which intelligence agencies, governments and militaries compete with combatants, activists and civilians to shape and define conflict narratives. Conflict narratives that were previously 'selected and "scripted" by national broadcasters and their gatekeeping practices' (Volkmer 2008: 92) are now produced by a variety of actors and dispersed across a globalized media sphere. This globalized public sphere challenges the dominance of national strategic narratives because, as Berenger (2006: 24) observes, 'the Internet is no respecter of national borders, of time, or, for that matter, unquestioned patriotism or nationalism'.

In the context of contemporary international relations, the concept of strategic narratives is frequently employed to analyse how powerful political actors 'construct a shared meaning of the past, present, and future of international politics [in order] to shape the behaviour of domestic and international actors' (Miskimmon et al. 2014: 1–2). The promotion of conspiracy theories can contribute to the advancement of various strategic narratives. For example, researchers have investigated Russian-sponsored propaganda in relation to Syria (Levinger 2018; Starbird et al. 2018; White 2018) and the strategic role of conspiracy theories for Russian diplomacy more generally (Aro 2016; Flaherty and Roselle 2018; Pomerantsev and Weiss 2014; Yablokov 2015). In his analysis of the state-funded broadcaster RT, Yablokov (2015) concludes that conspiratorial claims serve to legitimize Russia's domestic and foreign policies while delegitimizing the policies of the United States. At the same time, Russian narratives have been supported by political actors on the far-right (Flaherty and Roselle 2018; Starbird et al. 2018). In the process, conspiracy claims about international affairs intersect with far-right narratives of anti-Semitism and Islamophobia.

Moreover, conspiracy claims are often implicit as these media actors engage in a strategy of question-raising rather than an overt endorsement of conspiracy claims (Marwick and Lewis 2017; Starbird et al. 2018; Yablokov 2015). This strategy is highly suited to mediatized conflict as it raises doubt about the truth status of visual evidence and witness testimony.

The evidentiary power of images and witness testimony is frequently called upon by journalists, advocates and legal professionals to make human rights claims (Chouliaraki 2015; Ristovska 2018). In her analysis of contemporary conflict imagery, Chouliaraki (2015) contrasts the institutional norms of taste and decency that regulated mass-media photojournalism with the online exchange of amateur images and witness accounts. She argues that the latter are accompanied by radical doubt

> about the status of death images (are they authentic?), our relationship to them (what should we feel towards them?) and the power relationships within which they are embedded (who dies and how does this matter?). Central to these new challenges is the rise of 'amateur' recordings of conflict as a testimonial act – an act of representation that publicizes conflict death from the locals' perspective so as to mobilize emotion and invite a response, be this revenge, outrage, contempt, fear or empathy.
> (Chouliaraki 2015: 1362)

This epistemological uncertainty is troubling because the visual media 'produced by a range of information stakeholders are increasingly the main mode of accessing conflict zones and understanding human rights violations' (Ristovska 2018: 243). Citing the prominent role of eyewitness videos in news coverage of conflicts in Syria, Burundi and Myanmar, Ristovska examines the ethical challenges surrounding eyewitness footage on social media and the related rise of new specialist actors who authenticate this footage for news media.

Visual media are a powerful tool for communication because images are processed more easily than text and can be effective at attracting viewer attention and eliciting emotional responses (Lane et al. 1999). There is some evidence to suggest that shocking images of conflict and violence can prompt viewers to change their perceptions (Norris et al. 2004; Pfau et al. 2006). For example, Pfau et al. (2006) found that newspaper photographs of 2003 Iraq war casualties had some effect in reducing support for the US presence in Iraq. In this context, it is unsurprising that those intent on gathering support for a cause seek to exploit the persuasive power of images. Yet conflict images, whether produced by amateurs or professionals, must be open to contestation and interrogation. In reference to Iraq War footage, the documentary director Errol Morris (2004) argued that images 'provide a point around which other pieces of evidence collect. They are part of, but not a substitute for, an investigation'. In effect, Morris's argument foreshadowed the rise of the social media verification expert who interrogates and authenticates online footage. An early innovator in this area was the Storyful news agency, founded in 2010, and the best-known exponent of this practice in relation to war and conflict footage is Eliot Higgins who founded Bellingcat in 2014.

The epistemological issues discussed above were evident throughout the Syrian conflict, which was notable for attracting a wide range of conspiracy and conspiracy-like claims from actors across the ideological spectrum. As outlined below, conspiracy claims relied heavily on questioning the veracity of visual evidence. However, as the debate about evidence concerned intricate details about the engineering of rocket launchers and the chemical properties of sarin gas, it took place over a long time period and at a level beyond the capabilities and interests of most ordinary news consumers. Unsurprisingly then, a parallel debate concerned the integrity of the experts interpreting the evidence and the plausibility of the narratives they endorsed. As argued below, an evaluation of this debate is necessarily time sensitive. Experts who initially appeared to have high levels of credibility were subsequently found to be suspect in their intentions and practices. In the process, conspiracy claims that initially presented plausible questions for official narratives could be reinterpreted as reflections of a more entrenched conspiracy mindset.

Disputed evidence and the Syrian war

The 2011 Syrian revolution against the regime of Bashar Assad escalated into a multi-sided conflict with complex geopolitical dimensions. The fight against Assad encompassed a myriad of Syrian opposition groups as well as ISIS militants who captured territory in Eastern and Northern Syria. The fight against ISIS engaged Kurdish forces, the Gulf League and the United States while Assad was supported by Russia and Iran among others. For his part, Assad declared the uprising a foreign conspiracy to undermine Syria's national unity. Many critics of Western foreign policy echoed this view while other opponents of Western intervention questioned the intentions of Syrian opposition groups. Disputes about the naming of the conflict – as revolution, civil war, terrorism or conspiracy – typified the wider set of alliances and competing narratives at play. Throughout, the conflict was characterized by claims and counterclaims about death tolls, the role of ISIS and foreign fighters, the legitimacy of the White Helmets (officially known as the Syrian Civil Defence) and the responsibility for casualties. Moreover, the conflict prompted protracted debates about the appropriate response of major states and supra-national bodies such as the United Nations. These debates peaked in response to claims that the Syrian regime breached international law and violated human rights by using chemical weapons.

A central component of the competing narratives and associated conspiracy theories concerned the disputed nature of the evidence underpinning accusations of human rights violations. Much of the evidence emerged on social media and in the absence of independent journalists who might normally verify the veracity of claims. Shortly after the uprising, the Assad regime effectively banned foreign media from entering the state. Those that did faced considerable risk of targeting and capture by both ISIS and the regime. In consequence, journalists and news organizations were heavily dependent on the social media content produced by people in Syria. However, online content was produced by at least four different groups with their own agendas to advance: jihadist, Kurdish, pro-Assad and secular/moderate opposition communities (O'Callaghan et al. 2014). To complicate matters further, an analysis of YouTube footage found that different uploaders remixed original witness videos in order to support particular conflict frames (Smit et al. 2017). These included remixes that questioned the original footage and remixes that endorsed the footage 'to persuade publics to act, either morally or politically' (Smit et al. 2017: 303). These circumstances contributed greatly to the uncertainty of news reporting.

Evaluating the available online content presented a major challenge for Western journalists. To overcome this challenge, they became reliant on Syrian insiders and on a new kind of journalism actor: the verification expert. The Syrian diaspora took on the role of information broker by coordinating 'the information flow between otherwise disconnected groups and [framing] messages that speak to target audiences' (Andén-Papadopoulos and Pantti 2013: 2188). In their analysis of *New York Times* coverage, Wall and Zahed (2015) found that much of the coverage constituted a collaboration between journalists and Syrian activists. Naturally, relying on activists as sources was controversial as it raised questions about the independence and transparency of news sourcing practices (Mast and Hanegreefs 2015; Sienkiewicz 2014; Smit et al. 2017; Wall and Zahed 2015). Some on the left drew parallels with news coverage prior to the 2003 Iraq War and accused the news media of bias in favour of regime change. Exponents of this perspective included the journalism professor Piers Robinson, a co-founder of the 'Syria, Propaganda and Media' working group which investigates bias in media coverage (see http://syriapropagandamedia.org/).

The Syrian conflict also saw the rise of a new interpretative tier of news actors positioned between those who filmed original footage and the journalists who reported on it (Sienkiewicz 2014). This interpretative tier included Syrian activist organizations such as Shams News Network as well as Western-based verification outlets such as Elliot Higgins's citizen-journalism blog Brown Moses (later known as Bellingcat) and the social news agency Storyful. Higgins and Storyful both played a significant role by verifying online images and supplying this content to Western newsrooms. Moreover, a range of experts – across science, medicine, human rights and international relations – were called upon to provide interpretations of the social media footage. The nature of expertise and the relevance of different fields of expertise played a significant role in the ensuing debates about the use of chemical weapons and about the plausibility of conspiracy claims (see Leander 2014). In what follows, we can examine how this unfolded in relation to two prominent events: the 2013 gas attack on Ghouta and the 2017 gas attack on Khan Sheikhoun. Of key interest is the shifting context for evaluating the credibility of expert claims between the two events and the corresponding ability to draw a distinction between conspiracy-like claims that question official narratives and conspiracy theories that reflect a more entrenched tendency towards conspiracy thinking.

The 2013 gas attack on Ghouta

On 21 August 2013, news emerged of a major attack on Eastern Ghouta, a suburb of Damascus. The Syrian opposition accused the regime of using sarin gas. The use of chemical weapons crossed the 'red-line' warning issued by US president Barack Obama in 2012 and prompted the launch of airstrikes by a US, UK and French coalition. However, the British House of Commons and US Congress ultimately opposed military intervention. The Syrian opposition and many Western commentators attributed blame for the attack to the regime. Meanwhile, Russia and the regime argued that the attack was staged by the opposition to implicate the regime and instigate international intervention. In news coverage and commentary, speculative questions about plausibility took precedence over an analysis of the evidence. This speculation hinged on whether it was rational for the regime to use chemical weapons given the risk of US intervention and whether it was plausible for the opposition to stage an attack that might provoke US intervention.

In the absence of journalists, the only footage was created by the Syrian opposition and civilians. Distressing footage of casualties and survivors struggling to breathe attracted millions of viewers on YouTube (Smit et al. 2017). In the immediate aftermath, Russia suggested the footage was fabricated – a view grounded in assertions put forward by Agnes Mariam de la Croix, a Christian nun living in Syria. Referencing the videos of the attack uploaded to YouTube, De la Croix concluded that the victims were merely posing and that an event was staged prior to the stated time of the attack. De la Croix's conspiracy theory was easily discredited due to her misreading of YouTube timestamps, which she had used as evidence (Leander 2014). The following month, the UN concluded that the regime was responsible for the attack. This was based on scientific evidence, which concluded that the weapons were launched from the regime's territory (United Nations 2013). At this point, Russian authorities accepted that an attack had occurred but rejected the UN's conclusions and the independence of the scientific report.

A prolonged period of argument and counterargument ensued among competing experts who presented their own interpretations of the social media footage. Here, we may focus on three competing experts – Theodore Postol, Seymour Hersh and Elliott Higgins – who played a prominent role in media coverage of the Ghouta attack and subsequent attacks. Each of these figures has distinct claims to expertise and credibility. Theodore Postol is an expert in weapons systems and professor emeritus of science, technology and national security policy at Massachusetts Institute of Technology (MIT). Seymour Hersh is a veteran investigative journalist who won a Pulitzer Prize for exposing the massacre of unarmed civilians by US troops at Mai Lai during the Vietnam War. Elliott Higgins is a citizen-journalist who pioneered the use of open-source investigations and founded the open-source journalism website Bellingcat in 2014.

Theodore Postol conducted an analysis of the YouTube footage and concluded that Assad was unlikely to be responsible for the attack because the rockets appeared to be launched within opposition-held territory. Postol's critique of the official narrative was reported by the news media, including *The New York Times* (Chivers 2013), as the expert view of an MIT ballistics expert. Postol was also cited by Seymour Hersh (2014) in his *London Review of Books* article, which blamed a Syrian jihadi group for carrying out the attack to provoke US intervention. *Die Welt* also reported Hersh's claims. The conspiracy claims presented by Postol and Hersh were vigorously contested by Elliott Higgins and his growing team of open-source investigative journalists. By analysing the wider pool of online videos, Higgins established that the munitions used in the Ghouta attack were used previously by the Syrian Army but not the opposition. Higgins's conclusion, attributing blame to Assad for the attack, was featured in *The Guardian*, *The Telegraph*, *The New Yorker* and *Foreign Policy*.

Although the UN had officially recognized that Assad was responsible by September 2013, the issue of responsibility remained a matter of debate in major Western media outlets through the circulation of conspiracy claims. As such, an ordinary citizen with an interest in news from Syria was confronted with contradictory claims from different experts across the news media. They encountered competing theories about the possible motives of actors, competing claims of expertise and authority to interpret social media footage and competing citations of evidence grounded in arguments about engineering and weaponry. It seems unlikely that ordinary news consumers had the time or interest to pursue these investigations. What is significant is the presence of uncertainty in news reporting, despite the official (UN) version of the story, which opened up a space for subsequent conspiracy theories about Syria. At this point, however, the arguments of Postol and Hersh constituted conspiracy claims rather than conspiracy theories; that is, they concerned critiques of the official narrative by experts whose experience and knowledge conferred a degree of credibility for reporting those claims.

The 2017 gas attack on Khan Sheikhoun

In April 2017, news emerged of a sarin gas attack on Khan Sheikhoun, a town in the north-western province of Idlib. In contrast to the Ghouta attack, responses to the Khan Sheikhoun attack were more obviously integrated with the circulation of online conspiracy theories. A study of Twitter activity in the days following the attack identified two groups of media activists (White 2018). In one group, Twitter users coalesced around the hashtag #SyrianGasAttack to normalize the view that the regime was responsible for the attack. In contrast, people using the hashtag #SyriaHoax promoted the idea that the attack was a false-flag orchestrated by the opposition (White 2018). Importantly, the false-flag accusation was linked to other conspiracy theories which had gained prominence in the preceding years. These conspiracy theories attacked the integrity of the Syria Civil Defence/White Helmets and the integrity of mainstream new media more generally. There now existed a network of conspiracy-driven outlets and social media influencers ready to embrace the claim that the Khan Sheikhoun attack was a hoax (see Starbird et al. 2018). Propelled by Russian media outlets including *RT* and *SputnikNews*, claims about the Khan Sheikhoun hoax were taken up by major conspiracy outlets such as *Infowars* and *21st Century Wire*.

However, suspicions about the official story were not confined to overt conspiracy theorists. Suspicion was also expressed by actors representing a diverse range of ideological views including anti-imperialists, libertarians and the far-right. These actors were not necessarily pro-Kremlin, although they would now stand accused of fuelling Kremlin-backed conspiracy theories (Monbiot 2017; Shachtman and Kennedy 2017). Writing in *Die Welt*, Seymour Hersh presented evidence that the Khan Sheikhoun attacked was a conventional strike and not a chemical weapons attack. To support these claims, Hersch primarily relied on an anonymous US intelligence source. While the use of anonymous sources is common, journalists are expected to provide corroboration for any anonymous claims. The fact that Hersh failed to provide such corroboration left him open to significant criticism (see Bloomfield 2017; Massing 2018; Shalom 2017).

Furthermore, Hersh's reporting tested the limits of plausibility. Writing in *Jacobin* magazine, the political scientist Stephen Shalom (2017) observed:

> To accept Hersh's account requires us to believe that Assad and Russia never undertake unnecessary actions, that every respected NGO has compromised itself on behalf of Trump, that the UN and France are in Washington's pocket, that the [Organization for the Prohibition of Chemical Weapons] produces bogus reports,... and that even though many members of the military and the intelligence community are furious that Trump rejected and falsified evidence, Hersh could find no one willing to speak on the record.

Hersh's journalism had become characteristic of conspiracy thinking in that it proposed 'the unnecessary assumption of conspiracy when other explanations are more probable' (Aaronovitch 2009: 5). According to journalist Steve Bloomfield (2017), Hersh appeared to have internalized the idea that his government is always lying, which allowed him 'to jump from the fact that America has denounced an atrocity to suspecting that it never happened'. It was now possible to re-evaluate Hersh's earlier reports on Ghouta as the work of someone who had succumbed to a conspiracy mindset. While his previous conspiracy claims may have merited publication by virtue of his expertise, there was now compelling evidence to question the integrity of his journalism in relation to Syria.

For his part, the credibility of the MIT professor Theodor Postol was undermined by an association with conspiracy theorists. In response to the Khan Sheikhoun attack, Postol again accused the US government of using false information to justify airstrikes on Syria.

However, one of Postol's key sources was revealed to be a regular contributor to conspiracy theory outlets. Postol had characterized Maram Susli, a Syrian-Australian blogger, as a chemistry expert. Investigations by journalists revealed that the chemistry graduate was a regular Infowars contributor who had endorsed conspiracy theories about 9/11 and the Holocaust and has appeared on programmes with white supremacists including the leader of the Ku Klux Klan (Monbiot 2017; Shachtman and Kennedy 2017). As with Hersh, Postol's conspiracy claims now appeared to be driven by an ideological commitment to a conspiracy theory rather than any expert interpretation of the evidence.

However, if we think again about the perspective of an ordinary news consumer, responsibility for Khan Sheikhoun and, more pointedly, the legitimacy of the US airstrikes remained open to debate. A news report in *Deutsche Welle* (Schultz 2017) noted the division among EU leaders. It also cited the hesitation of Hans Blix, the UN Weapons who became famous for questioning the US evidence for invading Iraq in 2003. As quoted in *Deutsche Welle*, Blix was uneasy with the immediate attribution of responsibility based on social media footage: the 'pictures of victims that were held up, that the whole world can see with horror, such pictures are not necessarily evidence of who did it' (Schultz 2017). Where Blix merely expressed caution, others proffered conspiracy claims. A former British ambassador to Syria appeared on the BBC's *Today* programme and speculated that the Khan Sheikhoun attack was the result of a conventional airstrike hitting a jihadi arms dump (Today 2017). A few months later, *Newsweek* reported that US Secretary of Defense James Mattis acknowledged a lack of evidence for the regime's use of sarin gas (Wilkie 2018). However, this opinion article gave the false impression that Mattis was referring to previous attacks rather than the most recent attack (Higgins 2018). Thus, while the conspiracy thinking of Hersh and Postol had been exposed through investigation and analysis, the news media facilitated the articulation of a new set of conspiracy claims that amplified uncertainty and required further investigations to debunk.

Conclusion

The Syrian conflict exemplifies the epistemological challenges of defining and understanding conspiracies theories about mediatized conflict. Contemporary conspiracy claims cannot be treated in isolation from wider political narratives and wider activities in the media environment. They are a subset of broader information pathologies such as disinformation and strategic influence campaigns and they are an extension of legitimate debates about evidence and motivation for action. Such debates are a necessary feature of media coverage of, and discussion about, conflict. Moreover, debates of this kind will always invite controversy because they concern political truths about the intentions of states and attempts to legitimize power relations as much as they concern factual truths about the use of weapons. As Stephen Coleman (2019: 157) recently argued, the uncertainties of the post-truth era are a consequence of an erroneous understanding of political truth as something 'neutral, objective, or absolute'.

He contends that it is no longer feasible for news media 'to wish away discordant opinions'; instead, it is necessary to provide the 'time and space to recognise and evaluate the political standpoints of others' (Coleman 2019: 165). It would seem that the news media were providing such a space by reporting the conspiracy claims that challenged the official narratives of the Ghouta and Khan Sheikhoun attacks. The difficulty lies with the capacity to evaluate those claims given the uncertainties that underpin visual evidence and the long time period required to investigate that evidence and competing claims about it.

The epistemological uncertainty of conflict imagery is widely acknowledged. So too is the strategic value of images for those intent on gaining support for their position.

Consequently, visual evidence must remain open to investigation. This raises the question of who is trusted to undertake this investigation – particularly when the evidence involves complex knowledge that is beyond the interest and abilities of ordinary citizens. As outlined above, the debate surrounding the Ghouta attack pitted a ballistics expert from one of the world's most prestigious universities against a citizen-journalist with no training in ballistics. It seems reasonable that people might consider the former more credible and trustworthy.

Moreover, while the circulation of conspiracy theories is primarily associated with social media, reputable news media outlets facilitated the articulation of conspiracy claims that were taken up by conspiracy theorists.

If trained journalists and media outlets with reputations to protect – particularly in the age of 'fake news' accusations – struggle to negotiate competing claims about Syria, it is reasonable to assume that an environment of plausible doubt was created for ordinary citizens.

Conspiracy theories present a significant challenge for conflict journalism and for researchers of war and conflict media. Conspiracy claims are not clearly delineated from other kinds of claims making it difficult to distinguish between legitimate critiques of political affairs and the promotion of conspiracy theories. In the case of Syria, the contestation of conspiracy claims and the exposure of conspiracy thinking required significant effort on the part of a small group of journalists. It also took time, which means that judgements made need to be revised in light of new evidence. What is plausible and who is a credible expert can change substantially over time. This means that journalists and researchers may need to be open to conspiracy claims that question official narratives even though these claims may subsequently be exposed as proto-conspiracy theories – as was the case with the claims of Postol and Hersh about Ghouta. For the news media, this suggests that the routine practices of conflict reporting may need to be adapted to accommodate uncertainty. In the coming years, we are likely to see the institutionalization of social media verification practices across journalism. As part of this effort, it would seem vital that journalists communicate the nature of the verification process to their audiences while allowing that verification takes time and is itself open to debate and dispute.

References

Aaronovitch, D. (2009), *Voodoo Histories: The Role of the Conspiracy Theory in Shaping Modern History*, London: Jonathan Cape.

Aistrope, T., and R. Bleiker (2018), 'Conspiracy and Foreign Policy', *Security Dialogue*, 49(3): 165–82.

Andén-Papadopoulos, K., and M. Pantti (2013), 'The Media Work of Syrian Diaspora Activists: Brokering between the Protest and Mainstream Media', *International Journal of Communication*, 7: 2185–206.

Aro, J. (2016), 'The Cyberspace War: Propaganda and Trolling as Warfare Tools', *European View*, 15(1): 121–32.

Aupers, S. (2012), '"Trust No One": Modernization, Paranoia and Conspiracy Culture', *European Journal of Communication*, 27(1): 22–34.

Bennett, W. L., and S. Livingston (2018), 'The Disinformation Order: Disruptive Communication and the Decline of Democratic Institutions', *European Journal of Communication*, 33(2): 122–39.

Berinsky, A. J. (2017), 'Rumors and Health Care Reform: Experiments in Political Misinformation', *British Journal of Political Science*, 47(2): 241–62.

Berenger, R. (2006), 'Introduction', in R. Berenger (ed), *Cybermedia Go to War: Role of Converging Media during and after the 2003 Iraq War*, 23–35, Spokane: Marquette Books.

Bloomfield, S. (2017), 'Whatever Happened to Seymour Hersh?', *Prospect*, 17 July 2017. Available online: https://www.prospectmagazine.co.uk/magazine/whatever-happened-toseymour-hersh (accessed 19 September 2019).

Brotherton, R., C. C. French and A. D. Pickering (2013), 'Measuring Belief in Conspiracy Theories: The Generic Conspiracist Beliefs Scale', *Frontiers in Psychology*, 4. Available online: https://doi.org/10.3389/fpsyg.2013.00279 (accessed 19 September 2019).

Bruder, M., P. Haffke, N. Neave, N. Nouripanah and R. Imhoff (2013), 'Measuring Individual Differences in Generic Beliefs in Conspiracy Theories across Cultures: Conspiracy Mentality Questionnaire', *Frontiers in Psychology*, 4. Available online: https://doi.org/10.3389/fpsyg.2013.00225 (accessed 19 September 2019).

Byford, J. (2011), *Conspiracy Theories: A Critical Introduction*, Basingstoke: Palgrave Macmillan.

Cassam, O. (2019), *Conspiracy Theories*, Oxford: Polity Press.

Chivers, C. J. (2013), 'New Study Refines View of Sarin Attack in Syria', *The New York Times*, 28 December 2013. Available online: https://www.nytimes.com/2013/12/29/world/middleeast/new-study-refines-view-of-sarin-attack-in-syria.html (accessed 19 September 2019).

Chouliaraki, L. (2015), 'Digital Witnessing in Conflict Zones: The Politics of Remediation', *Information, Communication & Society*, 18(11): 1362–77.

Cohnitz, D. (2017), *Critical Citizens or Paranoid Nutcases? On the Epistemology of Conspiracy Theories*, Utrecht: Utrecht of University.

Coleman, S. (2019), 'The Elusiveness of Political Truth: From the Conceit of Objectivity to Intersubjective Judgement', *European Journal of Communication*, 33(2): 157–71.

Denith, M. (2014), *The Philosophy of Conspiracy Theories*, Basingstoke: Palgrave Macmillan.

Dickson, E. J. (2019), 'Will the Internet's War on Anti-Vaxxers Work?', *Rolling Stone*, 28 March 2019. Available online: https://www.rollingstone.com/culture/culture-features/anti-vaxxers-facebook-youtube-instagram-806504/ (accessed 19 September 2019).

Fenster, M. (2008). *Conspiracy Theories: Secrecy and Power in American Culture*, Minneapolis: University of Minnesota Press.

Flaherty, E., and L. Roselle (2018), 'Contentious Narratives and Europe: Conspiracy Theories and Strategic Narratives Surrounding RT's Brexit News Coverage', *Journal of International Affairs*, 71(1.5): 53–60.

Giddens, A. (1990), *The Consequences of Modernity*, Cambridge: Polity.

Goertzel, T. (1994), 'Belief in Conspiracy Theories', *Political Psychology*, 15(4): 731–42.

Grzesiak-Feldman, M. (2013), 'The Effect of High-anxiety Situations on Conspiracy Thinking', *Current Psychology*, 32: 100–18.

Gualda, E., and J. Rúas (2019), 'Conspiracy Theories, Credibility and Trust in Information', *Communication & Society*, 32(1): 179–94.

Harambam, J., and S. Aupers (2017), '"I Am Not a Conspiracy Theorist": Relational Identifications in the Dutch Conspiracy Milieu', *Cultural Sociology*, 11(1): 113–29.

Hardin, R. (2002), 'The Crippled Epistemology of Extremism', in A. Breton, G. Galeotti, P. Salmon and R. Wintrobe (eds), *Political Extremism and Rationality*, 3–22, Cambridge: Cambridge University Press.

Hern, A. (2018), 'Facebook, Apple, YouTube and Spotify Ban Infowars' Alex Jones', *The Guardian*, 6 August 2018. Available online: https://www.theguardian.com/technology/2018/aug/06/apple-removes-podcasts-infowars-alex-jones (accessed 19 September 2019).

Hersh, S. (2014), 'The Red Line and the Rat Line', *London Review of Books*, 36(8): 21–4.

Higgins, E. (2018), 'Newsweek Engages in Easily Debunkable Syria Chemical Weapon Trutherism with the Help of Ian Wilkie', *Bellingcat*, 9 February 2018. Available online: https://www.bellingcat.com/news/mena/2018/02/09/newsweek-engages-easily-debunkable-syria-chemical-weapon-trutherism-help-ian-wilkie/ (accessed 19 September 2019).

Hofstadter, R. (1964), *The Paranoid Style in American Politics, and Other Essays*, Cambridge: Harvard University Press.

Hoskins, A., and B. O'Loughlin (2010), *War and Media: The Emergence of Diffused War*, Cambridge: Polity Press.

Huneman, P., and M. Vorms (2018), 'Is a Unified Account of Conspiracy Theories Possible?', *Argumenta Oeconomica Cracoviensia*, 3: 247–70.

Keeley, B. (1999), 'Of Conspiracy Theories', *The Journal of Philosophy*, 39(3): 109–26.

Lane, R. D., P. M. Chua and R. J. Dolan (1999), 'Common Effects of Emotional Valence, Arousal and Attention on Neural Activation during Visual Processing of Pictures', *Neuropsychologia*, 37(9): 989–97.

Leander, A. (2014), 'Essential and Embattled Expertise: Knowledge/Expert/Policy Nexus around the Sarin Gas Attack in Syria', *Politik*, 17(2): 26–37.

Levinger, M. (2018), 'Master Narratives of Disinformation Campaigns', *Journal of International Affairs*, 71(1.5): 125–34.

Lewandowsky, S., U. K. Ecker and J. Cook (2017), 'Beyond Misinformation: Understanding and Coping with the "Post-Truth" Era', *Journal of Applied Research in Memory and Cognition*, 6(4): 353–69.

Marwick, A., and R. Lewis (2017), *Media Manipulation and Disinformation Online*, New York: Data & Society Research Institute.

Massing, M. (2018), 'Breaking News', *The Nation*, 27 September 2018. Available online: https://www.thenation.com/article/seymour-hersh-reporter/ (accessed 19 September 2019).

Mast, J., and S. Hanegreefs (2015), 'When News Media Turn to Citizen-generated Images of War: Transparency and Graphicness in the Visual Coverage of the Syrian Conflict', *Digital Journalism*, 3(4): 594–614.

Miller, J. M., K. L. Saunders and C. E. Farhart (2016), 'Conspiracy Endorsement as Motivated Reasoning: The Moderating Roles of Political Knowledge and Trust', *American Journal of Political Science*, 60(4): 824–44.

Miskimmon, A., B. O'Loughlin and L. Roselle (2014), *Strategic Narratives: Communication Power and the New World Order*, London: Routledge.

Monbiot, G. (2017), 'A Lesson from Syria: It's Crucial Not to Fuel Far-Right Conspiracy Theories', *The Guardian*, 15 November 2017. Available online: https://www.theguardian.com/commentisfree/2017/nov/15/lesson-from-syria-chemical-weapons-conspiracy-theories-alt-right (accessed 19 September 2019).

Morris, E. (2004), 'Not Every Picture Tells a Story', *The New York Times*, 20 November 2004. Available online: http://www.nytimes.com/2004/11/20/opinion/20morris.html?pagewanted=print&position=&_r=0 (accessed 19 September 2019).

Nicas, J. (2018), 'Alex Jones Said Bans Would Strengthen Him. He Was Wrong', *The New York Times*, 4 September 2018. Available online: https://www.nytimes.com/2018/09/04/technology/alex-jones-infowars-bans-traffic.html (accessed 19 September 2019).

Norris, P., M. Kern and M. Just, eds (2004), *Framing Terrorism: The News Media, the Government and the Public*, New York: Routledge.

O'Callaghan, D., N. Prucha, D. Greene, M. Conway, J. Carthy and P. Cunningham (2014), 'Online Social Media in the Syria Conflict: Encompassing the Extremes and the In-betweens', in *Proceedings of the 2014 IEEE/ACM International Conference on Advances in Social Networks Analysis and Mining*, 409–16, IEEE Press.

Oliver, J., and T. Wood (2014), 'Conspiracy Theories and the Paranoid Style(s) of Mass Opinion', *American Journal of Political Science*, 58(4): 952–66.

Olmsted, K. S. (2009), *Real Enemies: Conspiracy Theories and American Democracy, World War I to 9/11*, New York: Oxford University Press.

Payne, K. (2005), 'The Media as an Instrument of War', *Parameters*, 35(1): 81–93.

Pfau, M. et al. (2006), 'The Effects of Print News Photographs on the Casualties of War', *Journalism and Mass Communication Quarterly*, 83(1): 150–68.

PNAC (2000), *Rebuilding America's Defenses*. Project for a New American Century, Washington: PNAC.

Pomerantsev, P., and M. Weiss (2014), *The Menace of Unreality: How the Kremlin Weaponizes Information, Culture and Money*, New York: Institute of Modern Russia.

Ristovska, S. (2018), 'Expanding the Epistemological Horizon: Institutionalised Visual Knowledge and Human Rights', *Javnost-The Public*, 25(1–2): 240–7.

Schultz, T. (2017), 'EU Urges Diplomacy in Syria as Ex-weapons Inspector Says US Acted without Proof', *Deutsche Welle*, 7 April 2017. Available online: https://www.dw.com/en/eu-urges-diplomacy-in-syria-as-ex-weapons-inspector-says-us-acted-without-proof/a-38345413 (accessed 19 September 2019).

Shachtman, N., and M. Kennedy (2017), 'The Kardashian Look-alike Trolling for Assad', *The Daily Beast*, 7 December 2017. Available online: https://www.thedailybeast.com/the-kardashian-look-alike-trolling-for-assad (accessed 19 September 2019).

Shalom, S. (2017), 'The Chemical Attack at Khan Sheikhoun', *Jacobin*, 24 July 2017. Available online: https://jacobinmag.com/2017/07/syria-chemical-attack-assad-trump (accessed 19 September 2019).

Sienkiewicz, M. (2014), 'Start Making Sense: A Three-tier Approach to Citizen Journalism', *Media, Culture & Society*, 36(5): 691–701.

Smit, R., A. Heinrich and M. Broersma (2017), 'Witnessing in the New Memory Ecology: Memory Construction of the Syrian Conflict on YouTube', *New Media & Society*, 19(2): 289–307.

Sontag, S. (1977), *On Photography*, New York: Penguin.
Starbird, K., A. Arif, T. Wilson, K. Van Koevering, K. Yefimova and D. Scarnecchia (2018), 'Ecosystem or Echo-System? Exploring Content Sharing across Alternative Media Domains', in *Twelfth International AAAI Conference on Web and Social Media*, 25–28 June 2018, Palo Alto, CA. Available online: https://faculty.washington.edu/kstarbi/Starbird-et-al-ICWSM-2018-Echosystem-final.pdf (accessed 19 September 2019).
Swami, V. (2012), 'Social Psychological Origins of Conspiracy Theories: The Case of the Jewish Conspiracy Theory in Malaysia', *Frontiers in Psychology*, 3. Available online: https://doi.org/10.3389/fpsyg.2012.00280 (accessed 19 September 2019).
Swami, V., R. Coles, S. Stieger, J. Pietschnig, A. Furnham and S. Rehim (2011), 'Conspiracist Ideation in Britain and Austria: Evidence of a Monological Belief System and Associations between Individual Psychological Differences and Real-world and Fictitious Conspiracy Theories', *British Journal Psychology*, 102: 443–63.
Today (2017), [radio programme], 'BBC Radio 4', 7 April. Available online: https://www.bbc.co.uk/programmes/p04zb6yv (accessed 19 September 2019).
United Nations (2013), *Report on the Alleged Use of Chemical Weapons in the Ghouta Area of Damascus on 21 August 2013*, New York: United Nations.
Uscinski, J. E., C. Klofstad and M. Atkinson (2016), 'Why Do People Believe in Conspiracy Theories? The Role of Informational Cues and Predispositions', *Political Research Quarterly*, 69: 57–71.
Van Prooijen, J. W. (2019), 'Belief in Conspiracy Theories: Looking beyond Gullibility', in J. Forgas and R. Baumeister (eds), *The Social Psychology of Gullibility*, 319–32, Abingdon, Oxon: Routledge.
Volkmer, I. (2008), 'Conflict-related Media Events and Cultures of Proximity', *Media, War & Conflict*, 1(1): 90–8.
Wall, M., and S. E. Zahed (2015), 'Embedding Content from Syrian Citizen Journalists: The Rise of the Collaborative News Clip', *Journalism*, 16(2):163–80.
Washington, H. A. (2006), *Medical Apartheid: The Dark History of Medical Experimentation on Black Americans from Colonial Times to the Present*, New York: Doubleday Books.
West, H. G., and T. Sanders, eds (2003), *Transparency and Conspiracy: Ethnographies of Suspicion in the New World Order*, Durham: Duke University Press.
White, S. P. (2018), 'Information Warfare in the Digital Age: A Study of Syria Hoax', *Technology Science*, 13 November 2018. Available online: https://techscience.org/a/2018111302 (accessed 19 September 2019).
Wilkie, I. (2018), 'Now Mattis Admits There Was No Evidence Assad Used Poison Gas on His People: Opinion', *Newsweek*, 2 August 2018. Available online: https://www.newsweek.com/now-mattis-admits-there-was-no-evidence-assad-using-poison-gas-his-people-801542 (accessed 19 September 2019).
Wood, M. J., K. M. Douglas and R. M. Sutton (2012), 'Dead and Alive: Beliefs in Contradictory Conspiracy Theories', *Social Psychological and Personality Science*, 3(6): 767–73.
Yablokov, I. (2015), 'Conspiracy Theories as a Russian Public Diplomacy Tool: The Case of Russia Today (RT)', *Politics*, 35(3–4): 301–15.

5

Command and control meet the decentralized network: Conventional militaries, social media and the information environment

Kevin Foster

At a time when control of the information environment (IE) is seen as increasingly central to success in warfighting, no combatant force can afford to ignore its digital capability. As NATO's Strategic Communications Centre of Excellence observed in a report on *Social Media as a Tool of Hybrid Warfare*:

> Virtual communication platforms have become an integral part of warfare strategy. The recent conflicts in Libya, Syria, and Ukraine have demonstrated that social media is widely used to coordinate actions, collect information, and, most importantly, to influence the beliefs and attitudes of target audiences, even mobilize them for action.
> (Svetoka 2015: 4)

As a consequence, the Multinational Capability Development Campaign (MCDC), a NATO 'test-bed' for concept and capability development, argues that for conventional militaries fighting to influence both domestic and dispersed overseas audiences: 'The question is no longer *whether* to be on social media, but *how* to be there...Though it is difficult to control discourses or to shape perceptions, it is less dangerous than staying away from the digital IE' (MCDC 2016: 4).[1]

Despite acknowledging that the information environment is a crucial space of war, many conventional militaries have struggled to integrate digital and social media technologies into their systems and capabilities. While they have been comfortable laying out parameters for safe and secure use of social media by their personnel – a list of do's and don'ts – or advertising its benefits as a recruiting and reputation management tool, their progress towards its fuller integration as a tool of influence operations has been more tentative, marked by risk aversion and fear (see Maltby 2015; Maltby et al. 2015). The conventional forces who have overcome these institutional ambiguities have recognized the central role played by social media in the 'cognitive battlespace...a unified threat environment where both state and non- state actors' pursue a continual arms race to influence – and protect from influence – large groups of users online' (Kelton et al. 2019: 860). Here, militaries deploy digital capabilities to 'affect behaviors, protect operations, communicate commander's intent, and project accurate information to achieve desired effects' (United States Air Force 2003: 31). While conventional militaries have moved haltingly towards the integration of the digital, non-state actors have been trailblazers in its adoption and deployment and have enjoyed long periods of dominance in the information environment (Blaker 2017; Farwell 2014; Merrin 2019; Shaheen 2015; Singer and Brooking 2018; Winter 2019). Al Qaeda, the Taliban and ISIS each moved their operations into a digitized space of war, from where they communicated, motivated and organized, and continue to have an important presence (Merrin 2019; Rid and Hecker 2009).

This chapter examines contrasting approaches to the adoption and adaptation of social and digital media by militaries and considers why non-state actors have been so successful in the cognitive battlespace while their conventional adversaries have struggled. It analyses differing understandings of these spaces of war within longstanding organizational contexts and how these considerations have framed the deployment of social media and its coordination with traditional warfighting. It appraises how the relationship between digital systems and the cultural and organization norms of differing militaries and non-state actors helped or hindered their capacity to deploy social media assets into the information environment and what they can learn from one another about best practice.

The chapter uses empirical data from the Australian Defence Force (ADF), and semi-structured interviews with members of the US-led Multinational Capability Development Campaign (MCDC), and the Israel Defence Force (IDF) conducted mid- to late 2017. The interviewees had played a role in either preparing for the integration or managing the deployment of social media operations. They responded to questions about the origins of the organizational impetus to employ social media, the extent of command buy-in, selection and training of social media 'operators', organization and management of social media teams, and outcomes of the use of social media to date. As dictated by the terms of the ethics protocols, all interviewees remain anonymous.[2]

Command, control and the cognitive battlespace

Examining the experiences of a range of conventional militaries and non-state actors, two dominant approaches to the adoption and integration of social media emerge – an organic method, marked by bottom-up initiative from junior ranks, born of crisis, sensitive to and eager to exploit the affordances of digital media; and the command method, which is top down, planned, risk-averse and unconscious of the revolutionary potential of social media. The latter is exemplified in the work of the MCDC. Established in 2002, the MCDC is a US-led initiative comprising member militaries from North America, Europe and Asia, which operates under the auspices of NATO's Allied Command Transformation (ACT).[3] One of ACT's four core functions is 'development of capabilities' for which the MCDC serves as a laboratory, furnishing 'a platform for collaborative joint, multinational and coalition concept and capability development'.[4] To this end, it sponsors two-year multinational campaigns focused on issues most relevant to NATO's current operations. Its campaigns over the last decade have included 'Autonomy, Hybrid Warfare, Cyber, Medical, Logistics... Strategic Communication' and 'Social Media in Support of Situational Awareness' (MCDC 2016: 4).

During 2015–2016, the MCDC sponsored the Multinational Information Operations Experiment (MNIOE), tasking it to examine the integration and deployment of social media into military operations. The outcome of its investigation, the *Analytical Concept for the Use of Social Media as an Effector v1.0.*, was published in December 2016. 'The overarching challenge for security and defence actors', the authors observed, 'is to adapt to the changes in the digital IE and use the new technologies to meet their own objectives. Making social media an effective tool in one's own toolbox as well as integrating it into operations planning and execution will be one of [sic] military's future challenging tasks' (MCDC 2016: 4).

According to the MNIOE, the key questions that the militaries and other 'security actors' faced were focused on integration, adaptation and deployment. Can social media be integrated into the given military's existing information operations architecture? Can it be adapted to established cultural and organizational systems? If so, how can it be weaponized and deployed?

This focus on the adaptation of new platforms to an existing architecture implies the extent to which members of the MNIOE were ill-equipped to investigate the military affordances of digital platforms. This is further reflected in their lack of policy and doctrine around social and digital media adaptation and use in an operational context. As Interviewee 1, a member of the MNIOE, conceded, neither he nor his colleagues knew very much about social media and what little social media policy existed was almost entirely focused on how to 'use it carefully'. As a whole, he admitted, the 'military doesn't have anything... Everybody wants to do social media, and the military wants to do it as well.... [but] there is nothing on social media and military doctrine' (Interviewee 1, 12 October 2017). The publication of the *Analytical Concept* can be read as an affirmation of this. But how are we to understand and explain this failing?

Organizational cultures and conformity

Perhaps the first framework through which we can understand the MNIOE's inability to respond to, or integrate digital media into its current operational understanding, is the traditional and longstanding organizational conforming cultures of conventional militaries and the lack of responsiveness and creativity that they generate. As recent studies suggest (Allen and Gerras 2009; Möls 2010; Nazareth 2013; Serbu 2010; Young 2018), mid-ranking military personnel by the nature of their rank and length of service (e.g. Majors, Lieutenant Colonels and Colonels, indeed those who comprised the membership of the MNIOE) are more likely to be unresponsive – if not actively hostile – to radical innovations and the creative thinking these require. This is despite – as is contended in organizational analyses – the key role that creative thinking plays in the ability of organizations to manage change (see Higgins and Morgan 2000: 117). In conventional militaries however, conformity is prioritized. As Nazareth argues: 'The conditions of war demand that orders be obeyed promptly and without regard to one's own interests' (2013: 81). As a consequence, creative thinking is regarded with suspicion: 'A person is not selected to join the military organization unless he can fit into the system, and when he is enlisted or commissioned he is adjusted on a Procrustean bed to ensure his conformity' (Nazareth 2013: 82). This is true of battlefield conditions and peacetime which 'encourages the breeding of officers who rigidly follow rules' and eschew creative thinking, and is intensified in those militaries with a slow operational pace (Vego 2013: 84). Conventional militaries thus endorse conformity as an end in itself, regarding it as both the means to and an emblem of the proper functioning of the hierarchy. Moreover, for the modern military professional, conformity is demanded for success. Personnel 'do not dare take the initiative as complying with rules and being an obedient subordinate opens up a safe road to the top' (Möls 2010: 31). Put simply, 'one progresses up the ranks' by doing as one's predecessors did (Young 2018: 52). As a result, military systems, and the 'military authoritarian structure' that supports them, valorize and reward conformity, resist heterodoxy, and so operate as 'a deterrent to creative thinking' (Nazareth 2013: 83).

These postulations are borne out in Leon Young's (2018) study of creativity among officers in the Australian Defence Force. In that study, he defines creative thinking as 'the ability to produce ideas that are novel and useful in competitive environments' (2018: 48).[5] His use of a customized assessment framework to measure the prevalence of creative thinking across ranks revealed that 'creative thinking experiences a sharp increase from officers in training (rank 1) but quickly plateaus' before showing 'a continual decrease from rank 04 [Major] through to rank 07 [Brigadier]' (Young 2018: 48–9). In the ADF, the attenuation of creativity as one rises through the ranks is compounded by the fact that 'only the bottom cohort, in terms of creative thinking, is promoted from 05 [Lieutenant Colonel] to 06 [Colonel]' (Young 2018: 50). Furthermore, the data suggests that officers on the extremes, the leadenly unimaginative at one end and the highly creative at the other, 'are either being "normalised" or are leaving the service' – graphically illustrating the 'Procrustean bed' of conformity in action (Young 2018: 49). This leaves behind a core of what Young (2018: 50) terms 'conservative colonel[s]' occupying crucial positions of authority, with the power to smooth the progress or impede the implementation of key innovations. The work of Allen and Gerras (2009), Möls (2010), Nazareth (2013) and Serbu (2010) suggests that Young's findings are not unique to the ADF.

From centralized to decentralized structures

That it was just such a cohort of conservative colonels who were responsible for the MNIOE helps account for some but not all of the *Analytical Concept*'s failings. The second and possibly larger issue that MNIOE faced was the fundamental mismatch between the centralizing, hierarchical command and control structures through which modern militaries organize and communicate, and the decentralized networks that underpin digital culture and operations in the information environment. While conventional militaries routinely acknowledge, and in many cases applaud, the innovations brought about by the revolution in communications technology, they have struggled to adapt to or have resisted the integration of this technology into their own systems. Wedded to a broadcast-era

Web 1.0 model of production and distribution, conventional militaries continue to fixate – in Merrin's (2019: 112) terms – on 'mass producing content for mass distribution and mass consumption...on controlling the production and distribution of information for dutiful, passive audiences'. Yet as a result of digital architectures of (audience) participation made possible by technological evolution, 'passive' audiences are in decline, have evaporated altogether or survive only under authoritarian regimes – including militaries – in which digital systems are tightly policed. The dominance of a single, simple broadcast model thus no longer exists and, as Merrin contends, 'the arrangements, assumptions, models, structures, and economic and political power relationships of the broadcast era have been overthrown' (Merrin 2019: 112–13). Many militaries have failed to adapt to this cultural revolution and are in danger of excluding themselves from the information environment or arriving there with inadequate weapons.

Similarly, while the communications revolution has powered a radical transformation in conflict paradigms, marked in the shift from War 1.0 to War 2.0 (Rid and Hecker 2009), conventional militaries have yet to adapt to decentralized information flows in War 2.0. The primary focus of War 1.0 was weapons and intelligence – among other characteristics – executed through hierarchical top-down initiatives where the media and public were tangential to the execution itself. In War 1.0 information was protected, secret and intended for internal military consumption only (see Rid and Hecker 2009: 10). In contrast, War 2.0 is executed through decentralized structures, driven by bottom-up initiatives in which the media and population play a central role. To capture this shift in the spatial power relations, Hoskins and O'Loughlin describe this as 'diffused war' (2010: 2). Here information may be 'predominantly public, open-source, and intended for external consumption' (Rid and Hecker 2009: 10). Yet while most conventional militaries officially endorse and are committed to the principles of War 2.0, they have continued to invest in War 1.0-style vertical command and control structures, where power flows from the apex to the base and conformity and obedience are the cultural norm. This system is fundamentally incompatible with the 'distributed network of semiautonomous interlinked nodes' that characterize the operations of contemporary digital and social media, with its horizontal vectors and decentralized distribution of power (Hables Gray and Gordo 2014: 252).

The inability of conventional militaries to embrace fully the developments of War 2.0. lies in stark contrast to other sophisticated non-state actors like Al Qaeda and ISIS whose social connectivity, made possible by decentralized networks, has flourished in their execution of war. The transformation of Al Qaeda's organizational planning is noteworthy in this regard as an example of adaptation and responsiveness through digital technologies. In the wake of the 9/11 attacks, when US military and intelligence services turned their fire on Osama bin-Laden and his leadership team, Rid and Hecker (2009: 188) argue that Al Qaeda's 'command-and-control became impractical'. Large training camps were abandoned and, as Lia (2008a: 420) notes, 'it became exceedingly dangerous to communicate, be it face-to-face, by messenger, by mail, by telephone, or by electronic means'. As such, Al Qaeda were forced to adopt new organizational and communications systems to recruit, motivate, train and communicate with their personnel. Among those tasked with solving this problem was Abu Musab al-Suri, one of Al Qaeda's principal strategists, who searched for a method to gather, organize and direct supporters and soldiers for a cause 'which is susceptible to self-renewal and to self-perpetuation as a phenomenon after all its conditions and causes are present and visible to the enemy itself' (Lia 2008a: 420). That is to say, he was looking for a resilient 'operative system', not an 'organization for operations' (Lia 2008a: 17). This culminated in the generation of the non-hierarchical, decentralized 'jihad of individualized terrorism' (Lia 2008a: 393), in which small cells, acting autonomously, initiated 'single acts of terrorism' in the service of 'a common aim, a common doctrinal program' (Lia 2008b: 533). The success of this method was largely dependent on, and deeply integrated with, the technical affordances of digital media where self-motivated, nodal, non-state actors weaponized digital and social media networks to enable a sophisticated coordination of the information with the kinetic spaces of war.[6]

Risks, threats and limitations

The failure of conventional militaries to integrate and merge these differing spaces of war has, by comparison, rendered them ineffectual in the cognitive battlespace relative to non-state actors. Instead, digital and social media are predominantly understood as risk generating as much as they are critical to operational success. These perceived risks include the conviction that user-generated content is untrustworthy, that social media platforms are hostile environments for reputation management, that social media generates risks to personnel security and operational security, that being active on social media is time and personnel intensive, and that the speed of social media poses a challenge to accuracy and presence (MCDC 2016: 16–18; Maltby et al. 2015; Maltby and Thornham 2016).

This is reflected in the *Analytical Concept* in the treatment of the 'Risks, Threats and Limitations' of social media, particularly the discussion regarding the challenges posed by speed (MCDC 2016: 16–18). Here the authors express concern regarding the expectation that conventional militaries will or can initiate or respond to social media posts with the timeliness and frequency of other users. For them this 'poses a challenge to the hierarchical nature of the military' (ibid.). The *Analytical Concept* proposes two possible responses to this problem: either 'the chain of command has to approve every message that goes out in the name of the coalition' – the so-called one-star tweet[7]– or militaries reverse the trend whereby *only* senior personnel act as spokesperson and instead 'lower levels... speak for the coalition online'. This 'requires a strong reliance on Mission Command – the decentralized execution of the Commander's intent' in the information space, which the command and control model has adamantly resisted (MCDC 2016: 17). Again, what is evident here is a recourse to practices and assumptions embedded in their organizational and cultural norms that disable 'truly distributing power (to judge and originate ideas)' because it cannot coexist with conventional military chains of command (Hables Gray and Gordo 2014: 255). This allegiance to a rigid interpretation of hierarchy – that in turn resists the organizational logic of contemporary digital and social media technologies – and the lack of commitment to revise existing systems that new technical affordances require restricts conventional militaries in their ability to operate successfully in the information environment.

The IDF: Mission command, decentralized networks and a nation in arms

The most notable exception to the tendencies identified so far among conventional militaries is the Israel Defence Force (IDF). The IDF have now actively embraced mission command in their use of social media, successfully integrated social media into their systems and operations, and adapted their systems and structures to the organizational logic of the digital age. Here, the devolved enactment of the commander's intent has extended beyond the military and, as a result, Israel has enjoyed unusual success in mobilizing its civil base, both domestic and dispersed, to support its campaigns and promote its core messages via social media.

The extent to which the IDF can be regarded as a conventional military is hotly debated. Born into war, Israel has almost consistently been engaged in some form of conflict since 1948 (see Gal and Cohen 2000) and thus the IDF occupies a central, and unusually pervasive, role in the nation's civil society.[8] Military service is compulsory, three years for men, two for women, after which men are automatically transferred into the reserves which constitute the main Army force.[9] Most Israeli men and women thus spend a significant part of their lives in the IDF, and their experience of citizenship, according to Schiff, 'is dependent upon a traditionally non-civil activity: military participation' (Schiff 1992: 646). As a result, 'civilian-military boundaries remain porous or... virtually non-existent' (Gal and Cohen 2000: 224) which, in turn, means that the IDF's organizational structures are necessarily loosened by the regular flow of part-time reservists and the shifting civil society norms they bring with them, including a culture of bottom-up innovation. Yet it is not these unique features alone that have enabled the IDF to adapt itself to War 2.0. Instead, it was the combination of these features alongside a long organizational struggle that prompted a move away from hierarchical, reactive military information systems to a more responsive, decentralized and technologically informed military. It is through the transformative 'journey' of the IDF that we can further locate the adaptation and adoption of digital systems that more conventional militaries lack.

Though perennially admired as a paragon of organizational agility, critics have long argued that the IDF 'underperformed in its public communication activities' (Rid and Hecker 2009: 101; Shavit 2017).[10] In the years before the outbreak of the Second Intifada in 2002, it sought to control the flow of information by pursuing 'a reactive, ad hoc, defensive and denial of access approach to media management that centred on creating media blackouts and limiting media access to conflict zones' (Shavit 2017: 2). As new communications technologies reshaped the information ecology in the first decade of the twenty-first century, the IDF held onto a centralized communication model, failing to acknowledge the accelerated and dominating pace of digital networks. The media handling of the Hezbollah missile attack on the Israeli Corvette, INS *Hanit*, is a key example of this. On the night of 14 July 2006, in the first days of the Second Lebanon War, the *Hanit* was struck by a Hezbollah anti-ship missile while patrolling off the coast of Beirut, killing four Israeli sailors (Harel 2007). The IDF's public affairs leadership first heard of the strike during a press conference by which time it was too late to prepare a media briefing. Concurrently, Hezbollah broadcast a video of the attack which subsequently dominated Israeli media coverage (Rid and Hecker 2009: 119).[11] In light of instances like this, 'some critics credited Hezbollah with decisive victory on the media stage – in part, due to superior usage of cyberspace to deliver its political message to international audiences' (Stein 2012: 137).[12] As a result, the war was widely regarded as a defeat in Israel and the military inquiry's[13] appraisal of the IDF's performance castigated it for a lack of media coordination and preparedness.

This 'performance' was repeated in December 2008 during the IDF's assault on Gaza – Operation Cast Lead – where although the media policy showed every mark of coordination and preparedness, it still failed to integrate effective coordination of kinetic action with the information environment. While the IDF's focus on restricting media access to the fighting (by closing the Erez crossing into Gaza) enabled them to put out a consistent 'media' message, journalists were stubbornly unreceptive to it, and, according to Patrikarakos, they unofficially boycotted material disseminated by the IDF's Spokesperson's Unit (SU) (Patrikarakos 2017: 51).[14] Instead, journalists used stories prominent in the digital sphere – particularly mobile phone messages and social media communications from within Gaza, detailing the IDF's targeting of civil infrastructure. The publication of this material unleashed a 'tidal wave of international criticism' apparent in both mainstream and social media (Schechter 2014; Shavit 2017: 142). Material that would have helped the IDF cause in this regard – for example cockpit video showing Israeli Air Force jets aborting attacks when civilians come into view – was prevented from being posted online by 'conservative colonels' in the IDF who opposed experimentation with social media, unable to see its potential military application. According to Hoffman (2009), they considered social media primarily as an entertainment platform, 'a toy for kids' and ineffective as a dissemination tool. Within this context, Aliza Landes, a junior officer in the Spokesperson's Unit, who had six months earlier written a position paper on the importance of new media as an influence vector,[15] was given approval to establish a YouTube Channel to post pro-IDF video material that she had been previously posting on her own blog. Within a fortnight the site had attracted more than 1.7 million views and the IDF began to finally embrace social and digital media as part of a combined communications and warfighting strategy.

By 2012, when the IDF attacked Gaza in Operation Pillar of Defense, they demonstrated a sophisticated grasp of the information environment via their use of social media, particularly Twitter, through which they communicated with both the public and their adversary.[16] This successful coordination of digital with military action, cognitive with physical battlespaces, and the timely and diverse dissemination of information were powerfully influential. For the IDF, it facilitated closer integration of bottom-up domestic enthusiasm for the campaign with top-down military coordination of public messaging. Widespread public participation in Operation Pillars of Defense via social media reinforced the permeability of the civil and military spheres in Israel and was used to promote to domestic and international audiences two key themes about the nation's struggle – one centred on the potency and precision of IDF weaponry, the other on 'the suffering within Israel' (Cohen 2012: 22). For example, a series of Twitter images were posted mapping the reach of Hamas rockets and the numbers of Israelis under threat from them.[17] Another depicted missiles raining down on Sydney, London, New York and Paris, inviting audiences to consider 'What Would You Do?' and 'Share This If You Agree Israel Has the Right to Self Defense' (IDF 2012). Sharing online was, for Israel's geographically dispersed supporters, an opportunity to enter the digital space of war and play an active part in it. Throughout the eight days of Operation Pillar of Defense active operations, and for months afterwards, pro-Israeli groups used the full spectrum of social media platforms 'to share patriotic testimonials, to voice hatred towards anti-war "traitors," to track sites of wartime devastation within Israeli territory, and to employ hashtags to catalyze solidarity (#PrayforIsrael), all capitalizing on the narrative of Israeli victimhood' (Kuntsman and Stein 2015: 33–4).[18] On 15 November 2012, the Israeli Ministry of Public Diplomacy launched the 'Israel Under Fire' project on Facebook, providing its supporters with a dedicated platform for their advocacy, encouraging them to use the information provided and to re-disseminate it. They wrote: 'Our mission is to show the truth about Israel and how it's under attack by Arab neighbours as well as by Palestinian terror groups and parties. We'll inform you and you can help us share the truth to the world.'[19] This project, which continues to run with the direct support of the Prime Minister's Office and the Ministry of Foreign Affairs, is an exemplary form of *hasbara* which, as Reuven Ben-Shalom (2014) notes, constitutes 'Israel's main "soft power" tool, aimed mainly at external audiences'. Facebook and Twitter have thus extended Israel's conscription policies online, providing a space of war within which its supporters can take up its cause and participate in its struggles.

In the wake of Operation Pillar of Defense, the IDF formalized the role of social media within its communications structure, establishing a new Interactive Media Branch (IMB).[20] As Interviewee 2 noted, the IMB delegates junior officers to oversee the management of its social media presence and empowers its young personnel to produce the material that will resonate with its target audiences. This approach, around rank, age and the perceived risks of engaging in social and digital media, stands in stark contrast to that of more conventional military cultures.

> All of my soldiers that are in the social media department here range in ages between eighteen to, twenty-three. Twenty-three is like, on the old [side]...I'm twenty-nine, my deputy is twenty-five. We're a bit older again. We're not, thirty-five, forty, we're not at that life stage. We're a bit older. The head of the branch for instance is usually around forty years old. So, leadership tends to be a bit older. But I think that if you want to have creative, innovative, unique content on social media, it can't be done by, by forty-year-olds.
> (Interviewee 2, 13 June 2017)

These social media operators, under mission command, are given broad directives about the narratives to prioritize and the freedom to generate content and employ the most appropriate platforms to post and disseminate that content. Interviewee 2 claimed that the fact that this approach was possible, let alone successful, was because the IDF chain of command was more condensed and fluid than in other conventional militaries, enabling better adaptation and integration: 'The bureaucratic level of approval is, I think, much thinner and much narrower than it is elsewhere, which can sometimes be a disadvantage, but I think that when you're trying to introduce something new or start something new, it's definitely an advantage' (Interviewee No 2, 13 June 2017). The combination of these factors ensures that IDF initiatives, or responses to a specific event, are relevant, timely and coordinated and that the bottom-up spontaneity of the social media operators is married with the top-down direction of command. As such, in terms of organization and effects, the IDF's operations in the information environment are far closer to those of Al Qaeda or ISIS than to those of any other conventional military.

Conclusion

Landes's experiences, and the digital wave she initiated for the IDF, offer a textbook case of the organic uptake of social media. Its introduction and original deployment were bottom up, initiated and pursued by motivated individuals of junior rank. Born of crisis, necessity and command permissiveness in the context of active operations, its uptake was also driven and directed by the unfolding capacities of the new media of that moment. Though a risky venture, its successful adoption acted as a significant force multiplier, extending the opportunity to participate in the information environment to domestic and dispersed international audiences. By contrast, the MCDC approach sits at the opposite extreme, reflecting a top-down, command-centred, risk-sensitive, theoretically driven approach, run by personnel with little experience, understanding of, or intuitive feel for the new media. The older, more senior officers who directed this experiment, paralysed by risk-aversion, fearful of their innovative juniors' greater familiarity with social media, use command structures to stifle creativity and corral communications initiatives within the known parameters of legacy media approaches.

The IDF experience suggests that unless they are willing, and able, to radically reshape their organizational systems, conventional Western militaries will struggle to create a space of war where they can realize social media's potential as both a platform and a weapon. Their traditional command structures cannot regulate, or harness, the information that 'now pours onto, from, about and around the battlefield' (Merrin 2019: 196). The IDF's success over the last decade has rested on its sophisticated integration of communication with warfighting operations, but perhaps more so on its mobilization of civil society communities in 'a new mode of participative warfare' (ibid.). Exploiting 'routine social media practices', the IDF augmented the top-down command messaging of uniformed service personnel with the bottom-up participation of Israel's domestic and dispersed civilian support base in a potent display of 'digital militarism' (Kuntsman and Stein 2015: vii). In this new, always at war space, the religious, ethnic and cultural ties that bind military and civil society actors are mobilized by potent narratives that evoke and affirm their shared sense of purpose and identity. Posting at will in support of specific operational goals, and the deeper sense of self they underpin, the digital operators can be managed – insofar as they can be managed at all – only through an attenuated form of mission command. Given its limited capacity to control or mitigate risk, the IDF elected to trust and empower its digital operators. Thinning its bureaucracy and flattening the chain of command, it endorsed the social media operator's autonomy, speed and spontaneity and thus augmented its top-down messaging. Spooked by the obvious risks to reputation and operations security, the greater risk for conventional Western militaries is that fear will paralyse them from embracing digital militarism and fully engaging with the information environment.

Yet there is no question that the IDF experience is sui generis. For Israelis, the regular flow of personnel into and out of uniform creates uniquely porous civil-military relations (Gal and Cohen 2000; Rid and Hecker 2009; Schiff 1992). By contrast, for almost seventy-five years, Western militaries have been engaged in wars of choice, while the abolition of conscription and the move to smaller, professionalized forces has deepened the divisions between civil and military orders (Moskos 2000). Perhaps the greatest achievement of non-state actors during the 'war on terror' was the collapse of civil-military boundaries in recruitment, mobilization and targeting, that it instigated and exemplified. Exploiting the specific affordances of digital networks, Al Qaeda weaponized the information environment and scored a series of compelling victories thereby. Its success demonstrated that Western militaries not only lacked the organizational systems and cultural posture needed to compete in this space, but that they were allocating their resources and concentrating their efforts in the wrong places. Their dominant paradigm for operations, developed and exemplified in US military doctrine, comprises a six-phase planning construct, running from phase 0 ('shape') through to phase v ('enable civil authority'), with the principal focus of training and resources on the major combat operations of phase III ('dominate') (Scharre 2016). Yet while the United States and its allies ready themselves for battle, their adversaries, unable to match the firepower ranged against them, spread their resources to all phases of conflict. Non-state actors have enjoyed particular success when focusing their resources on the information environment where phase 0 operations are principally conducted. Here, drawing on the digital environment's 'distributed network of semiautonomous interlinked nodes' they establish the parameters and purposes of the conflict, shape its narrative, and so determine what victory looks like while mapping their own progress towards it. As long as Western militaries underestimate the importance of phase 0 operations, the information environment and the narratives that motivate and empower its actors, they will be forced to fight on the enemy's terms, on the enemy's ground, with disappointment and failure the inevitable outcomes. The IDF experience demonstrates that redirecting resources from combat operations to narrative curation while ensuring closer coordination between the two has powerful effects. It enables militaries to shape both the information and kinetic spaces of war to their advantage, position their adversaries to their own benefit, dictate the criteria for success and deliver them. The process by which militaries can actively shape the space of war brings the question of narrative sharply into focus. Freedman notes that 'for a narrative to have the desired effect it must relate in some way to the experiences, culture and concerns of its intended audience' (Freedman 2015: 19). Al Qaeda, ISIS and the IDF share potent, core narratives about what they fight for and why. Their narratives define the principal actors and events in conflict; they speak to the experiences, cultures and concerns of their members and supporters, and create meanings that reaffirm their identities (Freedman 2015). As the conflicts in Iraq and Afghanistan illustrate, the wars of choice that Western militaries have pursued over the past half century have largely failed to sustain such narratives and public support for these ventures has tailed off in response (Foster 2013; Maley 2015; Miller 2010; Oliphant 2018).[21]

Social media has given Western militaries the tools to dominate the information space, but they have not yet been able to adapt their organizational systems and cultures to empower their personnel and exploit the affordances of the digital environment's 'distributed network of semiautonomous interlinked nodes' to maximum advantage. They have much to learn from their friends and their enemies. Non-state actors and the IDF have shown that by committing resources to shape the information battlefield, one can channel public participation, mute one's adversaries, dictate what victory looks like and determine when it has been attained. Yet, above all else, their experiences reveal that without a compelling narrative that explains why they are on the battlefield, what they are fighting for, and how this struggle reinforces who they are, their publics are unlikely to amplify the combatants' core messages or support their struggle in the information domain. Without that support, as the experience in Iraq and Afghanistan demonstrates, no amount of firepower will bring victory.

Notes

1 The MCDC has since been superseded by the Capability Development Directorate. See NATO, 'Who We Are' website.
2 The interviews were conducted under the auspices of Monash University Human Research Ethics Committee Project No. 8347.
3 'Allied Command Transformation's mission is to contribute to preserving the peace, security and territorial integrity of Alliance member states by leading the warfare development of military structures, forces, capabilities and doctrines' (NATO, 'Who We Are' website).

4 The link to the original NATO site, http://www.act.nato.int/mcdc, has since been disabled.
5 'As a thinking process', Young argues, 'creativity has three distinct and testable elements: (1) divergent thinking (novelty), (2) convergent thinking (evaluation) and (3) analogical thinking (communication of the idea)' (Young 2018: 48).
6 Rid and Hecker point out the close parallels between al-Suri's vision of global jihad and the organizational logic of Web 2.0; 'both assumed entrepreneurial individuals as part of a global community of like-minded activists, self-motivated participation, decentralized networks, self-administration, a common purpose, and global collaboration' (Rid and Hecker 2009: 193).
7 This option is exemplified in the actions of the ADF. Every tweet has to be approved by the relevant Brigadier or equivalent depending on its content and target audience. From May 2018, under instructions from the Minister of Defence's Ministerial Executive Corporate Communication Division (MECC), the ADF began shutting down social media accounts belonging to individual units and commands. Social media accounts have since been consolidated at the highest level. Now, while each of the three services operates on a range of social media platforms, only the Chief and Vice Chief of the Defence Force and the Chiefs of Army and Navy are present on Twitter. The Chief of the RAAF has no social media presence. See ADF, 'Social Media': http://www.defence.gov.au/socialmedia/ (accessed 29 August 2019).
8 Tsahal, the name by which the Israelis know their military, is the Hebrew acronym for Tsva ha-Hagana le-Yisra'el, which translates as 'The Army of Defence for Israel'.
9 Reserves demand between twenty and thirty days of service per year up until the age of fifty-five for men, women's service in the reserves is voluntary.
10 Rid and Hecker (2009: 104–5) summarize IDF-Media relations from independence to the Second Intifada in 2000. Michal Shavit (2017: 2) analyses the IDF's media and information operations policies from 2000 to 2014.
11 For the broadcast see Hezbollah (2006). The sailors aboard Hanit were even quicker off the mark, using their mobile phones from the ship to call and text their families.
12 I have adjusted Stein's spelling of 'Hizbullah' to 'Hezbollah' to ensure consistency. See also Kalb and Saivetz (2007).
13 There were a number of inquiries into every aspect of Israel's performance in the war. Inquiries focused on the media included the Winograd Commission, the State Comptroller's report on the treatment of the press and a report from the Israeli Press Council. There were also a number of classified military inquiries into various aspects of the IDF's performance.
14 'The purpose of the IDF Spokesperson's Unit is to report on the accomplishments and activities of the IDF to the Israeli and international public, to nurture public confidence in the IDF, and to serve as the IDF's primary professional authority on matters of public relations and distribution of information to the public.' IDF Spokesperson's Unit: https://www.idfblog.com/about/idf-spokespersons-unit/ (accessed 3 February 2017).

15 Landes was highly critical of the IDF's failure to move into the digital battlespace in her paper but it was never published and her suggestions 'remained stuck in the chain of command' (Patriakarakos 2017: 53).
16 On 14 November 2012, the IDF announced via Twitter that an Israeli airstrike had killed Ahmed al-Ja'bari, Chief of the al-Qassam Brigades, Hamas's military wing in Gaza (Lappin 2012). A succeeding Tweet from the IDF recommended 'that no Hamas operatives, whether low level or senior leaders, show their faces above ground in the days ahead' (https://twitter.com/idf/status/268780918209118208?lang=en). The al-Qassam Brigades responded with the announcement of a counteroffensive, Operation Shale Stones and a threat of their own: 'Our blessed hands will reach your leaders and soldiers wherever they are (You Opened Hell Gates on Yourselves)' (https://twitter.com/idf/status/268780918209118208?lang=en).
17 See https://www.idfblog.com/facts-figures/rocket-attacks-toward-israel/hamasrocketrange/ (accessed 2 February 2017).
18 Thomas Zeitzoff argued that the IDF was highly sensitive to public opinion and that the number of likes and re-tweets its posts garnered directly affected its targeting (Zeitzoff 2018: 46–9).
19 See IDF 'Israel under Fire'. https://www.facebook.com/pg/IsraelUnderFireLive/about/?ref=page_internal (accessed 2 February 2017). During Operation Protective Edge, in 2014, Matthew Hall described the efforts of students from one private university north of Tel Aviv in 'challenging propaganda from Hamas' (Hall 2014). Notably, the structure of the volunteer groups they formed mimicked that of the Interactive Media Branch in the Spokesperson's Unit.
20 The Spokesperson's Unit appointed Avital Leibovich as its Digital Spokesperson and Director of the IMB. For an interview with her see Tomchin (2015). She commanded a thirty-five-person team of tech-savvy young IDF personnel who 'tweet, Facebook, blog, build apps, edit videos, snap Instagrams, and update Google+ posts' (Kerr 2014). The IMB now operates on more than thirty platforms in six languages – English, Hebrew, Arabic, French, Spanish and Russian. Its Twitter account has more than 1 million followers (https://twitter.com/idf?lang=en), while its Facebook page has more than 2.2 million followers and more than 2.1 million 'likes' (https://www.facebook.com/idfonline/). The Social Media page on the IDF Spokesperson's Unit website invites young Israelis anywhere in the world to join its International Social Media Desk, a virtual community of online 'conscripts', to advance the state's official messages around defence and security and to counter anti-Israeli sentiment wherever they find it online (https://www.idfblog.com/join/).
21 The Falklands Conflict provides an isolated case where, in both Britain and Argentina, the contending official narratives spoke to the experiences, culture and concerns of the differing audiences (Foster 1999).

Bibliography

Allen, C. D., and S. Gerras (2009), 'Developing Creative and Critical Thinkers', *Military Review*, 89(6): 77–83.

Bebber, R. J. (2016), 'Winning the Phase 0 War', *Foreign Policy*, 27 January. Available online: https://foreignpolicy.com/2016/01/07/winning-the-phase-0-war/ (accessed 30 September 2019).

Ben-Shalom, R. (2014), 'Hasbara, Public Diplomacy and Propaganda', *Jerusalem Post*, 12 June. Available online: http://www.jpost.com/Opinion/Op-Ed-Contributors/Hasbara-public-diplomacy-and-propaganda-358211 (accessed 28 February 2017).

Blaker, L. (2017), 'The Islamic State's Use of Online Social Media', *Military Cyber Affairs*, 1(1): 1–9.

Cohen, N. (2012), 'In Gaza Conflict, Fighting with Weapons and Postings on Twitter', *New York Times*, 21 November. Available online: http://www.nytimes.com/2012/11/22/world/middleeast/in-gaza-conflict-fighting-with-weapons-and-postings-on-twitter.html (accessed 2 February 2017).

Farwell, J. P. (2014), 'The Media Strategy of ISIS', *Survival: Global Politics and Strategy*, 56(6): 49–55.

Foster, K. (1999), *Fighting Fictions: War, Narrative and National Identity*, London: Pluto Press.

Foster, K. (2013), *Don't Mention the War: The Australian Defence Force, the Media and the Afghan Conflict*, Melbourne: Monash University Publishing.

Freedman, L. (2015), 'The Possibilities and Limits of Strategic Narratives', in B. De Graaf, G. Dimitriu, and J. Ringsmose (eds), *Strategic Narratives, Public Opinion and War: Winning Domestic Support for the Afghan War*, 17–36, New York: Routledge.

Gal, R., and S. A. Cohen (2000), 'Israel: Still Waiting in the Wings', in C. C. Moskos, J. A. Williams and D. R. Segal (eds), *The Postmodern Military: Armed Forces after the Cold War*, 224–41, New York: Oxford University Press.

Hables Gray, C., and Á. J. Gordo (2014), 'Social Media in Conflict: Comparing Military and Social-Movement Technocultures', *Cultural Politics*, 10(3): 251–61.

Hall, M. (2014), 'Israeli Propaganda Hits Social Media', *Sydney Morning Herald*, 18 July. Available online: http://www.smh.com.au/it-pro/government-it/israeli-propaganda-war-hits-social-media-20140717-ztvky.html (accessed 3 February 2017).

Harel, A. (2007), 'Soldier Killed, Three Missing after Navy Vessel Hit off Beirut Coast', *Haaretz*, 16 July. Available online: https://web.archive.org/web/20060718032259/http://haaretz.com/hasen/spages/738695.html (accessed 3 February 2017).

Hezbollah (2006), 'Hezbollah Shooting on Israeli Warship INS *Hanit* 2', *YouTube*, 21 July. Available online: https://www.youtube.com/watch?v=lR4KIJk5q0U (accessed 4 February 2017).

Higgins, M., and J. Morgan (2000), 'The Role of Creativity in Planning: The "Creative Practitioner"', *Planning Practice and Research*, 15(1–2): 117–27.

Hoffman, A. (2009), 'The "Kids" behind IDF's Media', *Tablet*, 20 November. Available online: https://www.tabletmag.com/jewish-news-and-politics/117235/the-kids-behind-idf-media (accessed 16 September 2019).

Hoskins, A., and B. O'Loughlin (2010), *War and Media: The Emergence of Diffused War*, Cambridge: Polity.

IDF (2012), 'What Would You Do?', *Twitter*, 16 November. Available online: https://twitter.com/idfspokesperson/status/269419585101512704 (accessed 2 February 2017).

Kalb, M., and C. Saivetz (2007), 'The Israeli-Hezbollah War of 2006: The Media as a Weapon in Asymmetrical Conflict', *The Harvard International Journal of Press/Politics*, 12(3): 43–66.

Kelton, M., M. Sullivan, E. Benvenue and Z. Rogers (2019), 'Australia, the Utility of Force and the Society-Centric Battlespace', *International Affairs*, 95(4): 859–76.

Kerr, D. (2014), 'How Israel and Hamas Weaponized Social Media', *C-Nets*, 13 January. Available online: https://www.cnet.com/au/news/how-israel-and-hamas-weaponized-social-media/ (accessed 4 February 2017).

Kuntsman, A., and R. L. Stein (2015), *Digital Militarism: Israel's Occupation in the Social Media Age*, Stanford, CA: Stanford University Press.

Lappin, Y. (2012), 'IAF Strike Kills Hamas Military Chief Jabari', *Jerusalem Post*, 14 November. Available online: http://www.jpost.com/Defense/IAF-strike-kills-Hamas-military-chief-Jabari (accessed 1 February 2017).

Lia, B. (2008a), *Architect of Global Jihad: The Life of Al-Qaeda Strategist Abu Mus'ab al- Suri*, New York: Columbia University Press.

Lia, B. (2008b), 'Doctrines for Jihadi Terrorist Training', *Terrorism and Political Violence*, 20(4): 518–42.

Maley, W. (2015), 'The War in Afghanistan: Australia's Strategic Narratives', in B. De Graaf, G. Dimitriu, and J. Ringsmose (eds), *Strategic Narratives, Public Opinion and War: Winning Domestic Support for the Afghan War*, 81–98, New York: Routledge.

Maltby, S. (2015), 'Imagining Influence: Logic(al) Tensions in War and Defence', in M. M. F. Eskjær, S. Hjarvard and M. Mortensen (eds), *The Dynamics of Mediatized Conflicts*, 165–84, New York: Peter Lang.

Maltby, S., H. Thornham and D. Bennett (2015), 'Capability in the Digital: Institutional Media Management and Its Dis/contents', *Information, Communication and Society*, 18(5): 1–22.

Maltby, S., and H. Thornham (2016), 'The Digital Mundane, Social Media and the Military', *Media, Culture and Society*, 38(8): 1153–68.

MCDC (2016), *Use of Social Media as an Effector: Analytical Concept for the Use of Social Media as an Effector V 1.0 2016*, Mayen, Germany: MCDC.

Merrin, W. (2019), *Digital War: A Critical Introduction*, London: Routledge.

Miller, C. A. (2010), *Endgame for the West in Afghanistan? Explaining the Decline in Support for the War in Afghanistan in the United States, Great Britain, Canada, Australia, France and Germany*, Carlisle, PA: US Army War College.

Möls, T. (2010), 'Critical and Creative Thinking: Are Innovation and Initiative Welcome in the Military?', *ENDC Proceedings*, 13, 7–17.

Moskos, C. C., J. A. Williams and D. R. Segal, eds (2000), *The Postmodern Military: Armed Forces after the Cold War*, New York: Oxford University Press.
Nazareth, B. J. (2013), *Creative Thinking in Warfare*, Atlanta: Lancer Publishers.
Oliphant, B. (2018), 'The Iraq War Continues to Divide the US Public, 15 Years after It Began', *Fact Tank: Pew Research Center*, 18 March. Available online: https://www.pewresearch.org/fact-tank/2018/03/19/iraq-war-continues-to-divide-u-s-public-15-years-after-it-began/ (accessed 27 September 2019).
Patrikarakos, D. (2017), *War in 140 Characters: How Social Media Is Reshaping Conflict in the Twenty-first Century*, New York: Basic Books.
Prensky, M. (2001), 'Digital Natives, Digital Immigrants Part 1', *On the Horizon*, 9(5) (September/October): 1–5.
Rid, T., and M. Hecker (2009), *War 2.0: Irregular Warfare in the Information Age*, Washington, DC: Praeger Security International.
Scharre, P. (2016), 'American Strategy and the Six Phases of Grief', *War on the Rocks*, 6 October. Available online: https://warontherocks.com/2016/10/american-strategy-and-the-six-phases-of-grief/ (accessed 27 September 2019).
Schechter, A. (2014), 'The Social Intifada: How Millennials and Facebook Beat the Almighty Israeli Army', *Haaretz*, 5 May. Available online: http://www.haaretz.com/israel-news/.premium-1.589032 (accessed 6 February 2017).
Schiff, R. (1992), 'Civil-military Relations Reconsidered: Israel as an "Uncivil" State', *Security Studies*, 1(4): 636–58.
Serbu, G. (2010), 'The Dangers of Anti-intellectualism in Contemporary Western Armies', *Infantry*, 99(4): 44–7.
Shaheen, J. (2015), '*How Daesh Uses Adaptive Social Networks to Spread Its Message*', Riga: NATO Strategic Communications Centre of Excellence. Available online: https://www.stratcomcoe.org/network-terror-how-daesh-uses-adaptive-social-networks-spread-its-message (accessed 6 August 2019).
Shavit, M. (2017), *Media Strategy and Military Operations in the 21st Century: Mediatizing the Israel Defence Forces*, London: Routledge.
Singer, P. W., and E. T. Brooking (2018), *LikeWar: The Weaponization of Social Media*, Boston: Houghton Mifflin Harcourt.
Stein, R. L. (2012), 'Impossible Witness: Israeli Visuality, Palestinian Testimony and the Gaza War', *Journal for Cultural Research*, 16(2–3): 135–53.
Svetoka, S. (2015), '*Social Media as a Tool of Hybrid Warfare*', Riga: NATO Strategic Communications Centre of Excellence. Available online: https://www.stratcomcoe.org/social-media-tool-hybrid-warfare (accessed 9 August 2019).
Tomchin, S. (2015), 'Going on the Digital Offensive', *Jewish Woman Magazine*, Winter. Available online: https://www.jwmag.org/sslpage.aspx?pid=3851#sthash.1evGaqfY.dpbs (accessed 4 February 2017).
United States Air Force (2003), *Air Force Basic Doctrine: Air Force Doctrine Document 1*, Washington: US Air Force.
Vego, M. (2013), 'On Military Creativity', *Joint Forces Quarterly*, 70(3): 83–90.
Winter, C. (2019), 'The Battle for Mosul: An Analysis of ISIS Propaganda', in O. Fridman, V. Kabernik and J. C. Pearce (eds), *Hybrid Conflicts and Information Warfare: New Labels, Old Politics*, Boulder, CO: Lynne Rienner, pp. 171–190.
Young, L. (2018), 'The Conservative Colonel: How Being Creative Killed Your Career in the ADF', *Australian Defence Force Journal*, 203: 47–56.

Zeitzoff, T. (2018), 'Does Social Media Influence Conflict? Evidence from the 2012 Gaza Conflict', *Journal of Conflict Resolution*, 62(1): 29–63.

Zur, O., and A. Walker (2011), 'On Digital Immigrants and Digital Natives: How the Digital Divide Affects Families, Educational Institutions, and the Workplace', *Zur Institute*. Available online: http://www.zurinstitute.com/digital_divide.html (accessed 9 August 2019).

Websites

ADF 'Social Media': http://www.defence.gov.au/SocialMedia/ (accessed 9 August 2019).

DND Canada 'Social Media Use': https://www.canada.ca/en/department-national-defence/corporate/policies-standards/defence-administrative-orders-directives/2000-series/2008/2008-official-use-social-media.html (accessed 6 November 2018).

IDF 'Facebook Page': https://www.facebook.com/idfonline/ (accessed 27 September 2019).

IDF 'Israel under Fire': https://www.facebook.com/pg/IsraelUnderFireLive/about/?ref=page_internal (accessed 6 February 2017).

IDF 'Spokesperson's Unit': https://www.idfblog.com/about/idf-spokespersons-unit/ (accessed 6 February 2017).

MCDC: http://www.act.nato.int/mcdc (accessed 5 October 2017, now disabled).

MCDC https://www.gov.uk/government/collections/multinational-capability-development-campaign-mcdc (accessed 20 September 2019).

MvD 'Social Media Use': https://www.werkenbijdefensie.nl/nieuws/social-media (accessed 4 February 2017).

NATO 'Who We Are': https://www.act.nato.int/who-we-are (accessed 9 August 2019).

6

The myth of a thousand westerns: Media and just war theory

Sean Aday

Introduction

On 3 August 1965, CBS reporter Morley Safer accompanied a company of US Marines to the South Vietnamese village of Cam Ne, which the military suspected of harbouring and supporting Viet Cong forces. Safer and his cameraman, Ha Tue Can, filmed as US troops forced villagers from their thatched-roof homes and systematically burned down most of the structures in the village, nearly incinerating at least one family, including an infant, hiding in fear underneath one of the houses. In his report that aired two days later, Safer expressed barely contained outrage at the wanton destruction, pointing out somewhat derisively that the mission had only yielded three elderly VC suspects.

The story generated outrage towards the network among many CBS viewers and from the military, which demanded Safer be removed from Vietnam and briefly banned him from covering US armed forces. Yet many media scholars and journalists see the Cam Ne report as a watershed moment in press coverage of Vietnam and of war generally. As Safer said in the PBS documentary *Reporting America at War* (PBS 2003),

> Cam Ne was a shock, I think....I think [viewers] saw American troops acting in a way people had never seen American troops act before, and couldn't imagine. Those people were raised on World War II, in which virtually everything we saw was heroic. And so much of it, indeed, was.

And there was plenty in Vietnam, too, that was heroic. But this conjured up not America, but some brutal power – Germany, even, in World War II....It was the end of a certain kind of innocence among the public, really.... For the most part I think American armies are awfully good in the business of protecting civilians, of not going over the line. It happens, *but not as policy* [emphasis added], not as, 'This is how we do things' ...
(PBS 2003)

As legendary *New York Times* reporter David Halberstam said of Safer's report in the same documentary: 'It went against the American myth of a thousand westerns in the movies. It is the Indians who are torturing women and children and the cavalry that rides up at the last minute to free them' (PBS 2003).

Safer's report shocked sensibilities because, as Halberstam notes, it contradicted the prevailing myth that an inherently virtuous America always fought virtuous wars virtuously. Interestingly, however, even decades later Safer still reflexively framed the GIs' behaviour as an aberration from, rather than a product of, US military policy. This despite his own follow-up reporting at the time that showed the opposite, and other reporting and histories since then that revealed actions like Cam Ne – and much worse – were a common tactic in US military policy during the war.

This chapter argues that US reporting on war – both as policy (e.g. declaring war) and practice (i.e. waging it) – has historically been implicitly, and often explicitly, based on the assumption that the United States always fights what are known in philosophy and in modern political and legal realms as 'just wars'. Furthermore, it argues that the press also frames the way US GIs fight in those wars as within the bounds of just war principles – even when they are not. Through a review of decades of mass communication research, and employing Entman's (2003; 2004) Cascading Activation Model, I will show that this pattern in mainstream media coverage stems from institutional biases related to journalism's place in American culture and to the news norms and routines that govern news work. This persistent tendency in coverage of war matters for several reasons, I argue, especially because it has the effect of buttressing the rhetorical power and legitimacy of policymakers' just war claims. This can make specific wars, and war in general, more palatable and likely. In addition, I will show how coverage of deviations from just war principles, such as America's post-9/11 embrace of torture, is consistently framed as aberrant rather than as policy, thus further exonerating political, military and other officials.

Ultimately, this tendency to accept and promote the notion of just war compromises the media's Fourth Estate watchdog function and creates what Entman et al. (2010) call an *accountability gap* that distances political and military leaders from questionable policies and tactics. Although due to space limitations this chapter will focus on the US media, its arguments likely apply to other countries and media systems (see, e.g., Robinson et al. 2010).

Finally, a vast literature exists exploring various aspects of just war theory, its potential applications, its shortcomings and its implications for policy. Throughout the centuries, the thrust of this literature has focused understandably on the theory's implications for leaders, policymakers and those in the military. This has continued into the modern wars of the twentieth and twenty-first centuries, during which time just war tenets have become norms accepted to some degree, at least in principle, by most of the world's governments and international bodies. Yet while scholars and other observers have written extensively about the various ways that military and political leaders often attempt to convince the world and their own domestic constituencies that they are adhering to just war principles, or the various ways they may evade or obfuscate troubling deviations from those norms, less attention has been paid to the institutional mechanisms by which this happens. In particular, the news media's role has been almost entirely ignored in the just war literature. Meanwhile, mass communication research has not explored the media's role in the philosophy and politics of just war principles. This chapter begins to fill these gaps by conceiving more holistically of an *institutionally* produced and reified *moral* space that serves to legitimize both war and conduct in war. Furthermore, the 'institutional' space in this case thus refers to a kind of meta-institution comprised of interconnected sub-institutional entities including mass media, government, think tanks and political parties (as well as more general institutions such as the education system) that combine to define and promote these legitimizing national and cultural myths and identity. Put another way, this institutionally created moral space is one in which a nation defines itself as just and righteous, regardless of its actions, which can have the ironic effect of legitimating unjust and immoral policies and behaviour.

Just war theory: Brief background and major tenets

Just war theory in one form or another dates back centuries and has dominated thinking about war to the point that, despite modifications and revisions, its fundamental tenets lie at the core of contemporary legal, moral and even political paradigms of warfare (Dill 2018; Taylor 2017). As the most important just war theorist of the late twentieth century, Michael Walzer, has written, the traditional theory of just war is 'an argument about the moral standing of warfare as a human activity' that attempts to wrestle with the twin propositions, or realities, that 'war is sometimes justifiable and that the conduct of war is always subject to moral criticism' (Walzer 2005, p. ix).

Yet as time went on, attitudes slowly began to change. The Enlightenment emphasized human rights, democracies began to replace monarchies, and philosophers like the nineteenth-century military theorist Carl von Clausewitz began to understand that war is policy, and total war is often counterproductive politically. Walzer's seminal book *Just and Unjust Wars* ([1977] 2015) reinvigorated discussion of the theory and has defined the terms of how it's been discussed and debated since. Although just war theory has served as a rebuttal to strict pacifism since its earliest roots in Augustine philosophy (Walzer 2005) and has generally been associated with a more realist perspective (Dill 2018), Walzer himself argued for a conceptualization that would be a rejection of mid-twentieth-century realist perspectives, which he saw as responsible for an amoral rationalization of the Vietnam War, colonialism, and other historical and contemporary foreign policy abuses ([1977] 2015; 2005). Still, his version of just war theory has become associated with a 'traditionalist' school whose 'central commitment is to provide moral foundations for international law as it applies to armed conflict: states (and only states) may go to war only for national defence, defence of other states, or to intervene to avert "crimes that shock the moral conscience of mankind"' (Walzer [1977]2015: 107). This perspective, which has taken root in political, academic, legal and military circles, has at its core protection of innocent civilians and respect for human rights, including those of combatants (Lazar 2017; Walzer [1977]2015). More recently, a critique of the traditional approach has come to dominate philosophy departments, although the traditionalist view is still more prominent outside of academia.

Just war theory applies to three stages of war or potential war: *jus ad bellum* (when it is justified to resort to war), *jus in bello* (restrictions on how to ethically wage war) and *jus post bellum* (what is required of belligerents after a war). Within each phase, there are certain tenets that determine whether a state and its forces are acting in accordance with just war principles (Taylor 2017: 717–18). For instance, wars must be fought for a just cause and as a last resort; proportionate force must be used and only against legitimate targets, with every care taken to limit non-combatant casualties; and victors must aid in the post-war reconstruction of the vanquished.

It is understood that not all of these requirements can necessarily be met at all times (Walzer [1977]2015), but the general view is that an *attempt* should be made to meet them. For our purposes, however, what is important is that most states and policymakers claim to be adhering to these principles (even if they don't use the phrase 'just war'). Fazal (2012) points out that since the mid-twentieth century the institutionalization of just war norms in international affairs has created domestic and global incentives for leaders to claim they are adhering to those principles or to try and keep their transgressions out of the public eye. That is to say, just war theory has a *rhetorical* value even if political and military officials often fail to live up to its requirements – many times intentionally. For instance, both the Bush and Obama administrations, despite coming from ostensibly oppositional positions, employed militarized drones as a tactic against Al Qaeda and ISIS despite the high likelihood of incurring sometimes heavy civilian casualties. Yet importantly, both also employed just war arguments to defend the tactic, arguing that (1) the US had legitimate authority to use the weapons, (2) they were necessary for attacking terrorist leaders in remote and otherwise inaccessible areas, (3) their use was proportionate to the threat posed by the terrorists, (4) the harm to civilians was outweighed by the benefit of preventing even higher civilian casualties in future terrorist attacks, and (5) they were discriminate in that they attacked high value targets at times when they were around the least number of civilians. A significant corollary argument was that drones were highly precise, bolstering the discrimination argument.

Regardless of one's view of drone warfare, what is most relevant is that these arguments were based on just war principles. In this way, they were consistent with how US policymakers and military officials have *always* described their actions in wartime.[1] For example, the argument that US technology allows it to bomb precisely and minimize civilian casualties is the same used in the Second World War to defend Allied bombing (Fussell 1989) and during the Persian Gulf War to defend against charges by Saddam Hussein that American bombs were destroying children's hospitals (Sharkey 2001). In fact, the same argument was used not only by Bush and, early in his first term, Obama, but again by Obama later in his presidency when new drone technology was developed *because the earlier drones had been so imprecise they were causing too many civilian casualties.*

Policymakers thus clearly see a rhetorical value in claiming their wars are just and that they are fighting them justly. Neither Bush nor Obama, for instance, was willing to simply dismiss civilian casualties as irrelevant in a time of war. Yet it is important to understand that these arguments would not have as much power if they didn't also have advocates. As this chapter argues, the mainstream press has historically served that function.

Virtually all just war theorists, however, including Fazal and Walzer, rarely if ever address the role of media in perpetuating just war rhetoric and rationales, and when they do, they tend to do so offhandedly and make the assumption that the proliferation of global media outlets will create transparencies that make these violations more difficult to hide. There is, in these writings, a naivety about the willingness of an independent press to fully embrace its watchdog role and hold leaders accountable in wartime. While there are certainly numerous examples of superb journalists covering war and war policy, decades of political and mass communication research afford a variety of reasons to think the faith Fazal and Walzer place in the modern media to help enforce just war principles is certainly exaggerated.

In theory, media are one of the best institutions for assessing the legitimacy of just war claims and holding leaders accountable for violations.

Yet as we'll see below, generally speaking mainstream media coverage has not served this function. Not only that, the ways in which media fail to do so have the effect of *abetting* these claims not only by leaving them largely unchallenged, but by actually buttressing them in many ways. This is *not* because the media are a propaganda tool of the government (at least not in the United States and other countries with independent media systems), but rather due to structural and institutional factors. Indeed, the power of the press to reinforce elite just war arguments is made all the more salient in a free society with an independent media system by transferring its own credibility as the Fourth Estate to policymaker claims.

Theoretical underpinnings: Elite-driven news and the cascading activation model

In order to better understand the dynamic by which media reinforce elite just war claims it is perhaps most important to understand the fundamental ways in which even an independent press behaves *dependently*. Scholars have consistently found journalism to be source driven (Sigal 1973) and coverage of foreign policy to reflect the biases and policy goals of elites (Hallin 1986). Bennett's (1990) 'indexing hypothesis', for example, argues that media coverage of foreign policy crises and war reflects the range of elite opinion and priorities (Bennett 1990; 1994; Bennett *et al* 2007; though see Hamilton et al. (2010) for exceptions). Specifically, research by Bennett and others shows that foreign policy elites in the White House and Congress dominate the framing of international crises employed by the media, with the former exerting the most influence (Entman and Page 1994). By contrast, alternative views from sources outside that narrow institutional framework (e.g. protesters, international elites) receive less attention in media coverage of foreign policy crises, especially early on (Entman et al. 2009; Entman and Page 1994; Wolfsfeld 2004). If a crisis stays on the agenda for a while – for instance a long war – then the press may branch out and seek other perspectives that invite counterframes.

The indexing phenomenon is especially heightened in the contemporary era of massive cutbacks in foreign news reporting and overseas bureaus, which have the effect of making foreign policy reporters even more dependent on official US sources and perspectives and reducing access to alternative sources, information and frames (Auletta 2001; Fenton 2005; Pew 2011).

The best model for understanding how and why media amplify just war rhetoric from elites is Robert Entman's (2004) 'cascade network activation model', which elaborates on Bennett's hypothesis. Entman's model shares indexing's belief that elites dominate the news about foreign affairs but at the same time synthesizes a wide variety of literature across multiple domains, most notably indexing, hegemony and social cognition. Consistent with the waterfall metaphor, Entman proposes a chain of influence with the White House as the prime mover at the top of the information 'waterfall', its frames and agendas 'cascading' down and dictating to a large extent the terms of debate for a secondary level that includes Congress and other official elites. Below this we find a third level that includes the media, which filters the elite conversation above it before the information flows to a fourth pool where public opinion is located. Importantly, Entman's model also posits 'feedback loops' at each stage of the cascade process that can influence or change the terms of debate. At the same time, the cascade metaphor makes clear that only the White House gets to be the prime mover in these debates; every other stage of the process is reacting to the frame put forth by the President.

Entman links his argument to the hegemony literature to explain that not all elite arguments are created equal. Rather, those that are 'culturally congruent' – or, put another way, consistent with mainstream attitudes, values and perceptions – are the most powerful influencers in the cascade process. By contrast, arguments and perspectives that are less culturally congruent – e.g. those that challenge widely held beliefs and myths – will be less influential.

Cultural congruence helps us understand why just war rhetoric is especially powerful and why the mainstream press is likely to reinforce these claims or at least leave them largely unchallenged. Citizens of many nations take pride in their history and think of themselves as forces for good in the world. Yet Americans are perhaps especially imbued with a well-developed sense of righteousness and a 'saviour' complex that extends back to the earliest days of European settlement and colonization (the 'City on a Hill') and continues through 'Manifest Destiny' and the wars (hot and cold) of the twentieth century. Hence, one of the most 'culturally congruent' arguments an American political elite can make is that the United States is acting justly because, to many Americans, the United States is inherently virtuous and thus has *always* acted justly. The Cascade Model shows us that these arguments are likely to be quite persuasive at the various points of the influence chain and that the mainstream press is likely to be less critical and more accepting of them.

By contrast, then, arguments that the United States is acting or acted unjustly are by definition lacking in cultural congruence. Applying the Cascade Model, this means they are likely to be less persuasive and more likely to produce counterframing from other elites *and* from the press. Importantly, these counterframes would be more powerful precisely because they are more culturally congruent.

The intersection of culture and media norms and routines

Entman's argument that culturally congruent arguments are more powerful is consistent with decades of mass communication research demonstrating the link between mainstream media coverage and dominant cultural values. Over the years scholars have consistently found that mainstream media tend to reinforce dominant sociocultural norms and values, confer status upon that which is covered (and thus relegate to 'nonevents' that which is not) and make decisions about coverage that are heavily routinized (Fishman 1980; Gans 1980; Gitlin 1980; Katz and Lazarsfeld 1955; Klapper 1960; Lazarsfeld and Merton 1948; Sigal 1973). The beat system, for instance, privileges institutional sources and perspectives.

A key finding in this literature is the social and cultural overlap between mainstream journalists and establishment sources. Occupational role theorists have consistently found that sources and journalists share common values and that their interactions are conducted against a common cultural backdrop (Gieber and Johnson 1961; Weaver et al 2006). One reason why journalists and sources get along so well, then, is that they tend to look alike, think alike and speak alike, what Tuchman (1980: 210) has called the mainstream 'news net'. Blumler and Gurevitch (1995) have discussed this in terms of a 'shared culture' in which journalists and sources accept certain rules of conduct and definitions of news. Indeed, Fishman has argued that 'journalists simply do not expose themselves to unofficial interpretive schemes' (Fishman 1980: 62). The common bond between source and journalist appears to go beyond routines and demographics and enter into a shared ideological perspective that limits and defines appropriate discourse.

We see these ideas and perspectives in what Gans (1980) termed the 'enduring values' of news. Looking at decades of news coverage, Gans found evidence of a bias towards certain underlying, in many ways subconscious, *values* in stories about the world. For instance, he found American news to be consistently ethnocentric, not only in terms of a kind of jingoism, but more importantly in seeing the rest of the world through an American prism. Hence, the conflict in Indochina was never seen as a civil war, but rather as part of the Cold War (not coincidentally the elite frame, too). Enduring values are critical for understanding the media's role in reinforcing just war rhetoric for a couple of reasons. First, they show that news is value laden and even ideological. Second, they show that these values are not located only in the media but instead are shared across the culture. For example, news is ethnocentric, and so is American culture.

Most importantly, the notion of enduring values reveals the media to be both products and reinforcers of these values. Mainstream journalists don't exist in a vacuum, after all; they are influenced by the culture in which they are raised and live. As Lazarsfeld and Merton (1948) argued in some of the foundational mass communication research, the media are agents of status conferral and canalization, and they are at their most powerful when they are reinforcing dominant cultural norms, values and perspectives (see also Gitlin 1978).

Strategic narratives and the use and misuse of historical analogies

This points to the importance of culture in understanding how media, policymakers and publics understand wars and foreign policy challenges. In particular, significant past historical events help shape both elite and media framing of these crises. This is consistent with both Entman's Cascade Model and its emphasis on the power of culturally resonant frames and with Gans's notion of the enduring values that underlie popular, political and media memory, interpretation, and framing. One of the most significant examples of these phenomena for war and conflict involves historical analogies, both their latent meaning and the meaning they transfer when applied to new events. Specifically, these analogies are often used to make wars seem just.

Scholars have consistently found that policymakers use – and often misuse – historical analogies both to frame contemporary international crises (usually in a way that justifies a course of action they already support) and to persuade the public to support the desired policy response (Jervis 1976). The Second World War (WWII) analogies have been especially common since 1945, with virtually every major US adversary being labelled a modern-day 'Hitler' when US policymakers seek to gain support for military intervention (Khong 1992; Petraeus 1987; Record 2002).

One reason for the prevalence of WWII analogies in elite rhetoric appears to be the powerful mythology surrounding WWII as 'the good war', a war that figures prominently in America's national narrative as the world's 'saviour' in the twentieth century.

This narrative was born in large part from the mix of patriotic journalism and heavy government censorship of both casualty images and most forms of critical coverage during the war. Fussell (1989) shows how the power of that national narrative of 'The Good War', a narrative he persuasively argues devolved into something more like mythology due to a combination of censorship and propaganda, has had enduring effects on American national consciousness.

Specifically, he argues that WWII became synonymous with virtue and those who fought in it with superhero levels of bravery and righteousness. Because the government didn't allow home front audiences to learn about the complexities of war – that soldiers were understandably gripped by fear, that they often complained about substandard equipment, and even that they occasionally committed war crimes, among other things that didn't fit the 'hero' narrative – Fussell says America never had a realistic accounting of the war, what it meant, how it was fought and the damage it did to its combat troops. This made it easier for political elites and others to leverage the *myth* of the war (and of those who fought in it) to marshal support for future interventions and to belittle those in opposition.

The WWII narrative is deeply ingrained into the American consciousness in a way that Vietnam is not. Vietnam is not remembered as a 'good war', and in fact its legacy includes numerous stories of American war crimes, veterans with PTSD and of course defeat. This points to the power of mainstream media's tendency to buttress elites' WWII rhetoric, especially in the lead up to war (Dorman and Livingston 1994). Importantly, that rhetoric carries with it the implied notion of a just war, as Fussell has eloquently written. Hence, media amplifying these analogic arguments implicitly also strengthen the just war argument.

Recent scholarship on strategic narratives amplifies these points. As defined by Miskimmon et al. (2017: 6): 'Strategic narratives are a means by which political actors attempt to construct a shared meaning of the past, present, and future of international politics to shape the behavior of domestic and international actors.' They cite David Campbell (1992) in making the point that certain preferred historical narratives can end up legitimating certain myths and privileged – even ideological – constructions of the past that have profound implications for interpreting the present. Or as Liao (2018: 112) puts it:

> As a pragmatic function of narratives, the structuring of historical storylines entails selective remembering and forgetting of certain parts of the past to fit the ontological reflection of the contemporary world. Given its malleability, the construction of collective memory tends to be collapsed into the enactment and legitimation of 'myth' in forming master historical accounts, which often reduces the complex and multifaceted historical process to a single-dimensional picture.

Miskimmon et al. (2017) point to the role of media in helping form and project strategic narratives in ways that typically do not challenge elite perspectives and culturally accepted assumptions. They argue that media are important actors in the formation and projection of these strategic narratives, which come in three types: system, identity and issue/policy. Arsenault et al. (2018: 203–4) elaborate on this point, writing that media act as 'legitimizing agents' that provide momentum to these narratives. Thus, media are a part of the institutional 'space' that collectively constructs strategic narratives, reifying them in a way that makes them more culturally congruent, linked to the culture's enduring values, and ultimately influential. This often has the effect of imbuing key dates like 1938, 1989 and 9/11 with powerful, even mythological, meaning, something O'Loughlin et al. (2018: 37–8) refer to as the 'strategic use of ambiguity' through the use of 'empty signifiers'.

Justifying unjust behaviour: The case of torture

To this point most of the discussion has focused on how and why mainstream news in the United States is institutionally predisposed to justifying and amplifying political elites' just war claims. Importantly, much of the argument is based on the premise that the media are both a product and producer of cultural norms and narratives, and in the United States those have a nearly 400-year history predicated on the notion that America is an inherently virtuous country that has not only set the standard for liberty and righteousness but on several occasions saved the world from forces opposed to those principles. President George W. Bush summed up this perspective following the 9/11 attacks when he spoke of a 'crusade' against 'evil-doers'.

By implication, if America is inherently virtuous, so too must be its people, including its military personnel. But what happens when this isn't the case? We can get a hint at the answer when we see that the United States is still debating (or ignoring) whether to celebrate the Confederacy, or the actions taken during the Indian Wars, with cultural artefacts from textbooks to movies mythologizing both through a gauzy, nostalgic lens. Note that these are both examples of history being recast into a mythology that is ideological and serves to rationalize and entrench a hegemonic reading of history and the perpetuation of the very power structures that led to the abuses of the past. This highlights the important role of hegemony in Entman's Cascade Model, in which it is precisely hegemonic arguments, frames and rhetoric that is most likely to be culturally congruent and thus exert powerful influence.

During the early years following the 9/11 attacks, US policy embraced torture as an interrogation technique, both by third-party countries through the policy of rendition and by American interrogators themselves at black sites, Guantanamo Bay prison and elsewhere.

The reaction to the revelation of the US torture policy offers another example of how the country rationalizes unjust behaviour in wartime and, notably, how the media abet this rationalization.

America's torture policy represents an interesting test case of the elite-driven news model discussed above. In an analysis of mainstream media coverage of the Abu Ghraib scandal in 2003, Bennett et al. (2007) showed that the press quickly took the Bush Administration's lead in refraining from using the word 'torture' and instead used the more palatable, and less legally culpable, term 'abuse'. Bennett et al. argue that the White House scored a significant victory in distancing itself from what would otherwise have been considered war crimes if 'torture' had become the consensus view. This victory was long-lasting, as for years thereafter the press avoided using the word 'torture' to describe the US interrogation programme unless it was in a quote.

Thus, we have the following dynamic: the United States, facing criticism from the international community that its war in Iraq was unjust and illegal, secretly expanded a hitherto unknown policy of torture and rendition adopted following 9/11 to Abu Ghraib and other detention facilities around the world. Eventually, a series of media reports revealed that American interrogators were utilizing techniques that *the United States itself* had forever maintained were illegal and fell under the category of torture, most notably waterboarding. Faced with these revelations, White House officials including the President himself defended the practices in a variety of ways, including (1) reframing torture as 'abuse'; (2) in the case of the initial stories from Abu Ghraib, minimizing the torture as the actions of 'a few bad apples' and thus not representative of the United States; (3) when evidence came out that torture was more widespread than just at Abu Ghraib, the tactics were relabelled with the more palatable euphemism 'enhanced interrogation techniques' (EITs); (4) EITs bearing a strong resemblance to what had previously been understood to be torture, such as waterboarding, were differentiated from other examples by saying they were done under medical supervision.

Although Bennett et al. (2007) argue that indexing is the best prism through which to view this case, the cascade model is even better at helping us understand *why* abuse was preferred. In the end, the Bush Administration's communication strategists did an excellent job of making the word 'torture' a *partisan* construction, thus ensuring that a press that defines 'objectivity' as 'he said-she said' detachment (largely for commercial and credibility reasons [Schudson 1978]) would avoid it lest news organizations appear to be taking sides. When President Bush said (numerous times) 'We don't torture', a media governed by a norm of two-sided objectivity is constrained to present it as one possible opinion, rather than as a lie.

Importantly, then, administration officials did not simply embrace torture as torture and defend it. Instead, they felt compelled to argue that what they were doing was justified and moral. In making this case they brilliantly exploited some of the journalistic norms and routines discussed above. First, news is driven by and reliant on official sources for news and for framing of that news. Second, news is governed by a particular definition of 'objectivity' that is operationalized as detached two-sidedness, rather than, say, what is 'objectively' true.

A different news model not as dependent on official framing and with a different understanding of objectivity, for instance, might have privileged the historical precedent of defining acts like waterboarding as torture over White House claims to the contrary. As the cascade model shows us, however, American media are institutionally incapable of doing so, predictably opting instead for a notion of 'balance' that pits the President of the United States' word against various less powerful critics. Even ombudsman at liberal media outlets such as National Public Radio defended organizational policy to avoid using the word 'torture' to describe waterboarding and other torture techniques on the grounds that the word had become 'partisan' (Shepard 2009). This is in part because of the well-established pathway of elite-driven news, but also, importantly, because torture is not a culturally congruent concept to Americans. Americans would rather accept a narrative of American exceptionalism and virtue. Hence why the administration felt it so important to avoid the word (but not the practice) and why the media went along. This combination of news norms (detached, two-sided objectivity) and cultural norms helps explain why the word 'torture' was not used to describe US abuses in Iraq and elsewhere until the war was over and a Congressional report stated declaratively that torture had in fact occurred (Waldman 2014).

Summary and discussion

There is a straight line from colonial visions of America as a 'City on a Hill', through the values expressed in the Declaration of Independence, through entrenched revisionism about the Antebellum South and the Confederacy, through 'Manifest Destiny' and enduring popular understandings of the West and Westward expansion, through the twentieth-century narrative of rescuing the world three times from global war and tyranny, all the way to the post-9/11 era of waging 'war' on evildoers. The common thread in this progression is the notion of the United States as a *virtuous saviour*. This enduring value, as Gans (1980) might call it, underlies US citizens' very sense of their essentialism and their country's fundamental national character. Hence, deviations are by definition aberrations, not 'who we are' or even simply darker elements of a complex national identity. Americans don't like to think of themselves and their country in such complex terms, and hence political and cultural institutions, which both respond to and mould these public attitudes, reflect these assumptions uncritically and often unconsciously. The result is a national mythology, based on a combination of historical fact and self-serving fantasy, that codifies this enduring value of the United States as the virtuous saviour in ways big and small but overall continuously. The implications are evident in many ways, but not least among them being how these political and cultural institutions levy these assumptions to justify American military intervention (for good and bad and everything murkily in between) and to further justify American behaviour during those conflicts.

As perhaps the 'core systems for the distribution of ideology' (Gitlin 1980), the news media play a significant but to date underexplored role in helping and abetting presidents' arguments that America's wars are just and fought justly. This role stems from the fact that since the Penny Press era (at least), media occupy a space in US society as both a product and a reinforcer of the dominant cultural values that underlie media values, public opinion, policy and America's understanding of itself.

This chapter has shown how and why the mainstream media reinforce policymaker just war claims. Employing Entman's Cascade Model, it argues that claiming to adhere to just war principles serves a powerful rhetorical function for political elites; that these claims are especially persuasive because they are culturally congruent; and that therefore they are particularly likely to shape political debate, media coverage and public opinion. Media coverage of war and foreign policy, being dependent on elite sources, are institutionally predisposed to reflecting those sources' agendas and frames. Finally, it is impossible to separate mainstream media from the culture in which they exist, and which influences the values, assumptions and myths held by journalists. We see evidence of this dynamic in numerous ways, including the way media echo or leave unchallenged elites' use of WWII analogies to frame crises, analogies that themselves are imbued with just war assumptions.

We also see it reflected in how deviations from just war principles, such as institutionalized torture, are often dismissed or minimized, but rarely understood as articulated policy or a reflection of structural defect. Like the examples of the Confederacy and the Indian Wars, how the United States handled this latest violation of just war principles fits a well-established pattern. First, violators, when possible, are framed as aberrant and atypical ('a few bad apples'). Second, they are contrasted with more virtuous examples, in this case 'the troops', who are seen as true representatives of American's military and culture. Fallows (2015), for instance, has written eloquently about how American society has since 9/11 fetishized its reverence for the troops in a host of ways permeating the culture, something that strongly resembles the mythological (and damaging) portrait of GIs in WWII discussed by Fussell.

The result is another example of an institutionally created moral space in which the media create what Entman et al. (2010) have called 'accountability gaps' between policymakers and citizens. In this space, media supporting and contributing to policymakers' just war claims distance the latter from responsibility for potentially unjust wars and unjust ways of fighting them. Indeed, the political, media and popular culture institutions that comprise, create and codify this self-serving moral space implicitly accept as a matter of course that there will be no accountability for these, *policy-level*, transgressions.

Hence, President Obama ends torture as a practice but says it's in the best interest of the country that no legal repercussions hang over perpetrators of torture policy and practice. To bring everything full circle, in spring of 2018 the US Senate approves the nomination of a principal architect and supervisor of torture to be the new director of the CIA. In 2016 the country elected as president a candidate who not only called for a return to torture (which to his credit, perhaps, he did not refer to with a euphemism), but defended it as a means of punishment and said it should even be used on suspects' children. And more recently, that president continued his predecessor's strategy for fighting ISIS but removed most of the restrictions in place to limit civilian casualties. The predictable result: the virtual levelling of Mosul, Iraq, with little concern for the principle of discrimination. In a repeat of a sad, old story, the Pentagon claimed that the strikes were precision in nature, guided by superb intelligence, in which only one in 157 airstrikes produced civilian casualties. A thorough analysis by the *New York Times*, however, discovered the number to be more than thirty times as high (Khan and Gopal 2017). Yet in the end the President declared victory.

Note

1 At least until Donald Trump, who notably does not even go through the motions of adopting just war rhetoric.

References

Arsenault, A., S. Hong and M. E. Price (2018), 'Strategic Narratives of the Arab Spring and After', in A. Miskimmon, B. O'Loughlin, and L. Roselle (eds), *Forging the World: Strategic Narratives and International Relations*, 218–45, Ann Arbor: University of Michigan Press.

Auletta, K. (2001), 'Battle Stations', *The New Yorker*, 10 December 2001: 60–7.

Bennett, W. L. (1990), 'Toward a Theory of Press-state Relations', *Journal of Communication*, 40(2): 103–25.

Bennett, W. L. (1994), 'The News about Foreign Policy', in W. L. Bennett and D. L. Paletz (eds), *Taken by Storm: The Media, Public Opinion, and U.S. Foreign Policy in the Gulf War*, 12–42, Chicago: The University of Chicago Press.

Bennett, W. L., R. Lawrence and S. Livingston (2007), *When the Press Fails: Political Power and the News Media from Iraq to Katrina*, Chicago: University of Chicago Press.

Blumler, J., and M. Gurevitch (1995), *The Crisis of Public Communication*, New York: Routledge.

Campbell, D. (1992). *Writing Security: United States Foreign Policy and the Politics of Identity*, University of Minnesota Press.

Dill, J. (2018), 'Just War Theory in Times of Individual Rights', in C. Brown and R. Eckersley (eds), *The Oxford Handbook of International Theory*, 221–42, Oxford: Oxford University Press.

Dorman, W. A., and S. Livingston (1994), 'News and Historical Context: The Establishment Phase of the Persian Gulf Policy Debate', in W. L. Bennett and D. L. Paletz (eds), *Taken by Storm: The Media, Public Opinion, and U.S. Foreign Policy in the Gulf War*, 63–81, Chicago: The University of Chicago Press.

Entman, R. (2003), 'Cascading Activation: Contesting the White House's Frame after 9/11', *Political Communication*, 20: 415–23.

Entman, R. (2004), Projections of *Power: Framing News, Public Opinion, and US Foreign Policy*, Chicago: University of Chicago Press.

Entman, R. M., and B. I. Page (1994), 'The News before the Storm: The Iraq War Debate and the Limits to Media Independence', in W. L. Bennett and D. L. Paletz (eds), *Taken by Storm*, 82–104, Chicago: University of Chicago Press.

Entman, R. M., S. Aday and J. Kim (2010), 'Condemned to Repeat: The Media and the Accountability Gap in Iraq War Policy', in S. Koch-Baumgarten and K. Voltmer (eds), *Public Policy and the Media: The Interplay of Mass Communication and Political Decision Making*, 194–214, London: Routledge.

Entman, R. M., S. Livingston and J. Kim (2009), 'Doomed to Repeat: Iraq News, 2002–2007', *American Behavioral Scientist*, 52: 689–708.

Fallows, J. (2015), 'The Tragedy of the American Military', *The Atlantic*, January/February 2015. Available online: http://www.theatlantic.com/features/archive/2014/12/the-tragedy-of-the-american-military/383516/ (accessed 13 October 2019).

Fazal, T. (2012), 'Why States No Longer Declare War', *Security Studies*, 21(4): 557–93.

Fenton, T. (2005), *Bad News: The Decline of Reporting, The Business of News, and the Danger to Us All*, New York: Collins.

Fishman, M. (1980), *Manufacturing the News*, Austin: University of Texas Press.

Fussell, P. (1989), *Wartime: Understanding and Behavior in the Second World War*, New York: Oxford University Press.

Gans, H. (1980), *Deciding What's News*, New York: Vintage Book.

Gieber, W., and Johnson, W. (1961), 'The City Hall Beat: A Study of Reporter and Source Roles', *Journalism Quarterly*, 38: 289–97.

Gitlin, T. (1978), 'Media Sociology: The Dominant Paradigm', *Theory and Society*, 6: 205–53.

Gitlin, T. (1980), *The Whole World Is Watching*, Los Angeles: University of California Press.

Hallin, D. (1986), *The 'Uncensored' War*, New York: Oxford University Press.

Hamilton, J. W., R. G. Lawrence and R. Cozma (2010), 'The Paradox of Respectability: The Limits of Indexing and Harrison Salisbury's Coverage of the Vietnam War', *The International Journal of Press/Politics*, 15(1): 77–103.

Jervis, R. (1976), *Perception and Misperception in International Politics*, Princeton, NJ: Princeton University Press.

Katz, E., and P. F. Lazarsfeld (1955), *Personal Influence: The Part Played by People in the Flow of Mass Communication*, Glencoe, IL: Free Press.

Khan, A., and A. Gopal (2017), 'The Uncounted', *New York Times*, 16 November 2017. Available online: https://www.nytimes.com/

interactive/2017/11/16/magazine/uncounted-civilian-casualties-iraq-airstrikes. html?_r=0 (accessed 19 May, 2018).

Khong, Y. F. (1992), *Analogies at War*, Princeton, NJ: Princeton University Press.

Klapper, J. T. (1960), *The Effects of Mass Communication*, Glencoe, IL: Free Press.

Lazar, S. (2017), 'Just War Theory: Revisionists vs. Traditionalists', *Annual Review of Political Science*, 20: 37–54.

Lazarsfeld, P., and R. Merton (1948), 'Mass Communication, Popular Taste, and Organized Social Action', in W. Schramm (ed), *Mass Communication*, 492–503, Urbana: University of Illinois Press.

Liao, N. (2018), 'The Power of Strategic Narratives: The Communicative Dynamics of Chinese Nationalism and Foreign Relations', in A. Miskimmon, B. O'Loughlin, and L. Roselle (eds), *Forging the World: Strategic Narratives and International Relations*, 110–33, Ann Arbor: University of Michigan Press.

Miskimmon, A., B. O'Loughlin and L. Roselle (2017), *Forging the World: Strategic Narratives and International Relations*, Ann Arbor: University of Michigan Press.

O'Loughlin, B., A. Miskimmon and L. Roselle (2018). "Strategic Narratives: Methods and Practice," in A. Miskimmon et al. (eds), *Forging the World: Strategic Narratives and International Relations*, 23–55, Ann Arbor: University of Michigan Press.

PBS (2003), 'Reporting America at War', [TV programme] PBS, transcript. Available online: http://www.pbs.org/weta/reportingamericaatwar/about/ep02_transcript.html (accessed 13 October 2019).

Petraeus, D. H. (1987), *The American Military and the Lessons of Vietnam: A Study of Military Influence and the Use of Force in the Post-Vietnam Era*, Princeton, NJ: A dissertation to the faculty of Princeton University in candidacy for the degree of Doctor of Philosophy.

Pew (2011), 'The State of the News Media', *Pew Research Center's Project for Excellence in Journalism*, Washington, DC: Pew Research Center.

Record, J. (2002), *Making War, Thinking History: Munich, Vietnam, and Presidential Uses of Force from Korea to Kosovo*, Annapolis: Naval Institute Press.

Robinson, P., P. Goddard, K. Parry and C. Murray with P. Taylor (2010), *Pockets of Resistance*, Manchester: Manchester University Press.

Schudson, M. (1978), *Discovering the News: A Social History of American Newspapers*, New York: Basic Books, Inc.

Sharkey, J. (2001), 'War, Censorship and the First Amendment', *Media Studies Journal*, 15(1): 20–5.

Shepard, A. (2009), 'Harsh Interrogation Techniques or Torture?' *NPR*, 21 June. Available online: https://www.npr.org/ombudsman/2009/06/harsh_interrogation_techniques.html (accessed 13 October 2019).

Sigal, L. (1973), *Reporters and Officials: The Organization and Politics of Newsmaking*, Lexington, MA: D.C. Heath.

Taylor, I. (2017), 'Just War Theory and the Military Response to Terrorism', *Social Theory and Practice*, 43(4): 717–40.

Tuchman, G. (1980), *Making News*, New York: Free Press.

Waldman, P. (2014), 'The New York Times Finally Comes around on Torture', *The American Prospect*, 8 August. Available online: http://prospect.org/article/new-york-times-finally-comes-around-torture (accessed 13 October 2019).

Walzer, M. ([1977] 2015), *Just and Unjust Wars: A Moral Argument with Historical Illustrations* (5th edn), New York: Basic Books.
Walzer, M. (2005), *Arguing about War*, New Haven, CT: Yale University Press.
Weaver, D. H., R. A. Beam, B. J. Brownlee, P. S. Voakes and G. C. Wilhoit (2006), *The American Journalist in the 21st Century: U.S. News People at the Dawn of a New Millennium*, Mahwah, NJ: Lawrence Erlbaum Associates.
Wolfsfeld, G. (2004), *Media and the Path to Peace*, Cambridge: Cambridge University Press.

/ PART TWO

War of Spaces

7

Liminality, gendering and Syrian alternative media spaces

Dina Matar and Kholoud Helmi

Introduction

The 2011 Syrian uprising has generated considerable debate about alternative protest media spaces and oppositional news practices that have emerged in a rapidly changing media environment and a long-term violent conflict – a debate that has largely become entangled with broader concerns around theorizing the role of media in conflict. Many of these discussions have focused on the potential of alternative/radical/protest/ counter-hegemonic media for citizen journalism (Wessels 2018), activism, voice, political participation, agency and empowerment, the production of counter-hegemonic narratives (Crilley 2017; Matar 2016) as well as their role in the emergence of radically different political subjectivities often discussed, in Middle Eastern contexts, as products of liberated political imaginaries or as digital cultures of contention (Zayani 2015). These debates have also informed some studies around Arab women's media work and activism and their foregrounding of gender questions in sociopolitical transformations, with some scholars, such as Radsch and Khamis (2013), arguing that Arab women's digital activism had helped young women achieve leadership and visibility in the media, along with challenging mainstream (state or official) media narratives in relation to women, while others, suggesting that the Arab Spring had helped launch digital feminist movements in predominantly patriarchal societies. Khamis (2018: 2) goes further in noting that just by engaging in multiple forms of struggle, Arab women contest and redefine 'gendered spaces, politically, legally, and socially', while Sreberny cautions that studies of women's digital activism need to be more nuanced and consider connections between gendered subjectivities and other social identities, as well as the relationship between women and the nation state which ultimately 'hinge on broader issues of equality and power' (2018: 112).[1]

In Syria, alternative protest media that burst into the Syrian public sphere at the beginning of the uprising without doubt provided Syrian women, as well as the wider population, with what Cammaerts (2012) calls 'mediation opportunity structures' to represent themselves, tell their own stories, exert agency, discuss socially taboo subjects in public and insert gender politics and practices into the agenda of the popular revolution. In doing so, these women built on pre-uprising processes that had seen the establishment of women associations and committees and formal and informal networks to challenge gender stereotypes, strengthen women's status and seek to amend laws that discriminate against women (al-Aous 2013). Such informal networks included websites such as *al-thawra* (www.al-thawra-sy.com) and the Syrian Women Observatory (www.nesasy.org), which are examples of some of the first websites that have provided knowledge on gender identity, women's lived conditions, improvement of women's and children's rights as well as youth, people with special needs, prisoners, environment, health and legal advice to women who suffer from domestic violence or threats to their lives (al-Aous 2013).

Acknowledging the agential potential of alternative protest Syrian media platforms post-2011,[2] this chapter moves out of discussions that focus on the role of these media for empowerment and agency or those that discuss the production of counter-hegemonic discourses. Instead, it uses the optic of liminality to address these platforms as essentially *liminal spaces of war* that provide new fields of possibilities for Syrian women (as well as other members of the society) to tell their own stories and experiences of the uprising and to construct and imagine new political and social subjectivities.[3] 'Liminality' is a term that refers to events, processes or individuals that are on the threshold of, or in the early stages of, new social processes, which anthropologist Victor Turner has theorized as stages of transition and in-between positions that liminal individuals occupy. For Turner, liminality is a position of social and structural ambiguity or as 'the Nay to all positive structural assertions, but as in some sense the source of them all, and, more than that, as a realm of pure possibility whence novel configurations of ideas and relations may arise' (Turner 1967: 97). In liminal conditions, such as uprisings, revolutions and war, subjects become removed from the 'familiar space, the routine temporal order, or the structures of moral obligations and social ties ... [and] ... enter a liminal time/space ... [in which] the transgression of norms and conventions becomes possible' (Yang 2000: 25), social markers disappear and subjects, differentiated along gender, sexual, ethnic, religious or racial lines, can imagine themselves as equal. This is because in situations when order and norms are dissolved and/or contested, lived experiences shape political consciousness and meaning making.[4] Focusing on the concept of liminality in relation to media work during times of transition, Zizzi Papacharissi (2015) suggests that liminality allows media workers (journalists, editors, media managers, etc.) to engage in processes of transition through collaborative news co-creation, which she proposes is in itself liminal particularly because this form of engagement relies on the temporary dismantling of news rituals so as to be able to collectively (re)produce new ones. As she argues (2015:32):

> Liminality is a middle point in a dialogue about what is news, in a society. It is a transitional, but essential stage in finding one's own place in the story and doing so from a position that allows autonomy and potential for agency.... [but]... in order for this dialogue to be rendered liminal, all previous hierarchy about what makes news must be abandoned, and therein lies the empowering potential of liminality... the very function of liminality is to abandon structure so as to permit activity that will result in the birthing of a new structure, and therein lie both potential empowerment and disempowerment.

The concept of liminality is particularly relevant to addressing women's media work in liminal conditions, such as the uprising-turned war by the Syrian regime against all its opponents and characterized by upheaval and a breakdown in social order. To illustrate the argument, the chapter uses the example of *Enab Baladi*, one of the most prominent Syrian alternative media platforms that emerged following the March 2011 uprising, and draws on a select number of interviews with some of its female founders/media workers, who were involved in its creation from the beginning. The chapter is divided into two main sections: The first section discusses *Enab Baladi* as a liminal space of war that provides new fields of possibilities for women media workers to overturn structure and insert gender into the revolutionary agenda. The second section discusses how the protracted liminal state in Syria, exacerbated by the longevity and complexity of the war, is both ambiguous and precarious, and, as such, provides new fields of possibilities for regime and other counter-revolutionary forces to reinstate social norms, re-institutionalize structure, suppress dissent and seek to re-integrate liminal actors into pre-uprising social structures. The chapter concludes by suggesting that liminality can help us theorize the role of media and conflict in protracted conflicts without overtly emphasizing the potential of media in social and political conflicts and change, but to ground this potential in temporalities and sociopolitical contexts.

Liminal spaces of war

Enab Baladi, which means 'the Grapes of My Country', is one of many alternative media spaces and websites initiated by Syrian women in the context of the Syrian 2011 uprising – these include *Souriatna*, Oxygen newspaper, the *Kibree*t blog, the *Dahnoon* blog and *Al Haq* newspaper. While these media initiatives grew out of the Syrian uprising against oppression and economic deprivation that began in March 2011, they built on and extended a number of pre-uprising small and scattered initiatives that had also harnessed digital spaces to improve women's social status as well as draw attention to the conditions of women in predominantly patriarchal societies. Many of these initiatives used the internet and social media platforms to disseminate their views and fight patriarchy – for example, *Musawa* (equality), an independent civil society organization founded in 2009 by a group of Syrian women to fight gender discrimination and enable effective participation of women in the political, social, economic and cultural spheres of Syrian society and the collective *Syrian Women for the Syrian Intifada*, a network of women initially aimed at supporting families of detainees and martyrs, which later broadened its activities to support grassroots' activists who had lost their jobs or of those who had gone into hiding for their political stances.

Enab Baladi started as a weekly printed newspaper distributed by hand with the aim of disseminating news and information of the popular uprising and to counter the regime's narrative which had dominated the media sector for more than forty decades. The paper was founded by young Syrian female and male activists, including the co-author of this chapter Kholoud Helmi, in the Syrian town of Daraya, one of the main Syrian towns where popular protests for political and human rights began. Since its foundation, the newspaper has focused on publishing first-hand personal narratives of the uprising and of ordinary people's lived experiences, aspirations and needs as well as reports on women's involvement and participation in the uprising and in building collaborative protest networks bringing together opposition actors. During its foundation phase, various roles and responsibilities, such as interviewing, editing, assigning news stories and reporting from the battleground, were distributed in basic ways among the amateur founders, with some individuals taking on several reporting and editorial duties at the same time. Organization of tasks was simple and voluntary, and questions of journalistic professionalism in news gathering and news telling were not pivotal particularly at a time when holding a camera was considered a state crime. Most activities and media work were underground, compared to later stages, where teams were more organized and structures more developed. By 2019, buffeted by support from the EU and by international recognition of its contribution, *Enab Baladi* had developed into one of the most important independent Syrian media institutions, both published in print in Turkey and shipped to northern parts of Syria where some opposition strongholds remain online through its website and Facebook page which attract about 2 million page views a month.⁵

In its early stages, *Enab Baladi*'s media workers were mainly composed of volunteers and citizen journalists, including women, who focused on telling the stories of ordinary lives in conflict and providing eyewitness accounts of unfolding events – tasks which one of its female co-founders, Afraa Sharbaji (2018), said in an interview were essentially concerned with providing facts and information of the unfolding events and 'an alternative view to that of the regime's while paying particular attention to the Syrian people, their fears, struggles, dreams and aspirations'. The fact that women were some of the main founders influenced the stories they chose to tell and had access to, particularly because Syrian women were willing to speak to the female journalists about sensitive topics, including rape by security forces and militias. But this fact also reflected, according to our informants, a deep change in popular perceptions towards women evident in the early days of the uprising.⁶ These perceptions, as Manal Shakashiro (2018), an *Enab Baladi* reporter and co-founder, said, were 'not only witnessed in women's media work, which brought them visibility, but also in other public roles women took on'. For co-author of this chapter and co-founder of *Enab Baladi*, Kholoud Helmi, women, particularly those who had been marginalized before or who come from conservative and low-income backgrounds, were encouraged into taking new social and public roles, including media work, because of the transformative potential of the uprising as well as support from male colleagues and male family members, helping them gain recognition in their local communities as they established networks with other communities for social and political support.⁷ As she said: 'Personally, I was empowered because (the revolution) showed me I could speak up and ask for my rights and the rights of others and allowed me to challenge gender norms institutionalized under a dictatorship' (Helmi 2018), underlining how these women occupied liminal positions as a stage of transition and in-between positions during times of upheaval.

During that stage⁸ and before the conflict became more violent, most of the informants said they did not feel they were different from men, particularly because they were all united by similar revolutionary goals, reflecting how liminal conditions also helped remove them from the 'familiar space, the routine temporal order, or the structures of moral obligations and social ties' and enter a liminal media space (*Enab Baladi*) in which transgression of norms and conventions became possible, social markers disappeared and subjects were imagined as equal. All the interviewees said that it was the revolutionary agenda that spurred their activism in ways that did not exist before – for example, they found themselves assuming influential, decision-making roles as activists, journalists, human rights defenders and advocates, and they became aware of other roles they could take outside their household, blurring the public/private divide. For Sharbaji, it was during this stage that her imagination of what it meant to be a Syrian woman contested the imagined Syrian woman imposed by the ruling Ba'ath Party's ideologies. As she put it, 'I was able to know what it means to be a Syrian woman because I was able to have my voice heard and to freely participate in its political and social life' (Sharbaji 2018).

It is in this sense that *Enab Baladi* can be understood, as we propose, as a *liminal space of war* in which women media workers engaged in practices and imagined themselves as subjects from a liminal point of access (or an in-between position), and it is from that position that they were able to insert gender into the agenda of the uprising. For example, they discussed socially taboo subjects, such as sexual violence against women, a common practice even before the uprising, (see The Day After 2018); women's lives in conflict, not only as mothers, daughters or sisters, but as equal social actors with men; the regime's violations against women and Islamic State's brutal punishment of women who do not meet the strict Islamic dress code it imposed or those who appeared in public. Indeed, the mere coverage of such sensitive issues defined alternative media spaces as new spaces for anti-structure and spaces in which social norms can be challenged, as evidenced in the stories and reports the newspaper covered since 2012 (for examples of these stories, see Enab Baladi (2019)). Importantly, as we suggest, *Enab Baladi* as a liminal space of war provides new possibilities for making visible the ways in which Syrian women carry on everyday life activities without male members to support them, the ways women refugees take the lead in caring for families in refugee camps and displacement sites, the use of women as weapons of war, the increasing practices of taking women as slaves and the practice of forcing young female orphans into early marriage, topics that are normally considered taboo in male-dominated society (Enab Baladi 2017).

Patriarchy and ideology

A deep understanding of how liminal spaces of war, such as *Enab Baladi*, provided new possibilities for Syrian women during conflict cannot be fully understood without discussing gender relations and ideologies and the social, political and economic context in Syria pre-2011, which is beyond the scope of this chapter. Briefly however, in her co-edited book *Women's Rights in the Middle East and North Africa: Progress Amid Resistance* (2010), Sanja Kelly suggests that in Syria, 'women had been treated as subordinate to men in the highly patriarchal culture, and social customs place gender-based restrictions on their rights' (Kelly 2010: 479). In Syria, men have traditionally dominated formal spaces, like politics, academics or religion, while most women have been more present in informal spaces, like the family, households, and in social community work. Even in the relative normality of life before the war in Syria, women suffered from institutional discrimination, particularly in relation to questions of citizenship, custody of children (after divorce or separation), freedom of movement and basic rights (Syrian women are not allowed to pass on their nationality to their children if married to non-Syrian men, whereas men have this right. Syrian women cannot travel without their husband's approval, while men can. In addition, Syrian women of all ages are required to have male guardians to contract their marriages, while adult men are free to contract their own marriages).

Broadly speaking, institutionalized gender norms and imbalances in gender structures extended to the media work women undertook in various media institutions that had been regulated and controlled by the Ba'thist Syrian regime since it came to power in 1963. These media institutions, such as the three main newspapers *Tishreen*, *Al-Ba'ath* and *Al-Thawra*, along with the Syrian Arab News Agency, state radio and television, did not allow much visibility or voice to women activists, restricting their attention to well-known women such as first lady Asma al-Assad or those who held official positions in the government, including membership of parliament. Indeed, despite the fact that Syrian women's political struggles and their vital participation in the anti-colonial independence movement had gained them the right to vote in 1949, a majority of women continued to have to make difficult choices about what roles to play within the (largely patriarchal) Syrian society controlled and regulated by the nationalist discourse of the ruling Ba'th Party as well as the regime's broader project of mass mobilization and modernization (Matar 2019; Wedeen 1999) which allowed it to maintain structural control of women's organizations (Meininghaus 2016). While on the face of it, the project was committed to improving women's conditions and achieving the regime's promise of gender equality, it did not represent any ideological commitment to a profound change in the nature of gender relations in Syrian society or the elimination of legislative discrimination against women (Kelly and Breslin 2010), which, along with the exclusion of women from the Syrian nationalist narrative, has served to maintain power relations and bolster gendered hierarchies in the national imagination while fragmenting women's efforts to form independent women's movements.

Like other nation states in the Arab world, women in Syria had often been used as symbols of the nation's development and modernization plans and represented in national discourse as the mothers, daughters or sisters of the Syrian Arab nation, thus concealing gender inequalities by attempting to justify them on the basis of family, religion, history or other cultural terms. The symbolic connection between the idea of woman and the idea of nation and the use of women as symbols of nations by nationalist and liberationist movements has been critical to the gendering of women's membership in national communities (Joseph 2010). Sara Ruddick (1997: 213) suggests that the association of motherhood with nation and fatherhood with state is dangerous, bringing in 'the worst of fatherhood: a right, often conjoined with real power, to intrude, humiliate, exploit, and assault'. While the forms of patriarchy change, the linkage of woman/mother to nation and man/father to state reinforces the production of gendered hierarchy and facilitates the institutionalization of gendered citizenship in state-building projects. In the original discourses and policies of the Syrian Ba'th Party, women were constructed and imagined as *'national subjects'* (own emphasis) who supposedly were allocated the same rights and duties as their male compatriots, a discourse that represented a specific form of 'state feminism' under the largely secularist discourse of the regime (see Sparre 2008). This form of state feminism constructed an image of the ideal Syrian woman as a modern, unveiled, educated and emancipated woman who performed citizenship and national duties as stipulated by the Ba'th Party rhetoric about who is a 'good citizen' (Wedeen 2013), a discourse disseminated in the regime-controlled media and which depicted good women citizens as outgoing, free and modern that occupy social roles. As one of our informants, Noura al-Jizawi (2018), suggested, such a discourse extended to narratives of what it meant to be a successful woman as that woman who contributed to and worked within regime-sanctioned structures, such as the General Union of Syrian Women. Prominent examples of these women are Najah al-Attar who served as minister of culture, and was appointed vice-president in 2006, an unprecedented move in the Arab World, and Buthaina Sha'aban, a member of the regime's political elites and political media adviser to the Syrian President Bashar al-Asad. In the official media – and the private media related to the regime – women were portrayed in three main ways: as wives and mothers; as modern, outgoing women who worked mainly in art and as hardworking women working in rural environments. After the Syrian uprising in March 2011, state media began to change some stereotypical images of Syrian women, representing them as having a key role in the regime's war against opponents – for example, successful and national Syrian women were discussed as those who send their sons to join the Syrian army to defend the country against what it called enemies. These discourses did not mean women were free to participate in independent women's movements nor that women concerns were discussed in the official state-run Syrian media.

Liminal ambiguity

It was not until the uprising that Syrian women felt empowered to challenge structural limitations and gendered discourses as part of broader processes calling for change and more political and social rights became possible, and it was during the early more peaceful stages of the popular protests that alternative protest media provided them with the spaces to contest norms and resist authoritarian power. As al-Jizawi said, *Enab Baladi* allowed her and other Syrian women to do things differently, move out of private places and thrust themselves into the public sphere. Another informant Manal Shakashiro went further to suggest that *Enab Baladi* was in itself similar to an '*intifada*' (uprising), providing a space for acts of transgression and anti-structure from which to engage in public acts of defiance against social norms and construct new ways of imagining what it means to be a Syrian woman. It is not surprising that revolutionary processes open new social and political spaces for women.

Indeed, as Nadje al-Ali (2012: 28) writes,

> If we speak of the Middle East, the most commonly cited examples are the Egyptian anti-colonial and independence movement at the turn of the twentieth century that gave rise to the Egyptian women's movement; the Algerian war of independence in the time of French colonialism; and the Palestinian struggle against Israeli occupation. Yet, history also teaches us that during political transitions, women are regularly marginalized and tend to lose many of the gains they might have acquired, or have been promised, at the height of a revolutionary struggle...the issue is not only the lack or very limited representation of women in crucial transitional bodies, such as the constitutional review committee, but perhaps more significantly, we see women's rights being actively violated and women's and gender-based issues sidelined, occasionally even ridiculed, sometimes by women themselves.

Indeed, as the popular protests shifted towards a violent stage of militarization which witnessed extreme violence and destruction, an increased risk of kidnapping, forced displacement, rape, sexual violence, torture and even enslavement, women began to experience marginalization in different ways. For our informants, gendered differentiations began to re-impose themselves in the newsroom and organizational practices, practices which coincided with the re-emergence of traditional normative beliefs about gender and the role of women in society along with the discursive instrumentalization of gender by various actors as part of their ideological battles over power.[9] In the newsroom, as some of our informants said, gendered differentiations manifested themselves in the allocation of tasks and positions, which saw a downgrading of women's roles from managers and decision-makers and the re-imposition of binaries between the public and private.

The seven women we interviewed for this chapter were some of the early pioneers who participated in creating media outlets after the 2011 revolution and for a short period of time had leading roles and responsibilities in *Enab Baladi* and other alternative protest media platforms. For co-author and media activist Helmi, gendering differentiations reasserted themselves in different ways and diverse spaces:

> Even when we took part in demonstrations, we began to hear voices calling on women not to participate in the demonstrations. In the media, we began to see men taking over leading roles, such as chief executive officers, editors in chief and managing editors. The change also happened on the ideological level when most of the media began to change the discourse...for example, we saw men reporters writing more about military issues and hard news and rarely focused on ordinary people' stories and experiences.

Gendering practices also began to be felt in the field. For example, when seeking to interview ordinary people and members of the opposition, Helmi reported that one young man, affiliated to the oppositional Free Syrian Army, asked for a male reporter to speak to rather than her. Another informant Manal Shakashiro said men did not take her seriously as a woman and some of those she interviewed requested that a man be sent to talk to them instead. For her, male colleagues took over leading positions in the newsroom because it was more socially acceptable for men to be in the same place operating together, while it was not socially acceptable for a woman to work alongside a man. With increasing violence, many of the female journalists and founders left for Turkey where they established an office in Istanbul in 2014 and connected with international organizations ready to give training and funding to media organizations in Syria.

Five of the women we interviewed for this chapter come from relatively conservative backgrounds where women had traditionally been expected to remain at home, but all said they were fully supported by their families to engage in opposition acts against the regime at the beginning of the uprising. Three of those interviewed belong to families that opposed the regime before 2011 and several come from vulnerable socio-economic backgrounds, corresponding to the findings of a recent report on alternative media platforms in Syria which showed that on average a high proportion of Syrian women media workers came from vulnerable socio-economic backgrounds (SFJN 2016). Most of the informants spoke of the challenges they faced following the escalation of violence, which brought new security challenges to the female journalists and their families. With increasing militarization of the conflict and the involvement of extremist religious groups, freedom of expression was curtailed and women media workers, particularly those with leading media positions, faced the additional threat of risk to their reputation and lives. Mais Qat, 30, a journalist who cofounded Rozana Radio, said: 'Being a woman who works with a lot of men during times of war, where violence and aggression are the dominating language in the street and work offices as well; it is a big challenge that I faced' (Qat 2018).

According to the report 'Women in Emerging Syrian Media: 2011–2016' (SFJN 2016), on average, 54 per cent of the workforce of what it called Emerging Syrian media (ESM) in radio outlets were women, and over a third of the ESM print workforce (35 per cent) were women. However, only 38 per cent of the women working in the ESM print outlets under review hold senior positions and only 4 per cent of senior ESM journalists are women. The survey shows that common perceptions of women media workers tended to reflect a lack of belief in women's capabilities, a conviction that women are followers of men, and the understanding that women can be utilized as a useful tool to raise sympathy when they are portrayed as victims. Relying on discourse analysis of text and image, the report noted that women were portrayed as active players in the public sphere; as non-existent or confined to the private sphere; as victims or as objects of beauty, incapable of political involvement. In line with this trend, women are portrayed in some instances as active and in need of solidarity and partnership, but in many others as themselves in need of protection, sympathy, advice and help. Most of our informants said that from 2012, they faced security challenges such as the fear of detention, being killed or arresting family members. Later, militarization, masculinity and religious mindset limited the freedom of expression. Women also were faced with aggressiveness towards reputation and ridiculing any work related to gender concepts and gendering the Syrian media to force them stop their activism, especially when these women are in leading positions.

A number of authors have noted that media production, generally speaking, is not gender neutral (e.g. Ross and Carter 2011) and that media work is characterized by a number of patterns of gender inequality that relate to informality, autonomy and flexibility (Gill 2002). In Syria the patterns of gender inequality were fundamentally exacerbated by the protracted liminal state in Syria, which opened new fields of possibilities for regime and other counter-revolutionary forces to instrumentalize gender as a tool of war while engaging in gender-based violence to deter women from joining the opposition forces.[10] These practices were also reiterated in official discourses about women, such as in the speeches of Syrian president Bashar al-Assad's wife Asma al-Assad in which she repeated the old Ba'thist discourse about what it means to be a good nationalist Syrian woman during the war against opponents. For example, in a speech on Mother's Day on 21 March 2018, she said: 'The Syrian heroines are those who defended Syria, postponed their dreams, left their families and put on military uniforms instead of wedding dresses....they carried the fun to defend the soil of their homeland' (al-Assad 2018). The instrumentalization of gender became a tool for several actors in the conflict, but most visibly in the regime's use of gender as part of its narrative of Syria being in a grips of a crisis provoked by outsiders and 'others' in order to render its violence against Syrian people more comprehensible and acceptable. As Szekely (2019: 2), writing about gender ideologies in the Syrian conflict, suggests:

While gender ideology may not be the most important point of division in the conflict, it gives those involved an easy reference point to use in positioning themselves in relation to the other participants in the war, and to signal that position publicly. This is particularly useful in that such signalling represents a low-cost way of indicating an actor's position in what is often a complex web of ideological divisions and alliances.

Conclusion

The Syrian conflict is one of the most complex conflicts in contemporary history.[11] The conflict, now in its eighth year, has been described as the most socially mediated war due to the excessive use by diverse actors of different media platforms to disseminate ideologies, political positionings and images of war and violence, and as the first networked conflict in contemporary history. Compared with other Arab uprisings and long-term conflicts in the Middle East, the conflict has featured spectacular forms of violence mediated through a wide range of digital and social media practices created by a variety of content by a host of political activists, witnesses, rebels, state agents and soldiers, underlining how media are part of social and political processes and are fundamentally implicated in practices of war as well as the battle over ideologies, image, rhetoric and politics.

Theorizing media and long-term conflicts such as Syria's remains an elusive task. This chapter does not make grand claims as it has limited itself to using the optic of liminality to discuss alternative protest media and gendering processes and, in doing so, their potential for the redefinition, but also reinforcement, of social norms and gender distinctions. Liminality, in this sense, allows scholars to address the risks and opportunities for individuals and organizations alike during liminal times when subjects are neither 'in' nor 'out' but are separated from familiar space, routine temporal order or hegemonic social structures. As such, liminality helps us understand lived experiences and actions and alerts us to the potential and limitations of alternative media spaces during times of upheaval and constant transformation, such as the conflict in Syria. While much of the literature has focused on the agential role these spaces play, this chapter has suggested that liminality can affect the role alternative media spaces play because it is ambiguous and precarious and because it can both provide fields of possibilities for transgressive public acts in order to disrupt structure and social norms, including gender norms and practices, as well as fields of possibilities for the reinstatement of social norms and the re-institutionalization of structure by counter-revolutionary forces. The approach taken here does not negate the role alternative media spaces have played in the Syrian war or its understanding, nor does it downplay the incredible bravery and agency of various Syrian actors in their opposition to entrenched systems of power. Rather, it has served to show the precarious conditions women media workers face during conflict and protracted conditions of liminality. Further research needs to be carried out on ideologies of gender in the Syrian conflict,[12] particularly because gender has received less attention than other cleavages in the conflict, and particularly because gender continues to hold a central place in the constellation of narratives defining the Syrian conflict ecosystem and for those involved in and experiencing the conflict.

Notes

1. One of the key theoretical contributions of feminist theory is the concept of intersectionality which provides the language and framework for examining interconnections between social categories, such as gender, and systems and offers explanations of the ways in which diverse members of specific groups, such as women, might experience lived experiences and the work place differently, depending on their ethnicity, sexual orientation, class or other social markers. The term was coined by Kimberle Crenshaw (1989), in her work on the intersection of race and gender in relation to African Americans.
2. Roughly 100 new Syrian media projects were established after March 2011, according to Syrian journalists working in them. There were as many as 298 newspapers being circulated in different parts of the country during various periods of the uprising, in addition to seventeen state-run or regime-affiliated newspapers (see Issa 2016).
3. There is no space here to discuss imposed subjectivities in detail, but crucially the regime's Ba'athist nationalist ideology constructed Syrian subjects as national Arab subjects and Syrian women invariably as women who served this ideology (see, e.g., Wedeen (1999)).
4. We follow Judith Butler (2004) in addressing norms as operating within social practices, and, as such, as providing implicit standards of normalization.
5. See Enab Baladi's website for further details at www.ennabbaladi.net or to view their story in English: https://enabbaladi.org/en/.
6. Most of the newspaper's founders, including co-author Helmi, have fled Syria. Some of its journalists were arrested, some were released and one died under torture, according to Helmi.
7. This is a phase during which men acknowledged women's role in general and particularly in reference to women's role in mobilizing non-violent movements and becoming citizens.
8. The stage lasted until mid-2013 when different actors joined the battle for control of the country. For details about the conflict and its consequences, see BBC News (2019).
9. We follow Butler (2004: 42) in her argument that gender does not refer to 'what one "is" nor to what one "has," but as an apparatus by which

	the production and normalization of masculine and feminine take place along with the interstitial forms of hormonal, chromosomal, psychic, and performative that gender assumes'.
10	Gender violence in wartime is a complex phenomenon and is generally regarded not only as referring to social practices during 'war' as opposed to 'peace', but as happening on a continuum. For example, Cynthia Cockburn, in her study of the persistence of violence before, during and post-conflict, further suggests there is a shift in discourse, especially in media representations, prior to political violence or armed conflict and that this discourse can 'stoke the violence of national patriotism against a rival nation, point a finger at "the enemy within," or deepen the sense of ethnic belonging in opposition to some "other" from whom "we" are different and by whom our culture or our religion, our very existences, is threatened' (2004: 32).
11	By the beginning of 2019, the Syrian conflict had entered a phase marked by a broad consensus that the Assad regime had practically defeated its opponents, regained control of most opposition-held areas and managed to sustain its long-standing mediated regime of representation.
12	In the Syrian conflict, the Kurdish PYD (Turkish Union Democratic Party) and its armed wings have deployed an explicit inclusive position on women's rights and participation, attracting widespread international media coverage of Kurdish women fighters. The role of women fighters has consistently been a central part of the party's messaging in publicizing and promoting some military operations. Radical Islamist groups, such as Islamic State (IS), also adopted ultra-conservative positions on women, issuing a memorandum on how Muslim women should do and act in the public and private space. As is the case for the PYD, IS's beliefs about gender constitute a central feature of its ideology. The organization adheres to and promotes a set of explicit, prescriptive beliefs about the roles of women and men in society and has used the enforcement of those laws as a means of signifying its authority in the areas it controls.

References

Al-Ali, N. (2012), 'Gendering the Arab Spring', *Middle East Journal of Culture and Communication*, 5: 26–31.

Al-Aous, Y. (2013), *Feminist Websites and Civil Society Experiences in Syrian Voices in Pre-revolution Syria; Civil Society against All Odds*, The Hague: Hivos.

Al-Assad, A. (2018), 'Syrian Heroine Soldiers and Their Mothers Honoured, Excerpts from Mrs. Al-Assad Statements', *PresidentAssad.net*, 21 March. Available online: http://www.presidentassad.net/index.php?option=com_content&view=category&layout=blog&id=165&Itemid=487 (accessed 30 September 2019).

al-Jizawi, N. (2018), 'Interview by Kholoud Helmi', *via Skype*, 10 June 2018.

BBC News (2019), 'Why Is There a War in Syria?', *BBC News*, 25 February. Available online: https://www.bbc.co.uk/news/world-middle-east-35806229 (accessed 10 October 2019).

Butler, J. (2004), *Undoing Gender*, London and New York: Routledge.
Cammaerts, B. (2012), 'Protest Logics and the Mediation Opportunity Structure', *European Journal of Communication*, 27(2): 117–34.
Cockburn, C. (2004), 'The Continuum of Violence', in W. Giles and J. Hyndman (eds), *Sites of Violence, Gender and Conflict Zones*, 24–44, Berkeley: University of California Press.
Crenshaw, K. (1989), 'Demarginalizing the Intersection of Race and Sex: A Black Feminist Critique of Antidiscrimination Doctrine, Feminist Theory and Antiracist Politics', *University of Chicago Legal Forum*, 140: 139–67.
Crilley, R. (2017), 'Seeing Syria: The Visual Politics of the National Coalition of Syrian Revolution and Opposition Forces on Facebook', *Middle East Journal of Culture and Communication*, 10(2–3): 133–58.
The Day After (2018), 'Enab Baladi Video Report on "Violence against Women" Workshop in Idleb Countryside', *The Day After*. Available online: https://tda-sy.org/en/content/229/617/tda-in-the-news/enab-baladi-video-report-on-violenceagainst-women-workshop-in-Idlib-countryside (accessed 10 October 2019).
Enab Baladi (2017), 'Syrian Women in the Vicious Circle of Violence', *Enab Baladi*, 9 December. Available online: https://english.enabbaladi.net/archives/2017/12/syrian-women-vicious-circle-violence/#ixzz61wk3ry4q (accessed 10 October 2019).
Enab Baladi (2019), 'Citizen Chronicles of the Syrian Uprising', *Enab Baladi*. Available online: https://hummusforthought.com/wp-content/uploads/2019/05/enabbbaladi-book-web.pdf (accessed 10 October 2019).
Gill, R. (2002), 'Cool, Creative and Egalitarian? Exploring Gender in Project-based New Media Work in Europe', *Information, Communication & Society*, 5(1): 70–89.
Helmi, K. (2019), 'Interview with Dina Matar', 20 June 2019.
Issa, A. (2016), 'Syria's New Media Landscape', *Middle East Institute*, 6 December. Available online: https://www.mei.edu/publications/syrias-new-media-landscape (accessed 10 October 2019).
Joseph, S. (2010), 'Gender and Citizenship in the Arab World', *al-Raida*, 129–30: 8–19.
Kelly, S. (2010), 'Hard-won Progress and a Long Road Ahead: Women's Rights in the Middle East and North Africa', in S. Kelly and J. Breslin (eds), *Women's Rights in the Middle East and North Africa: Progress Amid Resistance*, London: Freedom House. Available online: https://freedomhouse.org/report/women039s-rights-middle-east-and-north-africa/womens-rights-middle-east-and-north-africa-2010 (accessed 10 October 2019).
Kelly, S., and J. Breslin (2010), *Women's Rights in the Middle East and North Africa: Progress amid Resistance*, London: Freedom House. Available online: https://freedomhouse.org/report/women039s-rights-middle-east-and-north-africa/womens-rights-middle-east-and-north-africa-2010 (accessed 10 October 2019).
Khamis, S. (2018), *Arab Women's Activism and Socio-political Transformation: Unfinished Gendered Revolutions*, Cham, Switzerland: Palgrave Macmillan.
Matar, D. (2016), 'Narratives and the Syrian Uprising: The Role of Stories in Political Activism and Identity Struggles', in M. Zayani and S. Merghani (eds), *Bullets and Bulletins*, 89–107, London: Hurst Co. and New York: Oxford University Press.

Matar, D. (2019), 'The Syrian Regime's Strategic Communication: Politics and Ideology', *The International Journal of Communication*, 13: 2398–2416.

Meininghaus, E. (2016), *Creating Consent in Ba'thist Syria: Women and Welfare in a Totalitarian State*, London: Bloomsbury.

O' Brien, A. (2015), 'Producing Television and Reproducing Gender', *Television and New Media*, 16(3): 259–74.

Papacharissi, Z. (2015), 'Toward New Journalisms: Affective News, Hybridity and Liminal Spaces', *Journalism Studies*, 16(1): 27–40.

Qat, M. (2018), 'Interview by Kholoud Helmi', *via Skype*, 18 June 2018.

Radsch, C., and S. Khamis (2013), 'In Their Own Voice: Technologically-mediated Empowerment and Transformation among Young Arab Women', *Feminist Media Studies*, 13(5): 881–90.

Ross, K., and C. Carter (2011), 'Women and News: A Long and Winding Road', *Media Culture & Society*, 33(8): 1148–65.

Ruddick, S. (1997). The idea of fatherhood. In H. L. Nelson (Ed.).Feminism and families (pp. 205–220). New York: Routledge.

Ruddick, S. (1998) 'Woman of peace': A feminist construction. In: Lorentzen LA and Turpin J (eds.) *The Women and War Reader*. New York: NYU Press, pp. 213–226.

SFJN (2016), 'Women in Emerging Syrian Media, 2011–2016', *Stichting Female Journalists Network*. Available online: http://www.sfjn.org/research-en.pdf (accessed 10 October 2019).

Shakashiro, M. (2018), 'Interview by Kholoud Helmi', *via Skype*, 25 June 2018.

Sharbaji, A. (2018), 'Interview by Kholoud Helmi', *via Skype*, 15 June 2018.

Sparre S. (2008), 'Educated Women in Syria: Servants of the State, or Nurturers of the Family?' *Critical Middle Eastern Studies*, 17(1): 3–20.

Sreberny, A. (2018), 'Women's Digital Activism in a Changing Middle East', in M. Zayani (ed), *Digital Middle East*, London: Hurst, pp 109–24.

Sweeney, B. (2009), 'Producing Liminal Space: Gender, Age and Class in Northern Ontario's Tree Planting Industry', *Gender, Peace and Culture*, 16(5): 569–86.

Szekely, O. (2019), 'Fighting about Women: Ideologies of Gender in the Syrian Civil War', *Journal of Global Security Studies*. Available online: https://doi.org/10.1093/jogss/ogz018 (accessed 10 October 2019).

Turner, V. (1967), *The Forest of Symbols: Aspects of Ndembu Ritual*, Ithaca, NY: Cornell UP.

Wedeen, L. (1999), *Ambiguities of Domination: Politics, Rhetoric and Symbols in Contemporary Syria*, Chicago: Chicago University Press.

Wedeen, L. (2013), 'Ideology and Humour in Dark Times: Notes from Syria', *Critical Inquiry*, 39(4): 841–73.

Wessels, J. (2018), *Documenting Syria, Film-making, Video Activism and Revolution*, London: Bloomsbury.

Yang, G. (2000), 'The Liminal Effects of Social Movements: Red Guards and the Transformation of Identity', *Sociological Forum*, 15(3): 379–406.

Zayani, M. (2015), *Networked Publics and Digital Contention*, Oxford: Oxford University Press.

8

#shaheed: A metaphotographic study of Kashmir's insurgency (2014–2016)

Nathaniel Brunt

On a summer day in 2015 I watched as the lifeless body of Talib Ahmed Shah was carried through the streets of the village of Kakapora in northern India's Kashmir Valley. Shah, who was 21, had been killed the evening before during an encounter between Indian security forces and the small group of Lashkar-e-Taiba (LeT) militants to which he belonged.[1] Hundreds of people from surrounding communities gathered for the funeral procession, a collective spectacle of mourning, solidarity and respect for the young man and his newly acquired status of *shaheed* – martyr. Shah's corpse, still in bloodied and soiled clothes and strewn with the flower petals that mark a *shaheed*'s funeral, was thronged by a sea of spectators hoping to glimpse or perhaps touch his now venerated mortal remains. Over the following days photographs of Shah were shared on a variety of public social networking websites. Many of these images, often taken with mobile phones, depicted the corpse and the martyr's funeral procession. The photographs, posted by users, were accompanied by captions that memorialized Shah's divine and nationalistic sacrifice and congratulated him on his journey to the paradisiacal afterlife of the 'martyr'. Alongside these photographs of the body were images of Shah during his short life (see Figure 8.1 and 8.2).

Shah, like a rising number of young Kashmiri men who have joined the militancy in the disputed Kashmir Valley, had a stable family background, was well educated, was a 'normal' young man who loved football and had a deep passion for learning. A few days after the funeral, his brother Saeed

FIGURE 8.1 Hundreds of people gather in Kakapora, Kashmir, for the funeral of 21-year-old Talib Ahmed Shah, a Kashmiri Lashkar-e-Taiba militant. © Nathaniel Brunt.

FIGURE 8.2 Villagers document the funeral of 21-year-old Talib Ahmed Shah, a Kashmiri Lashkar-e-Taiba militant. Funerals of militants have become hyper-photographed events in the post-2013 period. © Nathaniel Brunt.

told me that Shah had both an MPED degree from an institute of physical education in Chennai and an MA in history from the Indira Gandhi National Open University and before joining LeT he was pursuing a diploma at an industrial training institute (Shah, S. 2015). Like others in the generation of youths from the Kashmir Valley who came of age during the early years of the insurgency in the 1990s, Shah had experienced an upbringing defined and forged by the trauma of a conflict that has resulted in nearly 70,000 deaths, between 8,000–10,000 enforced disappearances and numerous human rights violations.[2] In early 2014, he chose to join the insurgency after being humiliated, harassed and ultimately arrested by Indian security forces for participating in anti-government protests in 2008 and 2010.[3]

In 2013, I became drawn to documenting and understanding this region, its conflicted history[4] and the new generation of young men like Shah who have decided to dedicate their lives to the fight for it. The first part of this ongoing work, #*shaheed*,[5] began in 2014. During that summer, while working in Tral, a highly militarized sub-district in south Kashmir, I learned about the unprecedented proliferation in production and distribution of photographs and videos of militants, like Shah, on mobile phones and through social media. This digital archive of images of the conflict, taken by local people and often the militants themselves, was part of an alternative digital information space that was used as an inexpensive and effective means to promote recruitment, memorialize the dead, and encourage and assert active political resistance against the Indian state. Simultaneously this media was also used by those actively involved in the conflict, or witnesses to it, to record and preserve their personal experiences of day-to-day life in the region.

This digital material revealed a physically inaccessible and unstudied first-hand view of the insurgency and the lives and deaths of young men fighting in it. While many of these photographs exhibited propagandistic tropes of contemporary Islamic militant groups, many also presented a complex and deeply layered view that oscillated between the ordinary and extraordinary moments of these 'invisible' men's wartime lives. The intimate photos presented an uncomfortable view that complicated popular Western representations of men in these types of groups. These digital 'fragments', created by individuals directly affected by the insurgency, opened up a new space for documentary fieldwork and were critical elements of this conflict's visual history. While I continued to produce my own images of the region throughout this period, frustrated with the limitations of the singular perspective of the traditional documentary approach, I also began to collect and archive these vernacular digital images from local people's phones and from social media sources. Using this new reflexive 'metaphotographic' (Ritchin 2013) process of intertwining my own images with the larger contextual framework of these collected digital artefacts was reflective of the fragmented nature of the insurgency in the Kashmir Valley and the broader media ecosystem surrounding the conflict. Simultaneously the production of this project also revealed the complexity of documenting war in the 'post-photographic' age, where the role of the documentary photographer and the distinctions between the professional and the amateur, and digital information networks and the physical space of the battlefield, have all become deeply contested.

Documenting conflict in the post-photographic era

Over the last decade advances in mobile phone imaging technology and internet connectivity have allowed for the production of billions of new images and the immediate and infinite ability to access an unprecedented range of photographs at any time. This shift in values challenges the core principles of the image, which have fundamentally reshaped the way in which we create, disseminate and perceive photographs (Fontcuberta 2015: 10). As Stephen Mayes writes, 'Online imagery is centered less on presenting photographs as objects of memory and more on the sharing of current experience' (Mayes 2014: 33). In turn, the sharing and disseminating of highly personal and formerly emotionally reflective 'social' images of 'non-events' in the online public sphere have become a significant part of the collective photographic documentation of public life where 'lens-based image making has become a form of communication nearly as banal, instinctive, and persuasive (or profligate) as talking' (Ritchin 2013: 11). In this 'age of total visibility' (Carruthers 2015: 191) the traditional photographic focus on recording has given way to a milieu in which the photograph has also become an important form of day-to-day communication. Images of typically disregarded everyday moments of personal experience, or 'non-events', have become equally prominent as other forms of photographs in the online photographic discourse (Dong-Hoo Lee 2012: 173; Ritchin 2014).

This evolution has had a profound effect on the way in which images are produced, consumed and perceived, directly impacting the visual coverage of current news events. Perhaps the most profoundly affected has been documentation of modern conflict. In contemporary war coverage, the hierarchical relationship of the predominantly Western and male (see Taylor-Lind 2016) professional documentarian or photojournalist, taking images of passive subjects, has shifted to an increasingly lateral format in which amateur participants involved in the conflict, including both civilians and the combatants themselves, are active agents in the process of photographic witnessing and recording. According to Gates (2013: 9), the traditional 'hierarchical flow of information (from the content providers to the content consumers) has started to give way to a more level flow, [where] content consumers are now also content providers'. Simultaneously, the space between the physical and digital space of the battlefield has increasingly dissolved, as well as the understanding of the photograph as a solely mnemonic document recording a specific 'event'. With billions of amateurs carrying small, portable cameras with social media connectivity, the traditional media distribution channels have shifted to a progressively horizontal system involving non-professionals. As a result, breaking news events are now increasingly being documented by amateur journalists who are often locals directly affected by events and happen to be present instead of solely professional documentarians. As Ritchin (2014: 45) has claimed, 'Unlike professionals who often tend to emulate previous iconic imagery of war, those whose lives are affected by the violence, whether as soldiers or civilians, make images that can be more personally felt, diverse and at times more perversely horrific.'

While the significance of these digital photographic practices – as a new feature in the history of the documentation of war (Kennedy 2009: 819) – has been revealed through recent forms of citizen visual journalism (most notably during the uprisings in Iran and the Arab world and in the ongoing conflict in Syria), the increasing number of conflict portrayals by those actually involved in perpetuating conflict violence may be even more profound and potentially disturbing. As Liam Kennedy notes:

> This digital generation of soldiers exists in a new relationship to their experience of war; they are now potential witnesses and sources within the documentation of events, not just the imaged actors – a blurring of roles that reflects the correlations of revolutions in military and media affairs.
>
> (Kennedy 2009: 819)

In turn, 'photographs that are conceived from the perspective of "us" – the combatants or those caught in the conflict' have become, argues Ritchin, 'at least as common as those made of "them"' (2014: 42). Of course, these images do allow for a broadening of viewpoints of conflicts, but they are also problematic as documents due to their highly manipulatable nature, often-opaque provenance and lack of conformation to the ethics and peer scrutiny of professional media standards. This has led to their wide-scale production and distribution as tools of propaganda and misinformation during war. Contemporary militant organizations globally, most prominently ISIS, have created complex public relations and communications campaigns using these types of amateur vernacular images in tandem with social media platforms to 'dramatize and proselytize their views or terrorize through [the] use of imagery' (Kennedy 2009: 818) where photography, in effect, becomes a weapon of war. It is within this context that access to previously unavailable viewpoints of the battlefield has become visible and where new opportunities have been generated to explore and document the use of photography for both documentary practitioners and researchers alike. It is in this context that my work on #*shaheed* is situated.

The metaphotographic approach

I made my first trip to the Kashmir Valley in 2013. Working as an independent photographer I was interested in documenting the events and scars of the insurgency of the 1990s that pockmarked the valley's landscape and the bodies and minds of its inhabitants. When I arrived, the valley was engulfed in violent protest following a twenty-eight-day government-enforced curfew.[6] A few weeks earlier, the divisive Kashmiri public figure Afzal Guru was, controversially, executed by the Indian government in Delhi's Tihar Jail (Roy 2013). In the aftermath of the execution large groups of Kashmiri youths flocked to the streets to protest in Srinagar. Working with a local colleague, I photographed these clashes embedded with groups of young stone-throwers as they fought with security forces. My photographs reflected my experiences of these events, interactions with the protesters, the violence of these incidents, and the inherent shock, fear, and strange form of selfish excitement that accompanies a first foray into covering violence.

Simultaneously during this trip, I focused my lens on the legacy of the conflict and its painful effects on the society. I produced pictures of the unmarked mass graves which dotted the valley's landscape, the mothers of

FIGURE 8.3 A selection of photographs taken by the author in early 2013. © Nathaniel Brunt.

those who had disappeared and the families of the war's dead. I employed a traditional documentary aesthetic and method: acting as a witness by creating authoritative photographic records that could serve as a vehicle to convey 'objective' information about the conflict to my audience (Mayes 2014: 34). I also sought to communicate the pain, suffering and resilience of those I encountered who had been deeply affected by the conflict (see Figure 8.3).

But while these intimate photographs captured the intensity of the experience of those violent weeks, they said very little about the nature and history of the insurgency, the peoples or the place. As I began to edit this work I became increasingly aware of the limited capacity of the traditional photojournalistic approach to communicate the complexities of the mosaic-like experiences of the conflict and the region's history. Simultaneously, as an outsider, I felt deeply troubled with the burden of authoritatively representing the region and its conflict through my perspective alone. In short, I began to question my process: was my methodological approach reducing the complexities of the region's history and the events (I had witnessed) into a simplistic and reductionist narrative? Where and how did my images fit into the larger photographic narrative of the region's history? Towards the end of this first trip in the remote, mountainside town of Chittybandi, in the northern part of the valley, I had a realization that enabled me to address some of these concerns.

I had come to Chittybandi to photograph the wedding ceremony of Showkat, the middle son in the Ahmed family. The Ahmed's and the community had shown me warmth and hospitality, a trait ubiquitous with Kashmiri culture, and I returned to the family with the gift of some photographs I had taken at the wedding. As I entered the family's home, I noticed a wooden frame filled with a montage of family pictures sitting on a small shelf (see Figure 8.4). The vernacular pictures showed typical family moments: images of Showkat's father, his uncle and some of the oldest brother Mohammed as a young boy. However, there were also images that I had not expected to see: photographs of Mohammed as militant in the 1990s and pictures of his funeral a few years later. Looking at these photographs I realized that these amateur family images revealed an intimate and untainted view of everyday life and the impact of the insurgency on the population. I also realized that these were photographic fragments of the cultural history of the region and the conflict and were critical elements of the historical and political themes I wanted to examine and try to better understand. This experience and my frustration with the limitations of the traditional documentary process led to a methodological divergence that would lay the foundation for my subsequent work.

The methodological approach that I adopted was largely influenced by work of Fred Ritchin (2013). Ritchin argues that contemporary photographers need to adopt a metaphotographic approach in which they act as a photographic sieve, straining out important fragments from the

FIGURE 8.4 Showkat Ahmed and his mother display a collage of family photographs in their home in Chittybandi. © Nathaniel Brunt.

constant flow of online and offline imagery and contextualize them into frameworks fit for public consumption and education. This method challenges the positivist concept of the singular photographic viewpoint and allows for multiple individual perspectives, which creates new forms of perception and understanding of current and historic events. By including this variety of views, the photographic process moves towards a democratic methodology in which the amateur is actively encouraged to photographically participate and share her views. This change is a fundamental resifting of principles in which selection is valued over solely production.

Utilizing this approach and working in a place devoid of formal institutionalized photographic archives, I began to collect a variety of professional and vernacular photographs from family collections, and portrait studios in the valley from various periods in history. These were then digitized and the original images returned to their owners and no physical holdings were retained. This was specifically done to encourage participation but also to revise a historical legacy of outsiders looting historical objects from developing countries. I then selected a number of photographs and experimented by mixing them with my own images into a non-linear narrative of the region that situated my own small visual contribution within the much broader photographic history and ecosystem of the region and the conflict.

In addition to collecting images, I collaborated with writer, curator and educator Alisha Sett, and together we collected oral testimony from those who had either donated images or possessed knowledge about the subjects depicted in photos. With many of the images produced in the late nineteenth and early twentieth century, where historical witnesses were unavailable we sought out contemporary first-person accounts in textual sources to contextualize the images. These photographs and stories formed a mosaic of different thematic and temporal tangents that depicted a layered history of the region. This multi-perspective work steered away from the classic approach of top-down grand historical narratives by integrating both professional and vernacular material. As theorist and educator Paulo Freire writes, 'Historical themes are never isolated, independent, disconnected, or static; they are always interacting dialectically with their opposites' (Freire 1972: 91–2). Kashmir's history was no different. The fragmentation of society in the aftermath of conflict had made the region a battleground of competing opinions about the historical record. Over the next two years we continued to collect and archive physical images and oral testimonies of Kashmir's past. This was formalized in the creation of the collaborative project, The Kashmir Photo Collective, which Sett and I co-founded in 2014 (see www.kashmirphotocollective.com).

Coinciding with this was a re-intensification of the insurgency in a new form which directly converged with my change in practice. As a result, I also used the metaphotographic process of collection and curation, albeit in the digital online world, to investigate the contemporary re-emergence of the local insurgency in the valley, a work that became *#shaheed*.

#shaheed

The context of *#shaheed* began in 2014 where, after a lull in the insurgency of close to a decade, a trail of young Kashmiri men, often only in their mid-teens,[7] left their homes to join militant groups – notably Hizbul Mujahideen and LeT – predominantly in the southern regions of the valley. While the numbers of militants operating in the valley were much smaller than during previous phases of the insurgency, these young local men made up for their low numbers and limited operational abilities through a wide-scale, and virtual, public relations effort. Using mobile phone cameras and social media platforms such as Twitter, Facebook and WhatsApp, they began to photographically document and share their everyday experiences online and to encourage others to join them. This effort was a means of exerting control over the competitive media ecosystem of the insurgency and more broadly the perceptions of the local population. While the digital vernacular images that emerged from this were often propagandistic they also revealed an unprecedented view of the lives of members of these groups, who in previous phases of the insurgency had purposely chosen to remain largely invisible (Massod 2015). I encountered these photographs on local friends' mobile phones in Kashmir and later on social media accounts run by the militants, their accomplices (known as over-ground workers) or civilians. Using my network of contacts in the valley, a variety of social media search engines and often-used keywords such as '#shaheed', I began to collect and archive these images and videos. The material collected was predominantly propagandistic and used by the insurgent groups and their supporters as performative visual constructions to build and promote a romantic myth of heroism and devotion to their religiously and politically motivated armed struggle (Shah F. 2015). These images were representative of the expected visual spaces of conflict imagery evoking powerful associations (memorialization, mobilization, myth) and in this regard, an intrinsic aspect of the crafting of the militancy's public image.[8] Yet others were also intimate and deeply human, visual forms that resonated specifically with the motifs of imagery of the post-photographic era.

Dominant among the visual material produced by civilians were memorial photographs of the dead, or 'martyred' militants, at their funerals. These events, often attended by thousands of locals, have become hyper-photographed occasions. Images of the Shaheed's corpse, which was the dominant photographic interest, were created as visual evidence of the perceived cruelty of the state, memorials of heroic sacrifice and as a traditional mnemonic document of the individual's life and deeds. As the father of a young man who joined Hizbul Mujahideen and was killed during a skirmish with Indian security forces later told me:

> [Young people's] passion gets raised by such images, it remains as evidence of the past, our history and what India has done to our people. Everybody here has images of the militants and songs eulogizing them in their phones... Everybody has the pictures of the martyrs in their phones.[9]

Unlike the photographs taken by civilians, the photographs produced by the militants themselves depicted the men as sentient beings. These images predominantly followed many of the expected visual tropes of Islamic insurgents and often feature highly constructed images of tough-faced, bearded, young men brandishing Kalashnikov rifles in a hodgepodge of military apparel in performative rock star-like poses. Others, which were digitally altered, were strangely akin to the aesthetics of Western teen magazines and postmodern internet culture and clearly illustrated the impulse to create a cult of celebrity around these young men and turn them into heroes to encourage further recruitment. As journalists Ipsita Chakravarty and Rayan Naqash (2016) write, 'There was always a certain glamour attached to becoming a militant [in the 1990s]. But now, individual figures

FIGURE 8.5 A memorial banner featuring militant photographs is displayed above a martyr's graveyard in Pulwama district south Kashmir. © Nathaniel Brunt.

are thrown into sharp relief. Local memories and personal ties are hopped up on technology. This is the age of celebrity militants who are also folk heroes.' Key to these visual narratives of folk heroism were plots focusing on sacrifice, martyrdom and revenge, forms of expression that, as Patrick Colm Hogan has shown, deeply resonate in disillusioned and humiliated Kashmiri youth and are common to broader nationalist movements (Hogan 2016) (see Figure 8.5 and 8.6). This practice was most prominently and successfully utilized by Burhan Wani, a young and charismatic Hizbul Mujahideen militant commander from Tral in south Kashmir who became a local legend between 2014 and 2016 through the public image he cultivated using social media, photography and videos (Chakravarty and Naqash 2016). This lies in stark contrast to often 'faceless' depiction of insurgents in traditional media where – notwithstanding the exceptions among groups like ISIS fighters – militant groups from the Islamic world are almost exclusively depicted as a homogenized, dehumanized and incomprehensible collective forces instead of complex multidimensional individuals. As Susan Carruthers (2015: 205) writes, 'Having espoused "illicit" violence, the insurgent forfeits any right to consideration as fully human. Inhumanity is intrinsic to this ascriptive identity.' This was particularly the case in Kashmir during the 1990s where, as reported in local Indian news media, 'the face of the Kashmiri has dissolved into a blurred, featureless mask. He has become a secessionist- terrorist- fundamentalist traitor' (Bose 2003: 113).

FIGURE 8.6 Kashmiri militants Davood Sheikh, Hilal Ahad Wani, Junaid Mattoo, Mushtaq Ahmed Mir and Farooq Ahmed pose for photographs with their weapons. All the young men, members of militant groups Hizbul Mujahideen and Lashkar-e-Taiba, were later killed in 'encounters' with Indian security forces. The photographs were collected by Nathaniel Brunt in 2016. The collage was made by Nathaniel Brunt in 2017. Donated to the author by anonymous, Summer 2016.

Existing beside the propagandistic images was a collection of intimate photographs that had a purpose that was difficult to define (see Figure 8.7). These photographs featured scenes of mundane everyday moments: a group of young militants slicing up a watermelon to share among themselves, a young man bathing in a stream, two militants arm-wrestling and a group of young men embracing lovingly while looking towards the camera lens. These images, produced by the militants, were directly a product of the post-photographic age. Taken behind the lines of the conflict, these autobiographic images strikingly revealed a deeply humanistic portrait of the normalcy and monotony of these individuals' everyday lives and the male camaraderie that is specific to times of war. As Kim Sawchuk (1998) writes, 'Artefacts [whether physical or digital] communicate because of what is inscribed on them, but they also tell us something about the values at the time and place of their creation because of the media that were used.' Looking through these images I realized that the militants sought to create an alternative reality through the creation of this subversive media space that allowed them to express their masculinity, freedom, agency outside the control of the Indian state. Simultaneously, it was clear that these images

FIGURE 8.7 HM militants Davood Sheikh and Hilal Ahad Wani. Source: Donated to the author by anonymous, Summer 2016.

were directly representative of a new type of amateur visual perspective that is specific to the contemporary post-photographic landscape that allows photographs of everyday experiences of conflict, from those directly affected war, to also be produced and disseminated widely. While some of the former propaganda images were integrated into the exhibition #*shaheed*, it was these unexpected, deeply intimate 'post' photographs of Kashmir's militants that provided a powerful means to show the complex human side of these controversial young men.

Exhibiting #shaheed

Over a period of close to two years between 2014 and 2016, I collected and archived close to 1,500 digital images of members of Kashmir's Islamist militant groups, many of which depicted the complexity of these men and their lives. Using these intimate autobiographical images, as well as my own traditional documentary photographs taken in the region between 2013 and 2016, I sought to design an exhibition that challenged simplistic visual convictions about these groups and opened new routes of understanding that encouraged viewers to consider the complexity of contemporary global issues and these individuals' lives. In contemporary warfare, opportunities for face-to-face encounters with opposing forces often in irregular forces are rare. By presenting these images in a balanced but nuanced fashion, I hoped to create an intimate and uncomfortable face-to-face encounter between my audience and these unexpectedly vulnerable, and thoroughly human, young men in Kashmir's militant groups.

Between 2016 and 2017 I produced two solo exhibitions in Toronto, Canada, that showed separately for several weeks at Ryerson Student Gallery and CONTACT Gallery. Exhibiting #*shaheed* presented a complex challenge (see Figure 8.8). With a highly eclectic mix of hundreds of images and videos, including my own photographs, the task of connecting these elements into a framework that blended these drastically different materials into a coherent whole presented many hurdles. Over the course of 2016, I worked with curators to edit and sequence close to 300 photographs and numerous videos from a collection of images dating back to 2013. This material fell into two categories that were radically different aesthetically. The first was a selection of my personal photographs, standard and panoramic black-and-white 35-mm film frames, in a traditional photojournalistic aesthetic, documented day-to-day life in Kashmir's ongoing conflict. In addition, a sequence of these images depicted the procession and protests during the funeral of Talib Ahmed Shah. The second category of material for the exhibition was the collected social media photographs and videos of the militants. These digital images had virtually no standardization of dimensions, aesthetics or content. Naturally found in the digital sphere of the online world, this material was particularly difficult to faithfully translate to a gallery space. Yet by integrating these found images, many of which had been often overlooked, with my own photographs, I sought to situate and also directly acknowledge the limitations of my own singular viewpoint and began to construct a narrative told from a multiplicity of visual perspectives that was directly reflective of the broader competitive ecosystem of photographic production and dissemination that surrounded, and was an important part of, the ongoing conflict.

Due to their online provenance, the collected photographs represented a major departure from my own images. Unlike my photographs, these images were of low resolution, colour photographs and had a variety of dimensions. In an attempt to maintain their mode of viewing on the web, I printed them at their natural dimensions in a variety of small print sizes. The collected photographs were mounted as a mosaic of layered images that mimicked the torrent of social media imagery. Plucking these ephemeral artefacts from the flux of the virtual space and grounding them in a material and permanent format in the gallery space allowed time for audiences to explore them in depth, make connections between them and return to them again and again.

The final component of the exhibition was a collection of several mobile phones loaded with a catalogue of collected images and videos of the militants. The randomized order of the slideshows represented the

FIGURE 8.8 Installation view of Nathaniel Brunt, #shaheed, 2017. Photo courtesy of Toni Hafkenscheid.

constant flux of the ever-evolving nature and chaos of social media and the history of the conflict. Simultaneously, these images, which often repeated the photographs on the wall or the other phones, implied an idea about the infinite replication and reproduction inherent to the medium of digital photography.

By presenting the collected photographs, along with my own, in the gallery space for a Western audience, I sought to reveal the complexity and contradictions that were inherent to these men's lives, the way they represented themselves and the broader world of Islamic militancy in order to provoke questions about the simplistic manner in which we represent and understand these individuals in the West. As Susie Linfield argues, the specific ambiguity of the photographic medium can be used as a powerful means of discovery by encouraging audiences to make connections to the world beyond the image's frame. Instead of simply approaching photographs 'as static objects that we either naively accept or scornfully reject', she writes, 'we might see them as part of a process – the beginning of a dialogue, the start of an investigation – into which we thoughtfully, consciously enter' (Linfield 2010: 29–30).

Conclusion

At the time of writing, the tension, violence and uncertainty in the Kashmir Valley continue. Indeed, since I embarked on producing #*shaheed* the terrain of contemporary conflict in the region has radically shifted.[10] In one sense then, the work contained in the project is located in a specific time and place. In another, however, the work #*shaheed* transcends these specificities to tell a complex, fragmented and often contradictory narrative about the ongoing insurgency in the Kashmir Valley, Islamic militancy and the changing nature of war photography in the twenty-first century. Relatedly, the exhibition of the work sought to challenge audiences to think more broadly about issues of the visibility/invisibility of individuals in radical insurgent groups in conflict spaces and the need to understand them as complex multidimensional human beings. While this presentation of the work was about Kashmir, the broader issues extend well beyond its borders, as do the ethical and methodological challenges presented by this type of documentary project.

Indeed, #*shaheed* draws our attention to how the dichotomous photographic records of the young militants are intimate and deeply human, despite the knowledge of their violent actions and beliefs being troubling. As artefacts these images can inform us about the changing nature of photographs in the post-photographic age. As documents they can teach us important lessons about the complex and often contradictory nature of our 'enemies' and ultimately what it means to be human. Like social media itself, Islamic militancy, writes journalist Jason Burke (2015: 12), 'is diverse, dynamic, fragmented and chaotic'. Ultimately, in order to attempt to comprehend such groups and those that are a part of them, it is critical that we swallow our fear, shock and despair and face the difficult reality that the 'monsters' we create are human.

Notes

1. Lashkar-e-Taiba or 'Army of the Pure' is a Sunni Islamic militant organization based in Pakistan. Though they are often referred to as 'terrorists' by Indian media and 'freedom fighters' by Kashmiri media, in this essay I will use the term 'militant' to denote any combatant, both Kashmiri or foreigner, involved in the insurgency in the Kashmir Valley.
2. The International Peoples' Tribunal on Human Rights and Justice in Indian-Administered Kashmir and the Association of Parents of Disappeared Persons, Structures of Violence: The Indian State in Jammu and Kashmir, publication (Srinagar: International Peoples' Tribunal on Human Rights and Justice in Indian-Administered Kashmir (IPTK) and the Association of Parents of Disappeared Persons (APDP), 2015).
3. Since I began my research in the valley I have discovered a strong trend of militants experiencing violent personal incidents by security forces during their civilian lives. Many of these young men also participated in the mass protests in 2008, 2009 and 2010 and witnessed the killing of unarmed protesters by security forces during these years. While religious conviction is often an integral part of their rationale for joining the militancy, an imperative to take revenge for direct experiences of violence, humiliation and harassment, and indirect feelings of collective historical oppression of the population by the Indian state is a primary factor. As author and former conflict reporter Chris Hedges (2015) astutely writes, 'Fanaticism is bred by hopelessness and despair. It is not a product of religion, although religion often becomes the sacral veneer for violence. The more desperate people become, the more nihilistic violence will spread.'
4. Since the late 1980s, the former princely state of Jammu and Kashmir has been the site of a protracted insurgency. A long-growing discord culminated following a rigged election by the Indian state; the bilateral conflict between India and Pakistan over Kashmir evolved as many Kashmiris rose up against Indian control. Quickly the movement spawned a large, albeit fragmented, collection of armed militant groups that began a full-scale uprising. Seeing the insurgency as a proxy opportunity to weaken its opponent and possibly gain influence or control of the region, the Pakistani government, military and the Inter-Services Intelligences (ISI) provided support for militant groups. By the early 1990s, many young Kashmiri men travelled across the border into Pakistan, often as far as Afghanistan, to receive training and arms, and returned to the valley to create numerous militant groups with competing ideologies.

This expansion and fragmentation of the insurgency led to competition and in-fighting between local militants. As the uprising continued in the mid-1990s and early 2000s, foreign fighters from Pakistan, Afghanistan, Central Asia, Africa and the Middle East in radical jihadi groups, backed by Pakistan, also became involved in the conflict. In order to stem the growing militancy in the region, the Indian state responded both judicially and militarily to quell the uprising with a program of counter-insurgency. However, while these operations were successful in greatly reducing the insurgency over time, hard-line policies, and legal tools such as the Public Safety Act and the Armed Forces (Jammu and Kashmir) Special Powers Act (which are both still in effect today), allowed Indian security forces and their proxies to act with virtual impunity. Human rights organizations reported violations by Indian military and paramilitary forces against civilians as early as 1991. In addition, human rights abuses were also perpetrated by local counter-insurgent forces, known as Ikhwanis, and various local and foreign militant groups.

5 It is almost certain that all of these young men will be killed. Militants who are cornered by Indian security forces predominantly choose death over surrender. It is for this reason that I use the term *shaheed* to refer to both living and deceased militants.
6 Curfews are often imposed by the Indian government during times of heightened political tension. During a curfew the valley or sections of it are put under lockdown and movement is heavily curtailed by security forces.
7 The charismatic Hizbul Mujahideen militant commander and folk hero Burhan Wani was only 15 years old when he joined the militancy. He carried a 10 lakh bounty (approximately $20000 CAD) on his head until he was killed in 2016.
8 During the 1990s Kashmiri militants were photographed in professional portrait studios by colleagues or photojournalists. Few of these photographs exist today and many were lost or destroyed during the conflict.
9 Interview with anonymous relative of Hizbul Mujahideen militant. Interview by author. August 2016.
10 For example, the 2016 protests following the death of Burhan Wani, the emergence of new militant groups and Al Qaeda and ISIS proxies, the dissemination of execution videos online, the switch from platforms such as WhatsApp to Telegram, the Jaish-e-Mohammed suicide bombing in February 2019 and the revoking of Article 370 of the Indian Constitution in August 2019.

References

Bose, S. (2003), *Kashmir: Roots of Conflict, Paths to Peace*, Cambridge, MA: Harvard University Press.
Burke, J. (2015), *The New Threat: The Past, Present, and Future of Islamic Militancy*, London: New Press.
Carruthers, S. L. (2015), 'Why Can't We See Insurgents? Enmity, Invisibility, and Counterinsurgency in Iraq and Afghanistan', *Photography & Culture*, 8(2): 191–211.

Chakravarty, I., and R. Naqash (2016), 'The Legend of Burhan Wani: How the New Militants of South Kashmir Have Become Local Heroes', *Scroll*, 5 July. Available online: http://scroll.in/article/811059/the-legend-of-burhan-wani-how-the-new-militants-of-south-kashmir-have-become-local-heroes (accessed 10 October 2019).

Fontcuberta, J. (2015), 'The Post Photographic Condition', in J. Fontcuberta (eds), *The Post Photographic Condition*, 10–17, Bielefeld: Kerber Verlag.

Freire, P. (1972), *Pedagogy of the Oppressed*, Harmondsworth: Penguin Books.

Gates, J. (2013), *Uneventful: The Rise of Photography*, Edinburgh: Museums Etc.

Hedges, C. (2015), 'The Great Unraveling', *Truthdig*, 30 August. Available online: http://www.truthdig.com/report/item/the_great_unraveling_20150830 (accessed 19 October 2019).

Hogan, P. C. (2016), *Imagining Kashmir: Emplotment and Colonialism*, Lincoln: University of Nebraska Press.

Kennedy, L. (2009), 'Soldier Photography: Visualising the War in Iraq', *Review of International Studies*, 35(4): 817–33.

Lee, D. H. (2012), 'Mobile Snapshots: Pictorial Communication in the Age of Tertiary Orality', in J. Macgregor Wise and H. Koskela (eds), *New Visualities, New Technologies: The New Ecstasy of Communication*, 171–88, Farnham, Surrey, England: Ashgate.

Linfield, S. (2010), *The Cruel Radiance: Photography and Political Violence*, Chicago: University of Chicago Press.

Masood, B. (2015), 'Guns "n" Poses: The New Crop of Militants in Kashmir', *The Indian Express*, 26 July. Available online: http://indianexpress.com/article/india/india-others/big-picture-guns-n-poses/ (accessed 19 October 2019).

Mayes, S. (2014), 'Toward a New Documentary Expression', *Aperture*, 214, Spring: 32–5.

Ritchin, F. (2013), *Bending the Frame: Photojournalism, Documentary, and the Citizen*, New York: Aperture.

Ritchin, F. (2014), 'Of Them, and Us', *Aperture*, 214, Spring: 42.

Roy, A. (2013), 'The Hanging of Afzal Guru Is a Stain on India's Democracy', *The Guardian*, 10 February. Available online: http://www.theguardian.com/commentisfree/2013/feb/10/hanging-afzal-guru-india-democracy (accessed 19 October 2019).

Sawchuk, K. (1998), 'Materiality, Memory Machines and the Archive as Media', *Library and Archives Canada*, 9 July. Available online: https://www.collectionscanada.gc.ca/innis-mcluhan/030003-4050-e.html (accessed 19 October 2019).

Shah, F. (2015), 'Interview with Nathanial Brunt, by Telephone', 7 November.

Shah, S. (2015), 'Interview with Nathaniel Brunt', August, Kashmir.

Taylor-Lind, A. (2016), 'How a Lack of Representation Is Hurting Photojournalism', *TIME Lightbox (blog)*, 4 May. Available online: http://time.com/4312779/how-a-lack-of-representation-is-hurting-photojournalism/ (accessed 19 October 2019).

9

The Plain (a photographic work in progress)

Melanie Friend

As a child, visiting my grandparents' home in rural Kent, I was intrigued by the 'gun room' just down the corridor from the living room. Sometimes my grandfather would be sitting there silently, an array of guns displayed around him on the green walls. A quiet man, he had fought in the second Boer War and the First World War. My mother remembers how, on a couple of occasions, he entertained her with animated discussions of military strategies in the First World War, pushing a silver salt cellar and pepper pot around on the white damask tablecloth to demonstrate manoeuvres. Other than that, he was silent about his experiences. He'd risen to Lieutenant Colonel and then retired at the age of forty to the tranquillity of cherry orchards and the pleasures of country pastimes such as hunting and shooting. As a teenager in rural Dorset, I grew up with a visceral dislike of the Hunt, and I became acutely aware of the strange conjunction of beauty and violence in the English countryside.

Four decades later, I have returned to the countryside to focus on Salisbury Plain, near my mother's current home in Wiltshire, an English county characterized in parts by a pervasive military presence. A complex and ambiguous space, the chalk plateau of Salisbury Plain encompasses the UK's largest military training area as well as a conservation area valued by many, including botanists and lepidopterists, sites of great importance to archaeologists and swathes of agricultural land. My interviews with local inhabitants on the whole have revealed acceptance of the military presence, despite the disruption of firing noise and inaccessibility of the large 'impact area'.[1] Military ownership of approximately half of

FIGURE 9.1 From *The Plain*, © Melanie Friend. Original in colour.

the Plain prevents housing developers or industry moving in.[2] The army's presence is expanding, as 4,000 British soldiers and their families return from Germany to relocate on Salisbury Plain. By 2020, more than 17,000 troops will be based in Wiltshire; nearly a third of the British Army will be based on or close to Salisbury Plain (BBC News 2016a).

The army promotes its role as conservator – 'greenwash' as argued by geographer Rachel Woodward, and discussed with regard to Salisbury Plain by Marianna Dudley (Dudley 2010: 135–149) – but the landscape is in parts scarred by the military presence (Figure 9.1).

It is a place of contradictions and also of great beauty. During my first forays onto the Plain, I was struck by the quality of the silence (no sound of traffic/trains), which at times was suddenly disrupted by the sounds of a live firing exercise, the pounding of shells in the distance or the roar of a (civilian) off-road motorbiker. At times I came across sinister military structures (see Figures 9.2 and 9.3) in isolated spots on the Plain where I felt too unnerved to return alone. In contrast, the 'ghost village' of Imber, in the heart of Salisbury Plain, now attracts large numbers of visitors on the few days of the year when the village is 'open' to the public.[3]

FIGURE 9.2 From *The Plain*, © Melanie Friend. Original in colour.

FIGURE 9.3 From *The Plain*, © Melanie Friend. Original in colour.

The Plain is in part a constructed landscape and over the years numerous copses have been planted by the military to provide cover for exercises, as one of the interviewees for the project, a forester, makes clear:

> They [the military] have planted hundreds of thousands of trees on the Plain since I've been involved with it as a child... So, conifer forests were pretty much emulated to try and give them a feeling of what it would be like in Germany, or you know, Poland or Austria, or wherever the front could be, if the Russian advance came that way.
>
> But now there's more diversity; it's more... towards conservation as well... Before, we were always sort of engineering the woodlands as they developed so they had areas to park their tanks.

In my forthcoming exhibition, large-scale photographic images will reflect traces and signs of the military presence on Salisbury Plain (see Figure 9.4), as well as the more obvious impact on the landscape through brand new structures or buildings repurposed for military training (as above, Figures 9.2 and 9.3).

FIGURE 9.4 From *The Plain*, © Melanie Friend. Original in colour.

An ex-army officer, now a conservationist, reflects on the building of Copehill Down, a village constructed purely for military training on Salisbury Plain:

> On the top of the downs you see a mock village, it's on the highline, and it used to be known locally as 'the German village' because that was the days of the Cold War, and it was used to train soldiers in fighting in built-up areas, FIBUA, and now of course it's been adapted [to include] a mosque, it's been adapted for Iraq and Afghanistan training and I'm sure it will remain like that while we're so preoccupied with the Middle East. But that was terribly controversial when it was first mooted, and I remember vividly in the early 1980s…going to village meetings here where everybody was absolutely up in arms that they should destroy this beautiful landscape…with this rather ugly village. That's now been forgotten, everybody now is used to it. It still rather breaks my heart quite honestly and they have planted a number of woods to screen the village from the road.

The majority of the interviewees were habituated to the sights and sounds of the army's presence on Salisbury Plain. One local inhabitant, a retired journalist, admitted that he found the sound of gunfire at night reassuring:

> And I would lie in bed at night and sometimes the activity would go on till eleven o'clock or shortly after, and I actually found it quite comforting, which seems strange I know, that the sound of large guns firing would actually lull you to sleep (laughs) but I suppose the fact that they weren't being fired at me gave me some form of comfort. But having lived here for so long, it's part of the background, it's part of the wallpaper of the place, and I miss it when it's not there.

Another inhabitant, a retired mathematician, below, was very much aware of the military's impact on her daily life:

> Sometimes when they are having big military exercises, it goes on all night and yes, it rocks the house because it is really heavy-duty shells that they are firing. Because they need to practise distance for targeting and that kind of thing…when the army aren't exercising, mainly during August, we have the planes going over, jet fighters, and they are really scary because often they come literally across the top of the barn and so the noise doesn't hit you until they have gone past you…and there have been times when you duck down because the noise gives you such a fright.
> … I work in Salisbury for one day a week and once I just hit – not literally – a whole row of tanks just crossing the road and I was thinking 'I'm going to be late, I'm going to be late', but you couldn't do anything about it. Stream after stream after stream. Yes, you're very conscious of them [the military] much of the time.

By way of contrast, it was the very presence of the army in her village which contributed to one young woman's decision to join up:

> We used to have the army driving their tanks up the high street and I can still remember the sound and the feel of it happening. And my mother used to say: 'Oh that's the army!' and then we used to hear the guns firing on the plain and the windows vibrating, the window panes vibrating in the house, and mum used to say: 'Oh, there's the army again!' and I just always used to look up to it, and think it would be something, quite an adventure to join and do something like that in my life, in terms of a vocation as well.

The Plain exhibition soundtracks will comprise ambient sounds (artillery fire, larks) and excerpts from interviews, such as the above, with a range of local inhabitants, focusing on their attachment to the landscape of Salisbury Plain and their responses to the military presence. Additional voices will include those of a local farmer, a war tax resister, a Salisbury CND member, a storyteller and a retired lieutenant colonel.

Much of my work has used alternative documentary strategies to represent conflict. One of my earliest gallery exhibitions, *Homes & Gardens: Documenting the Invisible* (1994–1996), engaged with the aftermath of hidden state violence behind closed doors and used a soundtrack of voices in conjunction with images of domestic interiors and gardens in Kosovo/a.[4] *The Plain*, looking at the deep-rooted presence of the military in the Wiltshire landscape of Salisbury Plain, relates to an earlier body of work exploring the way that militarization has become normalized and embedded into the everyday. *The Home Front* (2013) focused on the staging of war as entertainment at air shows in the UK and on how militarization is 'woven into the fabric of civic culture' (Berland and Fitzpatrick 2010: 9).[5] Through the interplay of the large-scale images of Salisbury Plain with inhabitants' interview extracts, the exhibition will aim to explore the complexity of this landscape and to question the normalization of the military's presence in the English countryside.

Notes

1. The impact area is the zone where live firing is conducted.
2. 'The Army has been connected with Salisbury Plain since 1897, and the total area of the current estate is just over 36,000 hectares. It is 25 miles by 10 miles (40 km by 16 km) and occupies about one ninth of the area of Wiltshire.' From MoD UK landholding statistics report in 2015 (Gov.uk 2015).
3. Imber's inhabitants were forced to leave during the Second World War in order that the military could use the village as a military training area; they were never allowed to return to their homes (BBC News 2016b).

4 See my website for more on *Homes and Gardens: Documenting the Invisible* https://melaniefriend.com/homes-gardens (accessed 22 August 2019).
5 See my website for more on *The Home Front*, https://melaniefriend.com/new-page (accessed 22 August 2019).

References

Berland, J., and B. Fitzpatrick (2010), 'Introduction: Cultures of Militarization and the Military Cultural Complex', *TOPIA: Canadian Journal of Cultural Studies*, 23–4: 9–27.

BBC News (2016a), 'Salisbury Plain Military Homes Plan Approved', *BBC News*, 13 April. Available online: https://www.bbc.co.uk/news/uk-england-wiltshire-36037294 (accessed 22 August 2019).

BBC News (2016b), '"Ghost Village" on Salisbury Plain Opened to Public', *BBC News*, 20 August. Available online: https://www.bbc.co.uk/news/uk-england-wiltshire-37144240 (accessed 22 August 2019).

Dudley, M. (2010), 'A Fairy (Shrimp) Tale of Military Environmentalism: The "Greening" of Salisbury Plain', in P. Coates, T. Cole, and C. Pearson (eds), *Militarized Landscapes: From Gettysburg to Salisbury Plain*, London: Continuum, pp. 135–149.

Gov.uk (2015), 'MOD Land Holdings Bulletin 2015', *Gov.UK*, 20 August. Available online: https://www.gov.uk/government/statistics/mod-land-holdings-bulletin-2015 (accessed 22 August 2019).

10

This is not a bomb: Matériel culture and the arms trade

Jill Gibbon

FIGURE 10.1 Bomb stress ball. © Ricky Adam. Reproduced with kind permission.

FIGURE 10.2 Grenade stress ball. © Ricky Adam. Reproduced with kind permission.

FIGURE 10.3 'Welcome to Hell' sweet. © Ricky Adam. Reproduced with kind permission.

FIGURE 10.4 Tank. © Ricky Adam. Reproduced with kind permission.

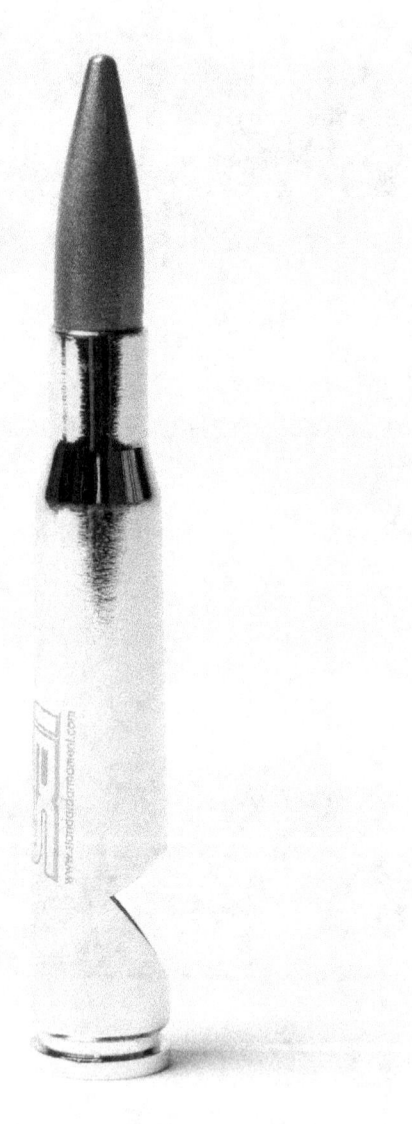

FIGURE 10.5 Ammunition shell. © Ricky Adam. Reproduced with kind permission.

FIGURE 10.6 Soldier stress ball. © Ricky Adam. Reproduced with kind permission.

FIGURE 10.7 'The ultimate protection' condom. © Ricky Adam. Reproduced with kind permission.

A general-purpose bomb sits by the reception desk leaving a slight indentation in the carpet. Next to it are three display cases, each mounted on a platform of blue light. The first has a selection of medium calibre ammunition, the shells arranged in ascending height with different coloured tips – yellow, mimosa, turquoise and indigo, with contrasting stripes. The second holds tank shells; the third, a single shining mortar. A rep notices I am looking and holds out a small bomb. He squeezes it and explains it is a stress ball (Figure 10.1).

This chapter concerns a selection of gifts that I have collected from arms fairs, trade shows for military equipment in London, Paris and

Abu Dhabi. They include stress balls in the shape of bombs, soldiers, and grenades; tanks made of foam rubber; facsimile ammunition shells; condoms; and toffees (Figures 10.1–10.7). I will suggest that the gifts reflect the way that weapons are regarded in the arms industry. The stress ball does not resemble a contemporary bomb. A black sphere with a string fuse, it evokes a cartoon idea of a bomb. It is a bomb imagined as a sign. Saussure (2013) argued that signs have shifting meanings. In an arms fair, bombs also have shifting meanings. They are presented as seductive objects, a focus for personal and state power, international cooperation, defence and jobs. In short, weapons are treated in the arms industry as commodities. It was Marx's (1867) insight that the 'use value' of a commodity is eclipsed by its 'exchange value'. A site of changing values and meanings, a commodity has a similar status to a semiotic sign. As Camus put it, 'The society of merchants can be defined as a society in which things disappear in favour of signs' (2018: 7). The stress ball is made from soft foam plastic, a material with shape-shifting properties resembling the changing meanings of weapons in the arms industry. Its function as a gift conveys the status of the bombs as commodities, objects of exchange. But of course, weapons are not simply commodities or signs. A bomb may be promoted as a focus of fantasies and desire, but when it is used, it has devastating material effects that are not open to interpretation.

The chapter explores what happens when the gifts are removed from the spaces of the arms trade and shown, instead, in spaces critical of that industry. For instance, I showed the stress balls, condom and sweet in *The Etiquette of the Arms Trade*, Bradford Peace Museum, 2018. What happens to the meanings of these objects when displayed on plinths or indeed as photographs in this book? In an arms fair, the gifts take part in a disavowal of the material properties of weapons. Is it possible to subvert this function, by using them to reveal processes of commodification in the arms industry? Or do the gifts continue to seduce viewers?

Materials are central to this discussion. The influence of militarized capitalism on materials is evident in the etymology of the word. Borrowed from the old French *matériel* and the Latin *materialis* in the early fourteenth century, 'material' was originally used as an adjective to describe the real, ordinary and earthly, and by the late fourteenth century as a noun to describe the components from which things are made. This sense developed a more specialized meaning in the early nineteenth century when 'matériel' was borrowed from the French again and used, this time with the original spelling, to describe military equipment. This new usage coincided with the emergence of industrialization and the mass production of armaments. It is as if, as the world was increasingly plundered and fought over, the etymological source word of 'material' had to be retrieved and redefined as the stuff of military campaigns. Now, in globalized capitalism, 'matériel' has been reimagined again as a commodity linked to a share price. The chapter title makes a play on these meanings, referring both to the culture of the arms industry and to the study of materials and things.

The chapter begins with a discussion of 'the material turn', a new focus on materiality in the arts and humanities, in reaction to the postmodern emphasis on signs and signification. In particular, I will use Karen Barad's (2003) performative understanding of meaning and materials to argue that the gifts enact the deceptions of the arms trade. The duplicity of the arms trade raises problems for empirical approaches, so I will then discuss methods, particularly the influence of Dada on the project. This is followed by a description of the gifts in the spaces of the arms trade and, finally, in spaces critical of war.

The material turn

It is not only in arms fairs that things are presented as signs. Academic discourse has focused on the social construction of meaning at the expense of the material properties of things since the 1980s in semiotics, postmodernism, post-structuralism. Academic work does not hover outside economics and politics but is intertwined within it. Fredric Jameson described postmodernism as the cultural logic of late capitalism and linked it to 'a whole new wave of American military and economic domination throughout the world' (1991: 5). The idea that meaning is entirely socially constructed colludes in the disavowal of materials at the heart of militarized capitalism. As Jane Bennett puts it in *Vibrant Matter* (2010): 'The image of dead or thoroughly instrumentalized matter feeds human hubris and our earth destroying fantasies of conquest and consumption' (p. ix). This is not to discount social constructivist approaches. As with most cultural developments, they can be understood as dialectical with the potential to be both radical and reactionary. The idea that meaning is socially constructed has been progressive in acknowledging marginalized voices and experiences and yet problematic in ignoring non-human material agency and in the potential for relativism where any account is given as much credence as the next.

In response, in what has become known as 'the material turn', a number of academics and artists have highlighted the agency of materials and things. An idealized realism runs through much of this work, with materials described as glowing with authenticity outside human structures of meaning. Bennett (2010) challenges 'the idea of matter as passive stuff, as raw, brute or inert' (p. vii) and emphasizes instead its 'vibrant materiality' (p. viii). As an example, she describes a set of objects – a glove, pollen, rat, bottle cap and stick that she encountered in the street and initially interpreted as debris, until they broke through her definition and 'started to shimmer and spark' (2010: 5). She explains, 'In this assemblage, objects appeared as things, that is, as vivid entities not entirely reducible to the contexts in which (human) subjects set them, never entirely exhausted by their semiotics' (2010: 5). The adjectives 'vibrant', 'vivid', 'shimmer and spark' suggest light and connotations of truth. The archaeologist Bjørnar Olsen also invests things with authenticity. Olsen argues that we need to understand 'things in "themselves"' (2010: 172). He acknowledges that things are often part of signifying systems but suggests we explore their role beyond this. He asks, 'What is their *integrity* so to speak?' And he continues, 'Things are not words, nor are they primarily signs to be read or products ready to be consumed or "sublated". Things possess their own nonverbal qualities and are involved in their own material and historical processes that cannot be disclosed unless we explore their integrity qua things' (2010: 172). But do things always have 'integrity'?

In contrast, Karen Barad argues that meaning and materials are entangled: 'The relationship between the material and the discursive is one of mutual entailment. Neither is articulated/articulable in the absence of the other; matter and meaning are mutually articulated' (2003: 822). She uses the work of the physicist Niels Bohr to argue for a performative understanding of meaning that incorporates the human and non-human, the social and scientific, materiality and discourse (2003: 808). She writes, 'Meaning is not a property of individual words or groups of words but an ongoing performance of the world in its differential intelligibility' (2003: 821). Barad challenges the Cartesian distinction between the knower and the known, but her concept of meaning is not so free-flowing as to leave out issues of responsibility. What is unusual in her account is that she maintains the idea of meaning as a performance, alongside the possibility of objectivity. She writes, 'What is important about casual intra-actions is that marks are left on bodies. Objectivity means being accountable to marks on bodies' (2003: 824). Barad is referring here to marks made as part of measurement; however, her remarks are equally applicable to the impact of weapons. If objectivity is possible in relation to 'marks on bodies', then, so too is deception. If matter and meaning are entangled in 'an ongoing performance of the world' (2003: 821), it is worth remembering that some performances are based on pretence. Borne out of the international arms trade, the gifts enact the capitalist disavowal of the material effects of weapons, of 'marks on bodies'. Objects may not be reducible to signs, but the stress-ball bomb masquerades as such. This raises a problem: how to research something that is always dissembling?

Dada as a method

This chapter is based on an art project – for the past ten years I have visited arms fairs by dressing up as a security consultant. The method is influenced by Dada, an art movement formed in 1916 in opposition to the First World War and, more particularly, the culture that validated the war. As such, Dada methods remain relevant.

In the introduction to *The Global Arms Trade: A Handbook* (2010) Andrew Tan notes a curious lack of research into the arms trade. He says that whereas there are important primary sources, there is little secondary analysis of the industry. He links this to a shift to post-positivist approaches in security studies and argues that 'a more positivist analysis' is needed to 'provide a better description of the current phenomenon that is the arms trade' (2010: 6). But perhaps the opposite is the case. Perhaps, the arms trade is under-researched because it slips out of view of academic methods, both positivist and post-positivist. The handbook contains an invaluable analysis of global trends in arms expenditure, exports and procurement, but whether this fully describes the 'current phenomenon that is the arms trade' (Tan 2010: 6) is another matter.

What many of the chapters show is the extent to which the globalized arms trade defies reason. Elisabeth Sköns (2010: 237) explains that at the end of the Cold War, it was widely expected that the American and European arms industries would shrink as part of a 'peace dividend', with military production converting to civilian uses. Instead, the arms industry went through a process of globalization with defence companies merging into multinationals, diversifying into security, and focusing on international sales including to repressive regimes and regions of conflict. The arms industry receives significant support from Western governments despite the international focus of sales, with high military spending in the United States, and subsidies and permissive export licences in the UK. Sam Perlo-Freeman (2010) suggests that this makes little economic sense.

The globalized arms industry contributes relatively little to UK jobs or the economy in comparison to the subsidies it receives. He accounts for government support in terms of the status of military production, and the influence of the 'military industrial complex' (MIC), a network of arms manufacturers, politicians and the military (Perlo-Freeman 2010: 261). This is a more globalized version of the military industrial complex than the network Eisenhower (1961) described. Since 1961 political influence has concentrated into the hands of fewer, larger arms corporations extending across national boundaries. Dunne and Sköns suggest, 'post-war restructuring may well have left an MIC that is just as pervasive and powerful, more varied, more internationally linked and less visible' (2010: 291). The 'pervasive and powerful, more varied' networks of influence Dunne and Sköns describe are sensuous rather than reasoned; they are enacted and felt as the seductions and threats of power, as bonds of loyalty, and a desire for status. They are authorized with a suit and lanyard, acknowledged with a handshake, sealed with a drink and complementary gift. These practices are aesthetic in the Greek sense of aisthesis, perceived with the senses and feeling rather than the intellect. So they remain always slightly out of sight, 'less visible' (2010: 291) to reason.

Here, Dada is useful. Dada developed a range of aesthetic methods to strip back the polite veneer of a corrupt culture. Dada was critical of the idea that art should be separate from society, concerned only with itself. As George Grosz put it, 'This art mused upon cubes and the Gothic period while military leaders painted in blood' (cited in Ades 2006: 310). In contrast, Dada used art as a critical tool. Hugo Ball, one of the founders of Dada, wrote, 'It can probably be said that for us art is not an end in itself – more pure naïveté is necessary for that – but it is an opportunity for true perception and criticism of the times we are living in' (1996: 58).

Dada was characterized by an emphasis on satire, parody and performance. Marcel Duchamp satirized rituals of art by exhibiting everyday objects or 'Readymades' on gallery plinths. The Readymade has since become an established method in art and no longer challenges gallery etiquette; however, the practice of placing an object on a plinth continues to offer a way of focusing attention on an item that might otherwise be overlooked.

Dada also satirized the dress, gestures and postures of respectable culture. George Grosz walked through Berlin dressed as Dada Death with a formal coat, cane and a skull mask; Hugo Ball recited poetry while wearing exaggerated outfits and waving flags. The emphasis on satire suggested that politics is far from logical, while the use of performance demonstrated that politics is played out through the body as much as in words. Ball wrote, 'The only thing left is the joke and the bloody pose' (1996: 66). For Ball, Dada was based on dissembling, 'The Dadaist... welcomes any kind of mask. Any game of hide-and-seek, with its inherent power to deceive' (1996: 65). The emphasis on masks and hiding in Dada highlighted the pretensions of wider society. The next section describes my attempt to reveal the deceptions of the arms industry by masquerading as an arms trader. In the final section, I return to the Readymade, using gallery plinths to draw attention to the gifts.

Meeting the military industrial complex

The military industrial complex meets regularly, if discreetly, at arms fairs, trade shows for military equipment. Emerging from the globalization of the defence industry, arms fairs provide opportunities for transnational networking. The world's largest fair, the Defence Security Exhibition International (DSEI), takes place every two years in London. It was established in 1998 and now hosts over 1,660 exhibitors from forty countries, with around 34,000 visitors (DSEI 2019). But, in spite of its scale, the event has a sense of exclusive membership. It is closed to the general public and surrounded by police and security guards. Inside, visitors share codes of dress and behaviour. I act the part by wearing a suit, formal shoes and fake pearls. I stroll up and down the aisles gazing at equipment and leaf through catalogues. The pretence is rewarded with gifts; as I walk around the stalls I am offered small sandwiches, a glass of champagne, a rubber tank (Figure 10.4). The gifts affirm my membership of the event. Lewis Hyde suggests, 'Gifts tend to be an economy of small groups, of extended families, small villages, close-knit communities, brotherhoods and, of course, of tribes' (2007: xxi). In return, I find myself nodding and smiling. Whatever misgivings lurk beneath the surface, no one shows them, including me.

Meanwhile, security cameras scan the hall for unusual behaviour. Critical reactions are shut out.[1] The reason that this is necessary is perhaps because the display of weapons in an arms fair is so strange. Separated from the defence needs of any one country, missiles, bombs and tanks are presented as products. And, as Marx (1867) explained, commodities are capricious, 'but, so soon as it steps forth as a commodity, it is changed into something transcendent. It not only stands with its feet on the ground, but, in relation to all other commodities, it stands on its head, and evolves out of its wooden brain grotesque ideas, far more wonderful than "table-turning" ever was' (Marx 1867: 47).

At DSEI weapons are presented as transcendent. Tank shells are displayed on plinths for viewing. Hand grenades are cut open and dramatically lit to show the precision of design and engineering. CS gas canisters are promoted as 'moral effect grenades'. A young woman in a short skirt leans against a tank, while businessmen take selfies alongside her. A Brimstone missile is suspended against an image of the London skyline under changing coloured lights. The promotional literature calls it 'the most accurate precision strike missile on the market. When you have to hit a target, stay within budget and don't have time to waste, Brimstone is your answer' (MBDA 2017). The Brimstone missile is currently being used by Saudi Arabia in airstrikes on Yemen, yet here, ballistics is presented as the key to efficiency in business. A wine reception is held around a case of bullets, the glasses leaving red stains on the display glass, while hostesses offer refills. On a nearby stand 'Team UK' offers advice on export licences with the slogans, 'government and industry working together' and 'international co-operation and partnerships'. Weapons are presented as facilitating success, power and collaboration.

The bomb-shaped stress ball that is not a bomb embodies these shifting meanings. Soft and pliable, it is first and foremost a gift, a token of contacts and good will. Its secondary function as a stress ball points to the challenges of business, flattering the hand that squeezes it that they are equal to the task. Other gifts suggest additional meanings. A gas mask manufacturer gives away condoms with the pun, 'the ultimate protection' (Figure 10.7). Here, military equipment is presented as a sign of patriarchal virility, reflecting the ways that weapons are sexualized in arms fairs, while punning on the claim that weapons offer 'defence'. Bofors, a subsidiary of BAE Systems, offers toffees with the slogan 'welcome to hell' as part of a promotion for a weapons-testing facility in Sweden (Figure 10.3). The typeface mimics the military stencilling traditionally used on boxes of explosives, while the caption echoes computer games where hell is a byword for entertainment. On a video screen, a military vehicle explodes alongside the slogan, 'hell for your product, heaven for your investment'. The impact of weapons outside the test site is never shown.

The Bofors slogan suggests that weapons are significant in the arms industry primarily as 'your investment'. This was evident at the 2018 AGM of BAE Systems when the chair, Roger Carr, welcomed investors with news about the share price, 'There is no doubt that 2017 was a successful year as reflected in our sales, profits and cash flow' (Carr 2018). The year was 'successful' partly due to sales to Saudi Arabia during the war in Yemen. Saudi-led airstrikes have destroyed civilian sites including infrastructure for water, health care, food and transport (Mundy 2018). Monitors allege that weapons and aircraft produced by BAE Systems have been involved in some of these attacks (Dearden 2018). But, when questioned about this, Carr explained, 'We separate ourselves from the war itself... we're not involved in any part of prosecuting, planning or executing the war.' He continued that the company provides equipment, servicing, maintenance and training but 'the use of that equipment is for others' (Dearden 2018). Here, Carr deftly separates the meaning of weapons as products, from their use and material impact on people, homes and communities.

Critical spaces

I have shown the gifts in several exhibitions critical of war: *Art the Arms Fair*, Maverick Project Space, 2019; *The Etiquette of the Arms Trade*, The Bradford Peace Museum, 2018–2019; *And This Too*, Platform Gallery, Belfast, 2017; and *Shock and Awe,* Royal West Academy, Bristol, 2014. In each case, the gifts were shown on plinths behind glass or Perspex, with a label explaining where they had come from. Clearly there are many factors influencing the meaning of the gifts in these settings, including the historical and social context of each gallery and the other work on show. However, I want to focus on the specific impact of removing the gifts from their original context in arms fairs and placing them on a plinth in a gallery or museum.

The method draws on the tradition of the Dada 'Readymade', as referred to earlier. Perhaps the most notorious example is Marcel Duchamp's *Fountain*, a urinal signed with the pseudonym R. Mutt and submitted to the Society of Independent Artists in New York in 1917. The submission was refused, lost and then reproduced as a series of replicas in the 1950s and 1960s that are now displayed on plinths in major galleries around the world. The disjuncture between the gallery setting and the apparently pedestrian object on display, along with the history of its refusal and subsequent celebration, raises questions about art, aesthetics and value. And there is something else. In addition to presenting a urinal as art, the installation shows how art works by removing an object from its usual location and interrupting its everyday function. Confronted with a urinal that can't be used, the viewer perceives the object differently, noticing a form with particular qualities, as well as being confronted by their own likely feelings of unease at its displacement.

Tyson Lewis argues that art opens up a space where objects can address us. He suggests that things 'have pedagogical power' (2018: 123) that is often overlooked in everyday life. Guided by phenomenology, he suggests that our perception of a thing is framed by our habitual uses of it. 'Normal everyday perception is structurally set up in a way to censor any attentiveness to such thing-power' (Lewis 2018: 126). But if we interrupt habitual processes of perception, we can 'become attentive to the call of things' (Lewis 2018: 127). Lewis suggests that art offers this kind of disruption. His examples are paintings; however, the simple act of placing an object on a plinth interrupts its usual function. Encountered on a pedestal, the urinal cannot be understood through habitual use. A museum setting also implies that an exhibit should be encountered in a particular way. Helen Rees Leahy (2012) describes a set of expectations that developed about visitors' behaviour in museums in the mid-nineteenth century – walking at a certain pace, viewing artefacts from a particular distance, not touching, talking in hushed tones – all of which contributes to the presentation of exhibits as objects of contemplation. Similar expectations have arisen in relation to galleries.

Since Duchamp many artists have used the physical restrictions and cultural expectations of museums to present certain objects for consideration. In *Nanoq: Flat Out and Bluesome* the artists Snæbjörnsdóttir and Wilson (2006) identified every taxidermied polar bear in the UK and then exhibited ten of the specimens at Spike Island, Bristol, each in an individual glass case. In contrast to Duchamp's *Fountain*, the exhibits were not signed. They were not presented as art objects; rather, the art space was used to turn scrutiny on the artefacts. The repetition of bears accentuated the awkwardness of their lifelessly lifelike poses, drawing attention to the disjuncture between the stuffed animals and their increasingly endangered living counterparts. Like a plinth, the glass cases prohibited any sensuous engagement with the bears except through observation.

Edwards, Gosden and Phillips are critical of the emphasis on vision in museums, linking this to 'pervasive colonial legacies' (2006: 1). Western museums have traditionally taken artefacts from their original cultures and displayed them behind glass, positioning both the artefact and its culture as exotic objects of study. This has led to the development of 'sensory museology' where sensuous engagement is encouraged in an attempt to retrieve something of an object's original function (Howes 2014: 261). In contrast, *Nanoq* retained the usual curatorial emphasis on vision, turning scrutiny on Western culture. The glass cases mirror the bears' sterile separation from each other and their natural habitat, and while this might seem to have exacerbated the Western disavowal of materiality, this is part of what was held up for consideration.

I attempt to use plinths in a similar way. The gifts have sensuous qualities redolent of their cultural function – the stress balls are pliable, inviting a squeeze; the toffees are sugary for eating; the condoms' spermicide-coated rubber facilitates sexual liaisons. Displayed on a pedestal, these qualities are out of reach. They cannot be used; they can only be observed. The method of display also parodies arms fairs, where shells, grenades and CS canisters are presented on plinths for viewing. Walter Benjamin argued that advertisements, seen slightly out of context, give a critical insight into capitalism, 'What, in the end, makes advertisements so superior to criticism? Not what the moving red neon says – but the fiery pool reflecting it in the asphalt' (2007: 86). Reflected in a puddle, a neon advertisement shows distorted flashing lights without the detail of promises. Displayed on a pedestal, the Bofors sweet offers the hell of war as a confection without the explanatory detail of the advertising campaign.

The photographs in this book also present the gifts primarily as objects to be looked at, but here there is an additional factor. A photograph can be constructed to direct the gaze in specific ways. The photograph of the bomb has been lit and framed to accentuate the rubber seam that runs around the circumference, giving away its rubber construction. The photograph of the sweet emphasizes the shiny paper, the twists at either end, the possibility of unwrapping it. Yet although this draws attention to the materiality of the objects, they remain out of reach. A photograph is smooth to the touch; the gifts can only be apprehended by vision. Michael Taussig suggests there is a tension in a photograph – it seems to be a faithful copy of its subject but it is not what is reproduced. A photograph makes an apparently exact image of something, and yet it is materially different from what is portrayed. As Taussig puts it, they are 'copies that are not copies' (1993: 115). 'Sliding between photographic fidelity and fantasy, between iconicity and arbitrariness, wholeness and fragmentation, we thus begin to sense how weird and complex the notion of the copy becomes' (1993: 17). Like Magritte's painting of a pipe that is not a pipe, the photograph of a bomb-shaped stress ball is not what it is an image of. And this perhaps points to the disjuncture between the gifts and the material properties of weapons they are modelled on and intended to promote.

Yet whether encountered on a plinth or in a photograph, the first reaction of many viewers to the stress-ball bomb is to laugh. The spherical shape, colour and fuse evoke a century of cartoon conflicts. Shape shifting with a stress ball, it also conveys the shared frustrations of work. The cultural references are so strong that for many viewers they survive the relocation in a new context. The bomb elicits a laugh even from the distance of a plinth. Objects have agency and not just through their physical impact. As Barad argues, matter and meaning are intertwined (2003: 822). Art can affect people in ways not intended by a curator. Christine Sylvester (2013) describes art in the Nazi Degenerate exhibition that attracted viewers in spite of the disapproving context, 'The audience and the thing become dynamic' (2013: 206). Benjamin Meiches argues that weapons seduce; they 'enchant, glimmer, and terrify' (2017: 15). The bomb-shaped stress ball seduces with humour rather than metal.

Conclusion

The globalized military industrial complex is largely invisible. It meets regularly in arms fairs but behind lines of police and security guards. Inside, it is hidden again in a more subtle way by a facade of respectability, with suits, handshakes and hospitality. The gifts are formed from this deceptive veneer. They beguile with humour, flatter with promises of career success and sexual conquest, and placate with sugar. They dissemble the material properties of weapons. Presented in a museum, gallery or book, the gifts can be re-appropriated to give an insight into this secretive industry. Yet they also have agency. Their sensuous qualities may be interrupted by a plinth or photograph, but they continue to perform their jokes. Whether we laugh in unease or complicity is an open question. As Freud suggested in relation to contentious jokes, 'We do not in the strict sense know what we are laughing at' (2002: 99).

Note

1 I have twice been asked to leave DSEI when security guards saw through my cover and then had to change my name and passport to get in again. A colleague was asked to leave because he took a sympathetic interest in a protest at the door.

References

Ades, D. (2006), *The Dada Reader, A Critical Anthology*, London: Tate Publishing.
Ball, H. (1996), *Flight Out of Time, A Dada Diary by Hugo Ball*, Berkeley, Los Angeles, London: University of California Press.

Barad, K. (2003), 'Posthumanist Performativity: Toward an Understanding of How Matter Comes to Matter', *Signs, Gender and Science: New Issues*, 28(3): 801–31.
Benjamin, W. (2007), *Reflections*, New York: Schocken.
Bennett, J. (2010), *Vibrant Matter, A Political Ecology of Things*, Durham and London: Duke University Press.
Camus, A. (2018), *Create Dangerously*, Milton Keynes: Penguin.
Carr, R. (2018), 'AGM 2018', *BAE Systems*. Available online: https://www.baesystems.com/en/article/sir-roger-carragm-2018 (accessed 28 December 2018).
Dearden, L. (2018), 'BAE Systems "Does Not Know" if British Weapons Used to Commit War Crimes, Chairman Admits', *The Independent*, 12 May. Available online: www.independent.co.uk/news/uk/home-news/saudi-war-crimes-yemen-british-weapons-bae-systems-know-agm-values-a8347736.html (accessed 1 December 2018).
DSEI (2019), 'Visiting'. Available online: https://www.dsei.co.uk/visiting (accessed 3 February 2019).
Dunne, J. P., and E. Sköns (2010), 'The Military Industrial Complex', in A. T. H. Tan (ed), *The Global Arms Trade Handbook*, 281–92, Abingdon, New York: Routledge.
Edwards, E., C. Gosden and R. Phillips, eds (2006), *Sensible Objects: Colonialism, Museums and Material Culture*, London: Bloomsbury.
Eisenhower, D. (1961), 'The Farewell Address'. Available online: www.eisenhower.archives.gov/research/online_documents/farewell_address.html (accessed 10 September 2018).
Freud, S. (2002), *The Joke and Its Relation to the Unconscious*, London: Penguin.
Howes, D. (2014), 'Introduction to Sensory Museology', *The Senses and Society*, 9(3): 259–67.
Hyde, L. (2007), *The Gift: Creativity and the Artist in the Modern World*, New York: Vintage.
Jameson, F. (1991), *Postmodernism, or the cultural logic of late capitalism*, London, New York: Verso.
Lewis, T. E. (2018), 'The Pedagogical Power of Things: Toward a Post-intentional Phenomenology of Unlearning', *Cultural Critique*, 98 (Winter): 122–44.
Marx, K. (1867) (translated into English 1887 Moore, S. and Aveling, E.) '*Capital, Vol 1*'. Available online: https://www.marxists.org/archive/marx/works/download/pdf/Capital-Volume-I.pdf (accessed 10 July 2018).
MBDA (2017), '*Brimstone: Air to Ground Missile*'. Available online: https://mbdainc.com/services/brimstone/2017 (accessed 8 January 2018).
Meiches, B. (2017), 'Weapons, Desire, and the Making of War', *Critical Studies on Security*, 5(1): 9–27.
Mundy, M. (2018), 'The Strategies of the Coalition in the Yemen War: Aerial Bombardment and Food War', *World Peace Foundation*, 9 October. Available online: https://sites.tufts.edu/wpf/files/2018/10/Strategies-of-Coalition-in-Yemen-War-Final-20181005-1.pdf (accessed 22 December 2018).
Olsen, B. (2010), *In Defence of Things*, Plymouth: Altamira Press.
Perlo-Freeman, S. (2010), 'The United Kingdom Arms Industry in a Globalized World', in A. T. H. Tan (ed), *The Global Arms Trade Handbook*, 250–65, Abingdon, New York: Routledge.

Rees Leahy, H. (2012), *Museum Bodies: The Politics and Practices of Visiting and Viewing*, London: Routledge.
Saussure, F. (2013), *Course in General Linguistics*, London: Bloomsbury.
Sköns, E. (2010), 'The US Defence Industry after the Cold War', in A. T. H. Tan (ed), *The Global Arms Trade Handbook*, 235–49, London: Routledge.
Snæbjörnsdóttir, B., and M. Wilson (2006), '*Nanoq: Flat Out and Bluesome*'. Available online: https://snaebjornsdottirwilson.com/category/projects/nanoq/ (accessed 14 November 2018).
Sylvester, C. (2013), 'Power, Security and Antiquities', in J. Edkins and A. Kear (eds), *International Politics and Performance*, 203–20, London: Routledge.
Tan, A. T. H. (2010), 'The Global Arms Trade', in A. T. H. Tan (ed), *The Global Arms Trade Handbook*, 3–11, London: Routledge.
Taussig, M. (1993), *Mimesis and Alterity, A Particular History of the Senses*, London: Routledge.

11

Dialogic spaces in the situation of conflict: Stepping stones and sticking points

Liudmila Voronova

Introduction

In July 2019, a Russian state-controlled TV channel *Rossiya-1* and a private Ukrainian channel *NewsOne* owned by Taras Kozak, a politician from Ukrainian party 'Opposition bloc', announced a 'Need to Talk' – a telecast 'bridge' between the two countries. In the situation of conflict and a 'war of narratives' (Khaldarova and Pantti 2016), the idea of a telecast by many was perceived as disturbing: in Ukraine, demonstrations took place at the office of *NewsOne*, and both politicians, including the President of Ukraine Volodymyr Zelensky, and NGOs condemned the initiative. The channel announced the cancellation of the telecast due to 'statements about protest actions near the channel's office, and [...] direct threats of physical violence against journalists and their relatives' (Iz-za pryamykh ugroz 2019).

The Prosecutor General's Office of Ukraine, in connection with the plans for a telecast, has registered a proceeding on the attempt to commit high treason, and both the owner of the channel and the presenter who made the announcement were called in for questioning (Ukrainskij kanal otmenil 2019). Simultaneously, Volodymyr Zelensky posted a video, in which he suggested to hold – instead of a telecast – a discussion with the President of Russia Vladimir Putin in Minsk, hosted by the President of Belarus Alexander Lukashenka, and in a 'company' of Donald Trump, Theresa May, Angela Merkel, and Emanuel Macron (Ukrainskij kanal otmenil 2019). According to Zelensky, the telecast was a PR tool to be used before the upcoming parliamentary elections and an attempt to divide the people of Ukraine (Ukrainskij kanal otmenil 2019).

Among the organizations that criticized the idea of a telecast was the National Union of Journalists of Ukraine (NUJU). Sergiy Tomilenko, its head, called on the *NewsOne* channel to comply with the Ukrainian legislation and media-regulatory norms that prohibit Russian TV channels broadcast in Ukraine. As cited by public channel *Hromadske*, he suggested that 'owners and leaders of the media should take into account that conscious collaboration with Russian state media may be a factor that will really lead to protest actions (and very probably to physical aggression)' (Natsionalna spilka zhurnalistiv zasudyla 2019).

Yet ultimately the NUJU did not deny the possibility of a dialogue with representatives of the Russian journalist community. As expressed by Lina Kuscsh, the first Secretary of the NUJU, the only possibility for such a dialogue is when it takes place between Ukrainian and *independent* Russian journalists in a *neutral* space and *mediated* by established international organizations (Chomu NSJU zasudyla 2019). The NUJU itself has recently been an object of criticism exactly for participating in a trans-border dialogue in a framework of the project Two Countries – One Profession. This project was initiated and supported by the Organization for Security and Cooperation in Europe (OSCE) in 2014-2017 as a part of an umbrella project Safety of Journalists and Reporting during Crisis. In the project, representatives of the Russian and Ukrainian professional journalist associations – the Russian Union of Journalists (RUJ) and the NUJU – met to discuss counteraction to propaganda, safety of journalists, professional standards and ethics, and sign appeals, and young journalists from the two countries worked in joint teams to produce documentaries on the 'neutral territories' of European cities. At home, their participation in the project was often met with criticism, and the purposes of the project were questioned. As such, in Ukraine a part of the media community labelled the project 'collaborationist' (see Rudenko 2016), and some politicians even named it 'anti-Ukrainian' (Rukovodstvo NSZhU praktikuet 2017). Instead of a space for trans-border dialogue the project was perceived by some as a platform for promotion of the 'Russian world' in European space (see Dunja Mijatovic kak povod 2016). In this sense, participation of the NUJU and the young journalists in the project became a sticking point in the internal struggle within the media community between supporters of Ukraine as a space for journalism on patriotic principles and those in favour of Ukraine as a space for journalism on universal principles (c.f. Budivska and Orlova 2017; Nygren et al. 2018; Orlova 2016).

The Two Countries – One Profession project was not unique with its idea of a trans-border dialogue. International organizations, such as International Federation of Journalists (IFJ), European Federation of Journalists (EFJ), Reporters without borders and Commission for counteraction to propaganda (CIS countries) have argued that propaganda of all kinds can be fought only with the help of professional journalistic standards that should remain the same even in the most difficult times of the conflict. Dialogue instead of disruption of communication has been named as a key strategy of counteracting propaganda and information war on different levels and in different types of projects. For example, on the regional level, the annual Donbas Media Forum has taken up issues of reaching to the audiences remaining in the non-government-controlled territories of Donbas (the self-proclaimed Donetsk and Luhansk 'people's republics') and re-integration of media professionals who remained in these territories. On an organizational level, public broadcaster *Hromadske* sees trans-border interactions as an inevitable part of their activities – including cooperation with the Russian independent newspaper *Novaya gazeta* (V ozhidanii 2019).

Individual journalists, too, initiate dialogue by creating specific media products, like Leonid Kanfer and Evgeny Lesnoy, who previously worked for the Russian media and after 2014 moved to Ukraine and produced documentaries problematizing the way the conflict and the war of narratives put an end to communication between the people of different regions and countries.

Inspired by the approach of this book, I see these attempts – by organizations and individuals – as interesting cases to discuss spaces and places for dialogue in the situation of conflict. My chapter poses a question whether and where in the situation of a conflict there is a space for dialogue: from a trans-border dialogue to an internal agonistic dialogue within the Ukrainian media community and from physical meetings between individuals to a dialogue at the level of the self. What is the role of journalism and journalists in the discursive construction of these dialogic spaces? In this chapter, I will focus on construction of the spaces for dialogue in – and around – the documentaries created by the mixed teams of young journalists in the informal part of the Two Countries – One Profession project, and in *Trudnosti perevoda* and *Kto nas razvel?* by their more experienced colleagues. I will highlight both the motivations behind and the challenges faced by organizations and individual journalists when initiating and participating in the trans-border dialogue in the situation of conflict. Both these documentaries and the discursive practices of their production and use become spaces for dialogue. In these spaces, dialogue is an aim, a process and a product to spread in the media spaces of Ukraine and Russia.

From spaces of war to dialogic spaces

Gould (1991; see also Adams 2017: 42) stresses the communicative and connective aspects of space and place. In this chapter, I look at how, in the situation of postmodern warfare (Hammond 2007), a space can be both connecting and disconnecting. The Ukraine conflict has been discussed as a 'war of narratives' (Khaldarova and Pantti 2016). In such a war, information is one of the main weapons (Hoskins and O'Loughlin 2010) and information management – technics of dissemination of disinformation and attempts to influence the media agenda – becomes one of the main dimensions of the conflict (Tumber and Webster 2006), blurring war and not-war (O'Loughlin 2015). In this situation, much attention of media scholars has been devoted to studying propaganda and actions in both Russia and Ukraine leading to disruption of communication and mediation (e.g. Nygren and Hök 2016; Pantti 2016; Szostek 2018). As suggested by Nygren et al (2018: 1075), research also needs to address how journalism can contribute to a dialogue and understanding as proposed, among others, by researchers wanting to promote 'peace journalism' in contrast to conventional 'war journalism'. Following this, I focus on the discursive construction of the spaces for dialogue in the situation of conflict.

Since 2014, Ukraine has moved symbolically 'closer to the EU than Russia' (Horbyk 2017: 32). Its borders with Russia and the EU changed their status and meaning after 'referendum' in Crimea and self-proclamation of the so-called 'People's republics' of Donetsk and Luhansk ('DPR/LPR').[1] In this situation, the trans-border dialogue initiatives also provide grounds for a continuation of a discussion on discursive construction of spatial relations (Jansson and Lindell 2018), as well as the relations between communication and place and space: place being a 'pause in movement' and space – the awareness of and 'the opportunity for movement or interaction' (Adams 2017: 42).

Ganesh and Zoller (2012) drawing from different traditions in dialogue inquiry identify three positions on dialogue: *dialogue as collaboration*, *dialogue as co-optation* and *dialogue as agonistic*. The first one tends to 'treat dialogue as a specialized form of communication involving consensus, collaboration, equality, and mutual trust' (Ganesh and Zoller 2012: 70). The second 'warns about the possibility that dialogue can be manipulated, co-opted, and limited by state, corporate, and other powerful agents' (Ganesh and Zoller 2012: 74). The last one – following Laclau and Mouffe (1985) – sees 'dialogue as a phenomenon closely intertwined with radical democracy that emerges out of difference, conflict, disagreement, and polyvocality' (Ganesh and Zoller 2012: 77). Mouffe (2013: 9) suggests that confrontation between different positions when 'played out under conditions regulated by a set of democratic procedures accepted by the adversaries' represents an agonistic model of democracy. A 'conflictual consensus' should be accepted (Mouffe 2013: 8).

Interestingly, a definition of *dialogic space* as it is introduced in the field of education studies seems relevant even for the study of media and conflict, and for analysis of such initiatives for trans-border dialogue as the ones this chapter focuses on. Wood and Su (2014: 364) define dialogic space as 'the site for dialogue to occur at the level of self (internal dialogue) and at the level of connected "interthinking" (Littleton and Mercer 2013) in collaboration with others'. Wegerif (2013) discusses how in education dialogue needs to be both a tool and an aim: dialogic education being education both for and through dialogue. Although Wood and Su's conceptualization of dialogic space is rather based on understanding of dialogue as collaboration, the idea that 'in the dialogic space, we are more concerned with exploring perceptions of meanings rather than proving "truths"' (Wood and Su 2014: 368) makes me assume that in the situation of conflict, dialogic space can also be constructed based on agonistic dialogue.

Truth seeking and truthfulness belong to the key issues discussed by journalist practitioners, experts and scholars in relation to professionalism and the values of objectivity (Schudson and Anderson 2009: 92). Possibility of fulfilling the ideal of objectivity and truthfulness, however, has often been questioned. Objectivity (as a normative category) is 'self-reflexively posited as an ideal never to be entirely realized in practice' (Allan 1998: 131).

A conflict can be viewed as a 'battle over truths' (Gutsche 2019: 242). Feldman (2019: 198) suggests to view war as a 'regime of truth', if the regime of truth is to be understood in Foucauldian sense, where '"truth" is linked in a circular relation with systems of power that produce and sustain it, and to effects of power which it induces and which extend it' (Foucault [1977]2005: 334). In this sense, a battle 'over' truths may be seen as nothing else than a will for 'recited truth', where social facts are produced through certain types of narratives and their repetition (Lentin and Titley 2011: 21). As Foucault ([1977] 2005: 334) explains, at any moment in a society:

There is a battle 'for truth', or at least 'around truth' – it being understood once again that by truth I do not mean 'the ensemble of truths which are to be discovered and accepted', but rather 'the ensemble of rules according to which the true and the false are separated and specific effects of power attached to the true', it being understood also that it's not a matter of a battle 'on behalf' of the truth but of a battle about the status of truth and the economic and political role it plays.

Turning to hermeneutical philosophers provides the necessary link between truth and dialogic space. For Gadamer a successful conversation is characterized by both partners coming 'under the influence of the truth of the object', which bounds these partners in a new 'communion in which we do not remain what we were' (Gadamer 1989: 379). For Habermas truth is to be searched through dialogue. A ground for the 'hermeneutic utopia of a universal and unlimited dialogue' is, according to Habermas, an agreement that unites subjects 'oriented to reaching understanding and thereby to universal validity claims, who base their interpretive accomplishments on an intersubjectively valid reference system of the worlds, let us say, on decentered understanding of the world' (Habermas 1984: 134). This suggests that, in the situation of conflict specifically, dialogic spaces allow if not for finding *the* truth, then for perceiving truth as historically and culturally constructed, understanding its situatedness and complexity, and recognizing a war of narratives as not only a 'battle over truths', but a regime of (a) truth from a critical standpoint. Dialogic space, thus, becomes a condition for deconstructing the narratives of war and for achieving a more balanced and critical reporting. In the context of war of narratives, or war between different regimes of truths, dialogic space opens up for a *'regime of truth seeking'*.[2]

For sure, dialogue and dialogic spaces – especially in the situation of conflict – should be looked at from a critical standpoint. As Ganesh and Zoller (2012) point out, the issue of power and hierarchical relations in the dialogue must be taken into account. Stokke and Lybäck (2018: 74), moreover, suggest that the concept of negotiations – rather than dialogue – 'more explicitly acknowledges asymmetric power relations, as between majority and minority'. The questions of who initiates the dialogue, who participates in it, and even in which language it is held are all of a crucial importance for the dialogue to take place – or not and to be accepted (and potentially continued) by other actors.

Some words on methodology

In the framework of a collaborative research project 'Propaganda and management of information in the Ukraine-Russia conflict: From nation branding to information war',[3] I conducted interviews and focus groups with representatives of the Ukrainian media community: journalists, heads and employees of professional journalist associations and NGOs working with media policies. Through my acquaintances, I learned about the Two Countries – One Profession project, and its idea of a trans-border dialogue as an antidote to propaganda seemed more than relevant to study. The materials for analysis of the project included observations of meetings between the RUJ and the NUJU at the OSCE Ministerial Council 2016 in Hamburg and the conference Media Freedom in Volatile Environments organized by the OSCE in Vienna (June 2017); two focus groups with the young journalists involved in the project conducted at these occasions (with six and seven participants respectively); four interviews and informal communication with representatives of the Office of the OSCE Representative on Freedom of the Media, the RUJ and the NUJU conducted in Hamburg, Vienna, and Kyiv, and additionally eleven interviews with representatives of other professional media associations and organizations in Ukraine conducted in

Kyiv. I also used brochures and online materials produced by the Office of the OSCE Representative on Freedom of the Media, documentary films produced by the teams of young Ukrainian and Russian journalists (particularly, *Guards of Freedom* (2016), *Nashmarkt* (2016), *Believe* (2017)) and their trailers, and negative and positive reactions to the project by the Ukrainian media community in the media. The good relations established with the participants of the project during the fieldwork could potentially influence my analysis. However, by obtaining information from the critics of the project through interviews and publicly available materials, as well as getting acquainted with a variety of discourses produced within the Ukrainian media community, I have hopefully achieved a proper distance from the project and its participants.

Searching for other trans-border dialogue initiatives, I found the documentaries by Leonid Kanfer and Evgeny Lesnoy and interviewed the two journalists in Kyiv in April 2017. All interviews and focus groups were semi-structured, and all of them were conducted in the Russian language and recorded – for which the informants gave their consent. The citations I use in this text – both from the interviews and from the media, except for materials originally in English – were translated by me. I chose to anonymize the young journalists who participated in the focus groups, while I provide names of all other informants I am citing. Thematic analysis was applied in order to analyse the materials, and I was focusing primarily on how the informants speak about places and spaces for dialogue, as well as motivations and challenges behind their decision to initiate and participate in trans-border dialogues.

Two Countries – One Profession: Dialogic space for professional journalists

The Two Countries – One Profession project (Two Countries – One Profession 2019) was based on the discussions between professional journalist associations in Ukraine and Russia and collaborative production of documentaries by young Ukrainian and Russian journalists. As expressed by Nadezda Azhgikhina, one of the participants, vice-president of the European Federation of Journalists in 2013–2019, and, in the beginning of the project, still one of the Secretaries of the Russian Union of Journalists, the dialogue between the professional associations of the two countries could be seen as an instrument for overcoming manipulations in the situation where the journalists are turned into state tools of informational confrontation (Azhgikhina 2016). The core ideas of this dialogue, as it was presented in a brochure about the project were 'a shared understanding of the rights of journalists and their responsibilities, commitment to professional values and a readiness to address ethical dilemmas encountered by the media in Russia and Ukraine in the current climate of conflict' (Two Countries – One Profession 2016: 4).

In the project's formal part, senior representatives of the National Union of Journalists of Ukraine (NUJU) and the Russian Union of Journalists (RUJ), the biggest in the countries' professional journalism associations, met to discuss ways to improve professional standards and safety of journalists. The meetings took place on a 'neutral territory', primarily, in Vienna, where the office of the OSCE Representative on Freedom of the Media is located.

The formats of the meetings varied: these were closed and public roundtables, press conferences and informal – behind-the-stage – communication. The format of the meeting defined how many representatives of the two associations were attending. The formal appeals, statements and action plans, in the first hand, were signed by the heads of the two associations.

In the beginning, apart from NUJU, there was one more Ukrainian professional association taking part in the project: the Independent Media Trade Union of Ukraine (IMTUU) that later left the project. As Ihor Chayka, the head of the IMTUU in 2016–2019, explained to me in an interview, there were several reasons for this decision. First, the IMTUU perceived as problematic the plan of the OSCE to send a monitoring commission to Crimea to observe the situation of media freedom and safety of journalists. The IMTUU did not accept inclusion of the Crimean Union of Journalists to the Russian Union of Journalists and were afraid that the commission would be deliberately misled by some kind of 'Potemkin village' picture in Crimea. Second, according to Chayka, the participants in the project from the Russian side were not 'real journalists', but 'propagandists loyal to Kremlin'. Finally, as expressed by Chayka, the NUJU expressed the opinion on behalf of the large part of the Ukrainian media community, while '90% of the members do not know what is going on under the aegis of the NUJU' (interview with Chayka, Kyiv, April 2017).

While the formal part of the project served primarily as a space for dialogue between institutions, the project also became a platform for dialogue on an individual level. The unions of journalists and their regional offices in the two countries spread the calls to the young journalists to participate in collaborative production of documentary films under guidance of Sergiy Tomilenko, the head of the NUJU, and Ashot Dzhazoyan, Secretary of the RUJ. The key idea of this part was that the young journalists from Ukraine and Russia should work together in mixed teams. It was decided that the young journalists would shoot documentaries on a 'neutral territory' as well: in Vienna and Sarajevo.

The filming groups of the young journalists came from a range of Ukrainian and Russian regions, not only Kyiv and Moscow. This, as expressed by the teams' participants, allowed them to also get to know colleagues from other regions in their own countries. Five documentary projects became a result of this work. Each film was produced by a different team of journalists, while leaders of the team remained the same. In the focus groups, there were representatives of different film production teams, as not all of them participated in the events in Hamburg and Vienna where the focus groups took place.

The documentaries they produced were on different topics, but what united them was that each was produced in and was about a place where different spaces come together and form some kind of dialogic space, *a space in-between*. For example, *Guards of Freedom* is about the office of the Representative for Freedom of the Media at the OSCE, an institutional space uniting people from different cultures, where a universal idea and ideal of freedom of the press becomes the common ground. *Naschmarkt* is about people from the post-Soviet space working at the market in Vienna famous for its multicultural character. *Believe* is about post-conflict life in Bosnia and Herzegovina. In this space, people of different ethnic groups and religions, yet with similar traumatic experiences of war, are searching for ways to live together, overcome stereotypes and build a common identity. There were also parallel projects that some of the young participants initiated. For example, in one of the teams, there were two photojournalists – one from Ukraine and one from Russia – who together made a photo project about refugees in Austria.

According to one of the leaders of this part of the project, Ashot Dzhazoyan, these films became media products that can be consumed in both the Ukrainian and the Russian media spaces. These spaces had been mutually penetrating until 2014 when the situation changed. According to Szostek (2018: 4), the presumed influence of the Russian state-controlled media in Ukraine and 'a conviction that narratives in the Russian media pose an existential threat to their country' have led to both state-led and journalist-led corrective actions in Ukraine. These actions include restrictive policies (such as a ban for broadcasting of Russian Federation channels on the territory of Ukraine and a limited or restricted access to certain media products coming from Russia) and patriotic-partisan approach to reporting (that is aimed at supporting the interests of the state as a priority, even if it hinders following international professional standards) (Szostek 2018). In 2017, only 7.9 per cent of Ukrainians used Russia-based TV channels for information (Survey of Russian Propaganda Influence 2017). However, the social media platforms *Vkontakte* and *Odnoklassniki*, email platform *Mail.ru*, and search engine *Yandex*, despite being forbidden on the territory of Ukraine like the TV channels broadcasting from Russia, remained relatively popular (Vkontakte snova pokinula top-10 2017).

As expressed by Dzhazoyan, the project with the young journalists served an aim to create 'a new language of professional collaboration and friendship' and overcome a certain 'declarativity' of the OSCE project:

You know, the young people are maximalists, they do not bear a heavy load of accusations of each other. And most importantly: they are very self-aware, they know that they create a genius story. [...] So this is an attempt to create a new thought, idea in the media space that says: one can *together* create, *together* live and *together* find stories [...] It is important for us that these journalists, in the beginning of their professional career, would meet each other and work with each other. They will never have any hatred to each other. They will not be able to lie to each other, because they participated in creation of a common product.

(Interview with Dzhazoyan, Hamburg, December 2016)

Dzhazoyan said that it was not easy in the beginning to coordinate the project, when in a time frame of two to three days one is supposed to shoot a documentary in a team of people who do not know each other. The solution was to first create spaces on the internet, where they could e-meet in advance, start communicating and decide on the idea, topic and scenario of the film. Later they met physically and started working.

The participants of the project said that before meeting each other they had had prejudice about situations in each other's countries. One of the young participants confessed that he had been expecting 'maybe even some kind of confrontation, but it was not there. I had a feeling that the young journalists are thinking not in the way that is imposed by the media' (focus group, Hamburg, December 2016). Another one mentioned that in the beginning she had been sceptical and thought that with the very different opinions the participants would never be able to work together. Yet in the very first days of collaborative work, she realized that 'we have one aim – to stop information war. So why should we be against each other?' (focus group, Vienna, June 2017).

Interestingly, this willingness to be together was expressed even on a physical level. As told by one of the young journalists, when their group met for the first time in the premises of the OSCE, they chose to sit in front of each other: Ukrainian team vis-à-vis Russian. Yet already the second time they met, they all sat on the same coach: 'They actually tried to make us sit apart, but we refused' (focus group, Vienna, June 2017). Dzhazoyan found this to be one of the most amusing moments that introduced a much-needed informality into the otherwise formal project:

When we were coming for the discussions as delegations [from the RUJ and the NUJU], we would always decorously sit on two different sides. When we gathered these young people, they sat in a jumble. They didn't even realize who is where. This tells that for them it is not the politics that matters, but relationship with each other. This is what matters. They do not have a political bias.

(Interview with Dzhazoyan, Hamburg, December 2016)

Yet the absence of political bias that Dzhazoyan suggested did not mean that the young participants tried to avoid any political discussions. As one of the participants told, 'We talked about politics and had discussions. We said: "This and this happened, and our media portrayed it this way, your media – another way". We tried to find something in between, some kind of truth' (focus group, Hamburg, December 2016). They actively discussed propaganda and its channels. The dialogic space, thus, also turned into a space where the young journalists could critically discuss the narratives produced in their relative contexts and question them, thus, as formulated by Wood and Su (2014: 368), learning to explore 'perceptions of meanings rather than proving "truths"'.

Both the participants and the project leaders highlighted that this part of the OSCE project for them was a way both to advance their professional skills, work in new conditions and with new people, and to develop personally. Leaving the known space for the unknown, according to the participants, opened up new possibilities for learning and entering a dialogue with oneself. As expressed by one of the participants of the *Believe* documentary team:

> I found it interesting that we touched upon all aspects of such a problem as a long conflict. [...] There were journalists [whom we interviewed for the film] who worked in the times of the [Yugoslav] war[s]. They told us a lot about their professional activities, about their problems and how they tried to solve them. This I found to be the most practical part – thanks to this I drew some conclusions and, perhaps, will not make mistakes. Actually in Ukraine journalism today is also functioning in the situation of conflict, and it is always better to learn on the basis on someone else's mistakes.
>
> (Focus group, Vienna, June 2017)

As participants enthusiastically told me in the focus groups, they actively continue to communicate with each other in the space of social media – both on professional and personal level, and they wholeheartedly believe in the power of such projects:

> In any case, we communicate with each other and tell about our dialogue. We write articles about it. My colleagues ask me how the colleagues from Russia are, and I tell them that not everything is lost. Of course, there is information war and propaganda. But we managed – particularly in this project, we managed. This little example shows that collaboration is possible.
>
> (Focus group, Vienna, June 2017)

Although primarily taking place online, communication after completing the work on the films sometimes happened in a physical space too. As one of the young journalists from Ukraine said, she participated in her Russian colleague's trans-border book exchange that even drew the attention of the media:

> We were posting books to each other, and there was even a story [about it] on our local TV-channel. The journalist who filmed this story, took an interview, [and also] posted a book to [the name of this Russian colleague].
> (Focus group, Hamburg, December 2016)

Dunja Mijatovic, at that time the OSCE Representative on Freedom of the Media, expressed in her speech at the OSCE Ministerial Council 2016 in Hamburg that the young journalists from the two countries participating in the project 'are the future. Not only for these two countries, but for all of us in the OSCE family' (Mijatovic 2016). In this sense, the participation of the young journalists in this collaborative project was not only about creation of a space for dialogue, but also about including these young journalists, on the one hand, into the institutional space of the European organizations, and, on the other hand, the European space overall. The young journalists, as they told in the focus groups, continued to communicate not only between each other, but also with the heroes and heroines of their documentaries residing in Europe, for whom the participation in the film shootings also became meaningful:

> The heroes of the film [*Nashmarkt*, about the multicultural market in Vienna] we were shooting were delighted. They wrote comments to us, they said it was cool. I congratulated one of the heroes of the film, who was selling fruits, on his birthday. And he called me back, asked about how I was doing, invited me to visit. They are waiting for us there.
> (Focus group, Hamburg, December 2016)

The places where the films were shot and where the OSCE events, to which the young journalists were invited, happened were very important not only in terms of what they signified (spaces in-between, spaces for dialogue), but also in terms of conditions or symbolical 'communicative affordances' that they provided the young journalists with. The places – Vienna, Sarajevo, Hamburg – turned into uniting spaces, with their museums, cafes and nets of streets. As expressed by one of the teams' members:

> It could also be added that we do not only work together, but also spend time beyond the conference. What united us were the visits to museums, that we ate and drank coffee [together]. Got lost and found [our way]. As a result our team is very close-knit. It's a pity to think that already in a couple of days the fairy-tale created by the OSCE will finish.
> (Focus group, Vienna, June 2017)

The 'fairy-tale' character of these meetings that this participant, perhaps unconsciously, noted and articulated points as well to the ambivalence of the media communities' perception of the possibility of trans-border dialogue in the situation of conflict. This ambivalence can be explained by the different roles that journalists ascribe to themselves (e.g. activist-observer, 'patriotic' journalism – journalism based on universal standards) in the current situation and leads to growing splits in the community (Budivska and Orlova 2017; Nygren et al. 2018; Orlova 2016). The seemingly impossible collaboration between journalists of the two countries happened in these neutral places and continues, at least for some, in the space of the social media. The end of the 'fairy-tale' might also refer to the different challenges of the reality that the young journalists faced as soon as they came back to the routine. At home, there were many critical voices that questioned whether the 'fairy-tale' dialogic spaces like the one produced by the OSCE has a right to exist in the situation of conflict. As it was formulated by one of the participants of the project at a press conference in Vienna,

> We started to face negative reactions in Ukraine, like that we are traitors. We wrote in the press-release that this is a dialogue. Probably people thought that we are here solving some political questions. But we are not politicians, we are journalists [...] We would love to change the political situation, but we are just 20 years old, and we do what we can do. Still, we are not out of the political. The OSCE has created all conditions for us to understand that we can work together.
> (Press conference, OSCE conference Media Freedom in Volatile Environments, Vienna, June 2017)

The head of the NUJU Sergiy Tomilenko made both public statements and told me in the interviews I conducted with him that the Two Countries – One Profession model provided the media community with a possibility to inform the international community about the situation in Ukraine and, thus, help Ukrainian journalists who face challenges, primarily, freeing journalists from captivity and helping internally displaced journalists from Crimea and the so-called DPR/LPR. In this sense, he saw it as a space for dialogue not only with the professional journalist community in Russia, but also with the colleagues and international organizations around the world:

> It is a platform for statements and demonstration of adherence to standards, counteraction to propaganda. [...] There are colleagues who oppose the dialogue, believe that it serves the interests of the Kremlin. They believe that we should not enter into a dialogue while the conflict is going on. We advise them to read attentively the statements we are making. We are committed to professional standards. And if colleagues believe that during the times of conflict we must depart from the standards, then

we think that this path is dangerous, it can lead to biased journalism. We cannot say anything definite about the future of the dialogue. A key argument is assistance in the release of journalists from captivity.
(Interview with Tomilenko, Hamburg, December 2016)

These challenges of being criticized in own media communities were acknowledged by the Office of the OSCE Representative on Freedom of the Media. As expressed by its senior adviser and professor in media law Andrei Richter, this was not unusual or surprising, as 'any public activities, especially in the situation of conflict, as Ukraine is living through now, get criticized' (interview with Richter, Hamburg, December 2016). He suggested that it was important to make this dialogue public as one of the strategies of implementation of what was discussed in its framework:

We should just continue doing our job and believe in our ideals. Reader, viewer, citizen can always himself understand whether someone is an 'agent' due to the fact that he is cooperating and discussing with journalists from another country.
(ibid.)

Despite the hope of the project's initiators and participants that the project – as expressed by Richter – would not have any borders, and that the dialogue between the representatives of professional journalist communities would continue, no matter on which platform, the project's activities ended in 2018. Until this happened, Two Countries – One Profession encountered a lot of criticism. In Ukraine, it was labelled 'collaborationist' (see Rudenko 2016) and 'contributing to the spread of Russian propaganda' (see Lubchak 2016). Its critics even united under the initiative of the 'Ukrainian journalism platform' that turned into 'the discussion space of independent professional communication on patriotic principles' (see Lubchak 2016). The trans-border dialogue of the Two Countries – One Profession, thus, became a trigger for the ongoing discussion of what the journalistic profession in Ukraine should be like (c.f. Budivska and Orlova 2017; Nygren et al. 2018; Orlova 2016).

Trudnosti perevoda (2016) and *Kto nas razvel?* (2015): Dialogic space by and for individuals

Unlike a space for dialogue between, in the first hand, institutions, documentaries *Trudnosti perevoda* (2016) and *Kto nas razvel?* (2015) were initiated by individual journalists and problematized communication between individuals. *Kto nas razvel? (Who deceived us?/Who turned us apart?* 2015) by Evgeny Lesnoy narrated several personal stories of relatives, friends and former colleagues who happened to be on different sides of the border and of the 'war of narratives'. Through interviews with 'heroes' in Ukraine and Russia the director not only showed the personal drama of the disconnected families and friends but also attempted to establish dialogue between them as representatives of two countries and ideologies. His own family story – with relatives moving in-between Ukraine and Russia – and ideological differences with his cousin residing in Lviv became a starting point and a red thread in the documentary. For all of the heroes of the Lesnoy's project – friends, brothers, sisters, nephews and aunts – the conflict became a reason for disruption of communication.

For example, Lesnoy interviewed two sisters – one in Ivano-Frankivsk in Ukraine, the other in Russian Voronezh – who stopped talking due to their disagreement on which country Crimea belongs to. Lesnoy showed how every time the sisters touched upon politics in their discussion, the dialogue came to an end, and how the narratives of war in the media damaged their personal relations. The director recorded 'video letters' and travelled with them from one heroine to another in order to become a 'bridge', a mediator connecting them, trying to make them hear and trust each other. Unlike all other characters in the documentary, as viewers learned at the end of the film, thanks to this effort, the sisters continued to communicate and even met physically: one sister crossed the border to celebrate the other's birthday.

It was Lesnoy's own initiative to produce the film, and it was primarily financed by his friends and one anonymous businessman (Katz 2015). A part of the documentary was shot by Lesnoy himself, and for some parts of it he hired cameramen – who were also 'mediators' of the trans-border dialogues. Some cameramen participated for free. As Lesnoy told me in the interview, he had not thought who his audience would be when creating the documentary. He had not hoped that it could be shown on any of the national channels in Russia, where he resided at the time. Yet, in Russia, it was shown on an independent TV channel *Dozhd*. In Ukraine, *UA:Pershyi* (at that moment *Pershiy Natsionalniy*), *5 Kanal* and *Espreso* broadcast the documentary.

Lesnoy believed that the documentary could be considered a 'textbook' that would be shown to students in twenty years as an illustration of the history of this conflict, as it 'vividly demonstrates the reactions'. As for the reactions to the film today, he told me that in Russia the film was considered pro-Ukrainian, although he claimed that he tried to show the situation from different points of view. Yet he himself confessed in the interview that producing the documentary he 'forgot that journalism is not a mission. I wanted to reconcile the people'. He said that on some occasions after the film was finished he was labelled 'traitor' in Russia. In Ukraine, most of the audiences reacted 'warmly, understanding its value and importance'. Yet on Facebook he encountered incriminations of being an 'agent of Kremlin'.

Trudnosti perevoda/Trudnoschi pereklada (*Lost in translation* 2016) was produced by Leonid Kanfer for the Ukrainian national channel *STB*. The project narrated a story of Vladimir Vinogradov, the main hero of several earlier documentary projects by Kanfer, who was invited by the director to visit Ukraine and debunk the myths about the country that Vinogradov had potentially been influenced by as he watched the Russian state-controlled TV channels. The documentary consisted of ten short episodes (approximately 10–12 minutes each) that were consequently shown in the news programme 'Vikna-novyny'. Each episode discussed one of the assumed myths of Russian TV about Ukraine (e.g. 'Ukrainian nationalism') by showing how Vinogradov travelled across Ukraine and back to Russia. Sympathetic and never at a loss of words, Vinogradov entered dialogues with different people in several Ukrainian cities and regions – dwellers of Odesa and Kyiv, those internally displaced from Crimea and the so-called DPR/LPR now residing in Lviv, parents of a young man killed during Euromaidan demonstrations, and journalists and officials. Kanfer commented on Vinogradov's reactions, trying to explain why certain things Vinogradov encountered felt provoking for him and not 'in his system of coordinates', reflecting on Vinogradov's inner dialogue. In each of the episodes, Kanfer also showed Vinogradov's reunion with the family and friends at a dinner where he was telling about Ukraine he had witnessed, without finding much trust and understanding in his nearest circle.

Unlike Lesnoy, Kanfer had not planned to 'reconcile anyone' (Andrejtsiv 2016). In an interview to *Detector Media*, he said that his aim was to give the viewers 'food for thought'; it was an attempt to reflect upon 'a huge disconnection at a human level. Many families broke off relationships; many do not understand: why? Why did (we) live together for 30–40 years, and then – suddenly – everything broke off? There is no answer to the question why this happened' (Andrejtsiv 2016).

In an interview with me, Kanfer spoke about how journalism and projects like *Trudnosti perevoda* differ from propaganda: unlike 'propaganda (that) suggests ready answers, journalism asks questions'. He believes that 'journalism cannot have any other mission except for a general humanitarian one'. Kanfer said that his primary aim was to show Ukraine through a Russian's eyes in the period of a sharp political conflict.

> I wanted to bring in a critically thinking person, but (one) influenced by propaganda clichés, and see whether he can change his opinion about certain things. We showed him the side about which he had not known, so that things balance in his head. An intrigue was: whether he will be able to change his opinion.
>
> (Interview with Kanfer, Kyiv, April 2017)

In a way, by doing this, Kanfer made an experiment, placing his hero in a different space, on a different side of the 'war of narratives' in order to see whether seeing and, especially, entering a dialogue with the people he meets on his way can be a tool for debunking myths by posing new questions to the narratives of conflict.

Kanfer said that he believed that the project would be interesting for Russian audiences. However, no channels in Russia broadcast it. Yet as it was accessible on the internet, he received reactions from both Russian and Ukrainian viewers. According to Kanfer, there came many negative reactions from the Russian side that, he believed, could have to do with the audiences' expectations: Vinogradov – based on his earlier appearance in Kanfer's documentaries and other media – has his 'fandom club' and a reputation of a 'joker'; yet this project was completely serious, and Vinogradov appeared in a new, unexpected role. In Ukraine, Kanfer said, he received a lot of positive feedback and acknowledgements; however, there were also 'far-right comments', he said.

Unlike the documentaries in the Two Countries – One Profession project, Kanfer and Lesnoy's documentaries were not shot on neutral territories. On the contrary, they attempted to establish and encourage dialogues in both the media spaces and the physical spaces of the two countries. Kanfer in *Trudnosti perevoda* did so by placing his hero Vladimir Vinogradov, 'an ordinary Russian man', into the territory of Ukraine. Lesnoy in *Kto nas razvel?* did so by initiating and negotiating the mediated contact between friends and members of the families who reside on different sides of the border. The viewers in both countries too were invited to participate in the dialogues, getting involved directly by leaving comments on YouTube where the documentaries are available and engaging in discussions. Moreover, Kanfer said that many of the Ukrainian viewers wanted to show his project to their relatives in Russia, with whom they stopped communicating: 'perhaps, someone would see it and evaluate [the situation] differently'. Thus, the documentary became for the viewers a tool for potentially re-establishing a dialogue.

Language of the dialogic spaces

The language of the trans-border dialogues that I focused on in this chapter was primarily Russian. One of the focus group participants – a young journalist from Ukraine who participated in the Two Countries – One Profession project – said that

> it would be much more fair and right if we all would speak English. We were amazed that in Vienna everyone speaks both German and English.

In Ukraine, we primarily know Ukrainian and Russian, sometimes English. One more advantage of this trip is that we saw how important the foreign languages are. A wrong or imprecise translation of even one word has a significance. In the end, we chose the Russian language.

(Focus group, Vienna, June 2017)

The documentaries the young journalists produced were also mainly in Russian (with some interviews in Ukrainian), with English subtitles. This created a challenge for some of the participants of the Ukrainian team. As one of the young journalists highlighted, 'It was very difficult to speak Russian. I think in Ukrainian and in parallel translate into Russian. I was very afraid that I can forget some words and phrases' (focus group, Vienna, June 2017).

The documentaries by Kanfer and Lesnoy were also in Russian – both due to the fact that the journalists moved to Ukraine from Russia recently and also considering the audiences and the accessibility of the media products in the media spaces of Russia and Ukraine. In Russia less than 1 per cent of the population possesses Ukrainian language skills (Federal State Statistics Service 2010). In Ukraine, as participants of the Two Countries – One Profession project suggested, 'almost everyone understands Russian'. A sociological survey conducted in 2015 showed that 60 per cent of Ukrainian citizens residing in the controlled areas consider Ukrainian as their mother tongue, 15 per cent – Russian, 22 per cent – both Ukrainian and Russian, and 2 per cent – other languages (Plokhotnyuk 2016). At the same time, news is primarily consumed in Russian (V ukrainskikh media 2016), although recently language quotas were introduced in the broadcast sector in order to popularize Ukrainian language media consumption (Richter 2018; Szostek 2018).

In one of the episodes of his project, Kanfer provoked his hero Vinogradov by organizing a full-day guided tour of Lviv in the Ukrainian language, although Vinogradov stated that he did not understand what he was being told and felt that the guide was making fun of him. Moreover, as Kanfer revealed in the same episode, when filming in the Ivano-Frankivsk region, someone approached Vinogradov claiming that the latter only would be able to speak Russian if they allow it, after which Vinogradov said that he wanted to go back home. In this sense, Kanfer's project critically approaches the issue of language and demonstrates that the language of the dialogic spaces cannot be taken for granted, which can be read already in its multivocal title, *Lost in Translation*. Similarly, Lesnoy reflects upon the language in the episode of his documentary when he meets one of his heroines who resides in Russia but speaks *surzhyk* – a mixed sociolect of Ukrainian and Russian languages.

It is important that in the process of the discursive construction of the dialogic space, the question of the language of dialogue is discussed and critically reflected upon by its participants and that there is an agreement between the participants upon whether the dialogue is understood as a final aim or a tool. If the idea of dialogic spaces can be applied in the studies of media and conflict, dialogue is established in order to be continued. In the case of the Two Countries – One Profession and Kanfer and Lesnoy's projects, it was important for the initiators and the participants of the trans-border dialogue initiatives that not only the direct participants of the dialogue understand each other, but the dialogue reaches out to broader audiences – potential participants in the dialogue – in both countries.

Discussion: Spaces for dialogue – outside and within?

Spaces connect people. They are a possibility for interaction (Adams 2017). However, spaces of war and conflict also disconnect them and disrupt dialogues on all levels. This chapter has shown how different actors within the Ukrainian media community participate in, construct and perceive dialogic spaces in the situation of conflict. In the case of Two Countries – One Profession, the OSCE has initiated the dialogue both physically – by inviting the participants to the neutral territory of European cities, and symbolically – by encouraging the organizations and journalists to continue to talk with each other after the physical meetings were over. In the case of documentaries by Kanfer and Lesnoy, television and, even more so, the internet provided a space for such an initiative and a potential affordance for continuation of dialogue between both the heroes of the films and the viewers of the documentaries.

Most importantly, a dialogic space needs to be distinguished from a 'monologic' space. A 'war of narratives' can be imagined as a struggle over space where *one* narrative will dominate. In this sense, it is interesting to go back to the 'Need to Talk' that I started this chapter with. The Russian state-controlled channel *Rossiya-1*, in the end, broadcast the programme – without the Ukrainian *NewsOne* channel as a conversation partner – from its studio in Moscow to which they invited one guest from Kyiv and had several interlocutors from Ukraine on Skype, the rest of the studio guests representing Russia ('Nado pogovorit' pochaly pokazuvaty 2019). As was immediately noted by some commentators on YouTube, instead of a dialogue the 'telecast' – presented as a 'project of Russia and Ukraine' – took the form of a monologue. Among the comments by the viewers of the programme on the official YouTube channel of *Rossiya-1*, one could read: 'I have been watching the program for 40 minutes already – there is no dialogue...Who are you talking to?', 'They talk to themselves. What a shame!', 'A bridge with one bank. Pity' (Nado pogovorit. Proekt

Rossii i Ukrainy 2019). These comments can be read as a criticism of the impossibility of a dialogue caused by the policies in Ukraine. However, such comments were primarily criticism of the initially manipulated character of what was presented as a 'dialogic space'.

In the situation of conflict, constructing dialogic spaces, instead of a monologic space of the war of narratives, is challenging but not impossible. The cases I focused on in this chapter show this. The chapter has also shown how dialogic spaces are created on different levels. For *trans-border dialogue* – the most abstract level – there are certain conditions, on which the dialogic space is based, for it to take place and be accepted – common values and ideals, 'neutral territory' where physical meetings take place, and an established mediator as in the case of the Two Countries – One Profession initiated by the OSCE; and willingness to listen to each other rather than trust the propaganda messages and think critically – as in the documentaries by Kanfer and Lesnoy. The trans-border dialogues I discussed had different missions: to reconcile particular individuals – as in Lesnoy's documentary, to pose questions and initiate a dialogue on the level of self – as in Kanfer's project or to counteract propaganda and diminish risks and threats for journalists in the situation of conflict – as in the Two Countries – One Profession project. What unites them is the way they attempt to pose questions rather than provide ready answers. Unlike the disinformation and propaganda techniques that blur war and not-war (O'Loughlin 2015), these projects attempted to deconstruct the 'war of narratives' in order to construct dialogic spaces. As expressed by Wood and Su (2014: 368), they are about 'exploring perceptions of meanings rather than proving "truths"'. It is also important that these dialogic spaces were not detached or 'freed from politics' (as it was suggested by the organizers of the 'Need to Talk' 'telecast' – Nado pogovorit. Proekt Rossii i Ukrainy 2019).

These trans-border dialogues were sometimes criticized at the level of the *national media communities* for being co-opted. The mediator – be it an international organization or individual journalists – became the main object of criticism. In the case of the Two Countries – One Profession project, the OSCE was criticized by some representatives of the Ukrainian media community for imposing dialogue and certain values that are – assumingly – not working in the situation of conflict. The most radical critics of the documentaries by Kanfer and Lesnoy saw the directors of the documentary projects as biased and promoting an antagonistic ideology, no matter which side of the border the critic was located on.

The reactions of the media community in Ukraine to the trans-border dialogue initiatives of Two Countries – One Profession, and Kanfer and Lesnoy's documentaries, make me think about how these dialogues move from transnational to national levels, from 'neutral spaces' of the European cities and shared spaces on the internet to the meetings with the members of one's own media community. This movement transforms trans-border dialogues from 'bridges' ideally transgressing the conflictual narratives into a 'trigger' for already existing debates within the media community. There are a lot of issues raising disagreement, for example, concerning the methods of counteracting propaganda (restrictions vs standards), journalistic roles (observers vs activists) and the possibilities of cross-cultural dialogue with Russian journalists (Budivska and Orlova 2017; Nygren et al. 2018; Orlova 2016). I suggest that the critical debates around trans-border projects can be understood as an agonistic dialogic space within the media community. As suggested by Mouffe (2013: 7), the agonistic struggle 'is the very condition of a vibrant democracy'. Thus, these debates can be understood as a possibility for its development.

Even when dialogues on the level of the countries, institutions and organizations are disrupted, *dialogues between individuals* may continue. However, for the dialogue to happen, what is needed – as the cases I have focused on show – is the ability to leave one's own space and critically reflect upon one's own assumptions. Physical movement – as in the Two Countries – One Profession where the young journalists from the two countries worked together in the European cities or as in Vinogradov's discovery of Ukraine – can assist in this. In the discussion of *Trudnosti perevoda* on YouTube, Vladimir Vinogradov wrote that he would like to go back to Ukraine to talk to people he met during the film production again.

Dialogue is certainly about a distance – not only between its participants but also about an ability to distance from own assumptions. As suggested by Wood and Su (2014), dialogic spaces should also be observed *at the level of the self*. In Kanfer's project, such a dialogue is, in a way, used as a tool for checking whether the myths can be debunked by physically re-placing a critically thinking person from one geographic – and ideological – space to another. Dialogue with the 'other' initiates a dialogue within oneself. In a way, all of the informants revealed that the dialogue they engaged in, or initiated, was a process that brought them somewhere else, both physically and symbolically. Leaving one's own space becomes a way to a dialogue (to start with, a critical dialogic reflection on the level of self). And vice versa, dialogue becomes a way to explore an unknown space.

Conclusions

Whereas propaganda can be understood as a triumph of monologue, journalism – at least ideally – with its ability to pose questions and inspire discussions, can be a triumph of dialogue. If a war of narratives can be viewed as a battle over or around 'truth', the journalists' objective to be truthful becomes questioned from all perspectives and in all senses: personal, political and philosophical. Entering a dialogue can allow for questioning 'truths', recognizing their situatedness and relation to power. This, in its turn, allows journalists a perspective above the fray, avoiding participation in the information warfare by deconstructing the narratives of propaganda rather than constructing and reproducing recited truths.

The role of journalists and journalist associations in the construction of the dialogic spaces in the period of conflict can be seen as crucial. Dialogic spaces in the situation of conflict can be created on different levels and constructed around both dialogue as collaboration and agonistic dialogue. However, it is important that the dialogic space is not manipulated and its conditions are critically reflected upon by both its initiators, participants and observers, who may also choose to enter a dialogue. Dialogic space might not be a way to end the conflict, but at least it can be made bigger, louder, more inclusive and enduring than monologic spaces of propaganda and information war.

Notes

1 The results of the referendum on the status of Crimea held in March 2014 have not been recognized by many countries, and the process has been largely referred to as annexation. The Ukrainian law on Donbas reintegration adopted in early 2018 defines the Russian Federation as 'aggressor' and the non-government-controlled areas of Donbas as 'temporarily occupied territories' (Ukraine's Donbas reintegration law 2018).
2 I would like to thank my colleague Jaakko Turunen (Södertörn University) for a critical discussion of the relation between dialogue and truth. He proposed the concept of 'regime of truth seeking' as best fitting to describe dialogue as a condition for more balanced reporting.
3 The project was funded by the Foundation for Baltic and East European Studies (2016–2018, project leader – Per Ståhlberg).

References

Adams, P. C. (2017), 'Mapping Geomedia: Charting the Terrains of Space, Place and Media', in K. Fast, A. Jansson, J. Lindell, B. L. Ryan and M. Tesfahuney (eds), *Geomedia Studies: Spaces and Mobilities in Mediatized Worlds*, 41–60, Milton: Routledge.

Allan, S. (1998), '(En) Gendering the Truth Politics of News Discourse', in C. Carter, G. Branston and S. Allan (eds), *News, Gender and Power*, 121–37, London: Routledge.

Andrejtsiv, I. (2016), 'Leonid Kanfer: "My ne sobiralis' nikogo mirit"' [Leonid Kanfer: 'We did not plan to reconcile anyone'], *Detector Media*, 25 November. Available online: http://detector.media/production/article/120905/2016-11-25-leonid-kanfer-my-ne-sobiralis-nikogo-mirit/ (accessed 25 July 2019).

Azhgikhina, N. (2016), 'Dve strany – odna professiya': Zametki na polyakh dokumentov dialoga' ['Two Countries – One Profession': Notes on the margins of the documents of the dialogue], *Agora*, 15: 64–8. Available online: http://kennankyiv.org/wp-content/uploads/2016/02/Azhgihina_werstka_Agora_V15_final-6.pdf (accessed 27 August 2018).

Believe (2017), [Documentary], 'Austria: OSCE'. Available online: https://youtube.com/watch?v=kGq7Xld4Gzk (accessed 7 October 2019).

Budivska, H., and D. Orlova (2017), 'Between Professionalism and Activism: Ukrainian Journalism after the Euromaidan', *Kyiv-Mohyla Law and Politics Journal*, 3(2017): 137–56.

Chomu NSJU zasudyla ... (2019), 'Chomu NSJU zasudyla ideyu organizatsii telemostu z telekanalom "Rossiya 24"', [Why NUJU condemned the idea of organization of a telecast with TV-channel *Rossiya-24 (sic)*]. Available online: http://nsju.org/index.php/article/8074 (accessed 25 July 2019).

Dunja Mijatovic kak povod ... (2016), 'Dunja Mijatovic kan povod dlya skandala i raskola' [Dunja Mijatovic as a cause for scandal and split], *Detector Media*, 4 August. Available online: https://detector.media/medialife/article/117464/2016-08-04-dunya-miyatovich-kak-povod-dlya-skandala-i-raskola/ (accessed 27 August 2018).

Federal State Statistics Service of the Russian Federation (2010), 'Language Proficiency of the Russian Federation Population', *Russian Census 2010*. Available online: http://www.gks.ru/free_doc/new_site/perepis2010/croc/Documents/Vol4/pub-04-05.pdf (accessed 25 July 2019).

Feldman, A. (2019), 'War under Erasure: Contretemps, Disappearance, Anthropophagy, Survivance', *Theory & Event*, 22(1): 175–203.

Foucault, M. ([1977] 2005), 'Truth and Power', in J. Medina and D. Wood (eds), *Truth: Engagements across Philosophical Traditions*, 332–5, Oxford: Blackwell.

Gadamer, H.-G. (1989), *Truth and Method*, Second edition, London: Sheed & Ward.

Ganesh, S., and H. M. Zoller (2012), 'Dialogue, Activism, and Democratic Social Change', *Communication Theory*, 22: 66–91.

Gould, P. (1991), 'Dynamic Structures of Geographic Space', in S. D. Brunn and T. R. Leinbach (eds), *Collapsing Space and Time: Geographic Aspects of Communication and Information*, 3–30, London and New York: Routledge.

Gutsche, R. E. Jr. (2019), 'Elevating Problems of Journalistic Power in an Age of Post-truth', *Journalism & Mass Communication Educator*, 74(2): 240–8.

Guards of Freedom (2016), '[Documentary] Austria: OSCE'. Available online: https://youtube.com/watch?v=3GQ1VI0g644 (accessed 7 October 2019).

Habermas, J. (1984), *The Theory of Communicative Action*, Boston, MA: Beacon.

Hammond, P. (2007), *Media, War and Postmodernity*, London: Routledge.

Hoskins, A., and B. O'Loughlin (2010), *War and Media: The Emergence of Diffused War*, Cambridge: Polity Press.

Horbyk, R. (2017), *Mediated Europes: Discourse and Power in Ukraine, Russia and Poland during Euromaidan*, Doctoral dissertation, Huddinge: Södertörn University.

Iz-za pryamykh ugroz ... (2019), 'Iz-za pryamykh ugroz fizicheskoj raspravy v adres kanala, zhurnalistov i ikh semej Newsone soobschaet ob otmene telemosta "Nado pogovorit"' [Due to direct threats of physical violence addressed to the channel, journalists and their families NewsOne announces the cancelation of the telecast 'Need to Talk'], *NewsOne*, 8 July. Available online: https://newsone.ua/news/iz-za-prjamykh-uhroz-fizicheskoj-raspravy-v-adres-kanala-zhurnalistov-i-ikh-semej-newsone-soobshchaet-ob-otmene-telemarafona-nado-pohovorit.html (accessed 25 July 2019).

Jansson, A., and J. Lindell (2018), 'Studies for a Mediatized World: Rethinking Media and Social Space', *Media and Communication*, 6(2): 1–4.

Katz, E. (2015), 'Evgeny Lesnoy: "Ya gotov brosit' kamen' v nashu liberal'nuyu obschestvennost"' [Evgeny Lesnoy: 'I am ready to throw a stone at our "liberal public"'], *Open Russia*, 30 March. Available online: https://openrussia.org/post/view/3852/ (accessed 4 September 2019).

Khaldarova, I., and M. Pantti (2016), 'Fake News: The Narrative Battle over the Ukrainian Conflict', *Journalism Practice*, 10(7): 891–901.

Kto nas razvel? [*Who deceived us?/Who turned us apart?*] (2015), '[Documentary] Dir. Evgeny Lesnoy'. Available online: https://youtube.com/watch?v=txb-PbLycgc (accessed 7 October 2019).

Laclau, E., and C. Mouffe (1985), *Hegemony and Socialist Strategy: Towards a Radical Democratic Politics*, London: Verso.

Lentin, A., and G. Titley (2011), *The Crises of Multiculturalism: Racism in a Neoliberal Age*, London: Zed.

Littleton, K., and N. Mercer (2013), *Interthinking: Putting Talk to Work*, Abingdon: Routledge.

Lubchak, V. (2016), '"Mova vorozhnechi" vs latentna bezpryntsypnist', ["Hate speech" vs latent unscrupulousness] Den, 25 March. Available online: https://day.kyiv.ua/uk/article/media/mova-vorozhnechi-vs-latentna-bezpryncypnist (accessed 27 August 2018).

Mijatovic, D. (2016), 'Presentation of the "Two Countries – One Profession" project at the OSCE Ministerial Council 2016, Hamburg, 7–9 December 2016.

Mouffe, C. (2013), *Agonistics: Thinking the World Politically*, London: Verso.

Nado pogovorit pochaly pokazuvaty … (2019), '"Nado pogovorit"' pochaly pokazuvaty na kanali "Rossiya 1" spochatku na Urali, piznishe u Moskvi' ["Need to Talk" started to show on channel *Rossiya-1* first in Ural, then in Moscow], *Detector Media*, 12 July. Available online: https://detector.media/infospace/article/168927/2019-07-12-nado-pogovorit-pochali-pokazuvati-na-kanali-rossiya-1-spochatku-na-urali-piznishe-u-moskvi/ (accessed 25 July 2019).

Nado pogovorit. Proekt Rossii i Ukrainy (2019), '"Nado pogovorit." Proekt Rossii i Ukrainy. Polnyj vypusk' [Need to Talk. Project of Russia and Ukraine. Full edition], *Rossiya-1*, 12 July. Available online: https://youtube.com/watch?v=xnceQDS06CA&fbclid=IwAR05BXkYH-XP19FZFhc84lKep8TKct7l48qBd_GQkuh6TyCUgfymOgGnM4E (accessed 25 July 2019).

Naschmarkt (2016), [Documentary], 'Austria: OSCE'. Available online: https://youtube.com/watch?v=QUnxarKb4dk (accessed 7 October 2019).

Natsionalna spilka zhurnalistiv zasudyla … (2019), 'Natsionalna spilka zhurnalistiv zasudyla provedennya "telemostu z Rosiyeyu24"', [National Union of Journalists of Ukraine condemned holding a "telecast with Rossiya-24(sic)"], Available online: https://hromadske.radio/news/2019/07/08/nacionalna-spilka-zhurnalistiv-zasudyla-provedennya-telemostu-z-rosiyeyu24 (accessed 25 July 2019).

Nygren, G., and J. Hök, eds (2016), *Ukraina och Informationskriget: Journalistik mellan Ideal och Självcensur*, [Ukraine and information war: Journalism between ideals and self-censorship], Karlstad: Myndigheten för samhällsskydd och beredskap.

Nygren, G., M. Glovacki, J. Hök, I. Kiria, D. Orlova and D. Taradai (2018), 'Journalism in the Crossfire: Media coverage of the war in Ukraine in 2014', *Journalism Studies*, 19(7): 1059–78.

O'Loughlin, B. (2015), 'The Permanent Campaign', *Media, War and Conflict*, 8(2): 169–71.

Orlova, D. (2016), 'Ukrainian Media after the EuroMaidan: In Search of Independence and Professional Identity', *Publizistik*, 61: 441–61.

Pantti, M., ed. (2016), *Media and the Ukraine Crisis: Hybrid Media Practices and Narratives of Conflict*, New York: Peter Lang.

Plokhotnyuk, N. (2016), 'Rosijs'ka mova dominue v media i sferi poslug, ukrains'ka - v osviti ta kinoprokati' ['Russian language dominates in media and service sphere, Ukrainian – in education and cinema'], *Ukrainskij reporter*, 20 November. Available online: http://ukrreporter.com.ua/politic/rosijska-mova-dominuye-v-media-i-sferi-poslug-ukrayinska-v-osviti-ta-kinoprokati.html (accessed 16 December 2019).

Richter, A. (2018), 'Cultural Security of Ukraine in Times of Conflict: Legal Aspects', in Y. Watanabe (ed), *Handbook of Cultural Security*, 461–86, Cheltenham: Edward Elgar.

Rudenko, A. (2016), 'Chy ye 'natsionalnyi kharakter' u Natsionalnoi spilky zhurnalistiv?' [Does the National Union of journalists have a 'national character'?], Den, 15 December. Available online: https://day.kyiv.ua/uk/article/media/chy-ye-nacionalnyy-harakter-u-nacionalnoyi-spilky-zhurnalistiv (accessed 27 August 2018).

Rukovodstvo NSZhU… (2017), 'Rukovodstvo NSZhU praktikuet dvojnye standarty' [The NUJU leadership practices double standards], *Censor.net*, 9 August. Available online: https://censor.net.ua/n451048 (accessed 27 August 2018).

Schudson, M., and C. Anderson (2009), 'Objectivity, Professionalism, and Truth Seeking in Journalism', in K. Wahl-Jorgensen and T. Hanitzsch (eds), *The Handbook of Journalism Studies*, 88–101, New York: Routledge.

Stokke, Ch., and L. Lybäck (2018), 'Combining Intercultural Dialogue and Critical Multiculturalism', *Ethnicities*, 18(1): 70–85.

Survey of Russian Propaganda Influence (2017), 'Survey of Russian Propaganda Influence on Public Opinion in Ukraine Findings', *Detector Media*, 13 February. Available online: https://ms.detector.media/detector_media_en/reports_eng/survey_of_russian_propaganda_influence_on_public_opinion_in_ukraine_findings/ (accessed 4 September 2019).

Szostek, J. (2018), 'Russia, Ukraine and Presumed Media Influence in International Relations', *BISA Annual Conference*, Bath, 13–15 June.

Trudnosti perevoda/Trudnoschi pereklada [Lost in translation] (2016), [TV-documentary] Dir. Leonid Kanfer, *STB*, 7–18 November. Available online: https://www.youtube.com/user/ViknaSTB/search?query=трудности+перевода (accessed 7 October 2019).

Tumber, H., and F. Webster (2006), *Journalists under Fire: Information War and Journalistic Practices*, London: Sage.
Two Countries – One Profession (2016), 'Materials from Meetings with Representatives of Russian and Ukrainian Journalism Organizations under the Auspices of the OSCE Representative on Freedom of the Media'. Available online: https://www.osce.org/fom/226351?download=true (accessed 27 August 2018).
Two Countries – One Profession (2019), Official Website of the Project, OSCE. Available online: https://www.osce.org/representative-on-freedom-of-media/184881 (accessed 7 October 2019).
Ukraine's Donbas reintegration law ... (2018), 'Ukraine's Donbas Reintegration Law Enters into Force February 24', *UNIAN*, 24 February. Available online: https://www.unian.info/politics/10020068-ukraine-s-donbas-reintegration-law-enters-into-force-feb-24.html (accessed 7 October 2019).
Ukrainskij kanal otmenil ... (2019), 'Ukrainskij kanal otmenil telemost s Moskvoj. Organizatorov zapodozrili v izmene' [Ukrainian channel has cancelled telecast with Moscow. Organizers suspected of treason], BBC News Russian, 8 July. Available online: https://www.bbc.com/russian/news-48907592 (accessed 25 July 2019).
Vkontakte snova pokinula top-10 ... (2017), 'Vkontakte snova pokinula top-10 samykh populyarnykh sredi ukraintsev sajtov' [Vkontakte has left the top-10 most popular websites among Ukrainians], *Telekritika*. Available online: http://ru.telekritika.ua/business/vkontakte-snova-pokinula-top10-samih-populyarnih-sredi-ukraintsev-saitov-677798 (accessed 12 October 2018).
Vozhidanii ... (2019), 'V ozhidanii Sentsova'. Pervyj podcast 'Novoj gazety' i 'Gromadskogo' ['Waiting for Sentsov'. The first podcast of *Novaya gazeta* and *Hromadske*], *Novaya gazeta*, 10 May. Available online: https://www.novayagazeta.ru/articles/2019/05/10/80473-v-ozhidanii-sentsova-pyat-let-posle-aresta (accessed 5 September 2019).
Vukrainskikh media ... (2016), 'V ukrainskikh media prodolzhaet dominirovat' russkij yazyk issledovanie' [The Russian language continues to dominate in Ukrainian media – research shows], *BBC Ukraine*, 8 November. Available online: https://www.bbc.com/ukrainian/rolling_news_russian/2016/11/161108_ru_n_language_rates (accessed 4 September 2019).
Wegerif, R. (2013), *Dialogic: Education for the Internet Age*, New York: Routledge.
Wood, M., and F. Su (2014), 'A Mission Possible: Towards a Shared Dialogic Space for Professional Learning in UK Higher Education', *European Journal of Higher Education*, 4(4): 363–72.

12

Perfect war and its contestations

Jolle Demmers, Lauren Gould and David Snetselaar

Introduction

War is a time at which violence is legitimized, institutionalized and deployed against a constructed enemy. Apart from horrific and atrocious, war is essentially a social phenomenon (Jabri 1996). It repeats and reproduces itself through imaginaries which render it acceptable and necessary and through institutional forms and social practices which serve as war-making machinery. As we will argue in this chapter, the 'normalization' of war needs constant work. War, truth and power are intimately related. State institutions and their coalitions and private advocates have vested interests in the shaping of knowledges and truths about war. 'Not only are effective militaries, and the knowledges required to constitute, govern, and use them, necessary for the survival and flourishing of polities, but political orders entail narratives regarding the authoritative and legitimate command of armed force' (Barkawi and Brighton 2011: 142). In particular because war is always a highly uncertain enterprise, fraught with failure, humiliation and defeat, 'public perceptions and public support can never be left to chance' (Griffin 2010: 8). In this chapter, we highlight how twenty-first-century remote warfare campaigns, such as the US-led anti-Islamic State intervention named Operation Inherent Resolve, although fought from a distance and shrouded in secrecy, do not remain insulated from the machinations of war propaganda.

Drawing on Foucault's notion of 'regime of truth', we aim to investigate the ways in which 'war' actors negotiate, utilize and compete over media spaces. More specifically, we examine the spaces of contention through which watchdog organizations such as Airwars make counterclaims to the anti-IS Coalition's legitimations of remote warfare as ethical, that is, as remote killings as 'moral acts of care'.[1] Although we here contribute to investigating the 'war of spaces' through the analysis of a particular case, we very much realize how important it is to look beyond the specific historicity of 'this war' (Balibar 2008) and to place this case in debates on the ontology of war as the (always uncertain) (re)working of meaning, truth and order through violent means.

The spatial reconfiguration of warfare and its conceptualizations

Over the past decades, remoteness in all its modalities (e.g. as distancing or outsourcing) has become a characteristic feature of warfare. Western democracies in particular have resorted to remote warfare to govern perceived security threats from a safe distance. From the 2011 NATO bombings in Libya, the US Africa Command's counterterrorism training of Ugandan soldiers, to the US-led coalition airstrikes against Islamic State (IS) in Syria and Iraq, violence is exercised from afar. Remote warfare is characterized by a shift away from boots on the ground. It involves coalition drone and air strikes, while on the ground military training teams assist local forces to fight and die on behalf of Western interests (Biegon and Watts 2017: 1). Violence is thus executed and facilitated, but without the 'exposure' of Western military men and women to opponents in a declared warzone under the condition of mutual risk. This spatial reconfiguration of war has been conceptualized in a range of ways from 'globalized war' (Baumann 2001) to 'everywhere war' (Gregory 2011), and more recently as 'coalition proxy warfare' (Mumford 2013), 'transnational shadow wars' (Niva 2013), 'surrogate warfare' (Krieg and Rickli 2018), and 'vicarious warfare' (Waldman 2017). What these conceptualizations have in common is an attentiveness to how conventional ties between war and space have become undone. Gregory (2011) emphasizes how we have to rethink late modern war in terms of space and territoriality. Whereas wars in the past were conducted in 'resolutely territorial terms', we now have to 'supplement cartographic reason by other, more labile spatialities' (2011: 239). War has become mobile. The concept of the battlefield in US doctrine is replaced by a multi-scalar, multidimensional battlescape (Graham 2010: 31). For Chamayou (2015), the geocentric concept of war is now opposed to a target-centred one, attached to the bodies of the enemy prey. Contemporary

Western-led military interventionism shuns direct control of territory and populations and its cumbersome order-building and order-maintaining responsibilities, focusing instead on flexible, open-ended operations, supported by remote technology and reliant on local partnerships and private contractors to promote and protect interests – a shift that we termed 'liquid warfare' elsewhere (Demmers and Gould 2018). What we emphasize in this chapter, however, is not the question of space/territoriality but an analysis of the war of spaces: how particular 'war' actors produce authoritative knowledges and 'truths' around remote warfare and civilian deaths. As we will discuss in more detail below, for Foucault (1980: 133):

> 'Truth' is to be understood as a system of ordered procedures for the production, regulation, distribution, circulation and operation of statements. 'Truth' is linked in a circular relation with systems of power which produce and sustain it, and to effects of power which it induces, and which extend it. A 'regime' of truth.

We will outline for the case of Operation Inherent Resolve how particular actors (embedded in the army, media and civil society) became engaged in the production of what Barkawi and Brighton (2011: 140) name 'War/Truth': the making and contesting of statements on, or around, the 'true' meaning of the violence enacted under Operation Inherent Resolve, in particular the violence done to civilians in these zones of war. Aiming to reinvigorate a focus on war as a social phenomenon we aim to do three things in this chapter. First, we emphasize the relevance of the term 'regime of truth' as a useful tool to investigate the war of spaces. Second, we lay out how in the case of Operation Inherent Resolve watchdogs such as Airwars are afforded a narrow space of contention to contest the anti-IS Coalition's discourse of precision and care for civilian casualties, largely due to their reliance on new digital technologies. Thirdly, in the conclusions we highlight how the emphasis on a 'politics of numbers' and techniques of counting is part of a de-politicization move and a further sanitization of war. With this we come to what perhaps is the essence of remote warfare: its ability to ward off political questions on how it has transformative effects, that is, on the capacity of remote military violence to be constitutive and generative, and how 'war making' also always includes 'world making'. We now first turn to a further unpacking of the concept of regime of truth.

Regime of truth

In his work on pogroms and riots, Paul Brass (1996) suggests focusing on the interpretative processes in the aftermath of violent practices. The core idea underlying this approach is to not simply identify the multiple contexts in which violence occurs 'because it can occur anywhere and can be organized or random, premeditated or spontaneous, directed at specific persons, groups, or property, or not' (1996: 2). Brass acknowledges that these aspects of violence must be identified insofar as possible. However, he claims that we also need to examine the discourses on violence and the ways in which participants and observers seek to explain incidents of violence. In his work Brass aims to go beyond analysing the violent struggle to investigate as well the struggle to interpret the violence. That is, 'the attempts to govern a society or a country through gaining not only a monopoly on the legitimate use of violence, but to gain control over the interpretation of violence' (1996: 45). For Brass, the contest for gaining control over the interpretation of violence is 'at least as important, and probably more important' than the outcome of specific struggles themselves (1996: 45):

> The struggle over the meaning of violence may or may not lead to a consensus or a hegemonic interpretation. It will certainly not lead to the 'truth' but at most to a 'regime of truth' which will give us a pre-established context into which we can place future acts of a similar type into the same context and for the reinterpretation of previous acts of violence in history.

Evidently, Brass's work is an attempt to translate and apply Foucault's notion of 'regime of truth' to concrete settings of violent conflict. In his interview on Truth and Power Foucault offers the following refined definition of the notion of regime of truth:

> Truth is a thing of this world: it is produced only by virtue of multiple forms of constraint. And it induces regular effects of power. Each society has its regime of truth, its 'general politics' of truth: that is, the types of discourse which it accepts and makes function as true; the *mechanisms and instances* which enable one to distinguish true and false statements, the means by which each is *sanctioned*; the *techniques and procedures* accorded value in the acquisition of truth; *the status* of those who are charged with saying what counts as true.
>
> (1980: 131, our emphasis)

In our analysis of the war of spaces we will select and operationalize aspects of this broader notion to investigate: (1) which techniques and procedures are accorded value in the acquisition of truth around civilian deaths as caused by Operation Inherent Resolve; (2) what are the mechanisms and instances utilized by 'war' actors to distinguish true and false statements about civilian deaths; (3) what are the means by which each are authorized or sanctioned; and (4) what status is afforded to those who are charged with saying what counts as true? In tracing the above dynamics of interaction, we use a variety of sources. We draw on a small body of academic work (Bonds 2019; Chamayou 2015; Schwarz 2016; Schweiger 2019) as well as human rights reports, US military statements, and newspaper accounts to map the ascendency of a discourse of 'precision and care' accompanying the US-led anti-IS airstrikes between 2014 and 2019. In addition, information was gathered through interviews held with various actors within watchdog organizations, in particularly Airwars and Amnesty International; through participant observation at workshops, roundtables, public events organized and attended by both 'military' and 'watchdog' actors; and through a range of primary sources (press releases, evaluation reports, briefings, military magazines).

Operation Inherent Resolve and the machinations of war propaganda

In 2014, a new player in the Middle East increasingly drew the attention of Western media. A group of jihadi fighters, referred to as Daesh and later the Islamic State (IS), was quickly expanding their territorial control across Iraq and Syria (Cockburn 2015: x–xi). By mid-2014, they had successfully captured the city of Raqqa in Syria and Mosul in Iraq. In September 2014, shortly after IS released a video of the beheading of American journalist James Foley, president Barack Obama declared that the United States had to act:

> There can be no reasoning – no negotiation – with this brand of evil. The only language understood by killers like this is the language of force. So the United States of America will work with a broad coalition to dismantle this network of death.
>
> (cited in Friis 2015: 737)

This broad coalition came to be known as the US-led anti-IS coalition, or simply the Coalition, and included over sixty countries and partner organizations. Its military division was named the Combined Joint Task Force – Operation Inherent Resolve. Herein, the United States, UK, France, Belgium, Australia, Denmark, the Netherlands and twenty other states forged a military alliance in the name of 'destroying ISIS's parent tumour in Iraq and Syria, combating its worldwide spread, and protecting all homelands' (McInnis 2016: 2). Led by the US Central Command (CENTCOM), it set out to achieve its goals by using 'coordinated airstrikes, training and equipping local security forces, and targeted special operations' (McInnis 2016: 2). Since its establishment Operation Inherent Resolve has engaged in extensive security cooperation with local partners such as the Iraqi military, Kurdish Peshmerga and the Syrian Democratic Forces, and engaged in over 34,000 strikes, firing over 100,000 munitions across Syria and Iraq.

Although a largely riskless, remote and mobile intervention, Operation Inherent Resolve still requires (and facilitates) particular spaces of war in which legitimizing narratives are produced, sanctioned and valued. Those in favour of the operation contrast the brutal and barbaric violence perpetrated by IS against local as well as Western innocent civilians, with the surgical precision with which its strongholds were targeted. Former US Secretary of State John Kerry described IS as 'ugly, savage, inexplicable, nihilistic, and valueless evil' (Friis 2015: 735), while former US Secretary of Defense James Mattis emphasized, 'We are the good guys [...] We do everything humanly possible consistent with military necessity, taking many chances to avoid civilian casualties at all costs' (CBS News 2017). This distinction between 'their' violence as vicious and barbaric and 'our' violence as clean and precise fits the classic tropes of war. Such statements suggest a good deal about how war actors like to understand their own violence. They establish a highly appealing contrast between borderland traits of barbarity, excess and irrationality, and metropolitan characteristics of civility, restraint and rationality (see Duffield 2002: 1052). To reinforce the latter image, representatives of the Coalition also draw on a set of medical metaphors. In this, IS is represented as a cancer that needs to be cut out of the sick body of the Middle East. As former US Secretary of Defense Ash Carter (2016) asserted: 'ISIL is a cancer that's threatening to spread. And like all cancers, you can't cure the disease just by cutting out the tumor. You have to eliminate it wherever it has spread, and stop it from coming back.'

The Coalition presents surgical strikes as one of the key 'cures' that is being executed with utmost care – by applying the principles of military necessity, humanity and proportionality and the most advanced smart technology (see Bonds 2019: 11). Taken together, this sanitized discourse to legitimize Western state violence is what Chamayou (2015) calls 'necro-ethics' (killing as a moral act of care) and Bonds (2019) refers to as 'humanitized violence'.

Precision warfare and spaces of contestation: Producing an alternative truth

As with any official story on certain acts of violence, this war discourse of 'barbarianism', 'humanitarianism', 'care' and 'precision' intersects with alternative interpretations and forms of public contestation. In the wake of the launch of Operation Inherent Resolve, we have witnessed the advent of a set of Western civil society organizations that monitor the harmful impact of this (and now other) international remote interventions. Not satisfied with how the Coalition assesses the number of civilians killed by its airstrikes through relying on internal military visual intelligence recorded from the sky, watchdog organization Airwars for instance has developed new remote sensing techniques and procedures to count the number of civilian casualties from Coalition airstrikes. Airwars' teams of journalists, graphic designers, architects, humanitarian aid workers, and refugees from Syria and Iraq use open-source intelligence (such as social media posts and satellite imagery) to track, triangulate and geolocate, in real-time, local claims of civilian casualties. Concurrently, Airwars monitors and archives official military reports on munition and strike statistics to measure them against the public record and grade the reliability of the claims made. This grading ranges from 'discounted' to 'contested', 'weak', 'fair' (according to Airwars) and 'confirmed' (by the Coalition).

Crucial to being able to reach a 'confirmed' grade that represents instances where Airwars' statements about civilian casualties are sanctioned by the Coalition as true is an exchange between Airwars' team of investigators and the civilian casualty (CIVCAS) cell at CENTCOM. The CIVCAS cell was officially organized in 2016 after intense lobbying efforts by Airwars for a central point of contact to submit allegations to. CIVCAS consist of a small team of analysts that assess allegations of civilian deaths based on flight logs, strike records and visual intelligence gathered by Coalition aircraft. Initially, the responses Airwars received were similar to the periodic press releases of the Coalition, containing little information, only indicating what incidents were credible. Over the year that followed, the team at Airwars worked to standardize their exchanges with CIVCAS. This included assigning each incident a unique code and supplying the CIVCAS analysts with extensive spreadsheets with detailed information, such as the exact coordinates and an explanation of how they collected and corroborated the open-source information. By comparing its database of allegations with the records of the Coalition, Airwars was able to improve its online archive and discovered that over time they became the source of two-thirds of all assessed allegations by the Coalition.

Although it is clear from the above that the knowledge produced through Airwars' new civilian harm assessment procedures has been increasingly shared with the Coalition, the statements made by each actor about the 'true' number of non-combatant body bags is still astonishingly disparate. Airwars current 'fair' estimate is that between 8,214 and 13,125 civilians have likely been killed in Coalition actions – with the Coalition itself presently 'confirming' only 1,335 non-combatants deaths from its air and artillery strikes (Airwars n.d.).

Another illustrative example of how watchdog organizations 'make visible' the hidden local realties of remote warfare and produce contrasting statements on its precise and surgical nature is the joint initiative by Airwars and human rights organization Amnesty International to assess the Coalition's campaign to retake the Islamic State-held city of Raqqa. In the four-month remote *Battle for Raqqa* (June–October 2017), the United States, United Kingdom and France fired over 40,000 air and artillery strikes that were called in by their local allies the Syrian Democratic Forces by identifying targets on iPads. The then Secretary of Defense, James Mattis, said in an interview with CBS that the Coalition would adopt 'annihilation tactics' (CBS News 2017) and Sergeant Major John Wayne Troxell boasted that 'they fired more rounds in five months in Raqqa than any other Marine artillery battalion since the Vietnam War' (Snow 2018). In the immediate aftermath the Coalition acknowledged just twenty-three civilian casualties yet refused to conduct any on-the-ground investigations. In response, Airwars and Amnesty International joined forces and set up a crowdsourcing data project called *Strike Tracker*.

This online project engaged over 3,000 digital activists from across 124 countries to help them trace and geolocate how the Coalition's bombings destroyed almost 80 per cent of Raqqa. This was supplemented by two years of on-the-ground investigations conducted by Amnesty's Senior Crisis Response investigator Donatella Rovera. Airwars and Amnesty compiled their evidence and built a database of more than 1,600 civilians reportedly killed in Coalition strikes. They were able to name 641, of which the Coalition has since acknowledged 159.

Reflecting on the ground evidence she collected on civilian casualties as well as the notoriously imprecise artillery ammunition fired by the Coalition, Rovera (2019) argued at a launch of the report:

> The Coalition was using technology, but they did not put enough resources into using it properly and they were not using other technology that exists for them; namely more sophisticated smaller impact radius weapons which would have had a less detrimental impact on the civilians. In future wars we would like them to use technology in a more responsible way, in a way that focuses on the protection of civilians, not just technology that allows them to wage a war less expensively, or in a way that only protects their own forces.

This narrative is in line with what Bonds found in his qualitative content analysis of human rights and media reports on Operation Inherent Resolve, namely that leading non-governmental critics call on Coalition members to be more precise and exercise more care when striking enemy targets and to improve their investigation techniques and acknowledgement of civilian causalities (Bonds 2019, 9).

Sanctioning techniques, status and procedures

Challenging the 'truth' about the precise and careful nature of Operation Inherent Resolve with alternative statements on the number of civilian casualties and the type of technology used has not been without consequences. A clear example of how watchdog organizations were undermined by the Coalition occurred while the Battle for Raqqa described above was in full swing. On 31 August 2017 Samuel Oakford, an in-house investigative reporter with Airwars, published a report in *Foreign Policy* criticizing the United States for being in denial about the high number of civilian casualties in Syria. Two weeks later (15 September 2017) the then commander of Operation Inherent Resolve, Lieutenant General Stephen Townsend, published a response in the same magazine in which he discredited Oakford's claims by stating that Airwars' statements about civilian casualties were 'hyperbolic' and in which he questioned the value of Airwars' techniques and procedures and its status through saying: 'Assertions by Airwars [...] and media outlets that cite them, are often unsupported by fact and serve only to strengthen the Islamic State's hold on civilians, placing civilians at greater risk'. In his response Townsend emphasized that the Coalition dealt in facts and that he challenged anyone to find a more 'precise air campaign in the history of warfare.... The Coalition's goal is always for zero human casualties'.[2]

The Coalition not only undercut Airwars discursively, but shortly after actively obstructed Airwars' vital knowledge production procedures after another critical article called 'The Uncounted' was published in *New York Times* in November 2017 (Khan and Gopel 2017). Herein, investigative journalists Azmat Khan and Anand Gopal address the large discrepancy between Airwars estimates and those of the Coalition concluding that, contrary to Townsend's claim, the United States has caused far more civilian casualties than it is willing to acknowledge. Soon afterwards Airwars received a message from the Coalition that all communication between CIVCAS and Airwars would end immediately, thereby terminating the exchange of information which was critical for Airwars to identify the credibility of the civilian casualty claims under investigation (Dyers 2019).

Co-opting an alternative truth

After months of lobbying and a change of spokesperson at CIVCAS, contact was re-established and the sharing of techniques, procedures and knowledge between the CIVCAS team and Airwars improved once again (Dyers 2019). When Airwars launched its new website in December 2018, the team noticed that CIVCAS was proactively visiting their website and contacted them with questions, making it no longer necessary for Airwars to send in allegations (Awater 2019). Furthermore, in February 2019 a declassified 'Civilian Casualties Review', commissioned by the Chairman of the Joint Chief of Staff, recommended systematically including NGOs in the reporting on civilian casualties and identified Airwars as an important source of information as it was 'the only NGO that provided consistent reporting' (2018: 11). The Pentagon even invited NGOs, including Airwars, to provide information on civilian casualty assessment procedures and to discuss the possibility of setting up ex gratia payments for victims of US airstrikes (Woods 2019). In its 2018 annual report on Civilian Causalities, the US Department of Defense defines ex gratia payments 'as a way to convey feelings of condolence or sympathy toward the victim or the victim's family' but underlines these are not '(1) required by law; (2) an admission of wrongdoing; or (3) for the purpose of compensating the victim or the victim's family for their loss' (2019: 17–18). This is what Gilbert (2015) refers to as the sharp difference between 'accounting' and 'accountability'. In her work on US military payments in Afghanistan and Iraq, Gilbert shows how 'it is precisely through affective appeals to sympathy and condolence that the needs and interests of the victims are suspended, and the imperial noose tightened' (2015: 405).

The shift away from dismissing civilian casualty reports as 'hyperbolic' towards acknowledging the value of the techniques and procedures developed by NGOs such as Airwars, thereby granting it status as a reliable source of information, is in the interest of the Pentagon. CENTCOM's previous claims about civilian casualties were, as Airwars researcher Sofie Dyers (2019) stated, 'simply not believable' and thus undermined its credibility. Co-opting Airwars' remote sensing technologies and proposing to set up ex gratia payments allows the Pentagon to continue to maintain its distance from the battlefield, but it can now claim not only to be using smart technology to wage war, but also to count and offer financial gifts for the civilian casualties it has caused. These expressions of 'compassion' and 'regret' add value to its discourse of 'precision' and 'care', further emphasizing a hierarchical relationship of benevolence between remote violent perpetrators and their unintended local civilian victims on the ground in Syria and Iraq. This way, status is enhanced, without having to acknowledge or be held accountable for the remaining 90 per cent of Airwars and Amnesty's allegations.

We conclude that the above 'politics of truth', or in this case 'politics of numbers', opened up a constrained space of contention in which watchdog organizations were able to contest the Coalition's discourse of precision and care for civilian casualties by producing contrasting numbers on civilian casualties. They did so by relying on smart technologies that allowed them to connect to the battlefield from a safe distance and extract local images and allegations of civilian casualties. In some cases, such as the Amnesty Raqqa investigation, this was accompanied by on the ground investigations.

Rather than question the logic of the violence and offer opposition, the knowledge produced by these watchdogs was subsequently used to call on the Coalition to take *more care* of civilians by using *more precise* technology when striking enemy targets as well as when counting non-combatant deaths. At first the Coalition resorted to thwarting the contesting numbers by questioning the value of the techniques and procedures used, undermining the status of those who developed them, and constraining vital information sharing practices. By early 2019 the Pentagon gradually shifted to co-opting Airwars' specialist remote techniques and procedures and opening the way for ex gratia payments. Hereby they further the production of a 'regime of truth' in which the constant application of new smart technologies allows for a form of perfect warfare, which saves and cares for the lives of both Western military personnel and friendly civilians on the ground.

Contesting the logic of the violence

This perfect war narrative, however, directs our attention away from what is essentially a political act: coalition state violence needs to be accounted for both legally and politically. This is what Duffield calls the 'paradox of connectivity' (2019: 191). The reliance on technoscience by both military and watchdog actors sidesteps complex political problems and fundamental questions, such as why and how was IS able to emerge in the first place? How was the West involved in creating the conditions for IS' explosive success? What was the international legal mandate for Operation Inherent Resolve? And, more complicated and painful perhaps, if the Coalition airstrikes are legally justified through references to 'collective self-defense', is this how Western democracies best protect their citizens against armed attacks in the future? What are the potential boomerang effects of destroying 80 per cent of a city such as Raqqa and killing thousands of civilians with 'utmost precision'?

Rather than addressing these political, legal and strategic problems they are transformed into more concrete and 'do-able' technical challenges, such as how can we make sure local proxies know how to use iPads to call in coalition airstrikes more accurately? How can we make sure our guided ammunitions do not have a 50- but 10-metre impact radius? How can we geolocate what buildings were destroyed by 40,000 artillery shells? How can we identify how many civilians were in those buildings? Duffield (2019: 191) observes that this displacement marshals the positive energy and empathy of innumerable actors in a quest for a technical solution – in our case human rights activists, journalists, geolocation experts, graphic designers, architects and thousands of digital activists. Yet the hard political problems remain.

The case of Colonel François-Régis Legrier further shows that those who do openly question the political and strategic logic of the Coalition's state violence executed during Operation Inherent Resolve are coercively sanctioned as traitors. In January 2019, Colonel François-Régis Legrier published an op-ed in the National Defense Review – *The Battle for Hajin: Tactical Victory, Strategic Defeat?*. Taking the battle of Hajin, one of the last strongholds of IS in Syria, as an example he argues that the use of excessive coalition air force will leave a 'disgusting image of what may be a Western-style liberation' and plant the seeds for an 'imminent resurgence' (2018: 71). Shortly after the op-ed was removed by the journal and Colonel Legrier was reportedly punished. When questioned about the colonel's critique in the Assemblée Nationale, the Chief of Staff of the French Army General François Lecointre responded as follows (2018: 29):

> I do not understand it. I try to put myself in the shoes of those soldiers who, for four months, obeyed his [Colonel Legrier] orders and implemented a strategy and then find that their leader publicly declares in an article that what they are doing is contrary to common sense, ethics, morality and military efficiency. If I were in the place of these men, I would be absolutely upset. It is for this reason, for this feeling of treason, that I punished Colonel Legrier. It was I who wanted to punish him and I maintain this point of view.

Conclusion

The spatial reconfiguration of contemporary warfare as remote and mobile intersects with the ways in which 'war' actors contest and negotiate the meaning of violence. For one, the distancing of warfare and the shift to 'riskless war' reduces the urgency of public scrutiny and debate within societies in whose names the violence is exercised. Yet our case study illustrates that remote warfare, like any war, still requires particular spaces of war in which authoritative knowledges and legitimizing narratives are produced, sanctioned and valued.

The dynamics of interaction outlined in this chapter demonstrates how for the case of Operation Inherent Resolve (media) spaces are carefully channelled and controlled. Engaging to negotiate, utilize and compete over media spaces of war, watchdog organizations largely relied on remote sensing and a 'politics of numbers'. Contestation centred around war's most painful and inconvenient 'truth': the bodies of innocent civilian casualties. As it turned out, however, it was exactly this focus on the 'counting of the dead', which in the end allowed for the encapsulation of critique by state institutions representing the Coalition such as CENTCOM and the Pentagon. The Coalition's sanctioning of information, its discursive embracement of the counterclaims of monitoring agents as 'not caring enough', as well as its adoption of specialist knowledge allowed for the enhancement of the technological 'perfecting' of warfare as precise, effective and caring. Ironically, and unintentionally perhaps, watchdog organizations are gradually brought inside the perfect war-making machine. We argue that it is this encapsulation of critique together with the moralization of violence as 'care', that is, as life-preserving practice and as medicine, which is furthering the de-politicization of this type of war.

Looking beyond the historicity of 'this war', we see how a regime of truth about remote warfare as precise and caring works to promote war rather than limit it. This should prompt us to look at the ontology of war as the (always uncertain) (re)working of meaning, truth and order through violent means, and the particular quality of remote violence to ward off political questions on how it has transformative effects. That is, on the capacity of remote military violence to (re)produce and sustain regimes of power which render war an act of benevolence.

Notes

1 Despite our repeated reference to the 'Coalition' we aim to refrain from representing it as a unitary body or actor. Rather, we understand the Coalition as assemblage: as a social formation of governance consisting of heterogeneous elements that forge alliances to exercise power (see also Demmers and Gould 2018: 367–77). In our analysis we at times refer to CENTCOM and the Pentagon as the main 'spokespersons' of this assemblage.

2 In a similar fashion, members of the Coalition tried to undermine the techniques, procedures and status of Amnesty after it made the evidence of its Raqqa investigation public. When questioned about Amnesty's findings, the UK Secretary of State for Defence Gavin Williamson replied: 'I must say that I was deeply, deeply disappointed by the Amnesty International report, which was not only disappointing, but disgraceful.[…] If it is going to produce reports, we want them to be accurate. We certainly do not want them to be calling into question the amazing professionalism of our Royal Air Force' (UK Parliament 2018).

References

Airwars, n.d., 'US-led Coalition in Iraq & Syria', *Airwars*. Available online: https://airwars.org/conflict/coalition-in-iraq-and-syria/ (accessed 31 October 2019).

Awater, M. (2019), 'Interview with Lauren Gould', *Utrecht*, 23 April 2019.

Balibar, E. (2008), 'What's in a War? (Politics as War, War as Politics)', *Ratio Juris*, 21(3): 365–86.
Barkawi, T., and S. Brighton (2011), 'Powers of War: Fighting, Knowledge, and Critique', *International Political Sociology*, 5(2): 126–43.
Baumann, Z. (2001), 'Wars of the Globalization Era', *European Journal for Social Theory*, 4 (1): 11–28.
Biegon, R., and T. Watts (2017), 'Defining Remote Warfare: Security Cooperation', *Remote Control* (November). Available online: https://www.oxfordresearchgroup.org.uk/Handlers/Download.ashx?IDMF=0232e573-f6d6-455e-9d34-0436925002d4 (accessed 1 November 2019).
Bonds, E. (2019), 'Humanitized Violence: Targeted Killings and Civilian Deaths in the US War against the Islamic State', *Current Sociology*, 67(3): 438–55.
Brass, P. R. (1996), *Riots and Pogroms*, London: Macmillan.
Carter, A. (2016), 'Remarks to the 101st Airborne Division on the Counter-ISIL Campaign Plan', *Speech delivered on 13 January 2016 at Fort Campbell, KY*. Available online: https://www.defense.gov/Newsroom/Speeches/Speech/Article/642995/remarks-to-the-101st-airborne-division-on-the-counter-isilcampaign-plan/ (accessed 31 October 2019).
CBS News (2017), 'Transcript: Defense Secretary James Mattis on "Face the Nation"', 28 May 2017. Available online: https://www.cbsnews.com/news/transcript-defense-secretary-james-mattis-on-face-the-nation-may-28-2017/ (accessed 31 October 2019).
Chamayou, G. (2015), *Drone Theory*, London: Penguin Books.
Cockburn, P. (2015), *The Rise of Islamic State: ISIS and the New Sunni Revolution*, London and New York: Verso Books.
Demmers, J., and L. Gould (2018), 'An Assemblage Approach to Liquid Warfare: AFRICOM and the "Hunt" for Joseph Kony', *Security Dialogue*, 49(5): 364–81.
Duffield, M. (2002), 'Social Reconstruction and the Radicalization of Development: Aid as a Relation of Global Liberal Governance', *Development and Change*, 33(5): 1049–71.
Duffield, M. (2019), *Post-humanitarianism: Governing Precarity in the Digital World*, Cambridge: Polity Press.
Dyers, S. (2019), 'Interview with Lauren Gould and David Snetselaar', The Hague, 3 May.
Foucault, M. (1980), *Power/Knowledge: Selected Interviews and Other Writings 1972–1977* (edited by C. Gordon), New York: Pantheon Books.
Friis, S. M. (2015), '"Beyond Anything We Have Ever Seen": Beheading Videos and the Visibility of Violence in the War against ISIS', *International Affairs*, 91(4): 725–46.
Gilbert, E. (2015), 'The Gift of War: Cash, Counterinsurgency, and "Collateral Damage"', *Security Dialogue*, 46(5): 403–21.
Graham, Jr. W. H. (2010), 'Learning from the Enemy-offensively, What IEDs Should Teach the US', *Massachusetts Institute of Technology Cambridge* (April). Available online: https://apps.dtic.mil/docs/citations/ADA545052 (accessed 31 October 2019).
Gregory, D. (2011), 'The Everywhere War', *The Geographical Journal*, 177 (3):238–50.

Griffin, M. (2010), 'Media Images of War', *Media, War & Conflict*, 3(1): 7–41.
Jabri, V. (1996), *Discourses on Violence: Conflict Analysis Reconsidered*, Manchester: Manchester University Press.
Khan, A., and A. Gopel (2017), 'The Uncounted', *New York Times Magazine*, 16 November. Available online: https://www.nytimes.com/interactive/2017/11/16/magazine/uncounted-civilian-casualties-iraq-airstrikes.html (accessed 1 November 2019).
Krieg A., and J.-M. Rickli (2018), 'Surrogate Warfare: The Art of War in the Twenty-first Century', *Defence Studies*, 18(2): 113–30.
Lecointre, F. (2019), 'Compte Rendu Commission de la défense nationale et des forces armées', *Assemblée Nationale*, Compte Rendu no. 42, 11 June 2019.
McInnis, K. J. (2016), 'Coalition Contributions to Countering the Islamic State', *Congressional Research Service, the Library of Congress*, 24 August. Available online: http://goodtimesweb.org/overseas-war/2016/R44135.pdf (accessed 31 October 2019).
Mumford, A. (2013), 'Proxy warfare and the Future of Conflict', *RUSI Journal*, 158(2): 40–6.
National Defense University (2018), 'Civilian Casualty (CIVCAS) Review', *National Defense University*, 17 April 2018. Available online: https://www.washingtonpost.com/u.s.-military%27s-2018-study-on-civilian-casualties/e39c5889-6489-4373-bd8e-ac2ca012e03d_note.html?questionId=7440959e-887e-4a55-b113-796da0b17af4 (accessed 31 October 2019).
Niva, S. (2013), 'Disappearing Violence: JSOC and the Pentagon's New Cartography of Networked Warfare', *Security Dialogue*, 44(3): 185–202.
Oakford, S. (2017), 'The U.S. Is in Denial about the Civilians It's Killing in Syria', *Foreign Policy*, 31 August. Available online: https://foreignpolicy.com/2017/08/31/the-u-s-is-in-denial-about-the-civilians-its-killing-in-syria/ (accessed 31 October 2019).
Rovera, D. (2019), 'Address at the Launch of the Raqqa Exposition', *The Hague*, 20 October.
Schweiger, E. (2019), 'The Lure of Novelty: "Targeted Killing" and Its Older Terminological Siblings', *International Political Sociology*, 13: 276–95.
Schwarz, E. (2016), 'Prescription Drones: On the Techno-biopolitical Regimes of Contemporary "Ethical Killing"', *Security Dialogue*, 47(1): 59–75.
Snow, S. (2018), 'These Marines in Syria Fired More Artillery Than Any Battalion since Vietnam', *Marine Corps Times*, 6 February. Available online: https://www.marinecorpstimes.com/news/your-marine-corps/2018/02/06/these-marines-in-syria-fired-more-artillery-than-any-battalion-since-vietnam/ (accessed 31 October 2019).
Townsend, S. J. (2017), 'Reports of Civilian Casualties in the War against ISIS Are Vastly Inflated', *Foreign Policy*, 15 September. Available online: https://foreignpolicy.com/2017/09/15/reports-of-civilian-casualties-from-coalition-strikes-on-isis-are-vastly-inflated-lt-gen-townsend-cjtf-oir/ (accessed 31 October 2019).
UK Parliament (2018), 'Counter-Daesh Update', *Hansard*, 644. 3 July 2018. Available online: https://hansard.parliament.uk/Commons/2018-07-03/debates/C3257BF9-9024-4037-9B06-575AA23CB9DC/Counter-DaeshUpdate (accessed 31 October 2019).

US Department of Defense (2019), 'Annual Report on Civilian Casualties in Connection with United States Military Operations', *US Department of Defense*, 2 May 2019. Available online: https://media.defense.gov/2019/May/02/2002126767/-1/-1/1/ANNUAL-REPORT-CIVILIAN-CASUALTIESIN-CONNECTION-WITH-US-MILITARY-OPERATIONS.PDF (accessed 31 October 2019).

Waldman, T. (2017), 'Vicarious Warfare: The Counterproductive Consequences of Modern American Military Practice', *Contemporary Security Studies*, 39(2): 181–205.

Woods, C. (2019), Interview with Lauren Gould, London, 2 March.

Conclusion: Where war inhabits

Sarah Maltby and Katy Parry

Everyday language is replete with war's spatial metaphors. We find ourselves talking of 'no man's land', the 'frontline' or 'homefront' within quotidian conversations about mundane activities, such that militaristic terms permeate everyday vernacular. More obviously, spatial metaphors have been used in the enactment of war but often in nebulous and intangible ways, for example, 'war zone', 'battle ground' and 'global war on terror'. The spaces evoked within such phrases are far from neutral and even challenge the notions of freedom and availability that the term 'space' might otherwise suggest. It is precisely because of these contradictions that we began this book with the bold declaration that space matters. Space is, as various theoretical conceptualizations have suggested, political. When we speak of mediascape (Appadurai), mediapolis (Silverstone), new media ecology (Postman) or mediatization (Cottle), then we are envisaging structures, processes, feelings and power relations that are critical to our understanding of spaces of war, and war spaces.

What we have tried to do in this book is broaden our ability to think about space as a concept that is distinct, unique and has utility; to move the reader beyond singularly focused studies of media, politics, memory and so on; to consider the wider, messier whole that constitutes the complexities of how the relations and practices of war and media are conditioned by space and create space.

Space as dynamic

As part of this endeavour we take the position that both space *and* time are critical dimensions for building explanations and understandings of war and media. Scholars producing comparative case studies of different conflicts or media systems may provide temporal snapshots in which a full space can be seen – a web of relationships at that given moment which produce similar or different outcomes in the different cases. But taking 'slices' of spaces can only take us so far (Hay 2002; Massey 2005). Process and change matter too. Central to our mandate here then is the task of explaining and creating understandings of the role of media in initiating, sustaining, ameliorating or preventing war and conflict. These occur through time – either synchronic snapshots of one or more spaces or diachronic narratives of a singular process through time. As a field, we need to build both and, through collaborations, begin to find ways to build combinations of how we treat space and time together.

Essential to this is the notion of process. Indeed, recent scholarship in media philosophy has emphasized that analysis is enlivened when we consider we are always in the middle of any process. As Grusin quotes of Emerson: 'Where do we find ourselves? [...] In a series of which we do not know the extremes... We wake and find ourselves on a stair; there are stairs below us, which we seem to have ascended; there are stairs above us, many a one, which go upward and out of sight' (Emerson 2000: 307, cited in Grusin 2015:129). There is never a wholly new media space; websites initially looked like newspaper front pages; television broadcasting struggled for decades to escape the conventions of radio and theatre. 'Old media rarely die', writes John Durham Peters, 'just recede into the background and become more ontological' (Peters 2015: 23). Any 'digital' space will thus contain continuities with prior spaces and will contain the seeds of whatever 'post-digital' space is created next. No system is complete, no process wholly exhausted. Space is always unfinished (Massey 2005).

This insight bears upon how we can treat space as dynamic. A space rests upon matter already existing and it will leave traces and layers that form the conditions of emergence for the next space. But how this works varies. Whether we take the internet or a forest, both are always evolving through the interactions of uncountable entities and actors, both may feature sub-spaces in which humans intentionally carve out a site for specific gatherings and purposes, both leave layers of searchable detritus, and both are open to continual change to come. Moreover, that change does not just happen. Instead, we can explain what aspects of those spaces – whether topographic material features or topological feelings, perceptions and relations – are or are not conditions for change or how they are instrumentalized for change through interactions determined by hierarchies of power.

In this concluding chapter, we reflect upon how the contributions in this book have enriched our understanding of war and media through the foregrounding of dynamic spaces in which war is encountered, enacted and contested. Critical to this is thinking through how the dynamic quality of spaces are altered and shift according to the various actors who inhabit them, their motivations for doing so and the accrual of their inhabitation. Below then, we return to the spaces mapped in the introduction – *institutional spaces, public spaces, resistant spaces, ambivalent spaces* – to review how the contributions in this volume speak to issues of process and inhabitation. It is noteworthy that we do not intend these typologies to be definitive, mutually exclusive or exhaustive. Rather, we offer them as a useful framework to examine how mediated encounters with war are shaped by certain infrastructures, practices and bodies (both human and non-human) in space.

Institutional spaces

We start with *institutional spaces* which are loosely defined by the inhabitation of institutional actors, namely militaries, governments, policymakers and the media. For all of these actors, battlespaces were traditionally discerned by physical space – land, air, sea and (outer) space – with the introduction of information and cyberspace as a fifth domain of war in the 1990s. In the conceptualization of this latter domain, the threat of violence and disorder has led to growing uncertainty regarding the boundaries of battlespace. This is evident in the characterization of multidimensional or 'full spectrum' warfare where increased security, policing and surveillance capabilities are harnessed as preventative and containment strategies in what Gregory (2011) defines as 'the everywhere war': 'Far from making the battlespace transparent, this new apparatus actively exploits another grey zone, the space between civilian and combatant that is peopled by the spectral figures that haunt the landscape of insurgency' (Gregory 2011: 242).

There are ethical and legal questions raised by 'everywhere war' and it is within this context that Aday's (Chapter 6) and Foster's (Chapter 5) explorations of institutional spaces are most resonant. Both explore them as spaces in which legitimation strategies for war are conceived and enacted, and moral authority asserted. What emerges most from their analysis however is the persistence, stasis and endurance of particular power dynamics in these processes, particularly because war is 'everywhere'. For Aday (Chapter 6), it is in the relational power of institutional spaces inhabited by policymakers and media that moral affirmations are made through carefully constructed 'culturally congruent' (and strategic) narratives, built upon shared meanings of the 'past, present and future of international politics' (Miskimmon et al. 2017: 6). Here, Aday points to a 'kind of meta-institution comprised of interconnected sub- institutional entities including mass media, government, think tanks, and political parties [...] that combine to define and promote these legitimizing national and cultural myths and identity' despite the harm generated in other spaces as result. His observations not only suggest to us that it is the sustaining of legitimacy that characterizes these spaces, but also that the sustaining of traditional, hierarchical, authoritative, political logics through which this can be achieved is of critical importance.

Similarly, for Foster it is the organizational and cultural logics of traditional military institutions, with their emphasis on conformity, centralization and traditional hierarchical structure, that has undermined the effective integration of social media and digital platforms into military work. Comparing the Australian Deference Force and NATO-led initiatives with those of the Israel Defence Force and insurgent groups like Al Qaeda and ISIS, Foster not only draws our attention to the importance of spatial power relations – in the form of blurred civil-military relations – in the effective conduct of information war campaigns, but also the capacity of enduring and accessible narratives to mobilize support. Overall, in Aday's and Foster's work we see a re-entrenchment of the defining powers of war, where organizational war logic remains central to the ways in which we spatially encounter war.

But there are other contributions in this volume that suggest otherwise, articulating a more dynamic, fluid – and at times reconciliatory – dimension to institutional spaces. Culloty (Chapter 4), for example, turns our attention from notions of power and influence to that of distrust and suspicion. Seeking to understand the appeal of conspiracy theories, specifically around Syria, in the global 'ecology of war media', Culloty finds that the uncertainty brought about by 'conspiracy thinking' has also engendered a counterbalancing force: social media verification expertise, which is becoming an 'institutionalized practice' in its own right. This has generated a space of alternative plausibility and competition over claims (and official narratives) that is ever changing.

Similarly, through her work investigating Russian and Ukrainian journalists and documentary makers, Voronova (Chapter 11) suggests that the institutional spaces of media can, over time, be reconciliatory despite the conflicting and competing claims that may circulate within them. Here, like Massey (2005), Voronova resists the tendencies to think of space through the specificity of place by showing that it is *only* when Russian and Ukrainian journalists are taken out of their local environments and put in a neutral and 'uniting' space that more textured understandings of each other's respective positions are formed, the outcome of which has wider global impact. Both of these chapters, while not necessarily suggesting neutrality, highlight the extent to which institutional spaces are not always constrained by static hierarchical power, but rather *can be* dynamic spaces of mutation, dialogue, co-production and unification.

Public spaces

We noted above that institutional spaces are predominantly populated by those actors who are directly engaged in the enactment and mediation of war (militaries, governments, policy makers, journalists and so on). What then of broader public engagement in spaces of war?

When using the term 'public' here we acknowledge how contentious this is. What, after all, delineates a public actor from, say, an insurgent, a civilian, an activist and so on? Similarly, when are war spaces/spaces of war *not* public? Even when accounting for hierarchies of power, it would seem to us that we are *all* public actors who are inhabiting public war spaces at one time or another, under varying conditions, with varying consequences. Despite this, a notional use of the term 'public' – as both actor and space – has utility here in unpicking some of the contributions of this book to our understanding of space, precisely because it allows us to consider actor inhabitation in broad, generic ways, that other terms may not. In so doing we are able to not only shift the focus away from actors who have particular power relations in the enactment and communication of war – like the military, government, media – but also shift the notion of inhabitation away from the communicative (as above) to the affective and the invested, to the emotional and the resonant – to the participatory.

As Crilley and Chatterje-Doody argue (Chapter 3) it is how media audiences give meaning to, build upon and are 'affectively invested' in representations of war that deserves critical attention. Here they consider 'audience' interactions with disparate and epistemologically incongruent online narratives of chemical attacks in Syria, across different genres. As part of this endeavour, they discern the significance of popular culture forms in world politics (see also Dodds 2015; Shepherd 2013), particularly with regard to the 'blurring' of boundaries between factual and entertainment media formats. They also speak to issues of connectivity, highlighting how conflict conspiracy theories can be deployed strategically by powerful actors, where in-group and out-group allegiances facilitate aggression and overt anti-Semitism, often framed by opaque motivations. More than this however, they extend our understanding of actor inhabitation beyond notions of spectatorship to show how audience endorsement of and affective investment in online 'public' war spaces is not only expressive of identity and community but accruing in the meaning it generates. It is in these 'public' spaces, inhabited by 'public' actors, that we are able to see the interconnections of institutional and public in a manner that forms the conditions and emergences of new spaces and new identities by virtue of the traces and layers left behind by inhabitation.

In a similar vein, but referring to quite a different space in terms of physicality and materiality, is Friend's photographic work on Salisbury Plain (Chapter 9). Friend's writing and photographs convey the 'complex and ambiguous space' of the Plain, both the largest military training area in the UK and a conservation area, which, in her own words, is a 'strange conjunction of beauty and violence'. Friend's visual assessment of the military presence on Salisbury Plain as pervasive shows it scarring the countryside and forming 'constructed landscapes' with woodlands designed for hiding tanks and a 'ghost village' that now attracts tourists. But beyond this assessment is the insight she offers about those who literally and metaphorically inhabit the physical space of the Plain itself. Here, she writes of the habituation of the 'public' and the residents to military presence ('part of the wallpaper of the place') and the sensorial consequences that result, especially the sound and feel of army presence. There is an emotional resonance in her account (of their accounts) that is at once suggestive of identification and struggle, investment and dispossession, all of which are layered with meaning of past, present and future imaginings of the Plain. It is perhaps here in particular, in Friend's work, that we can most clearly identify the 'traces' of dynamic war space that have both accrued meaning and generate meaning.

Resistant spaces

For all those spaces that are inhabited by actors with seemingly vague motivations, there are also those where the inhabitation is clearly defined, purposeful and accumulative. Based on the contributions in this book, we are terming these 'resistant spaces' – spaces in which activists and artists, among others, attempt to challenge dominant narratives of war and where their expressed concerns about corruption or injustice are transformed into action. As war and media scholars, we tend to focus on how media intervene in war, as an amplifier of certain messages which might exacerbate conflict, but here we draw attention to how media and artistic practice can also emphasize the continuing harsh realities for those trying to live in, and with, war. Alongside institutional and public spaces, resistant spaces are transformative spaces, but deliberately so. They are inhabited by actors whose inhabitation is wholly contingent on their desire to affect change as a justice project. In this sense, these spaces are decisively ethical and moral in dimension, made possible through the inhabitation of the space itself.

Take, for example, Matar and Helmi's work on the women behind *Enab Baladi*, an alternative protest media initiative that emerged following the 2011 uprising in Syria (Chapter 7). Helmi herself was one of those activists operating in a context where a lack of access for Western journalists in Syria offered her a 'brokering' role. Employing the optic of *liminality* – referring to the quality of disorientation, where norms can be contested in moments of transition – they explore the extent to which the inhabiting of new media platforms by Syrian women would or could 'provide new fields of possibilities' for the women as authorial voices and actors in the imagining and construction of their political and social subjectivities. While Matar and Helmi note the precariousness of these possibilities – by virtue of the protracted nature of the conflict and the ability of those with power to suppress dissent – the possibilities are themselves transformative in the spatial configuration that made them thinkable. Key to this is Helmi's own 'present' role in the relational configuration of this space, where Helmi becomes simultaneously actor, activist and power broker. Roles that we would suggest also extend to her writing for this book.

The utility and power of actor inhabitation is also apparent in Gibbon's work (Chapter 10) where she actively attempts to disrupt the physical spaces she inhabits as part of her art. Employing Dada methods, Gibbon enters the globalized defence industry by visiting arms fairs, masquerading as a security consultant. Here she collects gifts provided for delegates – stress balls in the shape of bombs, mini rubber tanks, toffees – and subsequently puts them on display in galleries and museums. In so doing, she attempts to emphasize the commoditization of weapons (through the 'readymade' artefacts) but also makes visible the 'deceptive veneer' of the respectability of the arms industry – who usually prefer to remain secretive – through the displacement of the objects into more critical spaces. There are real transformative qualities in the methods Gibbon employs here if we are to think about them in 'space changing' terms. Not only does she generate visibility from invisibility (of space, of object, of reputation) but she also generates potential for the disruption of the space in which she is no longer present – the arms fair.

And it is through this role of absence that Barsdorf-Liebchen draws our attention to spatial power relations apparent in the enactment of abhorrent and illegal violence in ordinary, everyday spaces (Chapter 2). Here she examines the work of artist and photographer Edmund Clark Here she examines the work of artist and photographer Edmund Clark who forensically visualizes civilian locations of torture and rendition in ordinary-looking neighbourhoods, home interiors and commercial airports, placing these visualizations alongside declassified documentation. For Barsdorf-Liebchen, Clark employs a 'cadastral way of seeing', where cadastral maps are typically used by town planners to record property boundaries and so embody a quotidian, legal and bureaucratic dimension lacking in other maps. With a focus on specific 'owned' spaces of war, the viewer is invited to investigate further in their own 'sleuthing' of sites of hidden human trauma. Again, we see issues of accessibility and place here where the 'black sites' of the CIA during the war on terror were inaccessible and once deniable places, only able to work through the corporate- militarist coordination of the CIA, private contractors and security firms in global, complex infrastructures. And by presenting building plans of sites of rendition, imprisonment and torture in particular cities, she reminds us that something as abstract, global and alienating as the war on terror was something ultimately enacted locally by humans in concrete locations amid ignorance or indifference from local communities passing through the same streets and transport hubs as those rendered. The local is a site of horror here (Cavarero 2009). Thus, in her characterization of Clark, Barsdorf-Liebchen, like Matar, Helmi and Gibbon, serves to emphasize the role of the actor as seeking the possibility of transformation (of space, narrative, experience, understanding) both in the space they inhabit but also beyond.

Ambivalent spaces

While we have considered both Gibbon's and Barsdorf-Liebchen's work under the category of resistant spaces in the above, it is noteworthy their work also traverses what we term here 'ambivalent spaces'. In marking out ambivalent spaces, we are drawing upon Wendy Kozol's notion of ambivalent witnessing where visual witnessing is 'the relational process between the photographer or artists, subjects of the image, viewer, and surrounding contexts' rather than a one-way mirror (Kozol 2014: 12). As Kozol writes, 'ambivalence calls attention to the instabilities inherent to boundary-making between self and other that has long been a cornerstone of Western cultures' (Kozol 2014). For Kozol, there is also a continuing ambivalence for scholars and practitioners about the ethics of making visible violence and human suffering, especially as witnessing practices take place in a globalized media economy prone to reasserting hierarchies of difference in race, gender, sexuality and class.

War artists often occupy ambivalent spaces, commissioned by military bodies or museums to document war through expressive means but simultaneously disturbed or even traumatized by their own (complicit) role. The contributions of artists are often contrasted with the overly familiar tropes of photojournalistic images of conflict. As Quinn writes (Chapter 1): 'Art which enables us to see the nature of war, and which releases its meaning slowly can shed a new light on our understanding of conflict. It has found ways of showing subterfuge, surveillance, secrecy and distortion.' There is not only temporality here – of the time required to produce art and for contemplation to appreciate its message – but also the sense that art reveals something that would otherwise be invisible. There are echoes of Gibbon here too, but Quinn demonstrates an interdependent relationship between media images and artistic interpretation through the artistic re-imagining of war images. Whether created from a smiling selfie-taking Tony Blair or the kneeling figure in an ISIS video, Quinn argues war art interrogates the 'value systems involved in depicting conflict and its effects'.

Similarly, it is the ethical and methodological challenges that artists inhabit in ambivalent spaces that are at the centre of Brunt's work (Chapter 8) on vernacular images of Kashmir insurgents. Here Brunt argues the limitations of a traditional photojournalistic approach which, often devoid of context and humanity, can lead to a reductionist, simplistic portrayal of subjects and their history. Utilizing a meta-photographic approach, Brunt integrates professional and vernacular material (online images and video of insurgents) in an attempt to better understand and represent the fragmented history of the region and those who live it.

Like others who occupy ambivalent spaces, Brunt draws attention to the uncertainties of the self and the other, the relational process between photographer and subject, but also the ambivalence – in Kozol's terms – of the hierarchies and ethical challenges apparent in making the violence and suffering of others visible. But for Brunt, it was the recontextualization of what he calls 'intimate autobiographical' images (as well as traditional photographic imagery) in a Western gallery space that was as ethically demanding as the process of accumulating the images. His ambitions for the #*shaheed* exhibition were to acknowledge the limitations of a singular viewpoint, to challenge audiences to think more broadly about issues of the visibility/invisibility of individuals in radical insurgent groups and to understand them as complex multidimensional human beings. His work echoes Quinn in this regard in its aim to reveal the hidden nature of war, but one in which the artist inhabits the process in order to realize its ethical potential.

Jolle Demmers, Lauren Gould and David Snetselaar also pose a question about how the hidden realities of warfare can be 'made visible', in this case by activists contesting the narratives of precision and care in 'remote warfare'. Watchdog organizations such as Airwars employ technologies like geolocation analysis to counter the Coalition claims about the number of civilian casualties in airstrikes and drone attacks. But by co-opting the knowledge and methodologies of these organizations the Pentagon have been able to assimilate the discourses of a more ethical warfare into their own rhetorical approach, thus conducting a 'perfect war' that depoliticizes the violence and hopes to 'save lives'. In appearing to respond to dissenting voices, the critique is folded into the Coalition's own discursive strategy.

Where does this leave us: Bodily inhabitation?

Let us be clear: none of the spaces suggested above are singularly distinct from each other. All overlap in one way or another; all co-constitute each other. And there are resonant themes that traverse them all: accessibility, connectivity, ethics, justice, authorship, power and visibility to name a few. Similarly, all our contributors return us to the centrality of time in our understanding of space, where dynamic process and change is critical, extending our understanding beyond temporal 'snapshots' and comparative histories to spaces that are never wholly finished or complete. In this regard, the narratives and actions that permeate all the spaces discussed above (as both temporal *and* spatial) are ever evolving (through and with information systems and actors) with different outcomes at different times and in different spaces. And thus, we come full circle because in turn, this is transformative of the very 'battlespace' in which war is enacted. Battlespaces are not only 'everywhere' – in Gregory's sense (2011) – that is, in all places or directions. They also have temporal dimensions including continuousness, repetitiousness, routineness and even stasis: they are, as noted throughout here, open to continual change.

But what really emerges from the evolving spatial and temporal dimensions of the spaces described above is the overarching theme of *bodies* and the fundamentally embodied nature of war and its relationship to space. We noted in our introduction, for example, how war spaces are central to the ordering of the lived human war experience (that is, soldiering, refugee movement, radicalization among others), but we can also see above that war spaces are also ordering of a more vicarious war experience (as spectator or participant). As Sylvester (2013: 5) reminds us 'everyone has war experiences' by virtue of the interconnectedness of global politics, media and migration. In this sense, the inhabitation of spaces of war (through bodily presence and absence) is a profoundly corporeal experience. And if we take as our starting point Mensch's (2009) contention that there is a direct correlation between bodily enactment and our ability to make sense of the world and our place in it, then the corporeal reality that is felt, lived and enacted in the inhabitation of war spaces has significant resonance for our understandings of war.

There are two key ways which we suggest we could think about this in relation to the spaces discussed in this volume: **bodily presence/absence** and **embodied participation**.

Bodily presence/absence

When considering the extent to which bodies are both present and absent in spaces of war, we are also exploring the implications of bodily presence and absence in relation to the dynamic transformative properties of the space itself. Let us take, for example, the distinct absence of bodies in some of spaces described above, particularly in Foster's and Aday's work. Similarly, in the remote warfare practices discussed in Demmers, Gould and Snetselaar's chapter, contestations of 'truth' are articulated through (disputed) counts of dead bodies, or the removal of combatant bodies in the spaces were war is enacted. All of these spaces speak to a de-corporealization of war as an outcome of the abstract, technological focused, rational strategic thinking required to legitimize war (see Norris 2000). There is a disavowal of bodily injury here and the corporeal reality of war (Scarry 1985; see also McSorley and Maltby 2012). Instead, the body is *only* present when it has utility as a vehicle through which political imaginings can be articulated and realized (Butler 2009; Maltby and Thornham 2012). It is thus the militarized body, the civic body, the technologized body that inhabits these spaces as an outcome of institutionalized authorship.

In contrast, some spaces in this book are defined wholly by bodily presence and embodied enactment. Here we see the *use* of bodies in both the orientation of the actors, and the articulations within the space, and in a manner where bodily absence can be understood very differently. We think of Helmi's activist body (among other Syrian women) inhabiting the resistant space of *Enab Baladi*, where she is 'being' in the space, living her experience through her inhabitation. Similarly, we think of Gibbon's performative, radical and embodied employment of the Dada method. Like all Dada artists, she uses her own body to disrupt the space (in this case arms fairs) and make an activist/artistic statement about it (see Maltby et al. 2012). Critically however, this disruption continues when her body leaves the space, particularly because she also removes objects from it, redisplaying them in another space. Like Helmi, she leaves her own bodily trace. Here then, bodily absence takes on a different significance. It is, what we might call, *'post-inhabitation'* – a post-bodily presence that is critical to the metamorphosis of space.

There are of course traces of bodies and post-inhabitation in nearly all of the spaces discussed in this book. In Brunt's photographs the bodies of Kashmir martyrs (dead and alive) once removed from combat sites take on renewed significance in the spaces of social media and galleries. In Friend's photographs and oral testimonies from The Plain, the bodies of soldiers leave a militarized trace, for, among other things, tourist consumption. But it is bodily absence and the post-inhabitation of the spaces in Barsdorf-Liebchen's work that is most striking. The bodies that were once present and tortured in these everyday spaces are now absent but traceable. Here, the corporeal reality of war – mutilation, injury, even death – becomes unveiled in a manner that is antithetical to the power relations exhibited in institutional spaces that attempt to de-corporealize. There is a reclaiming of bodies in the work Barsdorf-Liebchen discusses, indeed even an invitation for us to engage in our own embodied investigation that is both powerful and dynamic. Bodily trace begets more traceable bodies.

Embodied participation

That the bodies in Barsdorf-Liebchen's work are made visible to others through new mediated spaces – that *we too* can trace the absent tortured bodies that were once present in these maps – is testament to the extent to which mediation is critical to the collective corporeal experience of war through, in and with all these dynamic spaces. This is particularly so when digital and media technologies mesh with the concept of space. We noted in our introduction how the emergence of digital spaces has generated a proliferation of mapping (Oates and Gray 2019; Wilson et al. 2018) that directly intersects with where bodies are located (as those in combat, those fleeing, those connecting). We also noted the transformative qualities of technologies such as drones and wearables that can, for example, alter and accentuate our corporeal sense of risk and our own sense of body in space(s).

There is little then to dispute the corporeal impact of technologies and the embodied use of technologies in the context of war spaces. Indeed, we know that bodies are transformed in digital and media technologies spaces through the collapse of distance and proximity, detachment and intimacy, often where the affective and sensorial become privileged. While we may not literally smell, touch or taste war in these spaces, we *can* see and hear war, and we can *feel* it as an embodied extension of our spatial engagement – as pain, grief, shock, horror, fear or even elation. As McSorley (2012) notes in his concept of 'somatic war', a key aesthetic idiom through which we now understand war is through the multi-sensorial corporeal experience. Referring to our engagement with helmet cam footage – through television, online and gallery installation – he argues that the feelings and intensities we experience as a result 'may be complex, contradictory and, at times, sober […] but it is through this regime of sensory engagement and affective labour that the war is increasingly felt, and potentially undermined or sustained' (2012: 56).

Crucially then, war spaces invite us – in one way or another – to participate in the embodied enactment of war. This is resonant in most of our chapters here, but especially in Quinn and Crilley and Chatterje-Doody's work. While the employment of digital and virtual reality technologies (including flight simulator joysticks) in Quinn's artwork can be understood differently to the audience interactions of Crilley and Chatterje-Doody's work, both spaces are inviting participation in the form of sensorial and affective engagement and are, in effect, bodily extensions into the enactment of war.

Of course, we are not all refugees or drone operators, nor are we all cadastral mappers or Dada artists, but we are, by our very engagement and participation in war spaces, active in the spaces themselves and their evolution. As Scarry reminds us, war is the 'most radically embodying event in which human beings ever collectively participate' (Scarry 1985: 71). And we are participating. Thus, it is incumbent upon us to not only understand *how* (ours and others') bodies inhabit and develop spaces of war, but what the consequences of such engagement are for ourselves, for others and for the space itself.

We finish this chapter with the following opening from Friend's chapter:

Sometimes my grandfather would be sitting there silently, an array of guns displayed around him on the green walls. A quiet man, he had fought in the second Boer War and the First World War. My mother remembers how, on a couple of occasions, he entertained her with animated discussions of military strategies in the First World War, pushing a silver salt cellar and pepper pot around on the white damask tablecloth to demonstrate manoeuvres. Other than that, he was silent about his experiences.

We include this here because for us it encapsulates everything we have tried to discuss above. It is an account of an embodied (re)enactment of war, articulated through sensorial spatial and temporal dimensions. It is here that we see most clearly how the body is the site through which the war is felt, expressed, understood, where dialogue has become contingent on simulation and a corporeal re-living of embodied memory. The scene portrayed here is both evocative and unsettling, revealing and elusive – the very qualities that speak to all of the spaces we have discussed in this volume and the very questions that we need to be asking of them and other spaces of war.

References

Butler, J. (2009), *Frames of War*, London: Verso.
Cavarero, A. (2009), *Horrorism: Naming Contemporary Violence*, New York: Columbia University Press.
Dodds, K. (2015), 'Popular Geopolitics and the War on Terror', in F. Caso and C. Hamilton (eds), *Popular Culture and World Politics: Theories, Methods, Pedagogies. E-International Relations*, 51–62, Bristol: E-International Relations.
Emerson, R. D. (2000), 'Experience', in B. Atkinson (ed), *The Essential Writings of Ralph Waldo Emerson*, 307–326, New York: Random House.
Gregory, D. (2011), 'The Everywhere War', *The Geographical Journal*, 177(3): 238–50.
Grusin, R. (2015), 'Radical Mediation', *Critical Inquiry*, 42(1), 124–48.
Hay, C. (2002), *Political Analysis: A Critical Introduction*, Basingstoke: Palgrave.
Kozol, W. (2014), *Distant Wars Visible: The Ambivalence of Witnessing*, Minneapolis: University of Minnesota.
McSorley, K. (2012), 'Helmetcams, Militarized Sensation and "Somatic War"', *Journal of War and Culture Studies*, 5(1): 47–58.
McSorley, K., and S. Maltby (2012), 'War and the Body: Cultural and Military Practices', *Journal of War and Culture Studies*, 5(1): 3–6.
Maltby, S., and H. Thornham (2012), '"The Dis/embodiment of Persuasive Military Discourse," in Special Issue "War and the Body: Cultural and Military Practices"', *Journal of War and Culture Studies*, 5(1): 33–46.

Maltby, S., S. Pratt and J. Gibbon (2012), 'The War and Body Exhibition: Showing, Sharing, Shaping', in Special Issue 'War and the Body: Cultural and Military Practices', *Journal of War and Culture Studies*, 5(1): 105–15.

Massey, D. (2005), *On Space*, London: Sage.

Mensch, J. (2009), *Embodiments: From the Body to the Body Politic*, Evanston, IL: Northwestern University Press.

Miskimmon, A., B. O'Loughlin and L. Roselle (2017), *Forging the World: Strategic Narratives and International Relations*, Ann Arbor: University of Michigan Press.

Norris, M. (2000), *Writing War in the Twentieth Century*, Charlottesville: University of Virginia Press.

Oates, S., and J. Gray (2019), '# Kremlin: Using Hashtags to Analyze Russian Disinformation Strategy and Dissemination on Twitter', *SSRN*. Available online: https://ssrn.com/abstract=3445180 (accessed 1 November 2019).

Peters, J. D. (2015), *The Marvelous Clouds*, Chicago: University of Chicago Press.

Scarry, E. (1985), The Body in Pain: The Making and Unmaking of the World, Oxford: Oxford University Press.

Shepherd, L. (2013), *Gender, Violence and Popular Culture: Telling Stories*, London: Routledge.

Sylvester, C. (2013), *War as Experience*, London: Routledge.

Wilson, T., K. Zhou and K. Starbird (2018), 'Assembling Strategic Narratives: Information Operations as Collaborative Work within an Online Community', *Proceedings of the ACM on Human-computer Interaction*, 2(183): 1–25.

EDITOR AND CONTRIBUTOR BIOGRAPHIES IN ALPHABETICAL ORDER

Editors

Sarah Maltby is Professor in Media and Communication at the University of Sussex. Her work focuses on military media practice, and media memory and identity in and through military, journalistic and artistic work. She is the author of '*Remembering the Falklands War: Media, Memory and Identity* (2016), *Military Media Management: Negotiating the 'Front' Line* (2012) and co-editor of *Communicating War: Memory, Military and Media* (2007). She is Founder and Coordinator of the War and Media Network (www.warandmedia.org), an interdisciplinary networking forum that brings together academics and practitioners interested in the intersection between war and media. She is also co-editor of *Media, War and Conflict* (Sage).

Ben O'Loughlin is Professor of International Relations and Director of the New Political Communication Unit at Royal Holloway, University of London. His latest book is *Forging the World: Strategic Narratives and International Relations* (2017, University of Michigan Press, with Alister Miskimmon and Laura Roselle). He was Specialist Advisor to the UK Parliament's Select Committee on Soft Power, producing the report *Power and Persuasion in the Modern World*. In 2016 Ben and his colleagues won the Walter Lippmann Award for Political Communication at the American Political Science Association (APSA). From 2016 to 2019 he carried out studies on culture, conflict and influence for the British Council, Goethe Institute and European Commission. In 2019 he was Thinker in Residence at the Flemish Royal Academy of Arts and Sciences working on Disinformation and Democracy.

Katy Parry is Associate Professor in Media and Communication at the University of Leeds. Her work focuses on visual politics and activism, images of war and representations of contemporary soldiering. Co-authored books include *Visual Communication: Understanding Images in Media Culture* (Sage, 2019) with Giorgia Aiello; *Political Culture and Media Genre: Beyond the News* (Palgrave Macmillan, 2012) with Kay Richardson and John Corner; and *Pockets of Resistance: British News Media, War and Theory in the 2003 Invasion of Iraq* (Manchester University Press, 2010) with Piers Robinson, Peter Goddard, Craig Murray and Philip M. Taylor. She is co-editor of the journal *Media, War and Conflict* and co-convener of the Political Studies Association 'Media and Politics' Group.

Laura Roselle is Professor of Political Science and Policy Studies at Elon University. Roselle holds degrees from Emory University (Math/Computer Science and Russian) and Stanford University (PhD Political Science). She has served as president of the International Communication Section of the International Studies Association and of the Internet Technology and Politics Section of the American Political Science Association. She is the author of *Media and the Politics of Failure: Great Powers, Communication Strategies, and Military Defeats* (Palgrave, 2006 and 2011), and with co-authors Alister Miskimmon and Ben O'Loughlin, *Strategic Narratives: Communication Power and the New World Order* (Routledge, 2013) and *Forging the World: Strategic Narratives & International Relations* (University of Michigan Press, 2017). Roselle is co-editor of the journal *Media, War and Conflict* and co-editor of the book series, Routledge Studies in Global Information, Politics and Society. She won the 2017 Distinguished Scholar Award from the International Communication Section of the International Studies Association.

Contributors

Sean Aday is Associate Professor of Media and Public Affairs and International Affairs at George Washington University. His research focuses on the intersection of media, war, foreign policy, public diplomacy and public opinion.

Nicolette Barsdorf-Liebchen has been Editorial Assistant of *Media, War & Conflict* since 2013. Her research and publications focus inter alia on the critical and strategic visualization of state-corporate-military power and contemporary warfare, aiming to reinvigorate visual culture debates surrounding war and conflict by proposing critically recalibrated vocabularies for its representation in an increasingly neoliberal, globally corporatized world order.

Nathaniel Brunt is an interdisciplinary scholar, documentary photographer and educator. Brunt is currently pursuing a PhD in the Communication and Culture joint programme at Ryerson University and York University in Toronto, Canada. His doctoral research is supported by the Social Sciences and Humanities Research Council and The Pierre Elliot Trudeau Foundation. Brunt is a co-founder and co-director of the Kashmir Photo Collective.

Precious N Chatterje-Doody is Lecturer in Politics and International Studies at The Open University, UK. Her research centres on questions of global communication, perception and security, with a particular focus on Russia. She is the author of 'The Russian Identity Riddle: Unwrapping Russia's Security Policy' (Routledge, forthcoming) and tweets @PreciousChatD.

Rhys Crilley is Postdoctoral Researcher in Global Media at The Open University, UK. His research explores the intersections of social media, images and conflict. In May 2020 he is to begin a Leverhulme Early Career Fellowship at the University of Glasgow exploring narratives of nuclear weapons and how emotions shape policies of deterrence and disarmament. He tweets at @RhysCrilley.

Eileen Culloty is a Postdoctoral Researcher at the Institute for Future Media and Journalism at Dublin City University where she is research lead on disinformation for the H2020 project 'Provenance' and a member of the management team for the MSCA project 'JOLT' on journalism and technology. Her research has been published in *Environmental Communication*, *Digital Journalism*, *European Journal of Communication* and *Critical Studies on Terrorism*.

Jolle Demmers is Full Professor in Conflict Studies and co-founder of the Centre for Conflict Studies at the History of International Relations section of Utrecht University. She is the author of *Theories of Violent Conflict* (Routledge, second edition, 2017). Together with Lauren Gould she is currently running The Intimacies of Remote Warfare; among their recent publications is 'An Assemblage Approach to Liquid Warfare' (*Security Dialogue*, 2018).

Kevin Foster is Associate Professor and Head of the School of Languages, Literatures, Cultures and Linguistics at Monash University in Melbourne. Educated in the UK, Canada and Australia he has conducted original research with the Australian, British, Dutch, German, Israeli, Canadian and US militaries. He has published widely on war, memory, cultural history, national identity and combat photography, and his work has appeared in a range of national and international journals. He is the author of *Fighting*

Fictions: War, Narrative and National Identity (1999) and *Lost Worlds: Latin America and the Imagining of Empire* (2009). He edited *What Are We Doing in Afghanistan? The Military and the Media at War* (2009) and *The Information Battlefield: Representing Australians at War* (2011). His most recent monograph is *Don't Mention the War: The Australian Defence Force, the Media and the Afghan Conflict* (2013).

Melanie Friend is a photographic artist, and she is Reader in Photography in the School of Film, Media & Music at the University of Sussex. In the 1980s Friend worked extensively as a photojournalist, before focusing on the wider aspects of war through long-term projects, touring exhibitions and books. Earlier works include *No Place Like Home: Echoes from Kosovo* (Midnight Editions, USA, 2001), *Border Country* (2007, Belfast Exposed Gallery and The Winchester Gallery) and *The Home Front* (Dewi Lewis Publishing in association with Impressions Gallery, 2013). *The Plain* will be published in autumn 2020 (Dewi Lewis Publishing). See melaniefriend.com for details of forthcoming exhibitions.

Jill Gibbon is an artist and activist. She has written *The Etiquette of the Arms Trade* (2018) and has drawings in the permanent collections of the Imperial War Museum and Peace Museum. She has a BA from Leeds Polytechnic, MA from Keele University and a PhD from Wimbledon School of Art. She teaches Graphic Arts at Leeds Beckett University.

Lauren Gould is Assistant Professor in Conflict Studies at the Centre for Conflict Studies at the History of International Relations section of Utrecht University. Together with Jolle Demmers she is currently running The Intimacies of Remote Warfare programme; among their recent publications is 'An Assemblage Approach to Liquid Warfare' (*Security Dialogue*, 2018).

Kholoud Helmi is a Syrian gender and media expert and the co-founder and board member of *Enab Baladi* newspaper established in 2011. She won the 2015 Anna Politkovskaya Award for her work on Syria and the 2017 International Award Association's Courage under Fire Award for the documentary 'Cries from Syria'. In 2016, *Marie Claire* magazine called her 'the bravest woman in the world'. Kholoud holds an MA in Media and Development and is a Chevening Scholar.

Dina Matar is Head of the School of Interdisciplinary Studies at SOAS, University of London, and reader in Arab Media and Political Communication. Her work focuses on political communication practices in non-Western contexts, communication strategies in conflict, activism, representation, identities and narrative politics in the Arab world. She is author of *What It Means to be Palestinian: Stories of Palestinian*

Peoplehood (2010); co-author of *The Hizbullah Phenomenon: Politics and Communication* (2014); co-editor of *Narrating Conflict in the Middle East: Discourse, Image and Communication Practices in Lebanon and Palestine* (2013) and *Gaza as Metaphor* (2016).

Jane Quinn is a curator and writer. Formerly a BBC television executive producer and international adviser on the development of digital content, she worked in the media industry during the transition from analogue to digital technologies. A published author, in 2019 she completed her PhD in contemporary war art, at Birkbeck, University of London.

David Snetselaar is Assistant Research Fellow at the Center for Global Challenges at Utrecht University and studies how, despite the remote documentation of acts of violence made possible by open-source online investigation, state transparency and accountability remain limited and the spaces for contestation narrow. David is also part of The Intimacies of Remote Warfare team at the Centre for Conflict Studies.

Liudmila Voronova is Senior Lecturer in Journalism at Södertörn University, Sweden. Her research interests include gender and journalism, political communication, media and conflict, and, recently, photography and educational processes. In 2016–2018, she was a part of the research project 'Propaganda and management of information in the Ukraine-Russia conflict: From nation branding to information war', funded by the Foundation for Baltic and East European Studies.

INDEX

Abu Ghraib torture and prisoner abuse 26–7, 52, 56, 133, 134
abuse 133–5
   human rights 24, 26–9, 176 n.4
academic discourse 194
accountability gap 124, 136
Adam, B. 5
Aday, S. 8, 249–50, 256
aesthetic effect 16, 22–7, 30, 32
affective investments 62–5
   in RT's Syria coverage 70–5
aftermath art 22
agonistic dialogue 208
Airspace Tribunal 4
Airwars 232, 233, 235, 237–41, 255
al-Ali, N. 151
al-Asad, B. 150
al-Assad, A. 149, 153
Al-Assad, B. 65
al-Attar, N. 150
Al-Ba'ath newspaper 149
Al Haq newspaper 146
al-Jizawi, N. 150, 151
Allen, C. D. 107
Allied Command Transformation (ACT) 105
al-Nashiri, Abd al-Rahim 47, 52
al Nusra 65
Al Qaeda 104, 108, 109, 114–16, 250
al-Suri, Abu Musab 109, 117 n.6
al-thawra (www.al-thawra-sy.com) 144
Al-Thawra newspaper 149
Aluminium Waste Pond at Petkovici (Norfolk) 18–20
Amazon 41
ambiguity, liminal 150–4
ambivalent spaces 10, 254–5
ammunition whistle 190

Amnesty International 235, 238, 243 n.2
Analytical Concept for the Use of Social Media as an Effector v1.0. 105, 109–10
'An Assemblage Approach to Liquid Warfare' (Demmers and Gould) 263, 264
anti-Semitism 73, 74, 89, 251
Apel, D. 20
Apparent Horizon (Cotterrell) 23
Armstrong, N. 20–2
artists 13–15, 31
   Dada 257, 258
   digital technologies 8, 10
   interpretations of war 16
   military 19, 20
   response 16
Assad, B. 91–2, 94
audience encounter 30–3
audience engagement 71–2
Australian Defence Force (ADF) 104, 107, 117 n.7, 250
Azhgikhina, N. 211
Azoulay, A. 20

Babich, D. 68
'bad guys' 53–4
Badiou, A. 40
BAE Systems 199
Baghdad Calling (van Kesteren) 28
Ball, H. 197
Barad, K. 194, 195, 202
Barkawi, T. 233
Barker, T. 22
Barsdorf-Liebchen, N. 8, 253, 254, 257–8
Ba'thist Syrian regime 149
Ba'th Party 149, 150

INDEX

The Battle for Hajin: Tactical Victory, Strategic Defeat? 242
Battle for Raqqa 238, 239
'battle over truths' 209
Bellingcat 91, 92, 94
Benjamin, W. 201
Bennett, J. 194
Bennett, W. L. 128, 133, 134
Ben-Shalom, R. 113
Berenger, R. 89
biased journalism 218
Black, C. 37, 47
black sites 37, 44, 47, 253
Blair, Tony 25, 254
'a blatantly pro-Kremlin apologist' 68
Blix, H. 96
Bloomfield, S. 96
Blumler, J. 130
bodily presence/absence 256–7
Bofors slogan 198–9, 201
Bohr, N. 195
Boiko, P. 70
bomb stress ball 187, 193, 195, 198, 201–2, 253
Bonds, E. 236, 238
Brass, P. R. 233–4
breaking news 67, 69, 74, 75, 77, 163
Brighton, S. 233
Brimstone missile 198
British House of Commons 93
Bruder, M. 88
Brunt, N. 9, 254–5, 257
Bucharest 47–50, 52
Burke, J. 175
Bush, G. W. 127, 133, 134
Butler, J. 20, 64, 155 n.4, 155 n.9

cadastral 8, 35–6, 38–40, 44, 57
    events 40–2
    forensic approach 42–9, 56
    mapping 36, 39, 41–4, 47–9, 253
    Negative Publicity 37–8
    proxy measurement 44, 47–9, 52
    visualization 35–44, 49, 53–7
Cammaertz, B. 144
Campbell, D. 132
Camus, A. 193
Capa, R. 36

Carr, R. 199
Carruthers, S. L. 169
Carter, A. 236
Cascading Activation Model (Entman) 124, 128–9, 131, 133–6
CGI. *See* computer-generated imagery (CGI)
Chakravarty, I. 168
Chamayou, G. 232, 236
Chatterje-Doody, P. N. 8, 251, 258
Chayka, I. 212
Chouliaraki, L. 90
CIA 40, 52, 53
    'black sites' 37, 47, 253
CIA Rendition Flights (2001–2006) 43
'City on a Hill' 129, 135
civilian casualty (CIVCAS) cell 127, 137, 233, 237–40, 242
Clark, E. 27, 36–8, 40–4, 47–9, 53, 55–7, 58 n.7, 253, 254
Clausewitz, Carl von 126
ClipArt 77
ClipaRT with Boris Malagurski 67–8, 74, 77
Coalition 235, 243 n.1
    anti-IS 232, 233, 235
    co-opting Airwars 239–41
    machinations of war 235–6
    Operation Inherent Resolve 235–6
    precision and contestation 236–8
    regime of truth 233–5
    sanctioning techniques 239
    spatial reconfiguration of warfare 232–3
    state violence 241–2
Cockayne, J. 55
Cockburn, C. 156 n.10
Coleman, S. 97
collaboration dialogue 208
Commission for counteraction to propaganda 206–7
communication
    disruption 207, 208, 219
    mass 124, 125, 127, 130, 131
    political 4, 84
    revolution 108
    virtual 103
    visual media 90–1

complexity 16–18
computer-generated imagery (CGI) 20, 22
conflictual consensus 208
conformity 106–8, 250
conspiracy mentality 88
conspiracy theory 83–9, 97–8
    claims 86, 87
    defined 86
    de la Croix, Agnes Mariam 93
    endorsement of 87–8
    Ghouta attack 93–4
    Khan Sheikhoun attack 95–7
    and mediatized conflict 89–91
    9/11 terror attack 87
conspiracy thinking 85–8, 93, 96, 98, 250
contemporary warfare 10, 16, 37, 172, 242
contestation 236–8
Control Order House (Clark) 27, 37, 42, 46, 49, 50
conventional military 103–4
    decentralized structures 107–9
    failure of 109–10
    Israel Defence Force 110–14
    MCDC 105
    Multinational Information Operations Experiment 105–6
    organizational cultures and conformity 106–7
co-optation dialogue 208
co-opting Airwars 239–41
corporatization 35, 36, 41
Cotterrell, D. 15, 23, 24, 32
creative thinking 106, 107
Crenshaw, K. 155 n.1
Crilley, R. 8, 251, 258
crippled epistemology 88
critical spaces 199–202
CrossTalk 68
CS gas canisters 198
Culloty, E. 8, 250
culture
    congruence 129
    material 194–5
    and media 130–1
    organizational 106–7
curfews 176 n.6

Dada method 194–7, 199, 253, 257, 258
Daesh 18, 235
Dahnoon blog 146
The Daily Show 67
Dead Troops Talk (Wall) 20
decadastration 43, 48, 56
decentralized networks 107–9
de-corporealization of war 256–7
Defence Security Exhibition International (DSEI) 197, 198
Deghayes, O. 27
de la Croix, Agnes Mariam 93
Demmers, J. 10, 255
Designing Nuclear Weapons (2000s) 26
Detector Media (Kanfer) 220
Deutsche Welle (Schultz) 96
dialogic space 205–7, 223–6
    definition 208–9
    Kto nas razvel? 218–21
    language of 221–3
    positions 208
    professional journalism 211–18
    spaces of war to 207–10
    Trudnosti perevoda 218–21
    Ukraine-Russia conflict 210–11
Die Welt (Hersh) 94, 95
diffused war (Hoskins and O'Loughlin) 108
digital
    activism 143, 144
    camera 22, 25, 27
    militarism 114, 115
    tools 15, 16, 22–5
digital media 14, 17, 20, 28–30, 33, 84
    and mediatization of conflict 89–91
    social and 104, 106, 112, 113
digitization 25, 30, 31, 33
discrimination 88–9, 127, 137, 146, 149
Distillation of Terror (Keane) 17–18
documentation 162–4
Donbas Media Forum 207
Douma chemical attack, RT 66–70
Dozhd channel 219
DPR/LPR. *See* 'People's republics' of Donetsk and Luhansk
drones 4, 14, 127, 258
Duchamp, M. 197, 199–200

Dudley, M. 180
Duffield, M. 241
Duncan, D. D. 36
Dunne, J. P. 196
Dyers, S. 240
dynamic spaces 248–9
Dzhazoyan, A. 212–15

Edwards, E. 200
elite-driven news 128–9, 135
embodied participation 257–9
Emerging Syrian media (ESM) 153
Emerson, J. 43
empty signifiers 133
Enab Baladi 145–8, 151, 252, 257
enhanced interrogation technique (EITs) 134
Entman, R. 124, 128–31, 133, 136
Entman, R. M. 124, 136
Etiquette of the Arms Trade, The 193, 199
European Federation of Journalists (EFJ) 206
'events' 40–2

Facebook 113, 220
'fairy-tale' might 217
Falklands Conflict 118 n.21
Fallows, J. 136
false-flag operation 87, 95
Fazal, T. 126, 127
Fear sequence (Keane) 27
Feldman, A. 209
Fenster, M. 88
fictional narratives 20–2
Fishman, M. 130
Foley, J. 235
forensic approach 42–9, 56
Forensic Architecture 28–30
Foster, K. 8, 249, 250, 256
Foucault, M. 209, 233, 234
Fountain (Duchamp) 199–200
Freire, P. 167
Freud, S. 202
Friend, M. 9, 251–2, 257, 259
Fussell, P. 131, 132, 136

Gadamer, H. -G. 209
gallery spaces 10, 32–3

Ganesh, Sh. 208, 210
Gans, H. 130, 131, 135
Gates, J. 162
gender
    differentiations 151, 152
    equality 149
    inequality 149, 153
    instrumentalization of 153–4
    norms and imbalances 149
    practices 152
    violence 156 n.10
genres 32, 61–3, 65–7, 75, 77–8
    affective investments 70–5
    breaking news 67, 69
    and emotion 75–7
    late-night parody show 67–9
    satirical social media short 68–70
    talk show 68, 69
geospatial references 41
German language 48–9
Gerras, S. 107
Ghouta attack 93–4, 97, 98
Gibbon, J. 9, 253, 254, 257
Giddens, A. 84
Gilbert, E. 240
Global Arms Trade: A Handbook, The (Tan) 196
globalization 36, 84, 196, 197
Good War, The 131
Google 32, 41
Gopal, A. 239
Gosden, C. 200
Gould, L. 10, 255
Gould, P. 207
Gregory, D. 232, 249, 256
grenade stress ball 9, 188
Grosz, G. 197
Grusin, R. 248
Guards of Freedom 213
Gulf War 1 (1990–1991) 13–15
Gurevitch, M. 130

Habermas, J. 209–10
Halberstam, D. 124
hand grenades 198
Hanit 111
Hardin, R. 88
Hecker, M. 108–9, 117 n.6, 117 n.10

INDEX

Hedges, C. 175 n.3
Helmi, K. 9, 146, 147, 152, 155 n.6, 252–4, 257
Hersh, S. 94–6, 98
Hezbollah missile attack 111
Higgins, E. 91, 92, 94
historical analogies 131–3
Hizbul Mujahideen 167–70
Hoffman, A. 112
Hogan, P. C. 169
Hök, J. 208
Home Front, The (2013) 184
Homes & Gardens: Documenting the Invisible (1994–1996) 184
Hoskins, A. 3, 108
House of Osama bin Laden, The (2003) 22
Hromadske channel 206, 207
humanitarian intervention 70, 72
humanitized violence 236
humanity 5, 43
  absence of 42
  and arts 39
  fallibility 26
  and social sciences 5
human rights 4, 24, 26–30, 92, 161, 176 n.4
humour 70, 72, 76, 202
Hyde, L. 198

ICYMI channel 68–70, 72, 76, 77
ideological contrivance 56
IDF. *See* Israel Defence Force (IDF)
IMB. *See* Interactive Media Branch (IMB)
Imperial War Museum (IWM) 15, 16, 22, 32
Incoming (2016) 25
Independent Media Trade Union of Ukraine (IMTU) 212
indexing hypothesis 128
indexing phenomenon 128
information environment (IE) 103, 104, 114, 115
  decentralized structures 107–9
  failure of conventional militaries 109–10
  Israel Defence Force 111–12, 114

'information war' 62
inhabitation 255–6
  bodily presence/absence 256–7
  embodied participation 257–9
inhumanity 169
INS *Hanit* 111
institutional spaces 8, 10, 85, 249–50
insurgency in Kashmir. *See* Kashmir Valley, insurgency
integrity 48, 91, 95, 96, 195
Interactive Media Branch (IMB) 113, 118 n.20
International Federation of Journalists (IFJ) 206
internet 8, 16, 18, 31, 32, 146, 162, 214, 221, 223, 248
internet freedoms 41
intersectionality 155 n.1
In the Future They Ate from the Finest Porcelain (Sansour) 22
intimate autobiographical images 172, 255
in/visible spaces of war 35, 36, 38, 39, 49, 57, 57 n.1
Iraq
  and Afghanistan conflict 116
  PhotoOp 24–5
  United States and 90, 96, 134, 135, 232
  War footage 90–1
ISIS 91, 92, 104, 108, 114, 116, 127, 137, 163, 250, 254
Islamic State (IS) 65, 156 n.12, 235
  British Muslims 4
  coalition airstrikes 232
  Operation Inherent Resolve 231, 233–9, 241, 242
  in Syria 242
Islamophobia 89
Israel Defence Force (IDF) 104, 110–16, 117 n.14, 118 n.16, 250
'Israel Under Fire' project 113
IWM. *See* Imperial War Museum (IWM)

Jablonski, M. 41
Jacobin (Shalom) 95
Jameson, F. 194

journalism 207, 208, 218
　biased 218
　citizen 27–8, 30, 163
　Hersh, S. 95–6
　Kanfer, L. 220
　professional 211–18
　Ukraine 206, 215, 218
　verification expert 92
jus ad bellum 126
jus in bello 126
jus post bellum 126
Just and Unjust Wars (Walzer) 126
just war theory 8, 124–30, 132, 133, 136

Kanfer, L. 207, 211, 220–5
Kashmir Photo Collective 167
Kashmir Valley, insurgency 159–62, 174–5
　documentation 162–4
　metaphotographic approach 164–7
　#shaheed 167–74
Keane, J. 14–18, 22, 27, 31
Kelly, S. 148
kennardphillipps 16, 24
Kennedy, J. 236
Kennedy, L. 163
Kesteren, G. van 28
Khamis, S. 143–4
Khan, A. 239
Khan Sheikhoun attack 95–7
*Kibree*t blog 146
Kozak, T. 205
Kozol, W. 254, 255
Kto nas razvel? 218–21
Kuscsh, L. 206

Laclau, E. 208
Landes, A. 112, 114, 118 n.15
Langlands and Bell 22
language of dialogic space 221–3
Lashkar-e-Taiba (LeT) militants 159, 167, 175 n.1
Last Week with John Oliver 67
late-night parody show 67–9, 74
Latour, B. 4–6

Lavelle, P. 68
Lazarsfeld, P. 131
legitimizing agents 132
Legrier, François-Régis 242
Leibovich, A. 118 n.20
Lesnoy, E. 207, 211, 219–24
Letters to Omar (2010) 27
Lewis, T. E. 200
Lia, B. 109
Liao, N. 132
liminality 144–5, 154–5, 252–3
　ambiguity 150–4
　Enab Baladi 146–8
　Syrian women 148–50
Linfield, S. 174
liquid warfare 233
London Review of Books (Hersh) 94
Lorrain, C. 18
Lost in Translation 220, 222
Lowry, G. D. 32
Lukashenka, B. A. 205
Lybäck, L. 210

machinations of war propaganda 235–6
McCullin, D. 36
McQueen, S. 15
McSorley, K. 258
Mail 213
mapping 6, 36, 39, 41–4, 47–9, 57, 112, 115, 258
marginalization 88, 151
Marx, K. 193, 198
masculinity 153, 170
Massachusetts Institute of Technology (MIT) 94
Massey, D. 6, 250
Matar, D. 9, 252–4
material effects 193–5
Mattis, J. 96, 236
Mayes, S. 162
MCDC. *See* Multinational Capability Development Campaign (MCDC)
meaning and materials (Barad) 195
media 4, 5–10, 13–16, 127–8. *See also* social media

actors and 7–8
conflict 89–91
culture and 130–1
digital 14, 17, 20, 28–30, 33
elite-driven news and Cascade Model 128–9
historical analogies 131–3
news 3, 5, 19, 30, 84, 85, 90, 92, 94, 97–8, 125, 136
opportunity structures 144
production 153
in Syria 9
technologies 4
'torture' 133–5
verification 85, 91, 98, 250
war and 3–7, 64–5
mediatization 6, 57, 84, 89, 247
Meiches, B. 202
Mensch, J. 256
Merrin, W. 108
Merton, R. 131
metaphotographic process 164–7
Mijatovic, D. 216
militarization 36, 151–3, 184
military industrial complex (MIC) 196–9
military sublime 50
Miller, L. 36
Miskimmon, A. 132
mobile phone imaging technology 162
Mogel, L. 39
Möls, T. 107
Monsters of the Id (Cotterrell) 23, 32
moral effect grenades 198
Morris, E. 90–1
mortar bomb 191
Mosse, R. 25
Mouffe, C. 208, 225
multimedia 33
Multinational Capability Development Campaign (MCDC) 103–5, 114, 116 n.1
Multinational Information Operations Experiment (MNIOE) 105–7
Musawa (equality) 146
Mutt, R. 199

Nachtwey, J. 36
Nanoq: Flat Out and Bluesome (Snæbjörnsdóttir and Wilson) 200
Naqash, R. 168
Naschmarkt 213
Nashmarkt 216
National Coalition of Syrian Revolutionary and Opposition Forces 65
national media communities 224
National Registry Office for Classified Information (ORNISS) 48
National Union of Journalists of Ukraine (NUJU) 206, 210, 212, 217
NATO-led initiatives 250
Nazareth, B. J. 106–7
necroethics 236
Negative Publicity (Clark) 37–8, 41–4, 46–50, 53, 54, 56, 57
neutral territory 212, 223, 224
Neville, M. 15
'New Cold War' 62
news 32, 130
   audience engagement 71–2
   breaking 63, 67, 69, 74, 75, 77, 163
   coverage 90, 92, 93, 130
   elite-driven 128–9, 135
   Khan Sheikhoun attack 95–7
   media 3, 5, 19, 30, 84, 85, 90, 92, 94, 97–8, 125, 136
   uncertainty 85, 92
'news net' 130
NewsOne channel 205, 206, 223
newspaper 13, 16, 18, 90, 146, 148, 149, 207, 235, 248, 264
Newsweek 96
New York Times 92, 94
NGO 10, 95, 240
9/11 attacks 36, 87, 96, 108, 133–6
Nixon, R. 86
non-human nature 26, 38, 57
Nonoq 201
Norfolk, S. 15, 18–20, 22, 26, 37, 42, 50, 58 n.8
Novaya gazeta 207

NSA – Tapped Undersea Cables, North Pacific Ocean, 2016 (Paglen) 25–6
NUJU. *See* National Union of Journalists of Ukraine (NUJU)
Nygren, G. 208

Oakford, S. 239
Obama, B. 93, 127, 137, 235
objectivity 134–5, 195, 209
Obrist, Hans Ulrich 32
Odnoklassniki 213
O'Loughlin, B. 3, 5, 108, 133
Olsen, B. 195
one star tweet 110
online spaces 7–9, 31–2
Open Society Foundations 48
Operation Cast Lead 111
Operation Inherent Resolve 231, 233–9, 241, 242
Operation Pillar of Defense 112, 113
"operative images" 30
operative system 109
organizational cultures 106–7
Organization for Security and Cooperation in Europe (OSCE) 206, 213–17, 223, 224
Organization for the Prohibition of Chemical Weapons (OPCW) 66
ownership boundaries 41
Oxygen newspaper 146

Paglen, T. 25–6, 37, 42, 43, 56
Palestinian identity 20, 22
Papacharissi, Z. 145
partisan nature 76, 134, 135
peace journalism 208
Pentagon 137, 240, 241, 243, 255
'People's republics' of Donetsk and Luhansk (DPR/LPR) 208, 217, 220
Perlo-Freeman, S. 196
'perpetual war' 39, 40
Peters, J. D. 248
Pfau, M. 90
Phillips, R. 200
philosophy, conspiracy theories 86

PhotoCall (Brothers in Arms) (1991) 14
photographic process 166, 167, 173
aluminium waste pond 18–19, 201
Brunt, N. 257
Ghraib, A. 26–7, 52
image-making projects (Clark) 36
metaphotographic process 164–7
post-photography 8, 48, 55, 56, 58 n.7, 162–4
Salisbury Plain 179–84, 251–2
#shaheed 159, 161, 167–75, 255
photojournalism 36, 90, 165, 255
PhotoOp (2005) 16, 24
photoshopping 16, 20
Pinckers, M. 27
Plain. *See* Salisbury Plain
plausibility 87, 88–9, 95
pluralism of perspective 23, 24
PMSCs. *See* private security and military contractors (PMSCs)
policymakers 126, 127, 131, 136, 249
popularization 33
post-inhabitation 257
Postol, T. 94, 96, 98
post-photography 8, 48, 55, 56, 58 n.7, 162–4, 168, 170, 172, 174
Poussin, N. 18
Powers, S. M. 41
precision warfare 236–8
private security and military contractors (PMSCs) 41, 53, 55
Procrustean bed 107
professionalism 146, 209
professional journalism 211–18
proto-conspiracy theory 98
proxy measurement 44, 47–9, 52
psychology, conspiracy theories 86, 88
public contestation 236–8
public secrecy 56
public spaces 10, 43, 251–2
Putin, V. 205

Quinn, J. 8, 254, 255, 258

radicalization 4, 256
Radsch, C. 143

Rancière, J. 38, 64
Raqqa investigation 240, 243 n.2
Readymade 197, 199, 253
'real cyberwar' 41
red-line warning 93
Rees Leahy, H. 200
regime of truth 209, 210, 226 n.2, 232–5, 241, 243
Registers of Scotland: Cadastral Mapping Overview 41
religious mindset 153
remote warfare 10, 231–3, 238, 242, 243, 255, 256
Reporters without borders 206
Reporting America at War 123–4
resistant spaces 10, 252–4
Richter, A. 218
Rid, T. 108–9, 117 n.6, 117 n.10
Ritchin, F. 163, 165
Robinson, P. 92
Romania 47, 48, 52
Romanian Intelligence Service (SRI) 53
Rossiya-1 channel 205, 223
Rovera, D. 238
Rowlands, D. 19
RT 95
Ruddick, S. 149–50
Russia 93, 208, 212, 213, 217, 219, 221, 222. *See also* Russia Today (RT)
Russian-Ukrainian conflict 84
Russian Union of Journalists (RUJ) 206, 210, 212
Russia Today (RT)
  affective investments 70–5
  audience engagement 71–2
  and comments 75–7
  humour 76
  late-night parody show 67–9
  news 67, 69
  satirical social media short 68–70
  Syrian conflict 62–3, 65–7
  talk show 68, 69
  YouTube 66–8, 70–2, 77

Safer, M. 123–4
Salgado, S. 25
Salisbury Plain 179–84, 251–2

sanctioning techniques 239
Sansour, L. 20–2, 31
satirical social media short 68–70
Saussure, F. 193
Sawchuk, K. 170
Scarry, E. 258
Schiff, R. 110
Schmitt, C. 36
Seawright, P. 16
secondary witness 48
Second World War (WWII) analogies 131–2
securitization 5, 6
'sensationalised landscape of declared war' 23
sensory museology 200–1
Serbu, G. 107
Serota, N. 32
Sha'aban, B. 150
#*shaheed* 159, 161, 167–75, 255
Shakashiro, M. 147, 151, 152
Shalom, S. 95
Shams News Network 92
Sharbaji, A. 147–8
'shared culture' 130
Shavit, M. 117 n.10
Sköns, E. 196
Sleboda, M. 68
Sloan, Helen 32
Snæbjörnsdóttir, B. 200
Snetselaar, D. 10, 255
Snowden, E. 26
social marginalization 88–9
social media 5, 26, 63, 65, 68, 70–3, 75, 77, 78, 85, 91, 92, 103–5, 114–16, 117 n.7
  digital and 108–10
  Israel Defence Force 110–14
  Multinational Information Operations Experiment 105–6
  risks 109–10
Social Media as a Tool of Hybrid Warfare 103
social sciences 5
sociology, conspiracy theories 86
'Solid Evidence Douma "Chemical Attack" Was Staged – Lavrov' 67
Solomon, T. 64–5

somatic war 258
Souriatna 146
space and time 5, 7, 9
Space Exodus (Sansour) 20–2
space in-between 213
Space Odyssey 20, 22
Spokesperson's Unit (SU) 111
SputnikNews 95
Sreberny, A. 144
state-corporate-military power 37–40, 43, 48, 55, 57
state feminism 150
'state of emergency' 36
state of exception 36, 57
Stokke, Ch. 210
Storyful news agency 91, 92
strategic use of ambiguity 133
stress ball 9, 187, 188, 192, 193, 195, 198, 201, 202, 253
Strike Tracker 238
Su, F. 209, 215, 224, 225
superimposition 16
Sylvester, C. 202, 256
Syria
   Ba'th Party 149, 150
   conflict 61, 85, 91, 92, 97, 154–5, 156 n.11, 156 n.12 (*see also* liminality; Russia Today (RT))
   Ghouta attack 93–4
   Khan Sheikhoun attack 95–7
   public sphere 144
   RT and 65–7, 70–7
   Russia in 62–3
   war and disputed evidence 91–7
   woman 144–53, 155
'Syria Attacked' episode 68
#SyriaHoax 95
#SyrianGasAttack 95
Syrian Women for the Syrian Intifada 146
Syrian Women Observatory (www.nesasy.org) 144
system hidden in plain sight 37
Szekely, O. 153–4
Szostek, J. 213

Taliban 104
talk show 68, 69, 73–4
Tan, A. T. H. 196
tank 189, 193, 198
Taussig, M. 56, 201
'Team UK' 198
'technical sublime' 26
technology 4, 8, 10, 14, 15, 23, 26, 28, 31, 107, 108, 110, 111, 127, 233, 238, 240, 241, 258
terror-democracy 57
terrorist 18, 27, 53, 68, 70, 127, 175 n.1
'textbook' 219
'theatre of war' 14, 15, 22
Thelwall, M. 75
Tishreen newspaper 149
Today programme 96
Tomilenko, S. 206, 212, 217
'torture' 133–5
torture taxis project 43
Townsend, S. J. 239
trans-border dialogue 206–11, 216, 217, 219, 221, 223–5
Troxell, J. W. 238
Trudnosti perevoda 218–21, 225
truth 215, 224–6, 233, 234, 236–8, 256
   regime of 209, 210, 226 n.2, 232–5, 241, 243
truthfulness 62, 71, 97, 209
truth seeking 209
Tsahal 117 n.8
Tuchman, G. 130
Turner, V. 144
Twitter 95, 112, 113, 167
Two Countries – One Profession project 206–7, 210–18, 221–5

Ukraine
   crisis 62
   journalism 215
   Kanfer, L. 221
   media community 206, 224–5
   nationalism 220
   Two Countries – One Profession project 206–7, 210–18, 221–5
   'war of narratives' 208
'the ultimate protection' condom 192, 198

uncertainty 97, 249, 250
    news 85, 92, 94
    visual media 90
Uncounted, The (Khan and Gopel) 239
United States torture policy 133–4
unrepresentability 38
US Central Command (CENTCOM) 235, 237, 240, 243, 243 n.1
US Congress 93
US intervention 93
US-led anti-IS coalition 235

Van Prooijen, J. W. 88
Vibrant Matter (Bennett) 194
'Vikna-novini' 220
Vinogradov, V. 220–2, 225
violence 234, 236
    and aggression 152
    gender 156 n.10
    logic of 241–2
    military 9, 36, 39, 43
    remote warfare 10, 231–3, 238, 242, 243, 255, 256
    sexual 148
    war and conflict 35–6
virtual communication 103
virtuous saviour 135
visualization process 35–44, 49, 53–7
visual media 90–1
Vkontakte 213
Volkmer, I. 84
Voronova, L. 9, 250

Wall, J. 20
Wall, M. 92
Walzer, M. 125–7
war 8–9, 16, 38, 39, 55
    Airwars 232, 233, 235, 237–41, 255
    and conflict 4–5, 10, 25, 35–6, 39–40
    de-corporealization of 256–7
    journalism 208
    machinations of 235–6
    media and 3–7, 64–5
    somatic 258
    on terror 3, 6, 36, 37, 48, 49, 54, 56

war art 13–16, 30, 31, 254
warfare 3, 4, 10, 19, 33, 42
    contemporary 10, 16, 37, 172, 242
    corporatization 36
    drone 127
    liquid 233
    precision 236–8
    remote 10, 231–3, 238, 242, 243, 255, 256
    spatial reconfiguration of 232–3
War 2.0 model 108, 111
'war of narratives' 205, 207, 208, 210, 219, 221, 223–5
Washington, H. A. 88
watchdog organizations 232, 235, 237–40, 242, 243, 255
Watergate 86–7
weapon 25, 26, 70, 97, 193, 195
    Al Qaeda 115
    Bofors slogan 198–9, 201
    chemical 91, 93, 95
    DSEI 198
    information 208
    and intelligence 108
    Meiches, B. 202
Web 1.0 model 108
Wegerif, R. 209
'welcome to hell' sweet 189
Wellcome Trust 32
west
    breaking news 67
    CrossTalk 68
    hypocrisy of 70
    militaries 115, 116, 233
    museums 200–1
    Russia in the Syrian conflict 62, 68, 70, 73–7
While Modelling Physics inside an Exploding Nuclear Warhead (2000s) 26
White Helmets 74, 76
Williamson, G. 243 n.2
Wilson, M. 200
women
    digital activism 143–4
    Enab Baladi 252–3, 257

media work 145, 148, 152, 153, 155
Syria 144–53, 155
Women's Rights in the Middle East and North Africa: Progress Amid Resistance (Kelly) 148
Wood, M. 209, 215, 224, 225
Woodward, R. 180

Yablokov, I. 89
Yandex 213

Young, L. 107, 117 n.5
YouTube 66–8, 70–2, 77, 92–4, 112, 221, 223, 225

Zahed, S. E. 92
Zapatista Jungle (1995) 14
Zeitzoff, T. 118 n.18
Zelensky, V. 205, 206
Žižek, S. 40
Zoller, H. M. 208, 210

www.ingramcontent.com/pod-product-compliance
Lightning Source LLC
Chambersburg PA
CBHW072128290426
44111CB00012B/1821